Teaching Thinking Skills
A Handbook for
Secondary School Teachers

Barry K. Beyer

George Mason University

Allyn and Bacon

Boston   London   Toronto   Sydney   Tokyo   Singapore

Portions of this book first appeared in Barry K. Beyer, *Practical Strategies for the Teaching of Thinking* (Boston: Allyn and Bacon, 1987) and Barry K. Beyer, *Developing a Thinking Skills Program* (Boston: Allyn and Bacon, 1988).

Library of Congress Cataloging–in–Publication Data

Beyer, Barry K., 1931–
    Teaching thinking skills : a handbook for secondary school teachers / Barry K. Beyer.
        p. cm.
    Includes bibliographical references and index.
    ISBN 0–205–12797–5
    1. Thought and thinking—Study and teaching (Elementary)—Handbooks, manuals, etc. 2. Thought and thinking—Study and teaching (Secondary)—Handbooks, manuals, etc. I. Title.
    LB1590.3.B53   1991
    373.13′028—dc20   90–43819
                                                                            CIP

Printed in the United States of America

10 9 8 7 6 5 4 3 2   95 94 93 92 91

For
KURT RAYMOND BEYER

May he, his sister, cousins, friends, and contemporaries
be the ultimate beneficiaries of these pages.

Contents

Foreword

While the goal of developing the thinking abilities of students is certainly not new, renewed attention is being directed toward accomplishing this educational objective. This focus has been stimulated, in part, by the results of national and state assessments of student achievement, which reveal disappointing performances on those tasks, such as inferential reading, persuasive writing, and multi-step problem solving, requiring the thoughtful application of knowledge and skills. These results are confirmed by university reports stating that large numbers of entering students are inadequately prepared for the complex thinking required in higher education. Nearly all of the educational reform reports issued during the 1980s have cited these poor performances, along with such factors as the rapidly changing nature of modern society, the "information explosion," the challenges of global economic competition, and the needs of a democratic society, in their recommendations for an increased emphasis on the development of student thinking abilities.

Although the "call to arms" is widely heard, secondary teachers interested in responding are often hard pressed to find practical solutions to the problem of integrating the teaching of thinking within content area instruction. The challenge is complicated by the recognition that sophisticated thinking may not develop automatically as a by-product of "teaching the subject well." In fact, the traditional means for stimulating students to think about content may be inadequate. For example, simply asking higher-order questions does not ensure that students will possess the necessary knowledge and thinking abilities to answer them. Merely holding a classroom debate does not teach students how to structure an effective argument or assume a devil's advocate position. Likewise, the assignment of a problem or a writing assignment does not, by itself, explicate the strategies employed by capable writers or problem solvers. In each of these cases, a more explicit approach to the development of thinking may be needed.

Unfortunately, the traditional source of curriculum and instructional support for secondary teachers, the textbook, is generally deficient in providing the needed assistance. Few current textbooks provide substantive guidance to teachers interested in the explicit teaching of thinking skills and processes within the content areas. Although a growing number of thinking skills workbooks are now available, their "content-free" exercises rarely address the unique thinking demands of secondary subject areas. Given the present state of affairs, *Teaching Thinking Skills: A Handbook for Secondary School Teachers* provides a uniquely practical guide for infusing the teaching of thinking explicitly into the various content areas. In an extremely clear and comprehensive fashion, Barry Beyer addresses and assists practitioners in working out their answers to the major questions faced by teachers: *What are the key thinking skills I should—or could—teach? How can I effectively teach thinking in a way that supports the achievement of content objectives? What are the steps and strategies involved in the various thinking skills and processes? In what ways might I promote transfer? How do I create a classroom climate to support the development of thinking? How do I assess the growth of my students' thinking?*

The recommended procedures presented here by which teachers can identify, describe, teach, and assess the relevant thinking skills within their subject areas are among the most detailed and complete available. Through the use of illustrative examples and sets of teacher-developed lessons, the teaching of thinking is ''brought to life.'' One cannot read these in-depth lesson descriptions without learning something new about the nature of the thinking skills being taught and about effective ways to teach them. The accompanying teacher reflections, while acknowledging the uncomfortable feelings associated with instructional innovation, reassure the reader that the teaching of thinking *is* important and *can* be done.

The explicit teaching of thinking skills as a part of content area instruction is still in its infancy. With relatively few models to follow, secondary teachers committed to teaching thinking will appreciate the support provided by this handbook. Its use will promote reflective teaching, a thoughtful approach to subject matter, and more meaningful learning for students.

Jay McTighe

Preface

One way to help people become better, more effective thinkers is to help them become proficient in carrying out the skilled operations of which effective thinking, in part, consists. To do this, of course, requires considerable knowledge about the nature of thinking and of thinking skills. It also requires mastery of certain basic teaching skills and strategies.

Thinking and thinking skills are not synonymous. *Thinking* is the mental manipulation of sensory input and recalled perceptions (information and thoughts stored in memory) to make or find meaning—to reason about or with, to formulate thoughts, and to judge. We think for many reasons, including to resolve problems; to comprehend; to judge worth, sufficiency, or accuracy; to make decisions; and to conceptualize. These are complex, complicated mental activities that consist of multilevel processing and simultaneous, often recursive, use of a multitude of skilled operations as well as considerable knowledge and information.

Thinking skills, on the other hand, are the discrete, precisely delineated mental operations used in varying combinations as we think. Dozens upon dozens of such skills have been identified, such as remembering, distinguishing the relevant from the irrelevant, classifying, predicting, judging the strength of a claim, synthesizing, inferring relationships, and making conclusions. These and similar skills are the building blocks, or tools, of effective thinking. They are used over and over again in changing combinations to carry out any major thinking task, strategy, or process involving the production of meaning, insight, or knowledge.

If you wish to help students—or individuals of any age for that matter—to improve their thinking, you can do so by deliberately and continuously teaching them how to sharpen their expertise at executing the thinking operations most commonly used in thinking. Initially this means focusing attention and efforts on helping them master individual thinking skills.* Eventually, however, it means helping your students integrate these individual skills into smoothly functioning procedures of a highly complex nature to a point where your students can execute them in rapid, accurate, expert manner on their own initiative in a variety of contexts.

My experience at teaching thinking and helping others learn how to do so indicates that to teach thinking skills most effectively, you must be able to do at least four things well:

1. *Identify the attributes (features, ingredients, components) of the thinking skills that you seek to teach.*

---

*To minimize confusion, I use the term *thinking skills* throughout this handbook to include *all* classes of cognitive operations, including those also commonly identified as strategies and processes.

To teach any thinking skill well, you must know and understand its major attributes—the (a) procedure(s), (b) rules, and (c) criteria or other knowledge employed to carry it out. But for many of us, knowledge of these attributes of most thinking skills remains quite elusive. Not only is this knowledge often unclear to us, but it is rarely found already packaged for us to read and understand. Rather, we often have to identify skill attributes for ourselves. Being able to teach thinking skills requires, first and foremost, skill at finding out what these attributes are for any cognitive skill you might choose or be expected to teach.

2. *Plan and conduct lessons to help inexpert thinkers learn how to carry out these thinking skills effectively.*

Teaching thinking skills involves more than simply making students think or think harder. It involves purposeful, instructive mediation, or intervention, to help them become conscious of how they think and to sharpen the cognitive skills they employ in thinking. Such mediation includes explaining, modeling, cuing, and guiding practice in how these skills can be carried out, as well as helping learners apply and bridge these skills in a variety of combinations, for a variety of purposes, to a variety of contexts. It also involves helping students consciously think about how they think and purposefully plan and direct their own thinking. To do these things well, you must be skilled at planning and carrying out, on a continuing basis, lessons using instructional strategies and techniques that are well-suited to these purposes.

3. *Assess student proficiency in the thinking skill(s) being taught.*

In order to improve your own teaching, as well as to evaluate student learning of the thinking skill(s) you wish to teach, you must be able to identify and use valid, reliable thinking skill assessment instruments and procedures and to construct your own. Assessing student thinking directly is an integral part of teaching thinking skills. The results can be used to improve your own teaching, motivate student learning, and make summative judgments about the quality of your teaching and of student achievement.

4. *Infuse, or integrate, the teaching of thinking skills in existing subject-matter units, classes, or courses.*

Students seem better motivated to learn a cognitive skill when instruction in that skill is provided at a time they feel a need to know how to do it better than they can at the moment. What better time or place to teach thinking skills, then, than in the subjects where students need these skills to achieve the learning objectives that have been established! In fact, unless students are helped to apply these skills in different subjects, it is unlikely they will be able to do so very well on their own. To maximize the learning of thinking skills *and* the academic achievement of your students, you must be able to integrate the teaching of these skills into the subjects your students study.

It is the goal of this handbook to assist you in learning how to carry out these four teaching skills or in improving your abilities to do so.

To accomplish this goal the pages that follow present four kinds of information. The accompanying figure outlines these in the context of the contents of the entire handbook. Part I presents step-by-step procedures and activities that will enable you to learn how to identify the attributes of any thinking skill you wish to teach (Chapter 1); how to construct and teach lessons employing strate-

Contents and Structure of *Teaching Thinking Skills: A Handbook for Secondary School Teachers*

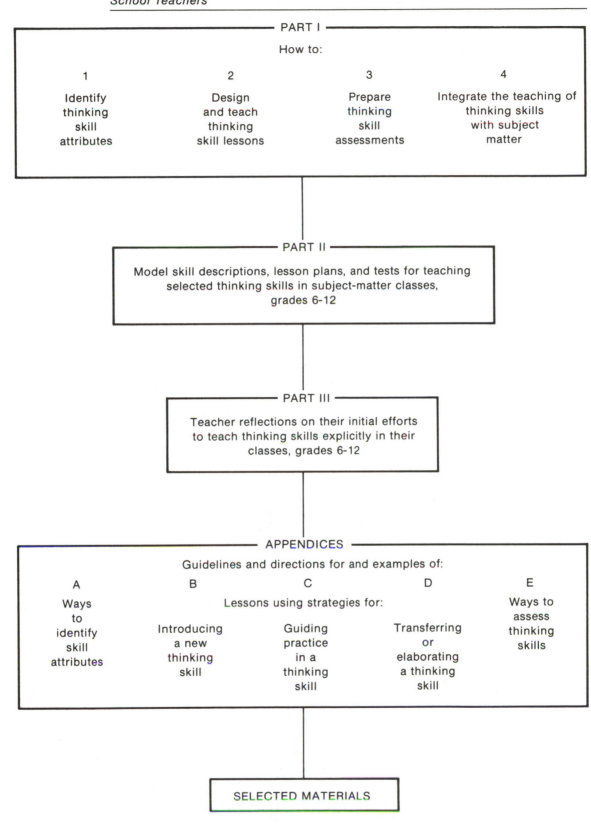

PART I

How to:

1	2	3	4
Identify thinking skill attributes	Design and teach thinking skill lessons	Prepare thinking skill assessments	Integrate the teaching of thinking skills with subject matter

PART II

Model skill descriptions, lesson plans, and tests for teaching selected thinking skills in subject-matter classes, grades 6-12

PART III

Teacher reflections on their initial efforts to teach thinking skills explicitly in their classes, grades 6-12

APPENDICES

Guidelines and directions for and examples of:

A	B	C	D	E
Ways to identify skill attributes	Lessons using strategies for:			Ways to assess thinking skills
	Introducing a new thinking skill	Guiding practice in a thinking skill	Transferring or elaborating a thinking skill	

SELECTED MATERIALS

gies appropriate to the teaching of any thinking skill in any subject area (Chapter 2); how to construct and conduct any of several different kinds of thinking skill assessments (Chapter 3); and how to integrate the teaching of thinking skills into your existing subject matter units, classes, or courses (Chapter 4). These procedures and activities are precisely those I would guide you through if you and I were working together on a one-to-one basis, or in a college course, or in a continuing inservice workshop dealing with the teaching of thinking skills. Upon completing this part of the handbook, you should be able to carry out these teaching skills on your own with some degree of proficiency.

The procedures presented in Part I have been used repeatedly—and refined extensively—over the past half-dozen years or so to help teachers become more skillful at teaching thinking skills. These procedures are derived from research in training, skill acquisition, and adult learning, and they apply teaching strategies generated by such research. Obviously, not everything you need to do to master the teaching skills taught herein can be included in these pages—the practice, coaching, revision, and continued application so critical to developing expertise in any skill are things you must continue to do once you have completed this handbook. However, the guidelines and procedures presented here will help you through the initial steps in learning how to carry out each of the four tasks so essential to the effective teaching of thinking skills noted above.

Part I of the handbook is not designed to be read through in a single sitting as you might do with an ordinary text. Rather, because it consists essentially of learning procedures and activities for you to use to develop the teaching skills noted above, you should read it and carry out the procedures presented a bit at a time. To assist you in doing this, I have divided it into convenient learning segments. Each segment consists of a major learning or planning task designed to help you to produce or understand something. Each concludes with an easily identified checkpoint. These checkpoints signal the end of a particular learning sequence and mark places where you can stop, sit back, reflect on and discuss with those of your colleagues who may also be using this handbook what you have learned or developed during your study of the segment just completed. Not all segments require equal time to complete. Some will require less than half an hour, whereas others will require a number of hours of reading, writing, practicing, reflecting, sharing, and revising, sometimes spread over several days or weeks. However, each segment comes to a close with a checkpoint where you can sum up what you have learned, done, or produced. Then, when you are ready, you can move on to the next segment.

The activities and procedures in Part I incorporate the principles of both collaborative learning and peer coaching. In learning how to teach thinking, two or more heads are usually better than one. The activities included here provide opportunities and guidance for such interaction and collaboration. Moreover, through these pages I have tried to do what a real coach would do to help you master the teaching skills and knowledge you will need to be a successful teacher of thinking skills in your classroom. Part I provides for explanation, demonstration, application, and practice of the teaching skills you choose to learn, as well as opportunities and procedures for receiving feedback on how you carry out these skills or complete these tasks when you try them. By the time you and your colleagues complete this handbook, you should have engaged in the kinds of activities and formed the kind of relationships that will enable you to continue on your own the kind of supportive, collaborative coaching relationship and activities so useful to improving teaching and so instrumental in successful efforts at improving the learning of youngsters in our schools.

Part I also provides numerous opportunities for you to reflect on how you think and how you carry out important teaching tasks. Research by Benjamin

Bloom, Ann Brown, Arthur Whimbey, J. H. Flavell, and others indicates that effective thinkers think about how they think before, during, and even after carrying out a cognitive task. This thinking about one's own thinking is referred to by experts as *metacognition.* Metacognitive thinking directs and controls the thinking we use to solve problems, make meaning, choose, and so on.

By reflecting on how you think, you raise your thinking to a level of consciousness where you can become acutely aware of what you are doing and how it works for you. As a result, you can deliberately and carefully dissect, redirect, modify, and improve how you carry out your thinking and take deliberate control of it. Consequently, as your thinking becomes more automatic and less conscious, it functions more smoothly and effectively. Thinking about how you do things—whether planning, teaching, testing, or thinking—helps you to understand these operations better and to take ownership of them. It is a higher-order cognitive activity and typifies experts in any field.

Part II of this handbook provides descriptions, lesson plans, and tests for selected thinking skills commonly taught in different subjects at different grade levels, 6–12. These skill-teaching materials have been prepared, reviewed, and used by teachers or teachers-to-be as they proceeded through activities and procedures like those presented in Part I of this handbook to learn specific strategies for teaching thinking skills. You can refer to these packets as you proceed through Part I for illustrations of these teaching strategies, but you may use them in other ways as well. For example, you may use these sample materials as models for similar materials you may wish to produce for teaching different skills of your choice to your students. Or, you may actually use these materials to teach these particular skills in your own classroom.

In Part III you will find essays by some of the authors of the skill packets in Part II as well as by other teachers or individuals training to be teachers, reflecting on their initial experiences in using various strategies for teaching thinking skills. In these brief accounts, these teachers tell how they felt in using new skill-teaching strategies for the first time, what worked and what didn't, and what they learned as a result of their teaching. By sharing their experiences with you, they hope to encourage you to feel more at ease with what you are learning. These accounts may also help you understand that everyone who tries something new experiences many of the same doubts, frustrations, and feelings that you may experience as you proceed to apply and try out teaching skills that may be new to you.

Finally, the Appendices present excerpts from my *Practical Strategies for the Teaching of Thinking* (Allyn and Bacon, 1987), which explain and illustrate classroom strategies for teaching a variety of different kinds of thinking skill lessons. Materials in the Appendices also illustrate a procedure by which you can identify the essential attributes or features of any thinking skill, as well as procedures for designing tests and other instruments to assess student proficiency in any thinking skills you might choose to teach. You will find this information useful in completing Part I of this handbook.

This handbook has multiple uses.* I designed it to help you learn particu-

---

*A companion to this handbook is also available for elementary school teachers. *Teaching Thinking Skills: A Handbook for Elementary Teachers* is identical to this handbook in structure. Part I is the same as Part I in this handbook. However, the skill-teaching materials in Part II and the teacher essays in Part III of the *Elementary* handbook present materials developed for use only in grades K–6 and the experiences of the elementary school teachers who designed and used them. Thus, it is possible to use this handbook in separate elementary and secondary courses or workshops or to use both handbooks in a common K–12 course or inservice class. Teachers at different grade levels will have immediate access to a considerable number of sample materials directly related to their own teaching responsibilities, while at the same time all engage in a common process to learn the same skills and knowledge related to teaching thinking skills.

lar strategies for teaching thinking skills, strategies that will enable you to teach within an instructional framework that research suggests is the most appropriate way to organize the teaching of thinking skills. These strategies provide direct instruction in thinking skills and can be used to teach any thinking skill using any subject matter to students of any and all ability levels or grade levels. They are presented in detail in my *Practical Strategies for the Teaching of Thinking,* which you may wish to study before or while using this handbook. But to facilitate as much as possible your access to these ideas, I have included excerpts from key chapters in that book here.

The skill-teaching materials in Part II also provide models of the lessons and strategies presented, analyzed, and demonstrated in the Appendices, and which you can learn as you proceed through Part I. Many educators, myself included, believe that mastery of these and similar strategies are absolutely essential to the effective teaching of thinking. Therefore, I have included information about and examples of these strategies as a starting place for you. Thus, this handbook is a *complete* instructional package insofar as this type of skill teaching is concerned. It contains all you will need to master a number of strategies useful in teaching thinking skills to your students right now!

You can also use this handbook to learn any other approaches to or strategies for teaching thinking presented in any other source. The learning procedures presented in Part I will guide you in understanding how to carry out *any* skill-teaching or assessment strategy, if you have additional material that explains, demonstrates, and analyzes that strategy or technique. So, while this handbook contains all the information you will need to learn one specific approach to teaching thinking skills, it also has broader uses. The *procedure* presented in Part I is quite independent of any specific teaching or assessment strategy and may be used to master any strategy for teaching thinking on which you choose to focus.

Indeed, I have tried to make this handbook flexible and to individualize it as much as possible. You may enter it at any point or use only that part that is of immediate interest to you without having to study what precedes it. For example, you may use only that portion of Part I that deals with assessing student thinking and only the sample tests in Part II if all you are interested in at this point is how to produce paper-and-pencil thinking skills tests. Or, if you wish, you may study and use the thinking skills materials in Part II as models for making your own lessons without referring to Part I. You may even pull appropriate materials from Part II and use the lesson plans and tests in your own classes, if they are appropriate to your interests. You may also use the procedures in Part I for learning specific skill identification, skill teaching, and test construction strategies other than those illustrated by the sample materials in Part II and the Appendices. Even within the procedure in Part I, you may skip or bypass certain steps depending on the extent of your experience and knowledge regarding the subject at hand. You may also use the procedures for infusing instruction in thinking skills into any subject or grade level as presented in Part III, quite independently of the rest of the handbook.

You may, in addition, use this handbook as a tutor to help you learn on your own and at your own pace how to carry out the key skills required for teaching skillful thinking to your students or you may use it in working with a group of your colleagues to learn these skills. It can be used as an individual study guide or as an instructional aid in a more formal course on the teaching of thinking or in a continuing inservice effort to accomplish the same goal. This text may serve *in loco instructor* but it can just as easily be used by or with an instructor to guide and supplement his or her own instruction in any approach to teaching thinking.

Regardless of how you choose to use this handbook, you should be aware of the assumptions upon which it is based:

1. Integrating the teaching of thinking skills with subject-matter teaching leads to improved student thinking *and* more meaningful content learning.
2. Most teachers want their students to be more skillful at thinking than the students seem to be if left on their own.
3. Most teachers or teachers-to-be have received precious little preservice training or instruction in how to teach thinking skills to any degree of proficiency using instructional and assessment strategies based on the latest research and theory.
4. Most teachers and teachers-to-be welcome an opportunity to improve their abilities to teach thinking skills, especially an opportunity that supports their own efforts to achieve this goal with skills of their choosing in subjects of their choosing.

Teaching Thinking Skills has been designed to provide this opportunity.

ACKNOWLEDGMENTS

This handbook represents the efforts and talents of many individuals. I wish here to acknowledge their contributions.

Many of the ideas and techniques presented in these pages were born or tested and elaborated on in courses and workshops I have conducted in school systems, at professional conferences, and in universities throughout the United States and Canada. I am indebted to all those who have participated in these efforts. I wish especially to thank the several hundred teacher candidates and experienced teachers who have enrolled in my courses at George Mason University and the teachers who participated in the summer seminars I have offered at Seattle Pacific University over the past few years or so. The insights they have contributed as to how to help teachers learn how to teach thinking skills as well as to how to teach thinking skills themselves have been invaluable.

I am also most appreciative of similar contributions from teachers with whom I have worked on a continuing basis in school systems throughout the United States, including the D. C. Everest Area Schools in Schofield, Wisconsin; the Monroe County Public Schools in Key West, Florida; Lynnhaven Junior High School in Virginia Beach, Virginia; the Walled Lake (Michigan) Consolidated Schools; the Amphitheater Public Schools in Tucson, Arizona; and the Weld County Schools in Greeley, Colorado. The learning experiences we shared have shaped these pages considerably.

Those teachers and teachers-to-be who have contributed the lesson plans and reflective essays featured in Parts II and III of this handbook deserve a special acknowledgment. They are identified in the section labeled "contributors" and their names appear on the materials they authored. Their enthusiasm and talents for teaching thinking are remarkable and, for the readers of these pages, I hope contagious. Without their willingness to risk trying new approaches to teaching and to share with others the products of their learning and classroom experimenting, this handbook would not have been possible.

I am especially indebted to seven colleagues in classrooms, administrative offices, state education departments, and research labs for their invaluable assistance in shaping this text and its contents. I was honored by their willingness to review this manuscript and pleased by the thoroughness of their evaluations. Their astute perceptions, positive and creative suggestions, and enthusiastic encouragement have contributed much to these final pages. To Marion Bennett, Ann Hutchinson, Toby Kline, Jay McTighe, Barbara Pressiesen, Al Wheeler, and Susan Whitten, I offer my sincerest thanks for all their help and advice. And to Erin McVadon Albright, my thanks, too, for her willingness to assist in the publication of this handbook.

Special gratitude goes to Jay McTighe for his dual contributions to this handbook. Not only did he take time from his busy schedule to review the original manuscript and make numerous, excellent suggestions for improving it but he also wrote the Foreword for this volume. Few educators are more knowledgable about teaching thinking or more accomplished teacher trainers than is Jay, and his insights into these areas have proven invaluable. I deeply appreciate his friendship over the years and his contributions to this handbook.

Two other individuals deserve special acknowledgment. Ernestine Meyer typed this manuscript—and retyped it again and again as it evolved. Her skill at this task was outstanding; her enthusiasm, unflagging; and her endurance, amazing. Her skill at weaving through my terrible handwriting and often confused notations makes her contribution to this handbook special. I appreciate more than words can say all that she did to help this handbook become a reality.

In addition, Mylan Jaixen, Executive Editor of Education at Allyn and Bacon, has been exceedingly helpful in engineering the publication of this handbook. I greatly appreciate his continuing support and helpful encouragement—and his welcome sense of good humor—in bringing this work to fruition.

In retrospect, I find it difficult to imagine any teacher-training publication that has benefited from the contributions of a greater range and more talented number of educators than has this one. Classroom teachers, staff developers, curriculum specialists, administrators and researchers, doers as well as theorists—all have had a hand in reviewing, creating, and producing this handbook. I have tried my best to interpret their ideas accurately, to incorporate their suggestions faithfully, and to accommodate their criticisms. To the extent that I have been successful in so doing, the credit is theirs. Where I have failed, the responsibility is mine.

To each and all who have contributed to this handbook, my most sincere thanks and appreciation. It would not *be* without you!

Barry K. Beyer

Contributors

Cynthia Abramoski
Middle school teacher
Prince George's County (Maryland) Public
  Schools

Elizabeth Calvert
Teacher candidate, secondary education
College of Education and Human Services
George Mason University, Fairfax,
  Virginia

Marijke deVries
Teacher candidate, middle school education
College of Education and Human Services
George Mason University, Fairfax,
  Virginia

Sharon Suzanne Gardner
Resource teacher
Prince William County (Virginia) Public
  Schools

Jack Green
Science Program Specialist
Fairfax County (Virginia) Public Schools

Carolyn Kreiter-Kurylo
High school English teacher
Fairfax County (Virginia) Public Schools

Peggy Recker
Teacher candidate, middle school education
College of Education and Human Services
George Mason University, Fairfax,
  Virginia

Jerome Robbins
Middle school teacher
Seattle (Washington) Country Day School

Cynthia Wood
Secondary school social studies teacher
Fairfax County (Virginia) Public Schools

Preparing to Teach
Thinking Skills

INTRODUCTION

In order to teach thinking skills, you should be able to:

1. Identify and describe the attributes of any thinking skill(s).
2. Design and teach lessons for teaching any thinking skill(s) in any subject matter of your choice.
3. Design and develop assessments of student proficiency in any thinking skill(s).
4. Infuse, or integrate, the teaching of thinking skills with instruction in existing subject-matter units, classes, or courses.

Each of the four chapters that constitute Part I of this handbook deals with one of these teaching skills. If you like to know in advance where you are headed when you embark on a journey, especially one through what may be a strange place, the chart in Figure 1.1 serves as a map of where these four chapters will take you. You can use this chart to keep track of where you are headed as well as where you are at any point in your learning journey through Part I.

Each chapter in Part I contains an even more detailed flowchart outlining the specific topics and procedures presented in that chapter. Reference to these advanced organizers can keep you from getting—or feeling—lost as you progress through this part of the handbook. These flowcharts may also encourage you in your progress by helping you understand how the topics and procedures presented interrelate and how each contributes to an understanding of the overall subject of the chapter.

Figure 1.1 Sequence and Procedures

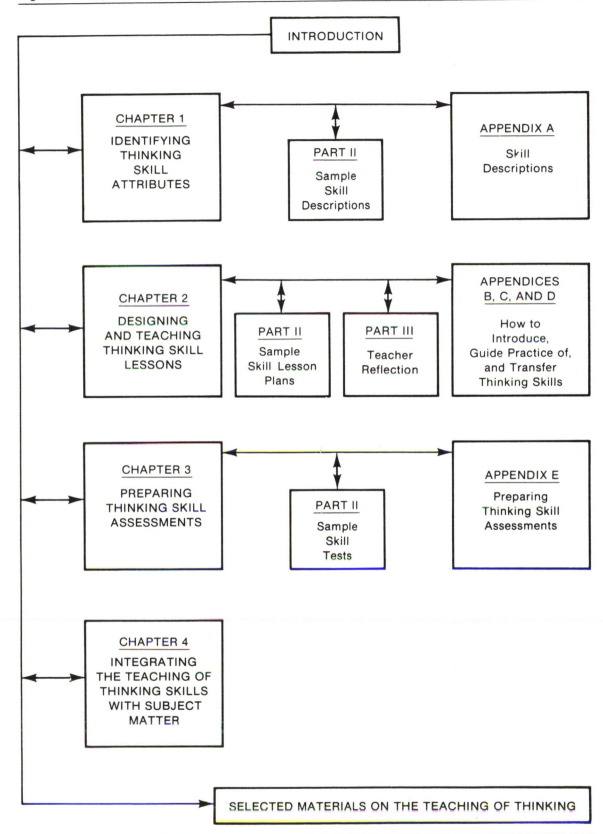

chapter 1

Identifying Thinking Skill Attributes

Good teachers know their subjects. This truism applies to thinking skills just as it does to any other subject taught in our schools. In teaching thinking skills, the subject is the thinking skill or skills you seek to teach. Effective teaching of any thinking skill requires you to understand—to know—as much as possible about this skill. This means not only being able to carry out the skill yourself in a reasonably expert, accurate fashion but also being able to explain to and show others who cannot do it well how to carry it out better than they presently do. To do these things, you must know the key components (attributes) of the skill. Thus, *producing a description of the major attributes of a thinking skill you plan to teach is the first step in preparing to teach that thinking skill.* This chapter will help you learn how to identify the significant attributes of *any* thinking skill so you can know what it is you are to teach. Having developed proficiency in this skill of identifying skill attributes, you can then plan and teach lessons that will have the best chances of helping your students become proficient in the thinking skill(s) on which you and they choose to focus.

When you have completed this chapter, you should be able to:

1. State and give specific examples of three major kinds of attributes of any thinking skill.
2. Describe and explain to someone else how to employ two different ways to identify the attributes of any thinking skill.

Figure 1.2 Chapter 1—Learning Modules and Procedures

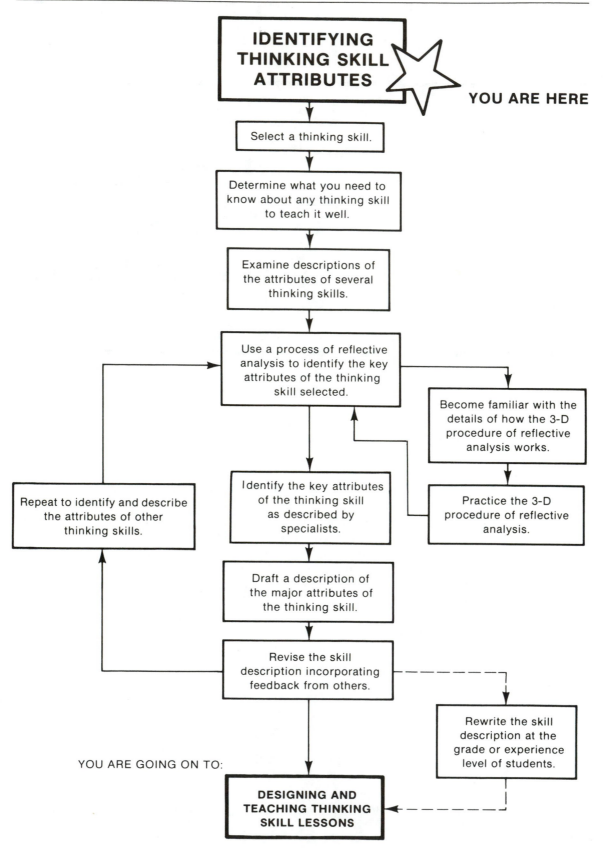

3. Apply these two procedures to describe in detail the major attributes of at least one specific thinking skill.

The following pages present procedures and information designed to help you achieve these objectives. Figure 1.2 outlines these procedures and the sequence in which they are presented in this chapter. You can use these procedures and information to learn about the major attributes of any thinking skill, to learn several ways to identify such attributes for any thinking skill, and to use these methods to identify the specific attributes of a thinking skill on which you can focus as you proceed through the remainder of Part I. The final written product of this chapter will be a description of the major attributes of a specific thinking skill that you have selected (or will shortly select), presented in enough detail so that someone who is not familiar with the skill can learn enough about the skill to introduce it accurately to his or her students.

The procedures in this chapter have been combined into learning segments, each concluding with a *Checkpoint*. Each *Checkpoint* provides you with an opportunity to pull together what you have learned or developed, to reflect on it, and, if you wish, to take a break before continuing your study of or preparation for teaching thinking skills. You can use these *Checkpoints* both as learning goals and, when completed, as mileposts to mark your progress through these pages.

---

note

Each of the sets of thinking skill materials in Part II begins with a description of the thinking skill that is the subject of those materials. These descriptions are based on guidelines presented in Appendix A and were developed by following the procedures presented in this chapter. You may wish to skim some of these descriptions now and to refer to them repeatedly as you proceed through this chapter.

This chapter consists of two sections. In the first section you will learn some information that will be most helpful in understanding the nature of thinking skills and how to describe them clearly. Here, you will also select a thinking skill on which to focus throughout Part. I. The second section will familiarize you with some procedures for identifying the major features, or attributes, of any thinking skill and then guide you in using these procedures to identify and describe for teaching purposes the significant attributes of the thinking skill you have selected.

IDENTIFYING WHAT'S IN A SKILL— GETTING STARTED

As noted earlier, the more you know about the subject you teach, the more of significance you can help your students learn about that subject. If you are teaching a thinking skill, this means you need to know as much as possible about it. If you know all the kinds of knowledge that exist about thinking skills, imagine how effective you could be in teaching these skills to others! Identifying this knowledge about thinking skills in general and about a specific skill in particular are important first steps in improving your abilities to teach both thinking and the subject(s) you are charged with teaching.

However, identifying the attributes of any thinking skill is not something easily done in the abstract or when you are not sure what you are looking for. Thus, before doing this, it is useful to do at least three things:

1. Select a thinking skill to concentrate on throughout your efforts here to learn how to identify thinking skill attributes, so you will have a specific example to refer to as you proceed.

2. Determine, in general, what you need to know about *any* thinking skill in order to teach it well.

3. Examine some descriptions of thinking skills so that by seeing specific examples of thinking skill attributes, you will know more precisely what to look for as attributes of the thinking skill in which you are interested and at the same time become familiar with a way to communicate these attributes to other teachers.

The pages that follow will assist you in accomplishing these three objectives. When you have completed this section, you can then use what you have learned to identify the important attributes of the thinking skill you have selected to focus on here.

1. Select a thinking skill.

For all practical purposes, teaching thinking skills starts with the selection of one or more thinking skills to teach. Learning how to teach these skills can best be done when you go about it with a specific thinking skill in mind. So, it is worthwhile right here at the beginning to identify a thinking skill on which to focus throughout Part I of this handbook. By doing so, you will have an actual thinking skill to which to refer as you apply theory to practice and reduce abstractions to concrete realities. By the time you complete this handbook, you will have virtually all the materials you need to actually teach this skill to your students whenever you choose to do so. The procedures you learn in this chapter for identifying skill attributes can be used to identify the attributes of this particular skill. The lessons you will learn how to teach in Chapter 2 and the assessments you can write in Chapter 3 can also focus on this skill. Thus, when you have finished these pages, you will have a complete instructional unit, ready for instant use in your own classroom. And, of course, the procedures and skills you learn and refine in completing this handbook will be useful in preparing similar materials for *any* thinking skills you may choose to teach in the future.

Sometimes selecting a thinking skill to teach is easy. In fact, if you are told by a state curriculum, or a district program of studies, or some administrative order which skill to teach, you do not have to make this decision at all. Perhaps, then, the only major decisions you have to make are how to identify the attributes of the skill or when to start teaching it and how. But if it is up to you to decide which skill(s) to teach, choosing it is an important task. How can you best make this decision?

First, you need to clarify your goals in learning more about the teaching of thinking skills. What you are trying to accomplish by using Part I of this handbook is likely to affect the kind of thinking skill you would find useful to focus on throughout your study. For example, if you wish to learn how to do something you can apply immediately to your teaching, you will want to select a skill your students are supposed to be learning. On the other hand, if you are simply interested in finding out how to go about carrying out the teaching skills presented in Part I, you will not find this criterion very helpful. Likewise, if your goal consists of improving student learning in a particular subject area, such as math or science, for example, you may want to select a thinking skill (hypothesis making and testing, for instance) that will help your students do this. But if you are more interested in helping your students develop schoolwide thinking skills, you may wish to consider skills of wider applicability, such as decision making or generalizing. Clarifying your goal is an important initial step in making any choice. Just what is it you wish to accomplish through your study of this handbook?

Once you have clarified your goal here, you need next to identify your options—in this case, the various cognitive skills from which you can choose one on which to focus. To identify these, you can consult any number of sources. For instance, you might examine books on the teaching of thinking to see what skills the authors recommend for instruction. Doing so might be especially useful if these sources also present general background on the nature of thinking and the various forms it takes, setting any recommended skills in a context that clarifies their interrelationships and relationship to thinking in general.[1]

There are other useful sources you should consult, too. These include the textbooks your students use or may use in the future, a program of studies from your district or from a district where you might someday teach, a state competency or standardized examination given to students in a grade or course you (might) teach, or lists of thinking skills recommended for teaching by some expert(s). You might even base your choice on some type of diagnostic assessment of your students or students to be.

Textbooks used by your students are often a good source of thinking skills to teach. For example, student texts at all grade levels often identify in the table of contents thinking skills that they purport to teach in special pages or in end-of-chapter exercises usually entitled ''For Further Thinking'' or ''Thinking Skills'' or ''Skills for Critical Thinking.'' If they include such features, they may also provide exercises that can be used to introduce and practice these skills. If the texts you use, or will later use, have these features, the task of deciding which skill(s) to select for instruction may be considerably easier than if such teaching aids are unavailable.

Additionally, state or district curriculum guides or programs of study sometimes specify selected thinking skills as learning objectives. Where none are specifically identified as thinking skills in these guides, you can study any learning objectives contained therein to identify the verbs they use. When you find statements like ''To analyze the life cycle of butterflies,'' the verb *analyze* denotes a thinking skill, the skill of analysis. Look for verbs that are, in fact, labels for thinking skills. You can consider choosing one that appears frequently in the document.

Other sources may be considered, too. Standardized or state minimum competency tests often assess thinking skills, as do reading tests. If your students are being tested for proficiency in any particular thinking skills and, if these test results are being used to evaluate teaching or curriculum, it seems only reasonable that you make an effort to help your students learn how to carry out those skills. You can examine the manuals for these instruments to identify such skills. Numerous specialists or experts in teaching thinking have also identified thinking skills they consider worth teaching. Some of these have been presented in some detail and arranged in some form to indicate their relationships to each other.[2] Consulting these sources will alert you to a wide range of thinking skills from which you can select.

You might even consult your students. Perhaps your school has data on them or on students like them (for example, reading test scores). Such data may reveal thinking skills in which these students appear to be weak. If no such data exist, you may, through your teaching or a simple assessment of your own design, identify some thinking skills that your students are unable to perform as well as you think they should. Basing your decision about which skill(s) to teach on some type of diagnostic assessment is especially useful, for there is little reason to devote all your attention and effort to teaching a skill or skills in which your students are already reasonably competent!

If it is difficult or impossible for you to consult these or most of these sources, you may find the information in Figure 1.3 useful. This figure presents some thinking skills commonly cited by experts on thinking as worthy of being ''mastered'' by graduation from high school. Some of these, of course, are more suited for introduction in certain grades than in others, at least insofar as formal instruction is concerned. Certainly the degree of sophistication of these or similar skills would change even if they were taught at all levels of a school curriculum. And other thinking skills might legitimately be added to this list, of course. These skills are presented here simply for your convenience, as skills you might consider teaching if you have no other sources to use or consider.

Figure 1.3 Some Thinking Skills Appropriate for Introduction at Selected Grade Levels

Grades K–2	Grades 3–6
Observing	Classifying
Comparing	Sequencing
Sorting (classifying)	Summarizing
Ordering (sequencing)	Decision making
Predicting	Problem solving
	Hypothesizing
	Drawing conclusions
	Identifying facts and value claims
	Identifying relevant information
	Determining the accuracy of a claim
	Identifying reliable sources

Grades 7–12

Analysis	Decision making	Distinguishing facts,
part/whole	Problem solving	value claims, and
themes	Conceptualizing	reasoned opinions
relationships	Argument making	Identifying:
structures/patterns		bias
Synthesis		unstated assumptions
making hypotheses		point of view
drawing conclusions		logical fallacies
generalizing		parts of an argument
Evaluation		Judging the strength of
		an argument
		Determining the
		credibility of a source

Notice that the skills in Figure 1.3 are listed according to the grade levels where they could be first introduced as major classroom learning objectives. Any skill appearing on this list more than once needs to be reintroduced where it is listed the second time in a form that is more elaborate or complex and using subject matter that is more abstract, or in a form that differs from how it was in its initial introduction.

The skills listed in Figure 1.3 deserve some additional explanation. Developmental psychologists are fairly unanimous in their belief that unless the skills of classifying (sorting) and sequencing (ordering) are mastered by the end of the first or second grade, a student will have difficulty in any task requiring higher levels or more complex forms of thinking.[3] Both of these skills require some proficiency also in the skills of observing and comparing. Thus, teachers in grades K–2 would be well advised to learn how to teach at least these skills to their students. Decision making, on the other hand, may be a particularly useful thinking skill to introduce explicitly in the middle or junior high school grades. Not only is there a perceived need on the part of students in these grades to be able to make better decisions but the subject matter often presented in these grades presents innumerable opportunities for teaching this skill. Other, more complicated skills, such as judging the strength of arguments, might best be reserved for introduction in high school subjects.

The point is that, except for the skills listed under grades K–2 in Figure 1.3, placement of thinking skills by grade level is rather arbitrary. There is no consensus among experts about precisely which thinking skills should be or are most appropriate for introduction at any particular grade level. Although almost any thinking skill could be taught in some detail to any youngster at any grade level, some skills are clearly better suited for explicit introduction in some grades than in others, given their levels of difficulty and the limited time available for teaching them at any grade level. Figure 1.3 indicates some grade levels where explicit introduction of selected thinking skills may be most productive. You may have other thinking skills in mind that may be equally valuable to students and quite appropriate to certain grade levels and subjects.

Once you have identified and explored your options (the range of skills you *could* teach), you need to choose the one you *will* focus on here. As you evaluate your options before making your final choice, you should keep at least two things in mind.

First, you must resolve to select a *thinking skill* rather than just any kind of skill, even if you do not feel comfortable in doing so because it may be somewhat unfamiliar to you. Many subject matter-related skills (such as finding latitude and longitude or distinguishing nouns from verbs) may command your attention and interest and do indeed involve some thinking, but they are not the kinds of thinking operations that are the focus of thinking skill instruction. Rather, the kind of cognitive skill you should select ought to be one that is widely used in a variety of thinking tasks and in a number of subject areas.

Second, you will need to use a number of specific criteria in making your final choice. In addition to some standards you may already have for making this decision, you should consider selecting a skill that also meets the following criteria:

1. It is widely used by students of the grade level where you would teach it *outside of school* as well as in learning school subjects.

2. It is used frequently by these same students in more than one academic subject at your grade level.

3. It is recommended for instruction by a number of recognized experts.

4. It can be readily taught using the subject matter you have to work with, where this subject matter provides plenty of opportunities and examples for using this skill.

5. Students have demonstrated a need to learn how to do it better than they do it at present.

Any thinking operation that meets all of these criteria is a good candidate for teaching and for choosing to work on as you move through Part I of this handbook.

After you have reviewed the list of thinking skills presented in Figure 1.3 and any other sources available to you and have considered which skills are *worth* teaching to your students, select one to serve as an object of study and practice throughout Part I. Actually, it may help at this point to select two or three on which you would like to focus, and then review these to see (1) if there are sufficient opportunities (as there should be) to teach them in the particular content you teach or will teach at your grade level or in your course; (2) if any of your colleagues are interested in any of them so several of you can work together in learning the teaching skills presented here; and (3) how much you already know about the skill(s) selected so you don't create too big a task for yourself. From these preliminary choices, you can then later select the skill on which to focus throughout the remainder of this handbook.

---

checkpoint

When you have selected a thinking skill to teach that meets the criteria listed in this section of the handbook, write the name of the skill on the line and check here:

☐

_____

Now, having made your choice of a thinking skill on which to focus in Part I, you can proceed to identify exactly what it is you need to know about the skill in order to teach your students how to do it.

2. Determine what you need to know about any thinking skill to teach it well.

What do you need to know about a thinking skill to teach others effectively how to do it? One way to answer this question is to ask—and answer—another, more practical, question: If you wished to learn a new thinking skill, one you did not know how to do at all or could not do very well, what would *you* want to know about that skill so *you* could become as proficient as possible in carrying it out? In other words, what would you want to know about the thinking skill you just selected in order to explain and demonstrate this skill to students who could not do it?

There are, undoubtedly, a variety of helpful answers to these questions. At the most practical level, however, what you would probably find most helpful would be knowing *how to do* the skill.

This means, in part, knowing what mental operations you need to engage in to carry out the skill and how to execute them with some degree of expertise. It also means knowing when and where it is appropriate to employ the skill, how to initiate its use, and what to do when you have trouble making it work. And, it means knowing any rules, principles, or other information that informs or guides the execution of the skill. If you possessed this *procedural knowledge* about any thinking skill, you would indeed be well on your way toward becoming proficient in the use of this skill. If you knew this about any thinking skill to the point that you could explain it as well as demonstrate it to others less expert in the skill than you, you would be well on your way to being able to design and conduct skill-learning lessons that would have the best chance possible of helping students to develop the degree of expertise in thinking—and the significant subject-matter learnings that result from skillful thinking—that are the ultimate goals of effective thinking skill instruction.

The most important features of any thinking skill are often referred to by information processing specialists as *attributes*. Briefly put, a skill attribute is a component or element of a thinking skill that is engaged or utilized in the process of carrying out that skill. Although experts have suggested a number of attributes typical of most cognitive skills, knowledge of three seems to be of major value in teaching any thinking skill. These are, as modeled in Figure 1.4:

1. A *procedure*—a series of steps and substeps (or a routine and subroutines) by which the skill is carried out by those who are reasonably proficient in it. In other words, a procedure is what one *does mentally* in *doing* the skill—what one does first, does next, then does next, and so on.

2. The *rules* or principles one follows which inform and guide the execution and application of this procedure. For example, thinking up as many alternatives as possible before deciding on one is an important procedural rule in decision making because it calls attention to the danger of neglecting *all* the possibilities and prematurely deciding on one when, with some further reflection, a potentially better alternative might be found.

3. *Criteria* or other *knowledge* is applied in carrying out the procedure or following the rules as the skill is executed. Criteria are standards or conditions that must be met for something to be judged an example of what it purports to be. For example, for a particular sweater to be the ''best alternative'' when purchasing a sweater, it may have to be a specific color, made of a particular type of material, be a particular size and style, and be within a given price range. Color, material, size, style, and cost are criteria for making this choice. As another example, one criterion of a reliable, credible source is that the author be an expert in or extremely well-informed about what he or she is writing. Many thinking skills use specific criteria, knowledge of which is required to carry out the skill well.

In addition to certain criteria, or instead of criteria, some thinking skills utilize other kinds of knowledge. Some thinking skills rely on knowledge of certain concepts. Decision making, for example, relies on one's understanding of the concepts of causation and probability. Some skills benefit from the use of content-specific concepts, as classifying information about any people's way of life benefits from use of concept categories such as social class, norms, roles, and similar subject matter of ''domain-specific'' concepts. Some skills are principle-directed. Such principles are often presented as heuristics or rules of thumb that can be used to guide the execution of the skill. In decision making, for instance, experts recommend deliberately looking for reasons or evidence *against* a fa-

Figure 1.4 Major Attributes of Any Thinking Skill

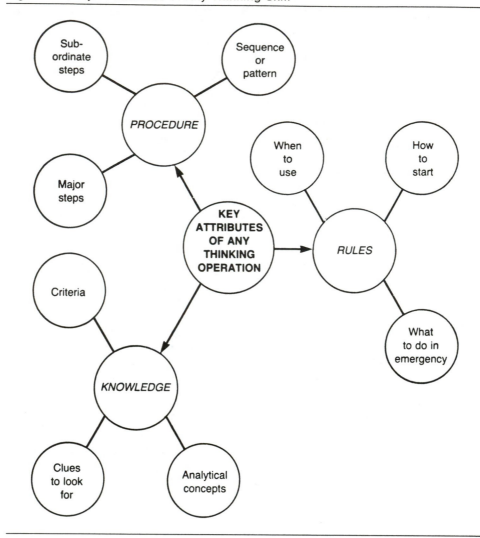

Source: Barry K. Beyer, *Developing a Thinking Skills Program* (Boston: Allyn and Bacon, 1988).

vored alternative as a way of preventing any initial bias in favor of the alternative from overriding an objective analysis of its consequences and value. Some skills include several of these kinds of knowledge, some only one kind, and others none at all. But to carry out any thinking skill with some degree of expertise usually involves the use of some criteria or other kind of knowledge closely associated with the skill.

Figure 1.4 depicts a generalized model of any thinking skill in terms of these three kinds of attributes: *procedure, rules,* and *knowledge.* Figure 1.5 shows how this model can be used to describe the major attributes of a specific skill—that of predicting. The three skill attributes presented here characterize virtually every thinking skill you may be called on to use or teach, whether it be as simple an operation as predicting or as complex as decision making.

The information presented about the skill of predicting in Figure 1.5 obvi-

Figure 1.5 Predicting: A Description

PREDICTING

DEFINITION	Stating in advance what will probably happen or be true next; forecasting, extrapolating, foretelling, prophesizing, projecting

PROCEDURE
1. State and clearly define what the prediction is to be about.
2. Collect/skim given data relevant to the prediction to be made.
3. Recall information you already know about the topic/situation.
4. Identify a pattern, trend, or repetition in the recalled data.
5. Map the perceived pattern(s) on the given data to imagine the next possible instances of the perceived patterns.
6. Determine the probability of each imagined outcome actually occurring.
7. Select the outcome most likely to occur.

RULES
1. *When to use?*
   - in hypothesizing or inferring about any topic or subject
   - in forming new categories or groups of any data
   - . . .

2. *How to start?*
   - ask yourself, "What could happen (or be true) next?"
   - arrange the data on paper or in a diagram
   - . . .

3. *What to do if . . .*
   - little relevant information exists? Think of similar situations, or of problems in the past, or of analogies.
   - it is difficult to generate possible outcomes? Brainstorm as many solutions as possible without regard to probabilities.
   - . . .

KNOWLEDGE
or
CRITERIA
1. Comparing, contrasting
2. Various types of patterns (such as temporal, spatial, numerical, cause-effect, functional, etc.)
3. Probabilities
4. Potential intervening conditions, variations, and influences related to the subject
5. Historical, analogical situations/problems/conditions

Source: Adapted from Barry K. Beyer, *Developing a Thinking Skills Program* (Boston: Allyn and Bacon, 1988).

ously does not represent all that experts know or assert about this thinking skill. But it does include some of the most important information about how this skill is presumed to work. Knowledge like this is virtually indispensable to effective instruction in any thinking skill.

Why is this procedural knowledge of any thinking skill so useful? It is exactly what you need to know in order to explain and demonstrate clearly how a particular thinking skill can be effectively carried out. Reference to this knowledge helps you, in teaching the skill, to keep students focused on the major attributes of the thinking skill rather than on anything about it that may happen to come up. Knowing this much about a thinking skill also helps minimize the dangers of accepting from students irrelevant, dysfunctional, or even erroneous ideas about what they believe to be rules or procedures involved in carrying out the skill. Furthermore, knowledge of the major attributes of a thinking skill enables you to design learning experiences in which students can engage successfully to generate this or similar knowledge and expertise for themselves. Such knowledge also proves useful in preparing tests or other kinds of thinking skill assessments. It is especially useful here, for example, in helping to pinpoint where students who are having trouble carrying out a particular skill may be going wrong. Clearly, any teacher who knows the major attributes of a thinking skill being taught is much more likely to be successful in teaching the skill than is a teacher who does not possess this knowledge.

---

checkpoint

When you can describe in some detail, giving specific examples, three different kinds of attributes of most thinking skills, check here. ☐

---

3. Examine descriptions of the attributes of several thinking skills.

One way to become familiar with the kinds of information that should be included in any explanation of the procedural knowledge or attributes of a thinking skill is to examine some already-prepared descriptions of different thinking skills. By identifying the skill-specific examples of each kind of attribute included in these descriptions, you can form a mental target or model of what you will need to look for in analyzing and then describing the thinking skill you have selected. Examining these descriptions will also familiarize you with a skill-description format that you can use in recording for yourself and reporting to others the attributes of the skill you have developed.

To be most useful, *any thinking skill description ought to present as explicitly as possible what those somewhat expert in the skill do mentally to execute the skill.* The description of the thinking skill in Figure 1.6 presents this essential information. Like the description of the skill of predicting in Figure 1.5, this description of decision making first describes the skill generally, in terms of a rather straightforward definition and synonyms. The description then presents more detailed information about the skill's procedural attributes, organized in terms of the *steps* someone skilled in carrying it out uses, some *rules* that guide and direct how one might execute the skill, and certain *knowledge* useful in carrying it out. Of course, this description is rather general and incomplete. At best, it represents what its author(s) believe to be how a particular mental operation is performed by those reasonably expert in applying it. The information provided under each of the three kinds of skill attributes exemplifies the kinds of information that should be included in any description of the procedural knowledge that characterizes any specific thinking skill. The *format* by which the information describing the skill is presented here serves as a useful format for describing

Figure 1.6 Decision Making: A Description

DECISION MAKING

DEFINITION Selecting an alternative from among a number of alternatives to achieve a goal *deciding*: choosing, picking, opting, selecting

STEPS
1. Identify and define clearly the goal(s) to be achieved.
2. Identify alternatives (options) by which the goal(s) can be achieved.
3. Analyze the alternatives in terms of criteria, such as:
   * goals(s)—long/short range
   * predicted consequences
     long range/short range
     consequences of consequences
   * costs
     real costs
     opportunity costs
   * resources
     available
     substitute
   * constraints
   * . . .
4. Weight and rank alternatives (in terms of the weights assigned to the criteria used)
5. Choose the top two or three alternatives
6. Evaluate the top alternatives in terms of selected criteria, such as:
   * risks
   * unanticipated consequences
   * strategies available to enact
   * values
   * . . .
7. Choose the best alternative

RULES
1. When to use?
   * in any "choice" situation, such as selecting a course of action to follow, something to believe, etc.
   * in attempting to resolve any problem involving values or divergent "potential solutions"
   * . . .
2. How to start?
   * brainstorm potential alternatives and alternatives to these alternatives
   * establish criteria to be used and relative weight of each
   * recall previous successful or comparable decision making cases
   * . . .
3. What to do if . . .
   * you are inclined early toward a specific solution? Look for additional options or for evidence against a favored option. Don't jump at the first seemingly "good" alternative that turns up!
   * you assume most alternatives are of equal weight? Identify relevant uncertainties and probabilities regarding alternatives.
   * you deal with various opinions and data sources? Apply critical thinking skills to determine their worth, accuracy, credibility, relevance, biases, etc.

KNOWLEDGE
1. Understand sources of decision-making interference, including impulsiveness, conflict of interest/bias, "ends justifies the means" mentality, irrational persistance of key beliefs
2. Understand conditions and forces likely to affect alternatives and their consequences in their future occurences

Source: Adapted from Barry K. Beyer, *Developing a Thinking Skills Program* (Boston: Allyn and Bacon, 1988).

these procedural attributes so teachers can design and teach lessons calculated to help youngsters learn a skill well.

Each of the sets of skill-teaching materials included in Part II of this handbook starts with a description of the thinking skill that is the focus of the lessons and test in that set. All these skill descriptions employ a format similar to that in Figures 1.5 and 1.6. To understand this format and to identify the kinds of information you can include in the description of the skill you will soon be preparing, you should examine several of these descriptions now. (In doing so, you should be careful to avoid looking at the description of any particular thinking skill you plan to develop, if this skill is included here, so you don't prejudice your own inquiry later.)

As you look at these skill descriptions, continuously ask yourself, ''Is this what I would want to know if I had to teach this skill to my students?'' Your answers to this question will help you determine if the information provided under the categories of *steps, rules,* and *knowledge* really do provide the procedural information you need. As you study these descriptions, also attend to the *format* of each presentation so you will later be able to describe the skill you select in this way. Detailed analysis of the substance of each skill can wait until later, when you may wish to teach those skills.

There are, of course, some cautions to be observed in making or using skill descriptions like these. First, these descriptions must be considered tentative. *By no means are they to be considered prescriptive.* They are often derived from limited applications of the skill to specific tasks—applications that in other tasks or contexts might be carried out somewhat differently and that almost certainly change as their users become more sophisticated in their use. Skill descriptions also vary considerably in quality, depending on the authors' expertise in carrying out the skill and their abilities to articulate what they are doing and why. For example, experts often carry out skills in fewer apparent steps than do beginners. Moreover, it is often difficult, initially, to become aware of and articulate clearly all that one does or knows in carrying out any specific thinking skill.

No thinking skill description should be presented as or considered to be *the* way any specific skill works for everyone. It presents just one way the skill *can* be executed. Other individuals may have different ways of doing it effectively and these procedures need eventually to be articulated and shared. But if you are teaching a skill for the first time or do not know much about how to execute the skill, having this much information about it is a big help. This knowledge can become an excellent springboard for developing your students'—as well as your own—understanding of the skill. Remember, however, that any description of a thinking skill is *not* to be considered or presented as something to memorize or slavishly follow without modification. It is simply a guide and takeoff point for *you* in providing instruction in the skill.

checkpoint

When you can describe in some detail the ingredients of a useful description of the procedural attributes of any thinking skill, check here:

—— **note**

If you already clearly understand the procedural attributes of the thinking skill on which you wish to focus—the significant rules and procedure by which it is carried out, and the criteria it applies or any specific skill-related knowledge or heuristics—you do not need to read pages 19–33 in this chapter. Instead, simply write out a detailed description of this thinking skill and put it in a form like that in Figure 1.6 as directed in Step 6 starting on page 33. Then complete the remaining pages of this handbook.

However, if you do not have a clear understanding of how to identify the major procedural attributes of a thinking skill you might wish to teach, or if you would like to clarify your understanding of a particular thinking skill, you should continue on here. The remainder of this chapter will help you accomplish these goals.

IDENTIFYING AND DESCRIBING THE ATTRIBUTES OF A THINKING SKILL

Teaching thinking skills starts with identifying and describing the procedural attributes of the skill you wish to teach. You can accomplish these tasks by doing the following for the thinking skill you selected earlier:

4. Use a process of reflective analysis to identify the key attributes of the thinking skill selected. (This consists of analyzing how the skill works in practice, by identifying what you and/or others who are ''good at it'' *do* mentally when carrying out that skill. If you do not know how to do this, then you need to learn a procedure that you can use to conduct this analysis.)

5. Identify the key attributes of this thinking skill as described by specialists.

6. Draft a description of the major attributes of the skill.

7. Revise the skill description incorporating feedback from others.

8. Rewrite the skill description as appropriate for the grade or experience level of your students.

Suggestions as to how to accomplish each of these five tasks are given on the following pages.

4. Use a process of reflective analysis to identify the key attributes of the thinking skill selected.

If this is the first time you have tried to identify or describe the attributes of a thinking skill or at least to think seriously about doing so, it would be most helpful at this time to join with one or two of your colleagues to work on the same skill and to proceed from this point on as a team. In this way, you can assist each other in analyzing the skill, preparing the skill description, and writing lesson plans to teach the skill. By engaging in the discussions that will be required to produce group-written products in each of these areas, you will learn more about the thinking skill you have chosen to work on, about teaching thinking skills in general, and about your own thinking than if you work alone. Teaming with others to carry out the tasks presented here provides the opportunity and support needed for such cooperative interaction to be most useful in learning.

There are several ways you can go about identifying the three major kinds of attributes of any thinking operation. One consists of actually performing the skill or strategy yourself and then, with several of your peers who have also just carried it out, reflecting on and reporting how you believe you did it. Another way is to find and study what specialists have written about the skill. Although there are other, more time-consuming ways to learn about a skill, these two are very practical ways to develop the kinds of insights into a skill you ought to possess before you try to teach it to others.

Either of these procedures can produce an initial understanding of a thinking skill you wish to teach. For best results, however, both should be used. Generally speaking, it seems most useful first to perform the skill yourself and analyze how you think you did it, and then to find out what specialists say about the skill. This prevents you from being locked in to one particular version of the skill before you try it yourself. However, it denies you the insights of experts or other specialists who have grappled with trying to understand the operation—insights that might alert you to how to improve and inform your own execution of the skill.

Whichever approach you use first, be sure to use *both* procedures to identify some of the major attributes of any thinking skill or strategy before planning lessons or tests on it.

Trying to execute a thinking skill yourself and then articulating how you believe you did it and why you did it that way is probably the best way to clarify the key attributes of any thinking skill. By doing so, you can discover what you already know about the skill and also establish a clear, experiential reference point for understanding what others, including your students, assert about the skill. Chances are that such reflection will be most enlightening. However, it is also somewhat risky. You might not be as good at performing this skill as you believe you are. Or you might be unable to verbalize exactly how you do carry it out. Indeed, you might even carry it out in a very inappropriate or dysfunctional way or be unable to do so at all. What you finally articulate about the skill may not be very helpful for teaching. Working with some colleagues as you try this approach can help you minimize these risks. Open-mindedness and tentativeness throughout this process are also helpful.

One way to carry out this task is to use a reflective procedure referred to as the 3-D procedure. It works this way:

1. **D**efine the skill to be studied.
2. **D**o it.
3. **D**escribe it in detail by discussing with others how each of you did it and why you did it that way.

Repeating this 3-D procedure *several times for the same skill* will enable you to develop extremely useful insights into how the skill *might* work and to generate a description of the major attributes of the skill.

note

If you know how to use the 3-D procedure or a similar procedure to identify the attributes of any thinking skill, skip to page 28. However, if this procedure for identifying skill attributes is unfamiliar to you, take time at this point to learn how to do it. The next few pages will guide you in accomplishing this goal. Once you have become familiar with the 3-D procedure, you can then use it to identify the attributes of the thinking skill on which you have chosen to focus, and, for that matter, the attributes of *any* thinking skill.

Becoming Familiar with the Details of How the 3-D Procedure of Reflective Analysis Works.   If you wish to learn to carry out the 3-D procedure of reflective analysis before using it to identify the attributes of a particular skill, you can start by finding out more about this procedure. Then you can practice it a few times, concentrating on how it works rather than on the product of its use. After you are comfortable with using this procedure, you can then use it to identify the attributes of your chosen skill. The 3-D procedure consists essentially of three major steps. Once you have selected a specific skill on which to concentrate:

- *Define the skill.*

With several colleagues, look up the definition of your selected skill in several reputable dictionaries and record these definitions. The most useful dictionaries for this purpose are large, unabridged editions because they give detailed, multiple definitions, examples, and synonyms of the terms they define. In collecting these definitions, be sure you find definitions of the skill label *as a verb* rather than some secondary or alternative definitions. *Under no circumstances* should you simply give a definition from memory or invent one off the top of your head. At this point, you need as accurate and reliable a definition as possible to help you understand the skill.

You may also wish to consult definitions of this skill prepared by different specialists in thinking. Four sources useful in this regard are:

Bloom, Benjamin, et al. *Taxonomy of Educational Objectives: Handbook I—The Cognitive Domain.* New York: David McKay, 1956.

Costa, Arthur L. (ed.). *Developing Minds.* Alexandria, VA: Association for Supervision and Curriculum Development, 1985, pp. 309–313.

Ennis, Robert. "A Concept of Critical Thinking." *Harvard Educational Review* 32:1 (Winter 1962), pp. 81–111.

Marzano, Robert, et al. *Dimensions of Thinking.* Alexandria, VA: Association for Supervision and Curriculum Development, 1987.

Collecting and analyzing definitions for a specific skill from *all* of the above sources, including several reputable dictionaries, will help you develop a sense of what the skill involves. It will also help you identify what the skill does *not* involve. With this information, you will be better able to carry out the skill.

After recording definitions of the skill from at least three different dictionaries and/or other appropriate sources, examine these definitions carefully to identify what seem to be the features of the skill common to all definitions.

Then, either adopt the definition that most clearly articulates the essence of this skill or write a new definition of your own that accurately and completely defines the skill. The latter is preferable because putting given definitions into your own words—paraphrasing them accurately and completely—helps you clarify in your own mind what the skill label really means.

Completing a definition following this procedure should take only about ten minutes or so. For example, assume you have elected to describe the skill *analyze.* You need to start this process by collecting definitions of this skill from three different dictionaries. Perhaps you and your partners might collect these definitions:

A. to separate an intellectual or substantial whole into its component parts (*Webster's New Collegiate Dictionary*)

B. to separate any material or abstract entity into its constituent elements and their essential relationships (*Random House Dictionary of the English Language*)

C. to determine by separation or isolation the fundamental elements of something; to determine by mental discernment the nature, significance and inter-relationship of the various parts, elements, aspects or qualities (*Webster's Third New International Dictionary*)

Now you should examine these definitions either to pick out the most accurate and complete one or to combine and rework these into one that is accurate and complete. Definition B is a pretty accurate definition. But you could also paraphrase the essence of all three into your own definition, which might read:

analyze—to separate a whole into its component parts in order to identify these parts and their relationships to each other and to the whole.

Suppose you want to look at another source in addition to the dictionaries. If you were to consult Arthur Costa's *Developing Minds,* you would find that he and Barbara Presseisen, two specialists in teaching thinking, define *analyze* as "to separate or break up a whole into its parts according to some plan or reason" (p. 309). This definition nicely summarizes the essence of the dictionary definitions noted above.

Although completing this task of defining a skill requires little effort or time, it is essential to learning about the skill, for it sets up what you need to do next. By generating a working definition of the skill, you develop a mental set that will enable you to execute that skill rather successfully—and rather faithfully. Without this type of preparation, jumping right into an effort to perform the skill may actually result in your doing a less-than-expert execution of the skill or unknowingly carrying out another skill instead. Any confusion at this point could lead to an inaccurate or quite dysfunctional understanding of the skill with serious negative results in the classroom later.

- *Do it.*

By yourself, do the skill. This means you have to have some data to process or a task to do that requires carrying out the skill. You should have the task or data prepared in advance so you can complete or use the skill immediately after agreeing on or writing the definition of the skill. If you do not have such a task already prepared, you will need to prepare it at this time. Whatever task you arrange, it should require a relatively short time to complete, three to five minutes at most. A skill-using task of any greater length is likely to make it impossible for you to recall later what you did mentally as you carried out the task. You and those working with you should all do the same task, but independently of each other, so you will have common referents on which to base the reflective analysis that is to follow.

An alternative to doing the task alone, especially when the skill being analyzed appears to be a rather complex one or one that takes a relatively long time (eight to ten minutes or so) to carry out, is to execute the skill with a partner. In doing this, one of you can execute the skill and report aloud what you are thinking and why (about every two to three seconds or so) while the other records these reports and prods the "doer" to report whenever he or she remains silent too long. This should take no more than ten minutes, depending on the complexity of the skill.

Continuing our example of "analyze," assume you found the following in your local newspaper's *Letters to the Editor. Analyze* it.

> It occurred to me recently that the biggest obstacle we must overcome in this country is general stupidity. While driving home from work the other day, I encountered two elderly women riding bicycles side-by-side in the middle of Fairmount Blvd., which is a heavily traveled route during rush hour. They seemed to be oblivious to the danger to themselves, as well as to those who had to maneuver around them. Not three miles later, I came upon another bike rider, this time a young man who fancied himself an Olympic hopeful. When I informed him (with a couple blasts of my horn) that he should move from the middle of my lane, I was greeted with an obscene gesture.
>
> At a recent softball game, one of the spectators let his dog run loose on the field. When informed that his pet was being a nuisance, he responded with an obscenity and told us we were dog-haters. Certainly, the dog was not to blame for its ignorance.
>
> Stupidity pervades all aspects of our society. Most of our politicians seem to be afflicted with the disease. Reagan is convinced that the way to deal with enemies is to blow them up. He thinks that force is a substitute for moral integrity.
>
> Perhaps we should institute mandatory classes in school to teach common sense, decency and courtesy. It is obvious that parents don't do a very good job of conveying these ideas to their children. How can they, when they are the biggest culprits in spreading the disease?[4]

The exercise you choose to engage in may involve using a letter to an editor like that above, a word problem, a children's story, a news article, an object, a painting, or some other type of data. Whatever you use should permit you to carry out the specific skill you are examining in a reasonably short amount of time.

- *Describe it.*

Once you and your peers have carried out the skill to complete the task you have designed, you can identify and then share with each other what you recall or observed doing mentally as you carried out the task. To assist you in doing this, keep asking yourself (or a colleague you may be helping try to recall what he or she did), "What did I (you) do first? Why? Next? Why?" and so on until you (or your colleague) have recalled and listed as much as possible about what was done mentally to carry out the skill. Then you should examine and discuss why you did what you did. These items may be recorded under the skill attribute headings of *steps* (what was done), *rules* (why it was done), and *knowledge*, or simply listed in random order to be classified under these headings after you have each recorded what you believe you did. After recording this information, analyze it to put what is listed under *steps* into some type of sequence or several parallel sequences. Then, infer the key skill rule and knowledge attributes from the rest of what has been listed, primarily the responses to the ''Why did I (you) do this?'' question. By articulating and examining information about the procedure you used to execute the skill, you can identify some of the more useful attributes of this skill.

In reflecting on and describing how you analyzed the letter to the editor presented earlier, you may recall that you perhaps initiated your analysis by skimming or reading the letter. As you did, perhaps you noticed that the author was making certain claims and providing statements intended to support his claims. So, maybe you then went back to identify each claim (such as ''the biggest obstacle we must overcome . . . is general stupidity'') and then examined each statement to see how it connected to the claim or to see if it was logical or factually accurate. In sum, you skimmed or read the letter, then proceeded to take it apart to identify the parts (claims and reasons or examples) in order to determine how the parts were related, and then judged the quality of the parts before judging the strength of the entire argument.

One of your partners who has analyzed this same writing sample may report the same process you did or may report that she believes she started analyzing it by deciding first what she was going to analyze it for. Having noticed a major claim in the very first sentence, she says she elected to read on to analyze the letter for its author's point of view. So, as she scanned the letter she tried to recall what clues to look for to determine an author's point of view. Remembering that the use of ''loaded'' words or special terms, as well as choice of facts provided, might be clues to point of view, she then looked carefully at each sentence to see if she could find such clues. Phrases like ''fancied himself,'' ''a couple blasts,'' and ''nuisance'' suggest a particular point of view—a cynic at best, a grouch at worst. As she accumulated evidence of these and other clues, she began to see a pattern and eventually described what she believed to be the author's point of view.

Much more will have been discussed in completing this step of the 3-D process, of course, before you and your partners have identified specific steps, some possible rules, and perhaps even some criteria or knowledge used as each of you carried out the skill. By articulating and recording these, you and your partners are on your way to identifying some major attributes of that skill, just as the individuals described in the example presented here were doing with the skill of *analyzing*.

In carrying out this final step of the 3-D procedure, you should follow several guidelines:

1. Do *not* try to get consensus as to a single series of steps or rules. Rather, identify several different procedures if you or your colleagues believe you each carried out the skill differently.

2. Be as specific and precise as possible. The first response to ''How did I do it?'' usually is a rather global statement. Although a useful way of initiating this reflective reporting, such a response is of little use in delineating the exact procedure you carried out. You must probe beyond the global to identify the *specific* components of this procedure.

3. Probe as deeply as you can. Ask yourself and those working with you, ''What did you do first? Why?'' Answers to the first question usually produce steps and procedures. Answers to the second question (''Why?'') often reveal

rules or principles, something you know that is guiding you through the task. Follow these two questions with a string of ''What did you do next? Why?'' questions, repeated, answered, and clarified until you have identified the key procedural attributes of the skill as best you can. Clarify each response as much as possible. It is useful to remember that you probably are not aware of all you did mentally to execute the skill. This is natural. The mind operates very rapidly, especially if you are already proficient in carrying out the skill. But by reflecting, probing, and asking yourself ''What did I do? Why did I do that?'' or ''How did I do that?'' and so on, you can uncover a great deal about what you seem to do to carry out any thinking skill.

4. Concentrate initially on identifying only the *major* steps of the skill and any obvious rules or knowledge needed to execute them. It is not necessary to incorporate in your description of the skill something fitting each type of attribute. Nor is it advisable to include everything everyone in your group believes they did to execute it. Furthermore, avoid what may appear to be rather idiosyncratic, at least for the time being.

5. Focus on the thinking skill rather than on the data or subject to which you are applying the skill. Avoid discussion of the data. Concentrate instead on *what you did mentally to perform the skill.* Articulate what you did in terms of mental operations and justify these operations in terms of rules for executing the skill rather than subject matter or content, data, or knowledge. The essential task is ''What did you do *in your mind* to carry out this skill—and why?''

6. Be sure that the procedure you identify tells as clearly as possible how to carry out critical steps in the skill procedure. For example, a description of *predicting* that states the procedure as ''determine what is to be predicted about, collect relevant data, and make a prediction about what will happen next'' is hardly useful in identifying what one does to ''make a prediction.'' A description of the procedure of any thinking skill needs to delineate clearly and exactly *what one does* to carry out the key steps of the skill.

7. Don't worry if you don't discover anything you might call a ''rule.'' It takes repeated tries at doing a skill to become aware of any habitual, consistent, or repeated practice by which you execute the skill. For the time being, include these under ''knowledge.'' After you have executed the skill several times, however, you may be able to identify some potential rules if you ask—and try to answer—these questions:

   a. What did I do first? Why?
   b. What problems or obstacles arose as I did this?
   c. What did I do when I first encountered this problem? How? Why?
   d. What could I have done to resolve this problem or overcome this obstacle? How would I do it? Why?
   e. Where would I ever use this skill? Why?
   f. What would I do after I finished using this skill? Why?

Responses to these and similar questions may assist you in identifying valuable heuristics (rules of thumb) or procedural rules for carrying out the operation in a rapid, expert manner. These can then be inserted into your skill description under ''rules,'' perhaps as ''when to use'' or ''how to start'' or ''what to do if . . . '' rules, three kinds of rules that can be identified for any thinking skill.

8. Generalize, if possible, beyond the data or immediate task. That is, don't tie the description to a specific data set or problem, but rather broaden it to include all kinds of data or applicable problems. For example, if you were using

predicting the weather as a task for identifying the attributes of *predicting*, don't specify the exact data needed to make a prediction (prevailing winds, weather fronts, yesterday's temperature, etc.). Instead, describe the attributes in more general terms, such as "data about similar events/conditions in the past," knowing that these will vary according to the topic about which one will be predicting.

One way to generalize a skill description is to do the skill again, using other kinds of data to see how it works with these different data. *Repeat this several times with different data sets each time.* Then try to identify the attributes of the skill procedure that seem to be common to the several appropriate tasks or data sets.

9. Remain tentative. Remember that what you are discovering is based on *your* experience and thus is limited. Use the resulting insights as guides, *not* as the only way to execute the skill. Be open to alternatives and especially to refinements and clarification of your initial perceptions about the skill. Change your description of the skill as you learn more about it to correct first impressions, to clarify initially vague thoughts, and to incorporate additional information such as newly discovered subroutines or rules.

You can conclude this 3-D processing by recording what you have learned about the skill, then categorizing your notes under the headings of *steps, rules,* and *knowledge/criteria.* Ideally, you should then try the skill several more times to see what else you can learn about the skill as well as to generalize it beyond a single, specific application. If you do this with a partner, switch roles so the one who recorded the first time is the one who actually executes the skill the next time and vice versa. The more times you apply and discuss the skill, the more you will discover about it.

To conclude the example of how to use the 3-D procedure to understand the skill of analyzing, assume you have other items you and your partners can analyze. For example, you might analyze a historical document or portion thereof, such as the preamble to the Declaration of Independence. After reflecting on and discussing how you carried out this task, all of you might then analyze a short poem or a newspaper ad, then a chart or graph, and, finally, perhaps a student's grades. In each instance, *be sure to focus on the skill,* not on the content of whatever is being analyzed. By analyzing and discussing what you did mentally to execute your analysis of each of these in turn, you will clarify, elaborate, and generalize how the skill of analyzing seems to work for you and your colleagues. Recording what you report under *steps, rules,* and *knowledge/ criteria,* you can assemble what you have discovered about the skill in a way that will enable you to prepare a clearly written descripton of the skill, using the format presented in Figure 1.8 on page 34.

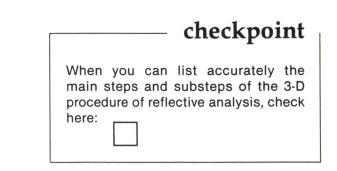

checkpoint

When you can list accurately the main steps and substeps of the 3-D procedure of reflective analysis, check here: ☐

Practicing the 3-D Procedure of Reflective Analysis.   Reading about the 3-D procedure is one thing; being able to do it is quite another. To achieve the latter goal, you should now practice this 3-D procedure several times before attempting to use it to identify the attributes of the skill you selected to work on earlier. Trying to use an unfamiliar procedure to learn about an unfamiliar skill is rather cumbersome, to say the least. But becoming familiar with the 3-D procedure first can allow you later to concentrate on the skill that you are trying to learn about because you will then be able to use this procedure rather automatically.

One way to practice the 3-D procedure is, first, apply it to a very simple skill. Doing it with a number of your colleagues is also helpful. Under the leadership of someone familiar with how to use this procedure, or someone responsible for carrying out the directions given above, apply it to learn about a relatively uncomplicated (and even nonthinking) skill. Have the group leader monitor or model the 3-D procedure as all of you work on this skill.

For example, what do you do to carry out the skill of *using an index*? Go through each of the steps of *Define it, Do it,* and *Describe it* to execute this task. For instance, imagine that you have been assigned to find out in your science text where Boyle's Law is explained. If you have no science text handy, do this in your imagination after you have defined *index* and *using an index*. To get you started at this, here are three different dictionary definitions of *index:*

A. anything that serves to guide or point out (*Websters Collegiate Dictionary*)

B. an alphabetical listing of names, places and subjects in a printed work that gives for each the page number(s) where it can be found (*American Heritage Dictionary*)

C. an alphabetical listing of places, names and topics that gives the page number(s) on which these are discussed or mentioned. (*Random House Dictionary*)

What is a good working defintion of *index*? Of *using an index*? After you have answered these questions, complete the 3-D procedure by doing and describing the skill of *using an index*. Conclude by outlining a description of *using an index* in a format like those in Figures 1.5 and 1.6.

---
note

You can find a description of what other teachers have done as they performed this task by referring to Appendix A. Read the first example to see how others worked through the procedure to identify the attributes of the skill *using an index*. As you study this example, focus on how the 3-D procedure is carried out, because what you are trying to learn here is this reflective analysis procedure, not any specific thinking skill.

Next, carry out this 3-D procedure with one or two colleagues to identify the attributes of another relatively uncomplicated thinking skill, perhaps the skill of *comparing*. After defining *comparing*, compare what school is like today with what it was like when you went to school. Then describe what you did mentally to make that comparison.

Each time you have completed this process, reflect on *how* you carried out this 3-D procedure. Remember, the purpose here is to become comfortable with the 3-D procedure rather than to learn about any particular thinking skill.

---

note

Additional examples of how this procedure works to analyze other thinking skills may also be found in Appendix A. Review these examples to identify how each step in the 3-D process is carried out. As you review this procedure, be sure to focus on the 3-D procedure itself rather than on the specific skills it is being used to investigate. If interested, you can take additional time later to find out more about these skills.

It is not easy to carry out a thinking skill and then reflect on how you did what you did and why, especially on your first one or two attempts. It is frequently difficult to recapture your thought processes unless you have trained yourself to reflect on how you think. It is also difficult to separate the mental operations performed from the data being used as vehicles for employing these operations. Moreover, many of us do not really carry out complex thinking operations—such as finding unstated assumptions, or identifying an author's point of view, or decision making—very well. Initial efforts to employ the 3-D procedure for identifying skill attributes may thus be quite challenging and even somewhat frustrating. However, by following the guidelines and procedures outlined above, by carrying out the 3-D procedure a number of "practice" times *before* you use it to analyze a thinking skill you really wish to understand, and by examining examples of how others have used this procedure, you can become quite good at it and comfortable in doing it.

---

checkpoint

When you can carry out and have explained to a peer, to his or her satisfaction, how to carry out the 3-D procedure for identifying the attributes of any thinking skill, check here:

☐

Identifying Thinking Skill Attributes by Reflective Analysis.   At this point, you should be comfortable with the 3-D procedure for identifying thinking skill attributes. With one or two others you can now use this procedure to identify the attributes of the skill you have selected. As you proceed, this is now the time to *focus on the thinking skill you are trying to learn more about.* Producing a detailed description of this skill similar in format to that shown in Figures 1.5 and 1.6 should be your ultimate goal.

Remember: In analyzing how the skill you have selected seems to work, you can proceed through these steps:

- Define the skill.
- Do it.
- Describe in detail what you (and your colleagues) did *mentally* as you carried it out and why you did what you did.

Be sure to repeat this procedure several times as you apply the skill to different kinds of data, so you can generalize or broaden your description of it beyond the context of any single kind of task or set of data.

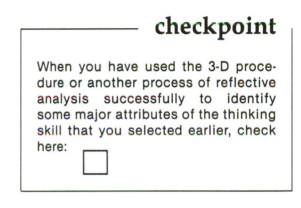

checkpoint

When you have used the 3-D procedure or another process of reflective analysis successfully to identify some major attributes of the thinking skill that you selected earlier, check here: ☐

5. Identify the key attributes of this thinking skill as described by specialists.

Another way of identifying the attributes of any thinking operation is to analyze what specialists have written about it. In recent years, a number of psychologists and educators have published descriptions of selected thinking operations. Unfortunately, however, these descriptions are of uneven quality. In some instances, they do not deal with how the operation is actually executed, which is precisely what you want to find out from such descriptions. All of these descriptions, whether based on protocol analyses or on theoretical reflection, are rather idiosyncratic and incomplete. Yet, if you can find a number of descriptions by *different* authors or researchers, you can combine relevant points they make with the results of your own inquiry to produce an even more accurate and detailed— *but still quite tentative*—description of the skill. Such a description will then be that much more useful in planning how to teach or test this skill.

Where can you find descriptions of or detailed information about thinking skills? Currently there are only two main types of sources to which you can turn. Figure 1.7 lists some books and articles that present information in some depth about selected thinking skills. These seem to be the best available on these skills, although additional similar sources may also exist.

Briefer, less detailed thinking skill descriptions can also be found in another type of source. These are books and articles prepared especially for teachers, which provide what essentially are outlines of the attributes of selected thinking skills. Although not in the depth of those sources listed in Figure 1.7, these additional sources provide what their authors consider to be essential procedural information about each of a number of different thinking skills, arranged

Figure 1.7 Selected Sources of Information about Thinking Skills

1. Bloom, Benjamin, et al. *Taxonomy of Educational Objectives—Handbook I: Cognitive Domain.* New York: David McKay, 1956.
   This volume describes the nature of different types of educational objectives presented in the form of a taxonomy of cognitive behaviors moving from recall to comprehension, application, analysis, synthesis, and evaluation.

2. Bransford, John, and Barry Stein. *The IDEAL Problem Solver.* New York: W. H. Freeman and Company, 1984.
   This volume describes and explains problem solving as consisting of five major steps, and analyzes skills related to problem solving such as memory, comprehension, critical analysis, creativity, and effective communication.

3. Damer, T. Edward. *Attacking Faulty Reasoning.* Belmont, CA: Wadsworth, 1980.
   In this small, college-level book, philosopher Damer describes fifty-eight common logical fallacies, providing for each a definition, several examples, and the way to attack it.

4. Ennis, Robert H. "A Concept of Critical Thinking." *Harvard Educational Review* 32:1 (Winter 1962), pp. 81–111.
   This classic analysis of critical thinking includes the identification of key critical thinking skills and a general description of various attributes of these operations.

5. Frederiksen, Norman. "Implications of Cognitive Theory for Instruction in Problem Solving." *Review of Educational Research* 54:3 (Fall 1984), pp. 363–407.
   In this summary of research studies into the nature of problem solving, Educational Testing Service psychologist Frederiksen analyzes various models of the process and how it is used with ill-defined as well as with clearly defined problems. He also explains a number of key implications for teaching problem solving.

6. Friedman, Michael, and Steven Rowls. *Teaching Reading and Thinking Skills.* New York: Longman, 1980.
   On pages 169–211 the authors describe some of the characteristics of different thinking skills including categorizing, fact/opinion, relevant/irrelevant, deductive reasoning, inductive reasoning, predicting, and conceptualizing.

7. Hayes, John R. *The Complete Problem Solver.* Philadelphia: Franklin Institute Press, 1981.
   This text in general problem solving for college students includes sections on problem representation, memory and ways to use it, learning strategies, decision making, and creativity and invention. This is best read after Polya's work (below).

8. Hurst, Joe B., et al. "The Decision-Making Process." *Theory and Research in Social Education* 11:3 (Fall 1983), pp. 17–43.
   Although less complete than Frederiksen's analysis of research on problem solving, Hurst's survey of studies and articles on decision making provides a useful insight into various models and components of this major thinking process.

9. Kepner, Charles H., and Benjamin B. Tregoe. *The New Rational Manager.* Princeton, NJ: Princeton Research Press, 1981.

One of the clearest and most detailed explications of a decision making process available, this large work presents a step-by-step description of decision making from problem analysis to decision analysis. It can provide a basis for teaching this process throughout a curriculum.

10. Nickerson, Raymond S. *Reflections on Reasoning.* Hillsdale, NJ: Lawrence Erlbaum, 1986.
    This exploration of reasoning explains in detail the nature of beliefs, assertions, arguments, and stratagems and then briefly describes twenty-one common reasoning fallacies. It concludes with ten basic rules for rational thinking.

11. Polya, Gyorgy. *How to Solve It,* 2d ed. Princeton: Princeton University Press, 1957, 1973.
    This classic explication of problem solving presents basic principles and procedures for problem solving with examples illustrating each major step.

12. Scriven, Michael. *Reasoning.* New York: McGraw-Hill, 1976.
    One of many good college texts on reasoning, Scriven's book describes and explains briefly the nature of reasoning and explains in detail key steps in analyzing an argument.

13. Siegler, Robert S. *Children's Thinking.* Englewood Cliffs, NJ: Prentice-Hall, 1986.
    In addition to dealing with language development, Siegler reports research on and analyses of memory development, conceptual development, and development of the academic skills of mathematics, reading, and writing. His analyses provide excellent insights into the attributes of selected thinking operations.

14. Toulmin, Steven, Richard Rieke, and Allan Janik. *An Introduction to Reasoning,* 2d ed. New York: Macmillan, 1984.
    An extremely clear introduction to argumentation, this text explains the structure of arguments and then how to determine the soundness and strength of arguments and how to identify common fallacies in argumentation. The authors then discuss applications of argumentation in different fields including science, the arts, and ethics. Examples, applications, and visual diagrams enhance understanding of the principles explained.

15. Wales, Charles E., and Ann Nardi. *Successful Decision Making.* Morgantown: West Virginia University Center for Guided Design, 1984.
    In this manual for college students Wales and Nardi outline twelve key steps in a useful process that combines problem solving and decision making as well as a four-part model of the essential components of problem solving.

16. Weddle, Perry. *Argument—A Guide to Critical Thinking.* New York: McGraw-Hill, 1978.
    In this guide, the author explains the nature of argument, selected fallacies, and the use of language in argumentation. He then examines the role of authority, generality, comparison, and cause. Numerous examples and applications are provided.

17. Whimbey, Arthur, and Jack Lochhead. *Problem Solving and Comprehension,* 3d ed. Philadelphia: Franklin Institute Press, 1982.
    This small book illustrates errors in reasoning and then provides instruction in problem solving, verbal reasoning, analogy making, analyzing of trends and patterns, and solving word problems; it is replete with examples, explanations, and opportunities for application.

in formats similar to those used in Figures 1.5 and 1.6 of this handbook. Of these sources, the following may be most valuable:

Beyer, Barry K. *Developing a Thinking Skills Program*. Boston: Allyn and Bacon, 1988.
In addition to general descriptions of different kinds of thinking (pages 56–68), this book contains one- and two-page detailed descriptions of each of 20 thinking skills, including analyzing, determining the strength of an argument, decision making, identifying point of view, problem solving, finding unstated assumptions, and 14 others (pages 317–352).

Fogarty, Robin, and James Bellanca. *Teach Them Thinking* (formerly entitled: *Mental Menus*). Palatine: Illinois Renewal Institute, 1988.
This book presents two- and three-page descriptions of 24 thinking operations divided into critical and creative thinking skills, such as attributing, prioritizing, solving for analogies, brainstorming, inventing, predicting, and dealing with ambiguity.

Marzano, Robert J. and Daisy Arredondo. *Tactics for Thinking: Teacher's Manual*. Alexandria, VA: Association for Supervision and Curriculum Development, 1987.
This volume presents detailed information about 22 procedures and skills related to and comprising thinking. The three- to nine-page explanations of each deal with such operations as goal setting, pattern recognition, extrapolation, nonlinguistic patterns, and invention.

Raths, Louis, et al. *Teaching for Thinking: Theory, Strategies and Activities for the Classroom*. New York: Teachers College Press, 1986.
Although concentrating on classroom activities for exercising various thinking skills, this volume (originally published in 1965) presents one- and two-page statements about 12 thinking operations, including comparing, interpreting, imagining, and applying.

In addition to these sources, each of which deserves to be consulted in trying to identify the major attributes of any thinking skill, other sources may also prove useful. Occasionally researchers publish articles or portions of articles on or about specific thinking operations. Among the more useful of these are the following:

Anderson, Valerie, and Suzanne Hidi. ''Teaching Students to Summarize.'' *Educational Leadership* 46:4 (December 1988–January 1989), pp. 26–28.

Brown, Ann L., Joseph C. Campione, and Jeanne D. Day. ''Learning to Learn: On Training Students to Learn from Texts.'' *Educational Researcher* 10:2 (February 1989), pp. 14–21 (brief section on summarizing).

Sternberg, Robert. ''How Can We Teach Intelligence?'' *Educational Leadership* 42:1 (September 1984), pp. 48–50 (brief section on analogy making/finding).

Once in a while you can find actual case studies of an expert executing a thinking task, analysis of which can provide unique insights into a particular kind of thinking. One such case study of problem solving can be found in my *Practical Strategies for the Teaching of Thinking* (Allyn and Bacon, 1987, p. 205). Sir Arthur Conan Doyle provides numerous examples and explanations of Sherlock Holmes's deductive reasoning in *The Speckled Band* and other adventures of this sleuth.

note

You may find that a description of the skill that you have been studying is also included in Part II of this handbook as the first page of a set of teaching materials on that skill. This would be an appropriate time to study it to identify what its author(s) discovered about it that you have not discovered.

As you study the explanations or descriptions of a skill presented in these or similar sources, look especially for information about the *steps* or procedure by which the skill is executed and for the *rules* and the *knowledge/criteria* assumed to constitute the skill. By arranging this information (where it is available) under these headings, you can readily identify some of the more salient procedural attributes of the skill. Then, by incorporating this information with what you discovered by repeatedly performing the skill and reflecting on how you did it, you can produce a description that can serve you well in planning for and teaching the skill to any students in any subject of your choice.

There are other ways—beyond the two described here—by which you can identify the attributes of a thinking skill or strategy. One recommended by researcher Robbie Case consists of making protocols (transcripts) of how several excellent students execute the skill and also of how several below-average students execute the skill in doing the same task. Having recorded in writing or on tape what they say they are thinking as they execute the skill, you can then analyze these protocols to identify the steps and infer the rules and knowledge they have employed to carry out the skill. This enables you to identify what the good students do that the less able don't and vice versa. Presumably, you could then simply teach the weaker students what it is the good students do differently, and then they will be able to match the better students in performing that skill. Making and analyzing such protocols require considerable expertise and time, however, and to some extent interrupt the thinking processes of the students. Additional ways to identify thinking skill attributes are outlined in my *Practical Strategies for the Teaching of Thinking* (Allyn and Bacon, 1987, pp. 51–62).

checkpoint

When you have found and read at least two essays or other explanations about or descriptions of the thinking skill on which you have chosen to focus (other than your descriptions of it), check here: ☐

6. *Draft a description of the major attributes of the thinking skill.*

At this point, you and your colleagues should prepare a written description of the thinking skill that you have selected to study. It does not need to be terribly

Figure 1.8 A Format for Describing a Thinking Skill

SKILL NAME

DEFINITION:

SYNONYMS:

PROCEDURE(S)
   (STEPS):

RULES:
   When to use . . .

   How to start . . .

   What to do if . . .

KNOWLEDGE OR
   CRITERIA USED:

elaborate but, at the very least, it must present one or more procedures used by those competent in doing the skill. It should also stipulate some rules they seem to follow (especially rules for when to use the skill, how to initiate it, and what to do if something blocks successful use of the skill), and any knowledge, such as concepts or criteria, that are used in executing the skill. A working definition and synonyms for the skill should also be included. The descriptions presented in Figures 1.5 and 1.6 illustrate a useful format that such a description may take. Use the form presented in Figure 1.8, or one like it, on which to write your description.

Of course, in describing your skill you may wish to provide information in addition to that presented in the format recommended here. Several exercises or data sets that require use of the skill might be included in the description, as could information about how the skill relates in a subordinate and superordinate way to other skills. A list of sources that provide useful data about the skill might also be included. A mnemonic device and/or a graphic organizer or "mind-map" of the skill might also be included to enhance recall. Regardless of what is presented about the skill, however, to be useful its description must include at least a definition of the skill, at least one routine or series of steps that individuals can or do go through in executing the skill, some rules that guide execution of the skill, and some of the concepts, knowledge, or criteria needed to execute the skill well.

In preparing thinking skill descriptions, it should be noted that your audience is not students but other teachers who may wish to teach the skill. Thus, in preparing your description, take into account the fact that you probably know more about the skill at this point than they do. Consequently, your description must use nontechnical language, must be clear and precise, and must present your information so they can easily distinguish the essential attributes from other kinds of skill-related information. Remember, too, that the description probably reflects how you and your colleagues executed the skill, not how second- or ninth-graders carry it out. Consider the description to be *tentative* only and subject to continuing revision. It represents not what students must learn but only a guide to you and other educators for use in planning classroom instruction and assessment.

checkpoint

When you have completed a draft of your skill description that presents key attributes of the skill as you understand them, check here: ☐

7. *Revise the skill description incorporating feedback from others.*

In order to be of maximum value, written thinking skill descriptions should be checked by others who are somewhat knowledgeable about the skill. Once a description has been drafted as a result of the efforts described above, it should be examined for clarity, faithfulness to the skill it is supposed to represent, and generalizability. Any initial description is the product of only a few minds and of application to limited experience and data. It is quite possible that a particular skill description could be very personal, or very subject-matter bound, or even flawed. Skill descriptions submitted to the analysis of your colleagues—or experts—can often be revised, filled in, or elaborated, all usually to the betterment of the description.

It is often useful at this point to trade skill descriptions with another group of your colleagues who have studied the same skill. Then, each group can revise the other's skill description to incorporate what they discovered about the same skill. Finally, two or three groups working on the same skill can pool their revised descriptions and produce a general description—still tentative in nature—that incorporates their consensus view of its key attributes. Such a description is likely to be a very useful outline of the major components of a thinking skill. And participation in the process of generating revisions of the skill description helps considerably in clarifying your understanding of the skill. In discussing, questioning, clarifying, defending, explaining, and challenging the contents of your or others' thinking skill descriptions, you come to learn a great deal more about the skill that you have been analyzing. Such interaction is at least as valuable to developing an understanding of the skill as are carrying out the skill, reflecting on it, and trying to articulate its attributes. Auden's ''How do I know what I think till I see what I write?'' might just as easily have been ''How do I know how I think till I try to explain it!''

The second place where sharing skill descriptions proves useful to producing accurate descriptions is after you and a number of your colleagues have taught several lessons on the skill. By discussing and revising your initial skill description at that point, all of you can include insights about the skill that have arisen in your teaching. The description that emerges from this analysis and revision will be even richer, more detailed, and more accurately descriptive of the skill than was the original description. Continued revision of a skill description over a number of years to incorporate what you and others have learned about it by repeated teaching also helps you learn more about the skill and improve your own teaching of it. As noted earlier, your knowledge of and expertise in carrying out a thinking skill will grow and develop in sophistication as you use and reflect on the skill for a variety of purposes in a variety of contexts over time. Skill descriptions should be continuously revised to reflect such growth in your understanding and expertise.

checkpoint

When you have revised your thinking skill description based on feedback from colleagues, instructor, specialists, or further reflective analysis, check here: ☐

8. Rewrite the skill description as appropriate for the grade or experience level of your students.

At this point, you may wish to prepare a version of the skill keyed directly to what you perceive to be the ability and experience levels of the students to

Figure 1.9 Comparing: Two Descriptions

General Skill Description	**Skill Description Revised for 1st-Grade Level**
LABEL: comparing	LABEL: comparing
SYNONYMS: likening, contrasting, differentiating	SYNONYMS: (words that mean the same): contrasting, likening
DEFINITION: to determine similarities and/or differences between two or more things	DEFINITION: finding what is the same and/or different between two or more things
STEPS: 1. Decide to compare. 2. Look at the things to be compared. 3. Notice the characteristics of the things being compared. 4. Choose a characteristic. 5. See if that characteristic is the same or different for all things. 6. Repeat the process.	STEPS: 1. Look at the things to be compared. 2. Choose a feature. 3. See if that feature is the same or different for all the things.
RULES: 1. When to compare? • to determine if two or more things are equal • to help make a choice between two or more things 2. How to start? • look at the things to be compared • note the most obvious characteristics first 3. What to do if . . . • you can't find any similarities? Note all differences first, then look for similarities. • you can't find any similarities (differences)? There may not be any. • there are too many similarities and/or differences to keep in mind? Write them down.	RULES: 1. When to compare? • to see if two or more things are equal • to help choose between two or more things 2. How to start? • look at the things to be compared • choose a big feature first 3. What to do if . . . • you can't find any features that are the same? There may not be any. • you can't find any features that are different? There may not be any.
KNOWLEDGE NEEDED: meanings of *similar* and *different*	KNOWLEDGE NEEDED: meaning of *feature*

whom you plan to teach it. Figure 1.9 presents just such a simplified thinking skill description, keyed to a selected grade level as well as the description of the skill as originally conceptualized by its author. The thinking skill you have analyzed, as you have described it, probably represents considerable experience on your part. But it may include too much detail or too many steps for understanding and use by young students or those who are complete novices in its use. Thus, a simplified description of the skill, accompanied by your more detailed version for teacher reference, would be extremely useful for anyone charged with teaching the skill to students at a particular grade or ability level.

In writing this second description, be sure to use words understood by the students to whom it is to be introduced. Reduce the number of steps to a manageable (for them) number and limit the number of rules to one or two key ones. In general, when rewriting thinking skill descriptions for young children or novices of any age, it is useful to (1) reduce the skill complexity and (2) build it out of everyday experiences appropriate to these students.

Once written, this simplified description can again be checked by your colleagues or against what experts offer about the skill. As you teach it to your students, you can also be alert to needed modifications in the description, so that it realistically represents what your students do and how they seem to do it.

checkpoint

When you have produced a simplified description of your thinking skill (if you have chosen to do so) keyed to the ability levels and experiences of your students, check here: ☐

SUMMARY

As a result of completing this chapter, you should now be able to:

1. Describe, giving specific examples, three major kinds of attributes of any thinking skill.
2. Describe and explain to someone else how to use two different ways to identify the attributes of any thinking skill.
3. Apply these two procedures to describe in some detail the major attributes of at least one specific thinking skill.

Can you do these three things without assistance? For example:

1. Given a new thinking skill (hypothesis making, for instance) can you identify and describe in detail its major attributes?
2. Given the task of identifying and describing a new thinking skill, can you carry out this task and produce a thorough and accurate description of the skill?

3. Can you explain in detail to someone unfamiliar with the 3-D procedure outlined earlier exactly how to carry out this procedure to identify and describe the attributes of a thinking skill of his or her choice and guide the person through this procedure?

If you cannot do any of these tasks, review the relevant sections in this chapter, perhaps repeating the procedures to describe a new thinking skill. When you can accomplish each of these three objectives, you are ready to explore and learn some ways to design and teach thinking skill lessons. To that task you can now turn.

Endnotes

1. See, for example, Barry K. Beyer, *Practical Strategies for the Teaching of Thinking* (Boston: Allyn and Bacon, 1987), pp. 13–14.

2. See Robert Marzano et al., *Dimensions of Thinking* (Alexandria, VA: Association for Supervison and Curriculum Development, 1987) for one such listing. Also, Barry K. Beyer, *Developing a Thinking Skills Program* (Boston: Allyn and Bacon, 1988), pp. 45–76 and 103–124 presents a number of skill lists and taxonomies developed by a variety of other experts and specialists.

3. See, for example, Robert Siegler, *Children's Thinking* (Englewood Cliffs, NJ: Prentice-Hall, 1986).

4. *Cleveland Plain Dealer*, August 19, 1986.

chapter **2**

Designing and Teaching Thinking Skill Lessons

Once you have identified in as much detail as possible the major attributes of a thinking skill you wish to teach, you can develop lessons to teach this skill. Designing and carrying out such lessons requires more than knowledge of or expertise in the skill, however. These tasks also require understanding the strategies that can be used to provide appropriate instruction in any thinking skill. This chapter will help you learn how to design and teach lessons employing these strategies.

There are many approaches you could take to help your students become proficient in any particular thinking skill. You could, for example, *stimulate* and *encourage* students to think by asking thought-provoking questions and by concentrating on subjects of interest to them. Or you could *foster* and *facilitate* thinking by asking carefully structured questions that move from data gathering to data processing or by providing inquiry-oriented classes. Or you could *exercise* student thinking by making students respond to questions, research tasks, or written assignments requiring different kinds of thinking.

All of these approaches to teaching thinking are useful—at the appropriate time. But, as commonly used, they fail to do what is needed most by students learning a new thinking skill. None of these approaches teach students *how to carry out* the thinking skills they are required to use when they respond to the questions you may ask them, the tasks you may assign them, or the opportunities and encouragement you may offer them. *Students benefit most from encouragement, teacher facilitation, and exercise when these are coupled with deliberate, system-*

atic instruction in how to carry out the skill being learned. Such instruction is known as *direct instruction* because it treats learning the skill as important as learning content, and because it focuses, especially in its initial stages, directly on the skill being taught rather than on the subject-matter learning generated by use of the skill.

Because interest in direct instruction in thinking skills is rather new and because this approach to teaching thinking appears to be so powerful for developing skillful thinking in students of all ages and in all subject areas, this handbook focuses primarily on how to design lessons that provide such instruction. You can use the procedures and guidelines presented in this chapter to learn how to plan and conduct classroom lessons that employ instructional strategies designed especially for the direct teaching of thinking. You can also use the procedures and guidelines presented in this chapter to learn how to plan and conduct lessons that employ other skill-teaching strategies.

When you have completed this chapter, you should be able to:

1. Examine any given lesson plan or observe the teaching of any thinking skill lesson and identify which principles of thinking skill instruction were reflected in or omitted from the lesson.

2. Examine a given lesson plan or observe the teaching of any thinking skill lesson and identify the steps in a specific skill-teaching strategy that were included, omitted, or in need of improvement.

3. Design and write detailed lesson plans for teaching different kinds of thinking skill lessons, each employing an instructional strategy appropriate to the skill-teaching function of the lesson.

4. Explain in detail to someone who is not familiar with the teaching of thinking how to design and write a lesson that will provide instruction in a thinking skill appropriate to a given stage in a research-based framework for thinking skills instruction and guide them in preparing such a lesson.

The following pages present procedures and information that will assist you in achieving the above objectives. Figure 2.1 outlines these procedures and the sequence in which they are presented. You can use these procedures and the information provided here, in Parts II and III, and in Appendices B, C, and D to help you learn how to design, write, analyze, evaluate, and conduct lessons for teaching any thinking skill to any teachable learners in any subject. The final

note

Each of the sets of thinking skill materials in Part II contains four lesson plans designed to teach a particular skill through the various stages of direct instruction, from introduction to guided practice and transfer/elaboration. These lessons are based on guidelines presented in Appendices B, C, and D. You may wish to refer to these sample lessons periodically as you proceed through this chapter. It might even be useful for you to examine one set of lessons in Part II now, *before* you start this chapter, so you will get an idea of what the chapter will help you learn to do. By the conclusion of Chapter 2, you should be able to write and teach lessons like these!

Figure 2.1 Chapter 2—Learning Modules and Procedures

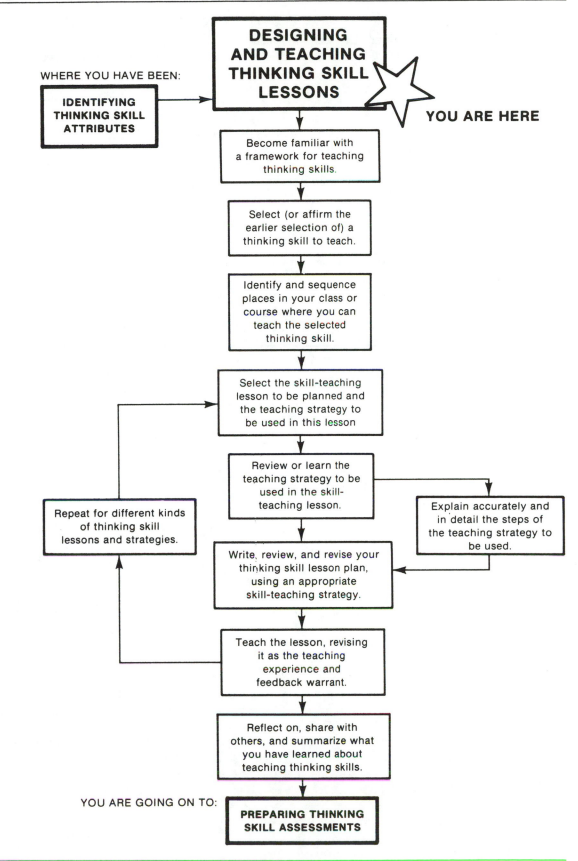

WHERE YOU HAVE BEEN:

IDENTIFYING THINKING SKILL ATTRIBUTES

DESIGNING AND TEACHING THINKING SKILL LESSONS

YOU ARE HERE

Become familiar with a framework for teaching thinking skills.

Select (or affirm the earlier selection of) a thinking skill to teach.

Identify and sequence places in your class or course where you can teach the selected thinking skill.

Select the skill-teaching lesson to be planned and the teaching strategy to be used in this lesson

Review or learn the teaching strategy to be used in the skill-teaching lesson.

Repeat for different kinds of thinking skill lessons and strategies.

Explain accurately and in detail the steps of the teaching strategy to be used.

Write, review, and revise your thinking skill lesson plan, using an appropriate skill-teaching strategy.

Teach the lesson, revising it as the teaching experience and feedback warrant.

Reflect on, share with others, and summarize what you have learned about teaching thinking skills.

YOU ARE GOING ON TO:

PREPARING THINKING SKILL ASSESSMENTS

written product of this chapter will be a lesson plan—or, if you repeat several times the procedure presented in this chapter, a sequence of plans—for introducing, guiding practice in, and/or initiating the transfer or elaboration of a specific thinking skill.

As in Chapter 1, each of the learning segments in this chapter concludes with a *Checkpoint*. Each *Checkpoint* signals an end to a particular learning task and offers you an opportunity to pull together what you have learned to that point, to reflect on it, and, if you wish, to take a break before continuing. These *Checkpoints* may thus serve both as learning goals and, when completed, as mileposts to mark your progress through these pages.

PLANNING THINKING SKILL LESSONS

Well-crafted, detailed lesson plans are indispensable to the effective teaching of thinking skills. This is especially true if you are just learning new strategies for teaching these skills. Without such plans and the mental preparation they require, you are not likely to do in your classroom the things your students need in order to learn a thinking skill to a high degree of proficiency.

Designing and writing detailed thinking skill lessons benefit you in at least two ways. First, the product—the actual plans that result from this endeavor—serves as a ready reference and effective guide for carrying out a lesson using a teaching strategy with which you may initially be unfamiliar. In effect, it is like a cue card that individuals might use when they are doing something for the few first times that requires them to remember to do very specific operations that they are just learning. A well-designed thinking skill lesson plan clearly indicates the key operations you should carry out and gives the significant moves you plan to make to complete these operations. It differs from the average lesson plan only in that it offers much more detail about what you actually propose to do.

Moreover, the process you go through in generating and writing a rather detailed lesson plan is as valuable as the plan itself. In order to produce such a plan, you must identify the key operations you want your students to perform, sequence them, identify exactly what you will say or do to initiate and direct them, and identify what your students must say or do to prove to you they have successfully carried them out. You must anticipate problems and make contingencies for dealing with these, or plan a way to avoid or minimize them altogether. Making such a plan is essentially an act of anticipatory teaching—a mental dress rehearsal for what you want to happen in your classroom.

To create the plan, you must identify what it is you wish your students to be able to *do* at the conclusion of the lesson. Then you mentally anticipate what you will do in the lesson to enable students to accomplish the established learning objectives. Such rehearsal of a teaching act helps you produce clear instructions, select appropriate learning tasks, and ensure that appropriate teaching operations have been selected. This rehearsal also helps you embed in your mind the routine by which you propose to carry out your lesson in class.

Writing lesson plans that use specific strategies to teach a thinking skill helps you actually practice these strategies, mentally, without having to execute them in front of a live class, where it is easy to forget a step, make a mistake, or get sidetracked. Even if you are an experienced teacher, detailed plans are useful when the teaching strategies they incorporate are likely to be somewhat new to you. Whether you are a beginner or an experienced teacher, you can use the procedures here to learn how to design and write lesson plans for teaching any thinking skill.

Before you begin to write a thinking skill lesson plan, however, there are several things you need to know or do. First, you should be familiar with a framework for teaching thinking skills that will enable you to create and sequence your lessons so they will have the best chance possible of producing the kind of skill learning you seek. Furthermore, you will need to figure out where in your class or course you can initiate instruction in a specific skill and where to provide followup instruction. You will also have to decide the kind of lesson(s) you wish to design and then review or, if you are not familiar with it, learn a strategy appropriate for use in this kind of lesson. The following procedures will assist you in accomplishing these tasks:

1. Become familiar with a framework for teaching thinking skills that is based on cognitive research and expert advice. Using this framework, you will be able to better organize your teaching of any thinking skill to bring about the skill-learning objectives you desire.

2. Select (or affirm an earlier selection of) a thinking skill to teach.

3. Identify and sequence places in your class or course where you can teach the selected thinking skill.

4. Select the type of skill-teaching lesson you wish to prepare and the teaching strategy to be used in this lesson.

5. Review or learn the teaching strategy to be used in the lesson to be prepared. This means reviewing especially the steps you want the students to go through to "learn" the thinking skill, and what you, as the teacher, will need to do to ensure that these steps are carried out. If you are unfamiliar with such strategies, you must at this point become familiar with them.

When you have completed these tasks, you will be prepared to design, write, and try out the thinking skill lesson(s) you wish to prepare!

1. Become familiar with a framework for teaching thinking skills.

If you wish to be successful at teaching thinking skills, it is important to recognize at least three things:

• Thinking skills are *not* learned as an automatic outcome of instruction that emphasizes subject matter learning.[1]

• No thinking skill is learned to any degree of proficiency as a result of only a single lesson or bit of instruction in that skill.[2]

• Students rarely transfer thinking skills on their own beyond the context or setting in which they are originally encountered or "learned."[3]

These generalizations summarize the findings of an increasing body of research in skill acquisition over the past 20 years. Indeed, research in skill learning and in cognition, as well as recommendations of specialists in teaching thinking, have identified a number of additional principles that have significant implications for teaching thinking skills. This research and advice indicate that:

- To be mastered, a skill should be overlearned initially.[4]

- In the initial stages of learning a skill, focus should be explicitly on the skill. Interference from subject matter and other skills should be minimized, if not eliminated altogether.[5]

- Initial instruction in a skill should be followed by frequent, intermittent, guided practice in the skill.[6]

- To facilitate transfer, skills should be applied in a variety of contexts and settings with appropriate instructional guidance.[7]

- Generalizing a skill may best occur by executing a variety of tasks, each requiring use of a variety of thinking operations.[8]

- Motivation to learn a skill is enhanced when instruction in the skill is provided at the time there is a perceived need on the part of students to be able to do the skill in order to accomplish a subject-matter goal.[9]

- Systematic, explicit attention to cognitive operations needed to understand subject-matter results in higher student achievement as measured by end-of-course subject-matter examinations.[10]

These findings and recommendations have been presented and elaborated elsewhere.[11] For our purposes here, their significance lies in a framework they suggest for structuring the teaching of any thinking skill. This instructional framework for thinking skills consists of six kinds of lessons, presented in this sequence:

1. Introduction
2. Guided practice
3. Independent application
4. Transfer and/or elaboration
5. Guided practice
6. Autonomous use

Any thinking skill can be learned to a high degree of proficiency when instruction in that skill proceeds through the kinds of lessons in this teaching framework. Lessons 1–3 constitute the first phase of teaching any thinking skill or strategy—introducing it and teaching it to independent use in a simplified form. Lessons 4–6, the second phase, complete this instruction by helping students transfer the skill to a wide variety of applications, to generalize it, and to internalize it in its more sophisticated, complex forms. A brief explanation of each of these kinds of lessons will clarify the nature of this framework.

Introduction.   Instruction in any thinking operation may be initiated whenever a teacher senses a need for students to be able to execute it better than they seem able to do. Such initial instruction can take the form of a single lesson anywhere from 30 to 50 minutes in length. The actual length of such a lesson will depend on the abilities of the students, the complexity of the skill to be introduced, and the degree of student proficiency in prerequisite skills. The purpose of this lesson is to introduce students to the major attributes or components of the new operation, if only at a rudimentary, rather simplified level. Instruction here focuses directly on the thinking skill or strategy being introduced as students not only see the operation modeled but also have one or more opportunities to engage in it with appropriate teacher guidance.[12]

Introductory lessons in a thinking skill obviously do not, by themselves, teach a skill. As a result of such a brief introduction, your students will not have developed any significantly increased proficiency in executing the operation being introduced. But they will have launched their study of it. This lesson is but one-sixth of the kinds of lessons needed to develop such proficiency. Subsequent lessons allow students to internalize their knowledge of the operation through repeated practice with the help of teacher and peers in reflecting on and articulating how it seems to work.

Guided Practice.   Once a thinking skill has been explicitly introduced, students benefit from a number of lessons in which they practice executing it *with instructive guidance.* In these lessons, students practice executing and applying the major attributes of the thinking skill being learned, always using the same kind of subject matter and the same media or same type of data used in their introduction to the skill. Experience suggests that these lessons should require relatively brief amounts of time devoted to actually applying the operation, accompanying such application with considerable teacher or peer-provided guidance, assistance, or direction in how to do so. Explicit attention to the skill is the major feature of this kind of lesson. Such attention may take the form of structured reviews or rehearsals of how the operation to be used can be executed, as well as followup reviews of how it actually worked in practice. In addition, graphic organizers, partially completed examples, procedural checklists, and carefully cued questions can be used to provide the instructive guidance needed by many students at this point in learning a new skill. These guided practice lessons should be spaced out intermittently over several weeks or months, as needed. They can also be easily incorporated into lessons that seek important subject-matter learning objectives as well.[13]

Unlike introductory lessons in which students must focus exclusively on the operation, guided practice lessons allow time and opportunity to deal with the subject matter used in the lesson and the substantive products of skill use. After discussing and analyzing how the thinking operation being practiced was employed, students can then use the insights generated by their application of it to carry forward the subject-matter learning in which they are engaged. Gradually, as students become more proficient with the new thinking skill, you can reduce the amount of explicit guidance to eventually little, if any, skill instruction.

The exact number of guided practice lessons needed to learn any thinking skill varies according to the skill being practiced and the abilities of your students. Such lessons should be provided until students demonstrate an ability to execute the operation, on request, without guidance. Once it has been introduced, you may have to conduct three, four, or even more guided practice lessons in a single thinking skill before moving on to the next kind of lesson.[14]

Independent Application.   As students demonstrate an ability to execute the thinking operation being practiced without assistance or guidance, you can then provide them repeated opportunities to use it on their own. These applications should continue to be in the same kind of data or subject matter or media in which the operation was originally introduced and practiced. When students independently apply the skill or strategy, as specifically required by you or the text, they integrate the various steps in the procedure by which it is made operational, and they begin to internalize the rules, principles, and other knowledge that inform it.[15] Such application is an important step en route to automatizing a thinking operation and to taking ownership of it.

This is the point in the teaching of thinking at which students can legitimately and productively be put into situations *requiring* them to think. It is at this time that encouragement and nurturance can contribute most to skill learning as students apply on their own over and over again the thinking operations they have been learning. Such opportunities for independent application of a thinking skill being newly learned may be combined with subject-matter learning and use of other skills in order to advance learning of both the thinking skill and subject matter.

Again, there is no precise rule for determining how many opportunities for independent application of a specified thinking operation are required to achieve a high degree of proficiency in executing it. But however many opportunities are required, they should be spaced out intermittently over several months.[16] Recurring use of the skill as an integral part of the subject-matter learning process helps to maintain it as well as to give it purpose and utility. Such lessons complete the initial phase of teaching any thinking skill.

Each of these first three kinds of lessons in this instructional framework—introduction, guided practice, and independent application—enable students to develop a degree of proficiency in a new thinking skill in the setting (or with the kind of data) in which it was first experienced. The entire sequence of lessons may number a half-dozen or more, depending on the complexity of the skill being introduced and the abilities of the students. Once students have demonstrated that they can do it on their own, you can then offer additional instruction designed to help them apply the operation in a variety of settings to thus generalize or transfer it beyond the introductory setting.

Transfer and Elaboration.   Showing students how to apply a previously introduced skill or strategy in new, unfamiliar settings or how to incorporate new rules or steps into the skill procedure launches the second phase of teaching any thinking skill. No instruction in thinking would be complete without considerable attention to this task. Thinking skills are not learned, in their most complex forms, once and for all, at a specific time, remaining unchanged thereafter. Learned initially in rather simplified forms and limited by the settings in which they are first encountered, the understanding of specific thinking operations grows and develops in sophistication as students repeatedly experience executing them in a variety of settings for a variety of purposes. As students learn how to apply these operations in settings, data, or media other than those in which they were first encountered, they learn more about the operations. This learning continues beyond school, but helping students to begin this process is an important function of this phase of teaching thinking.

Transferring a thinking operation consists of helping students learn how to execute a previously learned or introduced skill in settings other than that in which it was introduced. This means helping them identify the cues in these settings that signal the appropriateness of using the operation. It also means helping them identify any subtle changes in how to engage in the operation required by these new settings.[17] Lessons that launch such transfers are, in effect, reintroductions of the thinking operation but in new subject matter or with new kinds of data or media. In these reintroductions, students review what they already know about the operation being learned and then receive instruction in how to execute it in the new setting. As with the original introduction, focus remains on the thinking operation rather than on attaining any subject-matter goals. Because students have been doing the skill for some time, a transfer lesson may not require as much time as is required to introduce a completely new thinking operation—perhaps only 30 minutes or so. However, this depends on the complexity of the operation, the closeness of the new setting to that in which the operation was originally learned, the degree to which students mastered it in the original setting, and the extent to which students are familiar with the new setting. Every time it is appropriate to apply a previously introduced and practiced thinking skill or strategy with new data or in new subject matter, a lesson like this can initiate learning how to make the transfer.

Guided Practice. Once a thinking skill or strategy has been initially transferred—with instruction—to a new context, it must be practiced, again with your guidance, in that new context until students demonstrate appropriate proficiency in using it in this context.[18] The crucial ingredient of such lessons remains, as before, instructive guidance in how to execute the operation, provided, as needed, by you, the text, or student peers. As students become proficient in applying it in the new context, guidance can be reduced. Lessons applying a thinking skill or strategy in the original context can also be interspersed with lessons where students apply it in the newer context, always with teacher guidance as necessary.

Research provides no specific guidance for how many guided practice lessons are required for any particular thinking skill at this point. The number varies. Of course, all students do not develop proficiency at the same rate with the same types of instruction, so some may need more instructional help than others. Much instruction in this stage of teaching may be with individuals or small groups rather than with the class as a whole. But it readily becomes evident when students have become familiar enough with a new skill to be able to engage in it on their own, without assistance or correction.

Autonomous Use. Being able to use a thinking operation or strategy to generate knowledge on one's own is, of course, the major goal of the teaching of thinking. The sixth and final kind of lesson in the instructional framework presented here provides repeated opportunities for precisely this behavior. All the techniques useful for independent application in the first phase of learning a thinking skill are also useful in this stage of the framework. These include responding to questions, engaging in discussions and debates, writing, completing research or action projects, and so on. You must provide enough opportunities for students to engage in a specific thinking operation in a new setting to allow students to become proficient at doing so on their own.

One feature of practice at this stage deserves special note. The kinds of tasks in which students are asked to engage here ought not to be directed solely or explicitly at the thinking operation being worked on. As Professor Carl Bereiter asserts, students at this stage of skill learning should be confronted with tasks that require use—of their own choice—of any of a variety of the thinking operations they have been learning.[19] Thus, students in the midst of learning how to classify information might work at tasks that require classification as well as sequencing or other skills without receiving any cues from you as to which skills should be used or when. Knowing when to use a thinking operation and being willing to do so are very much parts of proficiency in thinking. Students need guidance and practice at this point in *selecting which* operations to use as well as in applying them accurately, efficiently, and effectively.

As important as autonomous use is in learning thinking skills and strategies, it should be clear that this also is only one-sixth of what is necessary to learn a thinking operation. Thus, providing opportunities for autonomous use is *no substitute* for the instruction required in the preceding lessons of the framework outlined here. Students need instruction in *how* to execute a thinking skill as well as guided and unguided practice in doing it. To develop student competencies in thinking to the highest degree of proficiency and to maintain this proficiency for the longest time possible requires instruction through all six kinds of lessons in the framework presented here.

Transferring or extending newly introduced thinking skills thus constitutes the second and final phase of this framework for the teaching of thinking. Unless students are assisted in learning how to execute a particular thinking operation in settings different from that in which it is introduced, they remain limited in their ability to use the operation on their own. By showing students how to transfer or elaborate a thinking skill in a variety of settings, by providing guided practice in executing it in these settings, and by offering repeated opportunities to apply it in these settings autonomously, you can help students to generalize the operation to the point where they can use it appropriately in a variety of novel settings and on their own initiative. The ultimate goal of teaching thinking skills is for students to be self-directed and self-starting skillful thinkers. This phase of teaching moves them toward this goal.

As you may have noticed, the lessons in this framework give differing degrees of emphasis or focus to skill-learning objectives and to content or subject-matter learning objectives. Figure 2.2 illustrates the relative focus of each type of lesson on each kind of objective and also the way in which this focus changes as you move through the sequence of lessons. Students in this framework learn thinking skills to understand better the subject(s) they are studying. At the same time, they use subject matter to help them learn more about the skill and become more proficient in its use.

This thinking skill teaching framework may be used to organize instruction in any thinking skill, in any subject, at any grade level. To put it into operation, you can:

Figure 2.2 Focus of Lessons in a Framework for Teaching Thinking Skills

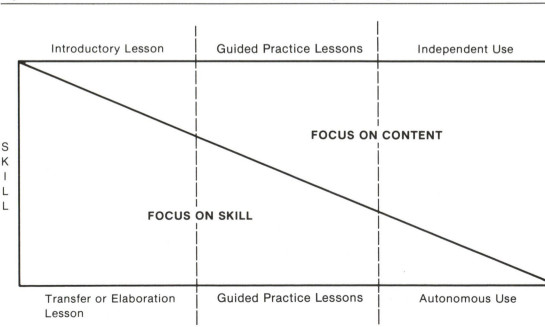

1. Introduce the thinking skill in a single lesson that focuses explicitly on the skill being introduced.

2. Provide guided practice in executing this skill in the same kind of setting as in the introductory lesson as many times as necessary for students to do it reasonably well on their own.

3. Provide repeated opportunities for students to apply the skill on their own in the same kind of setting or with the same kind of data as in the preceding lessons.

4. Show students, in another single lesson, how to execute the skill in a new context (or add a new attribute to it), again focusing directly on the skill (and doing this each time it is used in a new context).

5. Conduct additional lessons providing practice in executing the skill in each new context.

6. Provide additional lessons in which students can use the skill on their own in all the contexts in which they have been receiving instruction.

Figure 2.3 illustrates such a sequence of lessons. As shown in this figure, teaching any new thinking skill may require a dozen or more lessons over a semester or so as students move from introductory instruction through the remaining stages of the sequence. Exactly how many lessons will be needed to achieve a desired level of student proficiency will vary, depending on the extent to which students have mastered prerequisite skills, the complexity of the skill, their abilities, and your expertise in teaching the skill.

To illustrate this sequence, imagine that you wish to teach the skill of *predicting* to your students. If you were teaching in elementary grades, you might choose to teach the first three kinds of lessons—a total of seven lessons—in this skill in reading. You could introduce it as the students work on predicting what will happen next in a story. Subsequent guided practice in lessons could be taught as your students use their developing understanding of predicting to predict, with your guidance, what will happen next in other stories. As they become more proficient in doing this, they can then be asked, without assistance, to predict story endings and so on. Eventually, you or another teacher may wish to help these students transfer this skill to making predictions in science. In showing them how to do this, you may have them work in a transfer lesson (the eighth lesson in Figure 2.3) on predicting tomorrow's weather. After more guided practice in predicting the outcomes of various science experiments (for example, what happens if a "sick" plant is given water or sunlight regularly), the students can use the skill on their own to make and test hypotheses in science lessons. Later, you could even help them transfer the skill to social studies by repeating the last three kinds of lessons in the sequence to help them predict the effects of given historic events as they continue to learn better how to predict.

If you were a high school biology teacher who wished to teach the skill of *classifying,* you could sequence lessons in this skill by providing an introductory lesson in the skill early in your course when students need to distinguish between living and nonliving things. Such a lesson (Lesson 1 in Figure 2.3) could present data in the form of lists. Guided practice lessons in this skill could then follow (Lessons 2–4) when students need to be able to distinguish between various kinds of living organisms such as vertebrates and invertebrates; land, air, and water organisms; and so on (data that could always be presented in written form). After several opportunities to use the skill without any help from you

Figure 2.3 A Sequence of Lessons for Teaching a Thinking Skill

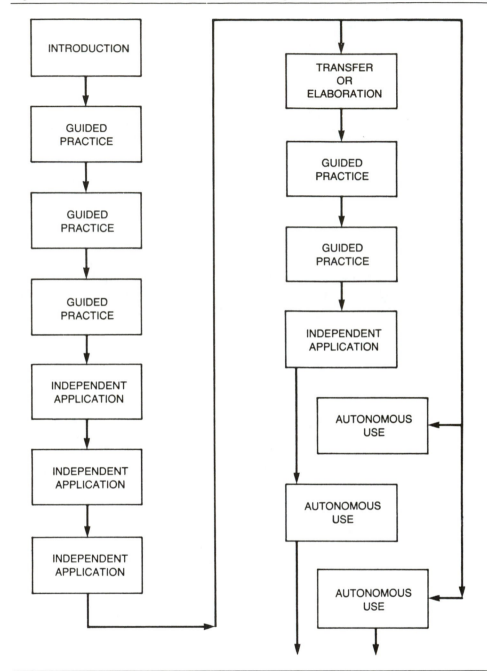

Source: Barry K. Beyer, *Practical Strategies for the Teaching of Thinking* (Boston: Allyn and Bacon, 1987).

(Lessons 5–7), you could then initiate transfer of the skill to pictorially presented data in a lesson (Lesson 8) when students study various circulatory systems. Again, several lessons could follow in which students receive guided practice in classifying other data presented pictorially—the respiration and nervous systems, perhaps. Finally, lessons could require autonomous use of the skill of classifying as well as other skills to develop generalizations about biological systems. Teaching the skill of classifying thus means conducting a number of lessons through each stage of this framework as students move toward proficiency in the skill over the duration of your course.

The number of lessons in a skill-teaching sequence using this framework will, of course, vary according to the difficulty of the skill, the number of new contexts into which the operation is transferred, and the number of new attributes to be added. Each new skill requires an introductory lesson, followed by enough guided practice and independent use lessons for students to begin achieving proficiency in this ''version'' of the skill. Each transfer lesson then requires followup guided practice lessons in the new context or in using the newly added dimensions of the operation, as well as repeated opportunities for autonomous use of it in the new as well as in the previously practiced forms and applications. You can develop a similar sequence for teaching any thinking skill, including the one you identified in Chapter 1. Doing this is an important step in planning to teach any thinking skill.

---

checkpoint

When you can explain briefly to a colleague the major types of lessons in this framework for teaching thinking skills, and the characteristics and rationale for each, check here: ☐

---

2. *Select (or affirm the earlier selection of) a thinking skill to teach.*

The pages that follow guide you through the process of designing effective thinking skill lessons or, if necessary, learning how to do so if you are unfamiliar either with designing skill-teaching lessons or with the strategies that could be used in these lessons. To make this process most productive, the plans you write and try out should be for the thinking skill you selected for analysis in Chapter 1. However, if you wish to teach a thinking skill other than that one, be sure you take time here to identify its major attributes and prepare a description of them just as you did for the skill identified in Chapter 1.

---

checkpoint

When you have selected a thinking skill for which you wish to write lesson plans and have described its key attributes, write the name of the skill on the line and check here: ☐

_____

3. Identify and sequence places in your class or course where you can teach the selected thinking skill.

Instruction in any thinking skill may be initiated in either of two basic ways: (1) spontaneously, when your students, in the midst of a regular lesson, reveal an inability to carry out a thinking skill required to complete the lesson and you consequently decide to introduce the skill right then and there; or (2) pre-planned, based on a decision in advance to introduce and teach a specific skill starting with a particular lesson, unit, or chapter.

Whichever way leads you to launch instruction in any specific thinking skill (most teachers find themselves using both approaches), it is important to remember one thing: No thinking skill is learned by students as the result of a single lesson on that skill, no matter how explicit the focus on the skill. As indicated earlier, it requires a number of lessons spaced over a period of time to teach any thinking skill so students can become proficient in applying it in a wide range of contexts or subjects. No matter what leads you to initiate instruction in any thinking skill, you need to provide a sequence of lessons in that skill. Planning that sequence is the subject of this section.

Having decided to teach a specific thinking skill and having identified its significant attributes, you need to determine where in your class or course you can "teach" it. Ideally, you need to find six to ten or more places over one to three months where activities in which the students will engage or material they are to study provide natural opportunities for them to use the skill you wish to teach. The initial four or five of these places ought to be fairly close together—no more than two or three days apart, for example. The remaining places can be spaced at increasing intervals—one or two lessons three or four days apart, with the next several lessons and others perhaps even further apart. In learning a new thinking skill, opportunities to practice the skill immediately following its introduction should be frequent and relatively close together; thereafter, practice can become increasingly intermittent. Although research suggests it may take up to 15 to 20 practice lessons—in some cases up to 53 practice lessons—to become proficient in a new skill, planning for about 10 to 14 lessons initially usually proves sufficient. Additional practice lessons can always be added later, as needed.

To produce a skill-teaching plan that meets these criteria, you can do three things:

1. Find places in your class or course that offer natural opportunities for your students to use the thinking skill you wish to teach.

2. Ensure that the time intervals between these places are appropriate for optimum skill learning, neither all bunched up at some point nor scattered randomly throughout the course or class.

3. Determine the specific type of skill lesson to be taught at each identified place in the sequence.

Identifying Opportunities for Students to Use the Skill.   Opportunities for skill use by your students are also opportunities for skill-*teaching* lessons by you. You can go about identifying these skill-teaching opportunities by referring to at least two sources. If you regularly use—or will use—a textbook for a particular subject, you can flip through the chapters of the text and its chapter-end activities to identify places where the skill you want to teach is required (for example, to answer certain questions in the text narrative or at the end of the chapter, or to complete various learning activities included in the chapter). You could also skim through the program of studies you use to find activities or tasks for the students that would require them to use the skill.

In identifying places in your class or course where use of the skill is possible or can be built into lessons, you should also consider carefully the content of these lessons. In order for your skill teaching to be most successful, the subject matter to be studied or used in the first half dozen or so skill lessons should meet three important criteria. In order for students to concentrate on learning the skill in these early lessons, the subject-matter content and the form of presentation (reading, pictures, graphs, or so on) of those lessons should:

- Be in the same form, or be translatable into the same form, as it was or is in the initial lesson on the skill.
- Be familiar, or capable of being easily made familiar, to your students.
- Be limited in quantity.

Each of these three conditions requires a brief explanation. First, it is especially important that the data or content used in your first several skill-teaching lessons be presented in the same form. That is, if the content in your initial lesson in the skill is presented in reading passages, then make sure the content to be used in the succeeding lessons on this same skill is also presented in the form of reading passages. If the content in the initial lesson is in the form of a chart, then be sure the content in subsequent places is (or can easily be redone) in chart form. In learning a new skill, you should not change the context (the form in which the content or data used by the student is presented) of the initial introduction of the skill until students have demonstrated proficiency in carrying out the skill in that context.

Thinking skills are tied closely to the context in which they are first introduced. In learning a new thinking skill, practice lessons in the skill should keep the context the same as that of the introductory lesson to minimize interference from having to learn how to deal with new forms of data presentation (such as films, graphs, poems, or tables) while simultaneously trying to learn a new thinking skill. When students are confronted with a new or unfamiliar mode of data presentation, they see the skill required to process that data in that form as unique and different from what they have been doing with the skill up to that point. Students need instructional assistance in understanding how a skill they have learned in one context is executed in new contexts. They do not generally pick up this knowledge automatically. The need to do so should be minimized or eliminated until your students have demonstrated how to do the skill, effectively and accurately, in the context in which it was originally introduced.[20]

Second, the subject matter in the place you select to introduce and provide initial practice in the skill ought to be familiar to or easily understood by your students. If students are not likely to understand the content to be used in an important thinking skills lesson, the preceding lesson can focus on this content. In the skill-practice lessons following its introduction, the content should also be familiar to the students so they can focus on the skill with a minimum of content interference. As students gain experience and expertise in carrying out the skill using familiar content, they can increasingly apply it to less familiar content and eventually transfer it to new contents.

Finally, the content to which the students are to apply the skill, in these initial lessons, should also be limited in quantity. It should require only ten minutes or less of student time to complete any initial skill-using task you assign them. The time devoted to doing the skill needs to be relatively short because in any of these lessons the students also need to do other things to help learn the skill. They will need time to preview how to do the skill before they apply it and more time after completing the task to reflect on, articulate, and share with others how they carried out the thinking skill required to complete the activity.

Identifying Where a Skill Can Be Used and Taught. Figure 2.4 illustrates the initial step in a plan for teaching a sequence of thinking skill lessons. Each number represents a lesson in the subject or course over the next 28 days. Assume each lesson requires a single class session, of whatever length of time is a normal class session (20 minutes, 45 minutes, or whatever). The checkmarks indicate those lessons where built-in opportunities perhaps already exist for students to use the thinking skill you seek to teach.

Spacing Time Intervals. Next, it is important to check the time intervals between the skill-using and teaching opportunities you have identified, to be sure they are appropriately spaced. In reviewing the checkmarks in Figure 2.4, notice that the time intervals between lessons are about right for providing the frequent practice needed to develop proficiency in the skill after it has been introduced—except for the gap between lessons 16 and 21. Thus, to ensure continued skill learning, it will be necessary to contrive a subject matter-related exercise about midway between these lessons, perhaps at lesson 18, in which students will have to use the skill. This will give you the needed opportunity to provide instructive guidance to them in how to carry it out and maintain the periodic attention to the skill required for effective initial learning. Thus, the X

Figure 2.4 Identifying Lessons Where a Specific Thinking Skill Could Be Taught

LESSON:	1	2	3	4	5	6	7
focus on the thinking skill			✓		✓		✓

LESSON:	8	9	10	11	12	13	14
focus on the thinking skill		✓		✓			✓

LESSON:	15	16	17	18	19	20	21
focus on the thinking skill		✓		✗			✓

LESSON:	22	23	24	25	26	27	28
focus on the thinking skill	✓		✓			✓	

indicates a skill-using opportunity that you will have to create in order to have an effective sequence of lessons in this thinking skill. This added skill-using activity will also have to keep subject-matter learning moving forward—it should use the content of the lesson to be taught at that point, if at all possible.

Determining the Type of Lesson.   Figure 2.5 illustrates the final step in this process of sequencing lessons in a thinking skill. It shows the *type* of thinking skill lesson to be taught at each of the places where students will be able to use the skill in their study of the subject at hand. To make this determination, you should refer to the thinking skill teaching framework outlined in the preceding section. This framework, you will recall, consists of the following kinds of lessons:

1. A lesson introducing the thinking skill
2. A number of guided practice lessons in the skill
3. Several lessons where students use the skill on their own
4. A lesson initiating transfer of or elaborating the skill
5. Additional guided practice lessons in the ''new'' context or skill attributes
6. Autonomous application of the skill

Figure 2.5 Identifying the Types of Thinking Skill Lessons to Be Used in Teaching a Specific Thinking Skill

LESSON:	1	2	3	4	5	6	7
focus on the thinking skill			Introduction		Guided Practice		Guided Practice

LESSON:	8	9	10	11	12	13	14
focus on the thinking skill		Guided Practice		Guided Practice			Guided Practice

LESSON:	15	16	17	18	19	20	21
focus on the thinking skill		Independent Use		Independent Use			Transfer or Elaboration

LESSON:	22	23	24	25	26	27	28
focus on the thinking skill	Guided Practice		Guided Practice			Autonomous Use	

As indicated in Figure 2.5, your sequence can consist of five guided practice lessons in the skill, following the introductory lesson. These will be followed by two opportunities for the students to use the skill independently, but at your direction. Then, if all goes well, you can transfer the skill to a different kind of data (for example, from using paragraphs throughout the preceding eight lessons to using maps) or subject (from social studies to language arts, perhaps, if you teach both). If transfer seems inappropriate here, you can elaborate the skill by adding new steps or rules or criteria to it. Then you can provide additional guided practice in the skill as modified or in the new context to which it is being transferred. Of course, additional lessons on this skill will have to be taught beyond these shown in this figure as you decrease the amount of instruction in it and increase the time intervals between these lessons. Eventually, your students will be carrying out the skill on their own in conjunction with other thinking skills as they use these skills to understand better the subjects they are studying.

In preparing any such plan, there is the very real possibility that it will not work—that your students will not be performing the skill as well as you wish by the conclusion of the final planned guided practice lesson. In this case, you will have to convert the next several planned independent-use lessons to guided practice and postpone transferring or elaborating the skill (here until lesson 27 or so) so they will have several opportunities to try the skill on their own before carrying it further. Flexibility in planning thinking skill lessons is a must, for it is often impossible to predict exactly how much guided practice students will need to become somewhat proficient in any particular thinking skill in any specific subject. Nevertheless, having a plan when you start teaching is essential in providing the kind of teaching necessary to help students become as proficient as possible in any thinking skill.

Once you have identified a sequence of places in your course where you could "teach" a thinking skill you have selected, you can proceed to design the specific teaching plans for each skill lesson. Learning how to design such lesson plans is the focus of what follows.

checkpoint

When you have identified a sequence of appropriately spaced opportunities for "teaching" the thinking skill you have selected to teach, check here:

☐

4. *Select the type of skill-teaching lesson you wish to prepare and the teaching strategy to be used in this lesson.*

Now that you have determined where the content lessons of your course or unit of study provide opportunities for students to use (and thus for you to "teach") the skill you have chosen, and have decided what kind of skill-teaching lesson seems appropriate to each of these places, you can turn to planning your actual lessons. To do this, you will have to decide which specific teaching strategies are best suited to the type(s) of lesson(s) you wish to design.

---

note

Part III of this handbook presents essays by several experienced teachers and individuals training to be teachers. They reflect on their initial experiences in writing and teaching thinking skill lessons like the one(s) you can learn how to prepare in this chapter. They followed the same procedures you can follow here. The lessons some of them produced may be found in Part II.

If you wish to see what they experienced in doing this—as an indicator of what you might experience—you may wish to read one or two of their essays at this point. Knowing what you could get out of all this may make your study here more worthwhile and help you realize that you are not alone in your reactions to this approach to learning how to teach thinking skills.

Many different strategies may be used to carry out any of the six kinds of thinking skill lessons listed in the teaching framework presented on pages 45–53. Figure 2.6 identifies some of the more powerful of these strategies. As the information in this figure indicates, if you wish to plan a lesson to *introduce* a new thinking skill to your students, you could use an inductive, a directive, or a developmental teaching strategy, depending on the complexity of the skill to

Figure 2.6 A Range of Strategies for Teaching Thinking Skills

Introducing a Skill	Guiding Practice in a Skill	Independent Use of a Skill	Transferring or Elaborating a Skill	Guiding Practice in a Skill	Autonomous Use of a Skill
Inductive	Explicit (PREP)	Guided discussion	Inductive	Explicit (PREP)	Research
Directive	Graphic organizer	Debates	Directive	Graphic organizer	Problem solving
Developmental	Cued questioning	Research	Developmental	Cued questioning	Concept making
		Cooperative learning			Decision making
					Creative production
					Argument production

be introduced, the ability levels and backgrounds of your students, and your own knowledge of the skill. An inductive skill-introducing strategy involves students in doing the skill and then reflecting at some length on how they did it as the class seeks insights into different ways to carry out the skill. A directive skill-introducing strategy calls for the teacher to explain and model the skill before having students attempt to carry it out and reflect on how they did it. A developmental strategy combines elements of these two: As students attempt to carry out the skill as best they can, the teacher looks for errors or obstacles and then intervenes to explain and demonstrate how to deal with these before allowing the students to complete the skill-using task.

If you wish to prepare lessons providing *guided practice* in a thinking skill already introduced, you can choose from a wide variety of other teaching strategies. For example, you could decide to use a rather explicit practice strategy known as PREP, which stands for the major steps in this strategy—Previewing the Skill, Reviewing or rehearsing how to do it, Executing the skill, and Pondering (or reflecting on) how it was or could have been better carried out. Or you might elect to employ some type of graphic organizer or questions cued or structured in some specific way.

If you wish to show students how to *transfer* to your class or subject a thinking skill they learned in another class or subject or how to apply it to another type of data, you could use an inductive, a directive, or a developmental strategy similar to those just described. The same strategies might be used to *elaborate*, or broaden, a thinking skill, too. Other strategies might also be employed to carry out other kinds of skill-teaching lessons in the framework as shown in Figure 2.6. Given the number of teaching strategies available, the combinations of strategies you could use to provide instruction from introducing a thinking skill to autonomous use of the skill is virtually endless.

Which kind of thinking skill lesson do you wish to prepare? What strategy will you use to conduct this lesson?

If you are not sure which kind of lesson to prepare, consider preparing an introductory lesson. Such a lesson is the first kind you should teach in helping students learn any thinking skill. It is also one of the most important in the entire instructional framework because how it is done shapes considerably the kind of instruction that will have to follow. So, if you have no inclination to the contrary, it might be most useful to start your planning by choosing to design a lesson to introduce to your students the thinking skill you selected in Chapter 1 of this handbook. If you prefer to develop another kind of lesson, just make your choice. Then determine the type of teaching strategy you will use to conduct that lesson and proceed.

checkpoint

When you have identified the kind of thinking skill lesson you wish to prepare (introductory, guided practice, transfer, or elaboration) and the type of teaching strategy you would like to use in this lesson, check here: ☐

5. *Review or learn the teaching strategy to be used in the skill-teaching lesson.*

At this point you can choose one of two options.

Option A. If you are already familiar with a teaching strategy appropriate to the kind of lesson you have chosen to plan, you should review it to be sure you remember the major steps of which it consists. It may also be useful to check any strategy you select against the general research-based principles for introducing, guiding practice in, and initiating transfer of or elaborating a thinking skill (presented in Figure 2.7) to be sure it is appropriate to the kind of lesson you wish to plan. Having these principles as well as the details of the strategy you plan to use clearly in mind will make writing and teaching the lesson plan you wish to prepare that much easier. If you know an appropriate strategy, you should proceed directly to page 66 to start writing your plan.

Option B. If you are not familiar with instructional strategies appropriate for use in the skill-teaching lesson you wish to plan, you should continue on here. The next few pages present a procedure you can use to learn this (or any other) strategy and how to write lessons that employ it to teach any thinking skill to students at any grade level using subject matter or academic content of your choice. Then you can proceed to page 66 to start writing your lesson.

The following procedure will assist you in learning about whichever kind of skill-teaching lesson and teaching strategy you choose to learn. The references under each step indicate information in the Appendices of this handbook that you may find most useful in learning the teaching strategy on which you have chosen to concentrate.

In order to learn any new teaching strategy, it is most helpful to go through the following procedure:

1. Listen to or read an introductory explanation of the strategy you wish to learn.

2. Observe a demonstration and/or analyze a case study of that strategy in use, looking specifically for how the strategy works in practice.

3. Analyze exactly how the strategy worked in the demonstration lesson or case study to identify and understand its key features.

4. Review the teaching plan for the demonstration lesson or case study to identify the key moves planned by the demonstration or case-study teacher.

5. Observe and analyze additional demonstrations or case studies and/or additional lesson plans that employ the same strategy to become aware of the key parts of the strategy and the varied ways they may be employed.

6. Review what you have learned about the strategy, making a list of

Figure 2.7 Research-Based Principles for Teaching Thinking Skills

General

1. Provide instruction at a time when the learner has a felt need to know how to execute the skill.

2. Minimize interference from content and other skills.

3. Cue skills as they are used to stimulate recall of information related to and the structure of the skill procedure.

Introducing

1. Keep the focus on the skill.

2. Emphasize the skill attributes.

3. Model/demonstrate the skill.

4. Have learners do the skill.

5. Have learners reflect on and share how they executed the skill.

Guiding Practice

1. Provide immediate feedback.

2. Provide frequent practice initially.

3. Space practice out intermittently after initial practice.

4. Keep application short.

5. Keep the context similar to that of the initiating experience.

Transfer/Elaboration

1. Focus on attributes/elements of the context that are like the familiar/original context/media/situation.

2. Show the structure of comparable situations.

3. Use familiar knowledge or information.

4. Provide rules to accompany examples.

5. Have students articulate and share principles, explanations, and analogies.

guidelines for you to observe when planning—and teaching—a lesson using this strategy.

The next several pages guide you through these steps so you can become familiar with whatever teaching strategy you wish to learn.

Step 1.

Listen to or read an introductory explanation of the strategy. Before watching a demonstration of any teaching strategy—or before reading a case study of how such a strategy was implemented in an actual class—it is helpful to be aware of the salient features and steps of that strategy. Awareness of these will help you better attend to the important aspects of the demonstration or case study. One way to do this is to listen to someone knowledgeable about the strategy explain these points briefly. Another way is to read a written explanation of them. If you cannot do the former for a strategy you wish to learn, you can do the latter by referring to the appropriate pages in some significant source on teaching thinking. For instance, Appendices B, C, and D in this handbook present three different kinds of strategies for teaching thinking skills:

For an Introductory Explanation of:	**See:**
1. An inductive strategy for introducing a thinking skill	Appendix B, p. B-2
2. A directive strategy for introducing a thinking skill	Appendix B, pp. B-8–B-9
3. A developmental strategy for introducing a thinking skill	Appendix B, p. B-16
4. A strategy for guiding practice of a thinking skill	Appendix C, pp. C-1–C-2
5. Strategies for initiating transfer or elaboration of a thinking skill	Appendix D, pp. D-1–D-2

As you read or listen to the explanation of the strategy about which you wish to learn, be alert to the major steps, important principles, guidelines or ''rules,'' and the knowledge essential to carrying out the strategy.

Step 2.

Observe a demonstration or analyze a case study of the strategy being used. Keeping in mind the explanation of the key attributes of the teaching strategy you are studying, you should now observe how that strategy works in action. Ideally, you should watch it demonstrated or modeled by someone proficient in its use. However, if this is not possible, you should read a description or case study of how it works in practice. To do the latter for some strategies appropriate to the thinking skills teaching framework outlined earlier, you can consult the following pages in the Appendices:

For a ''Case Study'' Description of:	**See:**
1. An inductive strategy for introducing a thinking skill	Appendix B, pp. B-2–B-6
2. A directive strategy for introducing a thinking skill	Appendix B, pp. B-9–B-11
3. A developmental strategy for introducing a thinking skill	Appendix B, pp. B-16–B-17
4. A strategy for guiding practice of a thinking skill	Appendix C, pp. C-2–C-3
5. A strategy for initiating transfer or elaboration of a thinking skill	Appendix D, pp. D-3–D-6

Remember, as you observe the demonstration or read the written description of the teaching strategy, look carefully to identify where, when, and how the major steps, principles, and knowledge that comprise the strategy are applied in actual practice.

Step 3.

Analyze how the strategy worked. Consulting with others who have seen the demonstration or read the same case study or description, if possible, identify and analyze where, when, and how in the lesson the various elements of the strategy were executed. In focusing on the steps of the strategy, ask yourself, ''What did the teacher do first? Why? What did he or she do next? Why? Next?

Why?'' and so on. See if you can determine if and where the basic research-based principles for this type of thinking skills lesson, as listed in Figure 2.7, were employed and what form their application took. Identify what it was the teacher knew or believed that led him or her to execute each step of the strategy or apply each principle as he or she did—or why these might *not* have been applied at all. By carefully considering and discussing these points with repeated reference to the demonstration or written description, you can become quite familiar with the teaching strategy you are studying. You may also check your analysis of the strategy listed above against analyses of this strategy by an experienced observer by consulting the following pages in the Appendices:

For an Analysis of:	**See:**
1. An inductive strategy for introducing a thinking skill	Appendix B, pp. B-6–B-8
2. A directive strategy for introducing a thinking skill	Appendix B, pp. B-11–B-12
3. A developmental strategy for introducing a thinking skill	Appendix B, pp. B-16–B-17
4. A strategy for guiding practice of a thinking skill	Appendix C, pp. C-3–C-5
5. A strategy for initiating transfer or elaboration of a thinking skill	Appendix D, pp. D-3–D-8

Step 4.

Review the teaching plan for the demonstration lesson or case study. Examine the lesson plan used by the individual who demonstrated the strategy to identify the steps and principles followed to carry out the lesson as you observed or read about it. If you are using the Appendices of this handbook as your source of information, you can consult the following:

For a Lesson Plan for:	**See:**
1. An inductive strategy for introducing a thinking skill	Appendix B, pp. B-12–B-13
2. A directive strategy for introducing a thinking skill	Appendix B, pp. B-14–B-15
3. A developmental strategy for introducing a thinking skill	Appendix B, pp. B-18–B-20
4. A strategy for guiding practice of a thinking skill	Appendix C, p. C-4
5. A strategy for initiating transfer or elaboration of a thinking skill	Appendix D, pp. D-6–D-7

Step 5.

Observe and analyze additional demonstrations or analyze other descriptions or lesson plans employing the same skill-teaching strategy you are studying. Use what you have learned about the skill-teaching strategy you are studying to analyze additional demonstrations, descriptions, case studies, or lesson plans that indicate they are employing this same strategy. As before, look for the steps being executed (where, when, and how they are carried out), any principles employed, and what it was the instructor knew or believed that made or let him or her execute the strategy as he or she did.

---

note

If you wish, you may examine the teaching materials in Part II of this handbook to add to your knowledge of these strategies. Each set of materials includes two introductory lesson plans—one that uses the inductive strategy and one that uses either a directive or a developmental strategy. Although you would only introduce a specific skill once, using only one of these strategies, three kinds of strategies are illustrated in these lessons so you can see how they work with the same skill. Also included in each set is a sample guided practice lesson and a lesson for elaborating or initiating transfer of a thinking skill. These sets use strategies explained in Appendices B, C, and D. By examining the appropriate plan, you will learn more about the teaching strategy and also something more about the lesson plans for guiding use of the strategy in a classroom somewhat like yours. You can examine as many of the relevant plans in each set of skill materials as you wish or need to, to understand the strategy as thoroughly as you can.

Step 6. *Review what you have learned about the strategy.* With others who have been engaged like you in the preceding activities, reflect on what you have learned about the strategy. One way to pull all this together is to make a list of ''dos and don'ts'' or guidelines for employing the strategy in any classroom. Focus on the steps—what to do and what not to do—rules, guidelines, or principles that ought to be (almost) always followed, and what you or any teacher needs to know in order to carry out the strategy most efficiently and effectively. When you have completed this, you may also wish to read the following in the Appendices:

For a Review or Summary of:	See:
1. Strategies for introducing a thinking skill	Appendix B, pp. B-20–B-27
2. Strategies for guiding practice in a thinking skill	Appendix C, pp. C-6–C-7
3. Strategies for initiating transfer of a thinking skill	Appendix D, pp. D-7–D-9

The above procedure can help you learn about any strategy used for teaching any thinking skill, if you have the resources and materials appropriate for the task. Strategies other than those cited here may also be learned following this same procedure.*

---

*Strategies for other kinds of lessons in the framework described here can be found in Barry K. Beyer, *Practical Strategies for the Teaching of Thinking* (Boston: Allyn and Bacon, 1987). These include

One aspect of teaching thinking skills often overlooked is that related to metacognition and ways to help students engage in "thinking about their own thinking." As you may have noticed in studying any of the strategies mentioned here, an important part of each of them is having students reflect on how they carried out a thinking skill, articulate what they did and why, and share this with each other as they strive to clarify how to carry out the skill. Such an instructional practice raises students' thinking to a level of conscious awareness so they can better understand what they are doing, take ownership of it, and be able in the future to execute it at their own initiative and direction. Study of information about metacognition at this point may clarify how attention to this aspect of thinking is useful in carrying out each of the teaching strategies you could or should use in teaching any thinking skill.*

Undoubtedly, there are many other strategies for effectively introducing, guiding practice in, stimulating independent application of, and initiating transfer of any thinking skill. You could probably produce numerous variations on these strategies and those presented here. However, if any of these strategies are new to you, it is most useful to first try to execute them as they have been modeled. When you have mastered them as they have been demonstrated for you and when you feel comfortable in using them in that form, then you should feel free to revise or modify them, adding your own ideas, trying new approaches, and creating your own variations of them. But as you alter them, keep in mind the general principles and guidelines (presented in Figure 2.7) on which they are based. *In teaching thinking skills, not just anything will do.*

---

checkpoint

When you can describe to a colleague or peer the kind of thinking skill lesson you propose to write and explain accurately in detail the basic steps of the teaching/lesson strategy you propose to use to conduct that lesson, check here:

DESIGNING AND TEACHING THINKING SKILL LESSONS

A lesson plan is a statement of intent. It is not a script or set of directives to be followed blindly no matter what happens, but a guide for carrying out a lesson that may be modified as the lesson unfolds. Designing and writing detailed lesson plans to use a specific skill-teaching strategy appropriate to the function

---

strategies for independent application and autonomous use of a skill (pp. 150–161 and 177–178). Other sources may be consulted for information on other skill-teaching strategies. Arthur L. Costa and Lawrence F. Lowrey, *Techniques for Teaching Thinking* (Pacific Grove, CA.: Midwest Publications, 1989), for example, provides guidelines for using questioning as a teaching technique.

*Barry K. Beyer, *Practical Strategies for the Teaching of Thinking* (Boston: Allyn and Bacon, 1987), pp. 191–216.

of a given type of lesson contribute immensely to understanding the teaching strategy around which it is built as well as to effective execution of that strategy later in your classroom.

In order to design, write, and teach—and learn how to design, write, and teach—effective thinking skill lessons that employ the most useful teaching strategies, you can do three things:

1. Write, review, and revise a lesson plan, using an appropriate skill-teaching strategy to teach the selected thinking skill to your students.

2. Pilot-teach the lesson, revising it as the teaching experience warrants, and reteaching (and rerevising) it as many times as necessary until it works the way you want it to.

3. Reflect on, share with others, and summarize what you have learned about the teaching strategy and type of thinking skill lesson and how to use them.

The pages that follow guide you through these steps and provide suggestions that will help you design effective skill-teaching lessons and be able actually to teach them with ease in your, or any, classroom or subject.

Beginning teachers find it useful to write detailed lesson plans because this helps them think through what they will do. It also helps keep them from neglecting what they should do to carry out their plans when confronted with a real class of lively students. Experienced teachers who have internalized a great deal of what to do in a classroom as a result of their experiences often feel comfortable with rather sketchy plans. But when learning a new teaching strategy, as is usually the case in learning how to teach thinking skills directly, even experienced teachers benefit from writing detailed plans. No matter whether you are experienced or inexperienced in teaching in general, producing a very detailed lesson plan using a new teaching strategy helps you rehearse—and thus better remember—how to conduct a new kind of lesson as well as produce an accurate guide you can use in teaching the lesson. This lesson plan can then help ensure against your forgetting or shortchanging any essential steps or things you need to know or do to carry out the lesson in your classroom when you teach it. Continued reflective teaching of these lessons can help you understand and take ownership of the strategies you are using. The procedures that follow here will assist you in accomplishing both of these goals.

1. Write, review, and revise your thinking skill lesson plan, using an appropriate skill-teaching strategy.

You can develop expertise in preparing lesson plans that incorporate thinking skill teaching strategies like the one(s) you just reviewed or examined by doing these things:

1. Review the elements of a useful lesson-plan format.

2. With a group or class of your colleagues, orally produce a plan using this format to teach a lesson for introducing a particular thinking skill.

3. With a partner, write your own plan for using this same kind of lesson to "teach" a thinking skill of your choice to your students in a subject of your choice.

4. Check your plan to be sure you have included the essential elements

of a good plan and the steps essential to the teaching strategy it is supposed to incorporate.

Here is one way to carry out each of these steps.

Step 1.

Review the elements of a useful lesson-plan format. Although there are many formats for lesson plans, not all are useful under actual classroom conditions. To be most useful, a lesson plan should clearly communicate to you (the user) (1) the objectives of the lesson, (2) the key moves you are to make in carrying out the lesson, and (3) the key moves or responses the students should make to let you know they are ready to go on to the next part of the lesson. Moreover, the plan should be written so that you can easily spot where you are in the lesson while you are actually teaching it.

The lesson-plan format used in the model plans in Appendices B, C, and D and in Part II of this handbook illustrate these criteria well. Figure 2.8 highlights the major features of a lesson presented in this format. The complete lesson plan, of which this is the first page, may be found in Appendix B. The remaining two pages of this plan (not included here) are simply the continuation of this plan for introducing a thinking skill. A review of the plan will familiarize you with this format and make it easier for you to use it as a format for the lesson plans you are about to write!

A word or two of explanation may be useful in understanding this format. Notice, first, that the teacher and student "moves" appear in separate columns. Keeping the two separated like this allows you easily to spot whichever you wish while you are teaching. No lengthy reading of the plan is necessary at a time when you really can't afford to do so anyway. Note also that the teacher and student entries are not a word-for-word literal script of what you think students are likely to say, nor do they give the lengthy introductions or explanations you plan to give in class. These entries are simply shortened versions of

---

note

Perhaps reviewing additional plans that use the teaching strategy you seek to use in your lesson may be useful at this point. You will find several such plans in Part II of this handbook. Each set of thinking skill materials in Part II includes four sample lesson plans for a specific thinking skill:

* an inductive skill-introducing lesson
* a directive or developmental skill-introducing lesson
* a guided practice lesson
* a transfer or elaboration lesson

You can turn to that part of the handbook now and examine lessons like the one you wish to design to clarify the teaching strategy as well as the lesson plan format highlighted in Figure 2.8. Examining lessons using the strategy you plan to use in your lesson will also help you understand what your lesson plan should look like when it is completed.

Figure 2.8 A Lesson Plan Format

The overall purpose for teaching this lesson.

What the students are to learn as a result of this lesson, stated in terms of what the students will know or be able to do as a result of the lesson that they didn't know or couldn't do before the lesson.

Materials to be used by you and by the students during the lesson.

Major steps in the teaching strategy used in the lesson as a reminder of what you are trying to do!

The first step can include motivating activities and review as well as the previewing of the skill to be "taught" in the lesson.

What you will say or do to move the lesson along at key points.

What students ought to say or do in response to your directions, key questions, or on their own initiative that indicates they understand the task and are ready to go on to the next step or activity.

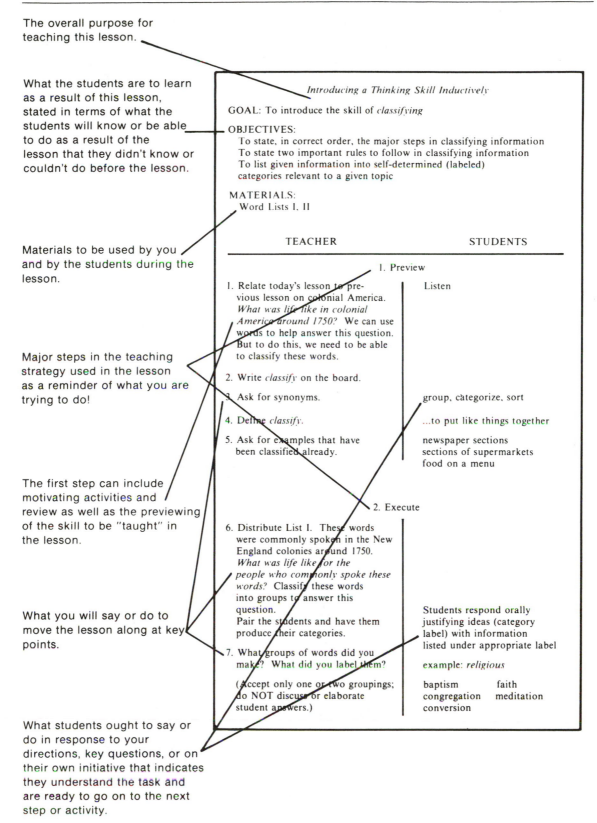

Introducing a Thinking Skill Inductively

GOAL: To introduce the skill of *classifying*

OBJECTIVES:
To state, in correct order, the major steps in classifying information
To state two important rules to follow in classifying information
To list given information into self-determined (labeled) categories relevant to a given topic

MATERIALS:
Word Lists I, II

TEACHER	STUDENTS
1. Preview	
1. Relate today's lesson to previous lesson on colonial America. *What was life like in colonial America around 1750?* We can use words to help answer this question. But to do this, we need to be able to classify these words.	Listen
2. Write *classify* on the board.	
3. Ask for synonyms.	group, categorize, sort
4. Define *classify*.	...to put like things together
5. Ask for examples that have been classified already.	newspaper sections sections of supermarkets food on a menu
2. Execute	
6. Distribute List I. These words were commonly spoken in the New England colonies around 1750. *What was life like for the people who commonly spoke these words?* Classify these words into groups to answer this question. Pair the students and have them produce their categories.	Students respond orally justifying ideas (category label) with information listed under appropriate label
7. What groups of words did you make? What did you label them? (Accept only one or two groupings; do NOT discuss or elaborate student answers.)	example: *religious* baptism faith congregation meditation conversion

what you expect to do, see, hear, and so on, put there to remind you that these are to be done or sought. The desired student responses are especially important; they serve as clear signals to you, when you hear or see them, that you may move the class on to the next step in the lesson.

In writing any lesson plan—especially a plan using a teaching strategy new to you—you should write it as if it is for a substitute teacher, who knows *less* than you about the strategy you wish to use. Doing this will help you be more precise and specific in the teacher directions you include. It will also help you realize the importance of including the key student responses (''right answers'') that will enable the lesson to move along. Writing the key steps of the strategy you will use in the lesson down the center of the plan, as if you are telling the substitute as clearly as possible ''this is what you are doing,'' helps you remember to include these steps, and when you use the plan, it provides obvious reminders to you of what you are trying to do.

Step 2.

With a group of your colleagues, orally create a lesson plan that uses the skill-teaching strategy that all of you would like to try. Regardless of what particular strategy you choose to incorporate into the plan, it ought to be the same strategy you and a partner will use in the plan you will later write for the skill you have already chosen. This will help you transfer the strategy to your own particular teaching situation when you try to write your plan for the skill you propose to teach. And you might have the plan deal with a relatively simple thinking skill, such as predicting, so you can focus on the steps in the skill-teaching strategy rather than on the thinking skill presented in the plan. Working together as a large group and simply telling each other what the plan should say helps give everyone involved a sense of what is entailed in this task, helps them rehearse what they will do next with their partner, minimizes the effort they have to make to create their own plans, and allows them to hear different ideas that could be incorporated in different parts of their own plans. In effect, this is a ''dry run'' for what you are about to do next—create a lesson plan of your own using this same teaching strategy and lesson-plan format.

In completing this large-group ''warm-up'' task, it is especially useful for someone to record the evolving plan on the chalkboard or on a transparency to be projected on an overhead projector. The recorder should make sure the group completes each part of the plan (the goal, objectives, materials [a task best left until the end when you know exactly what you used and thus will need], and key teacher moves and key student moves to carry out the strategy selected) and the key parts of any lesson (the motivation, preview or introduction, body of the lesson, final review, and any assignment). Actually seeing one of these plans take shape on the chalkboard or overhead as you and your colleagues generate it helps you see what you have to do in planning your own lesson and also see what such a lesson ought to look like. You can check the group plan by comparing it to the format described in Figure 2.8 or to an actual plan in Appendices B, C, or D or in Part II.

Step 3.

With a partner, write a lesson plan using the same teaching strategy as the large group used in its ''warm-up'' lesson plan to ''teach'' the skill you selected earlier. This may seem a difficult task, but if you have successfully completed the above procedures, you should be able to do it. Of course, there may be hitches and even false starts. But don't be reluctant to ask others for advice or to see how they are doing or have done this with the skills they have chosen. Remember, completing this task really requires two activities—writing your lesson plan and preparing the materials to be used by you, the teacher, and by the students during the lesson.

If you wish, you may use the blank teaching plan presented in Figure 2.9 on which to write your plan, duplicating as many extra copies of the second page as you need for your complete plan. On the horizontal lines in the center of each page, write the name of the step in your teaching strategy that includes all the moves between that line and the next one following it. On the first line of the first page, you can write ''Introduction'' or ''Motivation,'' and on the next, ''Preview.'' These will be fairly standard steps for all strategies used in teaching any thinking skill. The steps you write on succeeding lines and pages will vary according to the strategies you use.

As you create your plan, be alert to several cautions. First, before you start, key your plan to the sequence of places in your text or course (identified earlier) where you could ''teach'' the skill you wish to teach. If this is to be an introduction of the skill, it should be at the first point in the sequence you selected; if this is to be a guided practice lesson, it could be in any of the next several places in the sequence. An independent-use lesson might be at the sixth or seventh place in the sequence, whereas a transfer lesson might be toward or at the end of the sequence. In writing this plan, use content that would be appropriately used in the lesson in your course sequence where this lesson will or could be taught.

If necessary, refer to the sample lesson plan in Appendices B, C, or D or in Part II that uses the teaching strategy you wish to use as a model for your plan. Also use the guidelines in the Appendix associated with that strategy as an aid in completing your plan. If necessary, it is all right the first time through to copy a sample or model plan, if you wish, simply changing some words to fit the skill or lesson you have chosen instead of the one in the sample plan. However, it would be better if you at least rewrote the essential elements of the sample lesson in your own words. Translating the sample helps you internalize the ideas expressed in the words of the sample plan. Feel free to modify the sample plan as long as you use an appropriate format and as long as you include the major steps of the teaching strategy selected and/or the basic principles from which the strategy was derived, as noted in Figure 2.7.

Your plan will be incomplete without the materials you and your students will need to carry it out. These materials are an important part of any lesson plan designed to provide instruction in thinking and must be developed or secured at the time the plan is written, while it is clear to you what you are trying to do. If a worksheet is required, it should be written or photocopied at this point; if a visual is needed, a reasonably accurate sketch of it should be prepared now. A copy of whatever materials you or the students will need to proceed through the lesson, as designed, should be attached to the completed plan. Without these materials, it would be impossible to execute the plan or, prior to its use, even judge the extent to which it might work as designed.

Student materials for use in your lessons should meet five criteria. First, they must clearly require the students to carry out the thinking skill that is being ''taught'' in the planned lesson. Second, they should be appropriate to the thinking skill being ''taught'' in the lesson; that is, they must obviously exercise this skill and not be a subtle version of it. Third, these materials should not require much time to use, perhaps five minutes or so for most thinking operations other than the most complex strategies like problem solving, decision making, conceptualizing, and so on. Fourth, they should use subject matter familiar to the students, especially in the first two or three lessons on the skill and, after

Figure 2.9 A Thinking Skill Lesson Plan

TEACHING PLAN

Thinking skill: Teacher:

Type of lesson: Date of lesson:

Teaching goal:

Learning objectives:

Materials to be used:

TEACHER	STUDENTS

Figure 2.9 A Thinking Skill Lesson Plan (*cont'd*)

Thinking skill: Type of lesson: Page:

TEACHER	STUDENTS

the very first try at the skill, should use subject matter that the students are studying.

Finally, if being used in a practice lesson, the materials must be of the same form as the materials used in the introduction of the skill. That is, if the skill was introduced using information presented in the form of a map, then subsequent practice lessons should use materials in the form of maps. It is important to keep the data or information students use in practicing a new skill the same as that used in the introduction of the skill. Remember, transfer is not automatic. However, once students have demonstrated proficiency in executing the skill in one type of data, they can then be helped to transfer and generalize the skill to other kinds of data and contexts.

Step 4.

Check your lesson plan. At this point you should review your lesson plan to be sure it contains the essential elements and that it accurately and clearly incorporates the teaching strategy appropriate to its purpose.

The purposes of this check are threefold: (1) to determine if you understand the teaching strategy you propose to use, (2) to ensure that your lesson contains all the elements essential to a useful lesson plan, and (3) to determine how likely it is that the plan, if executed as designed, will actually work in a class.

You can conduct this check in either of two ways. You could exchange plans with another team of your colleagues who have also been writing a similar kind of lesson plan and have them check yours. Or you can review your own plan. Regardless of whether you use peer or self-review, the review can be facilitated by comparing the plan to a model plan or to guidelines for the type of lesson or strategy you are using. As you do either, look carefully to see that the teaching strategy used incorporates the steps, principles, and knowledge essential to that strategy and that all the elements essential to an effective lesson are included and are accurate or appropriate to the type of lesson it purports to teach.

If you are preparing a lesson using one of the strategies explained in the Appendices, you may recall that some guidelines for using the strategy are included there. You can check your lesson against these guidelines:

For Guidelines on:	See:
1. An inductive strategy for introducing a thinking skill	Appendix B, p. B-6
2. A directive strategy for introducing a thinking skill	Appendix B, p. B-10
3. A developmental strategy for introducing a thinking skill	Appendix B, p. B-17
4. A strategy for guiding practice of a thinking skill	Appendix C, p. C-2
5. A strategy for initiating transfer or elaboration of a thinking skill	Appendix D, pp. D-4–D-5

The lesson plan checklist in Figure 2.10 has been prepared especially to highlight the principles of effective teaching and of the direct teaching of thinking skills. You should find it useful in helping you check your own lesson plans or those prepared by others to ensure that they include the key teaching operations that need to be performed by a particular lesson. You may also find this checklist to be useful in designing future thinking skill lessons, by using it as a

Figure 2.10 A Thinking Skill Lesson Plan Checklist

	Yes	No
1. The purpose of this lesson is clearly stated.	___	___

2. The student *learning* objectives:

	Yes	No
2.1 Are stated in terms of observable behaviors or measurable products.	___	___
2.2 Focus on the thinking skill to be taught.	___	___
2.3 Are appropriate to the purpose of the lesson.	___	___

3. The teacher materials to be used, if any:

	Yes	No
3.1 Are clear.	___	___
3.2 Are appropriate to the purpose.	___	___
3.3 Are accurate.	___	___

4. The student learning materials:

	Yes	No
4.1 Provide clearly stated directions.	___	___
4.2 Are appropriate to the purpose for which they are intended.	___	___
4.3 Require execution of the skill being taught.	___	___
4.4 Are of an appropriate degree of complexity.	___	___
4.5 Require an appropriate amount of time to complete.	___	___
4.6 Use subject matter familiar to the students.	___	___
4.7 Use subject matter from the course.	___	___
4.8 Are appropriate in terms of form or context.	___	___
4.9 Are clear/legible.	___	___

5. The teaching strategy used is appropriate to:

	Yes	No
5.1 The stated purpose of the lesson.	___	___
5.2 The presumed ability level and experience of the students.	___	___

6. The main steps in the teaching strategy being used are:

	Yes	No
6.1 Clear.	___	___
6.2 Prominently displayed.	___	___
6.3 Accurate.	___	___
6.4 Complete.	___	___
6.5 Appropriate.	___	___

7. The teacher-given:

	Yes	No
7.1 Directions are clear.	___	___
7.2 Information is accurate.	___	___
7.3 Information is what is needed at the time it is provided.	___	___
7.4 Examples are relevant to the skill.	___	___
7.5 Examples are relevant to the students.	___	___

8. The key desired student responses or activities are:

	Yes	No
8.1 As specific as possible.	___	___
8.2 Accurate.	___	___
8.3 Appropriate.	___	___

	Yes	No
9. The time allocated to each step of the overall strategy is appropriate.	___	___

10. The plan:

	Yes	No
10.1 Provides for mediation by the teacher or students.	___	___
10.2 Includes demonstration of the skill.	___	___
10.3 Provides for application of the skill by students.	___	___

10.4 Provides opportunities for students to:

	Yes	No
a. reflect on how they carried out the skill.	___	___
b. articulate how they carried out the skill.	___	___
c. share how they carried out the skill.	___	___
d. justify, explain, contrast what they did.	___	___

(*continued*)

Figure 2.10 A Thinking Skill Lesson Plan Checklist (*cont'd*)

	Yes	No
10.5 Keeps the focus on:		
a. the skill.	____	____
b. the key steps of the skill.	____	____
c. important rules or principles related to the skill.	____	____
d. important criteria or other skill-related knowledge.	____	____
10.6 Provides a final review that:		
a. focuses on the skill.	____	____
b. has students articulate key attributes of the skill.	____	____
c. bridges the skill to other contexts.	____	____
11. There is congruence between the objectives, the instruction provided, and the review.	____	____

COMPLETE:

This plan is especially good at:	This plan can be improved by:

guide in writing your plan from the beginning. Obviously, not all items apply to every kind of thinking skill lesson you might wish to try, but the items that are included do apply to strategies for use in teaching thinking skills directly. The final section of the checklist provides space for you to note the strengths of any thinking skill lesson you have just examined as well as things that need to be improved and how they could be so improved.

Once your plan has been reviewed (and you have discussed with your reviewers their feedback, if it was a peer review), you should make whatever changes, revisions, or additions that have been recommended or seem advisable to improve the lesson. This may mean a major rewrite or redesign of the plan, a revision of the teaching strategy it incorporates, and/or a redesign of the associated teaching or learning materials. Or it may require only some editorial changes. But whatever is suggested should be seriously considered and accommodated. The lesson plan and materials that emerge at this point should be as thorough as possible and incorporate the essential features of an effective thinking skill lesson.

checkpoint

When you have written a lesson plan that incorporates the basic principles of skill teaching appropriate to the type of thinking skill lesson you have selected and that accommodates feedback from colleagues and, if possible, expert evaluation of the lesson, check here: ☐

2. *Teach the lesson, revising it as the teaching experience and feedback warrant.*

Once you have a completed lesson plan that is accurate, thorough, and workable, you should teach your lesson. In fact, you should teach it several times, revising it each time to reflect what actually happens as the lesson is taught or what you need to do to ensure that the lesson comes off as intended. The more you "practice teach" this lesson, the better you will understand the teaching strategy you are trying to use and the more comfortable you will feel in using it. And, happily, the better you will also come to understand the thinking skill on which your plan is focusing!

Using a new teaching strategy for the first time can be a risky and frustrating experience. Learning how to do anything new for the first time usually is. But if you want to learn how to do something new and useful, you have to start sometime. There are several things you can do to ease into the use of a new teaching strategy or lesson:

1. "Teach" the lesson to your colleagues.
2. Teach the revised lesson to students.
3. Practice using the strategy and reviewing with others how they used the same strategy.

Some suggestions that will make this advice easy to implement follow:

Step 1.

"Teach" the lesson to your colleagues. Presenting your lesson to a group of your colleagues is a useful way to try out a new lesson plan, especially if they have been engaged, like you, in learning how to use the teaching strategy you wish to try. Not only are they likely to be especially supportive of you in carrying out the lesson, but they all may share similar feelings about teaching to one's colleagues. They may not all be experts in the subject matter you wish to use in your lesson, but this actually works in your favor because they are less likely to sidetrack your lesson by shifting its focus to the subject being studied. Because they may all be learning the teaching strategy you are learning, they will also be more alert to the steps in the strategy and, in fact, often deliberately help you in carrying out the lesson.

The advantage of teaching a new kind of lesson or teaching strategy to your colleagues is that it helps you find gaps or errors in your lesson plan and in your knowledge of the strategy you have selected to use. When you actually try to carry out what you have written, you become (sometimes painfully or embarrassingly) aware of vague directions, skipped steps, redundancies, inaccuracies, and the like. It is very useful to make these discoveries *before* teaching your lesson to a real class where the resulting learning "counts." Demonstration or "trial teaching" will help you clarify your plan and revise it to be more practical and accurate when it is eventually used in a real classroom.

If you are uneasy about trying your lesson with a large group of other teachers or even about actually teaching it as a lesson, you can simply talk it through to a small group (4 or 5) of your colleagues. Rather than execute the plan as teacher with students, tell your colleagues step-by-step what you intend to do in the lesson and report how you will do it—what you will do first, then what the students should do in response, then what you will do next, how the students should respond, and so on. Write on the board some of what you would write if you were actually teaching the lesson. But in doing this, you don't need to make it a real teaching lesson at all. This should take only fifteen minutes or so to complete.

Another way to try out your lesson with your colleagues is simply to teach it to them (whether five or twenty or more in number) as if they are your students and you are *their* teacher. Without any editorial or other kinds of remarks, just conduct the lesson as a regular lesson. Consider your colleagues your students and teach accordingly, following your lesson plan as closely as possible. If you have to carry the lesson plan in your hand, that is perfectly all right. Everyone will understand that teaching this kind of lesson is new for you. Complete the entire lesson before talking about it. Try not to let anyone sidetrack the lesson while it is in progress to discuss the strategy or content being used. Save this type of discussion until after the lesson has been completed.

You will find the lesson observation forms reproduced in Figures 2.11 and 2.12 to be useful in conducting such a trial lesson. Participants can use these checklists to help them attend to the skill-teaching strategy you may be using for these checklists, incorporating the basic principles of skill teaching as outlined in Figure 2.7. During or after your teaching, participants can check off the various procedures or operations you use (or omit). Upon completing your demonstration, participants can refer to their checklists to guide them in reviewing what happened and in making suggestions for improvements.

Of course, the discussion about your lesson that should follow your demonstration teaching will be as valuable, if not more, to you as the actual teaching of it. Here, you can ask for help on what you *should* have done at any point in the lesson where you wish help. Such discussions can also call your attention to significant omissions of part of the teaching strategy you were trying to employ, to errors in content being used, and so on. As long as the discussion focuses on the execution of the lesson and the teaching strategy being used, such discussion will be very useful. All involved should strive to keep this ''debriefing'' focused on the extent to which your teaching of the lesson executed the steps and followed the guidelines of the teaching strategy. Your ''class'' may wish to use one of the observation forms presented in Figures 2.11 and 2.12 to guide them in their analysis and discussion of your demonstration, for it will keep their focus on your teaching, as is desired.

One way to initiate useful analysis of a demonstration lesson is for you, as the ''teacher,'' to respond to questions like the following:

1. How do you feel the lesson went? What made you feel that way?
2. What in your judgment worked well? Why?
3. What was a problem? How did you deal with it? What else could have been done to deal with it?
4. What will you do differently when you teach this lesson again? Why?

Similar or related questions almost invariably emerge from responses to these questions. Answers and followup discussion produce very useful insights—especially for the individual who taught the lesson being analyzed.

Once the concerns and issues implied by these questions have been aired and (at least some of them) resolved, the debriefing should focus on the specific teacher and student moves by which the teaching strategy moved the students through the lesson. Here is where the observation forms in Figures 2.11 and 2.12 come in especially handy. The items on these forms serve as reminders of what to focus on here. You should discuss the extent to which the operations listed on the appropriate checklist were carried out in the lesson. Avoid discussing the content or subject matter used. Rather, *concentrate on whether or not the*

Figure 2.11 An Observation Checklist for Lessons Introducing or Transferring/ Elaborating a Thinking Skill

Teacher _____ Observer _____

Subject _____ Date _____ Time start _____ end _____

	Yes	No
A. *Conduct of the lesson*		
1. The purpose for attending to the skill at this point is:		
1.1 clearly stated.	_____	_____
1.2 appropriate.	_____	_____
2. The skill is clearly introduced by:		
2.1 giving its label.	_____	_____
2.2 defining it.	_____	_____
2.3 giving synonyms for it.	_____	_____
2.4 giving appropriate examples of its use		
• in everyday life.	_____	_____
• in previous coursework.	_____	_____
2.5 relating it to other skills.	_____	_____
3. The skill is modeled/demonstrated.	_____	_____
4. The major components of the skill are explained, or re-viewed, including:		
4.1 key procedures for using it.	_____	_____
4.2 its key rules/principles.	_____	_____
4.3 knowledge needed to use it.	_____	_____
5. Students engage in the skill:		
5.1 prior to its explanation or demonstration.	_____	_____
5.2 after having it explained or discussed.	_____	_____
6. Students explain/discuss what goes on in their heads while using the skill:		
6.1 as they engage in the skill.	_____	_____
6.2 after they engage in the skill.	_____	_____
7. If there are several skill applications in this lesson, the data/media to which the students apply the skill are in the same form.	_____	_____
8. Students:		
8.1 modify given skill components.	_____	_____
8.2 suggest major skill components.	_____	_____
9. In concluding the lesson, *students:*		
9.1 define the skill.	_____	_____
9.2 give synonyms for it.	_____	_____
9.3 tell when/where it can be used.	_____	_____
9.4 articulate its key components.	_____	_____
9.5 relate it to other skills.	_____	_____
B. *Components of the lesson*		
10. The focus of the lesson was:		
10.1 clearly on the skill.	_____	_____
10.2 consistently on the skill.	_____	_____
11. The teaching strategy used was:		
11.1 inductive.	_____	_____
11.2 directive.	_____	_____
11.3 Other _____.	_____	_____

Source: Adapted from Barry K. Beyer, *Developing a Thinking Skills Program* (Boston: Allyn and Bacon, 1988).

Figure 2.12 An Observation Checklist for Lessons Guiding Practice in a Thinking Skill

Teacher _____ Observer _____

Subject _____ Date _____ Time start _____ end _____

	Yes	No	Notes

A. *Conduct of the lesson*

1. The purpose for using the skill at this point is:
   1.1 clearly stated. _____ _____
   1.2 appropriate. _____ _____

2. The skill is clearly introduced by:
   2.1 giving its label. _____ _____
   2.2 defining it. _____ _____
   2.3 giving synonyms for it. _____ _____
   2.4 giving appropriate examples of its use
       • previously in class. _____ _____
       • in everyday life. _____ _____

3. The major components of the skill are articulated *before* the skill is used, including:
   3.1 its key procedures. _____ _____
   3.2 its rules/principles. _____ _____
   3.3 the knowledge needed to use it. _____ _____

4. The skill is deliberately applied to relevant content. _____ _____

5. The major components of the skill are articulated and justified *after* the skill is used, including:
   5.1 its key procedures. _____ _____
   5.2 its rules/principles. _____ _____
   5.3 the knowledge needed to use it. _____ _____

6. Modifications and/or additions in the skill components are articulated, considered, made. _____ _____

7. Where and when the skill can be used is discussed. _____ _____

B. *Components of the lesson*

8. The focus is clearly on the skill throughout the above portion of the lesson. _____ _____

9. The media/content form in which the skill is applied is similar to that in which it was initially presented (or extended). _____ _____

10. The components of the skill are reviewed *before* students discuss the content results of using the skill. _____ _____

Source: Adapted from Barry K. Beyer, *Developing a Thinking Skills Program* (Boston: Allyn and Bacon, 1988).

steps and principles of teaching a skill listed on these checklists were evident—if not, why not; if only vaguely, how they could have been better executed, and so on. Keep the focus on the teaching strategy and *not* on the demonstration teacher, subject matter, or nature of the skill itself.

One interesting, sometimes unanticipated, result of such a demonstration lesson is that you and your colleagues may gain new insights into the thinking skill being taught. There may be a real temptation by all involved to want to discuss this at this point. Such a discussion is very useful but should be separated from discussing the *teaching* of the lesson. You often learn a great deal about your own thinking and about the thinking skill being taught as a result of such teaching and followup discussion. Take advantage of it when it occurs, but hold such discussion until after you have debriefed the teaching itself.

The value of a teaching demonstration lies in two things—the extent to which you and your colleagues can focus on the strategy being used in the lesson and the extent to which you incorporate the resultant insights and suggestions into a revision of your lesson plan. The result of this teaching demonstration should be a *thoroughly revised* lesson plan, one ready to be used in your (or someone else's) classroom with the kind of students for whom it was designed.

Step 2. *Teach the revised lesson to students.* Of course, the quality of any thinking skill lesson plan is ultimately determined by the extent to which your students will achieve the learning objectives of the lesson. The only way this can be determined is to teach the lesson to the kinds of students for whom it was designed. These students might well be your own class or a comparable class of another teacher who is willing to let you try your lesson with them. You do not need to use an entire class; instead, you might arrange to teach a half dozen or so students (hopefully students of mixed abilities in the same grade level). Sometimes, teaching a new kind of lesson for the first time is easier to do with a small group of students because behavior problems are virtually nonexistent and you can concentrate on the teaching strategy you are using. If you do try this microteaching approach, videotape it or ask another teacher to watch it (with a copy of your lesson plan or the appropriate observation checklist in hand so he or she can note what might be altered in reteaching the lesson). At the conclusion of the lesson, you should review the videotape yourself or with the observer—and with the students if they are at all tuned into teaching—and reflect on and analyze what worked well, what didn't work well, what needs clarification or resequencing, and so on. The debriefing of a demonstration lesson often provides the most valuable learning of the entire experience.

Teaching your plan to a regular-sized class eventually ought to happen, of course. The class could be your own or that of another teacher. The first time you try the lesson, perhaps in your own class, you may wish to do it without any observer. But it might help to videotape the class; you can look at the tape later, in private, to analyze how the lesson went and whether or not you carried out the teaching strategy as intended. After revising the lesson, you ought then to teach it again to a comparable class. Again, you should videotape it or have another teacher observe your teaching. After the lesson, you can review the tape or go over the lesson with the observer to analyze your use of the teaching strategy employed. Again, the debriefing and revision of the plan based on the experience are musts.

---

checkpoint

When you have taught your lesson at least twice and revised it to incorporate feedback from your colleagues and from your own reflection on your use of it with students, check here:

☐

Step 3.

Practice using the strategy and reviewing with others how they used the same strategy. The more you use the same thinking skill teaching strategy, the better you will be at it. But it takes time to feel comfortable with a new teaching strategy and to be able to carry it out without worrying or thinking much about it. Bruce Joyce and Beverly Showers, two prominent educational researchers, report that it may take fifteen to twenty tries to learn a new skill, and this applies as much to any teaching strategy you are trying to learn as to any thinking skill you are trying to help the students learn.[21] Instant success is rare. The more lessons you create and teach using the same strategy, and the more you observe others teaching similar lessons and/or evaluate their lessons, the more proficient you will become at its use. From this point on, trying the strategy with different classes, analyzing what you did in retrospect, revising the lesson plan, observing others teaching the same strategy and helping them analyze what they did and revise their lessons over and over again will eventually enable you to internalize an effective way to execute the strategy.

Then you can select another strategy and start this process all over again! Learning never ends—for students *or* for teachers!

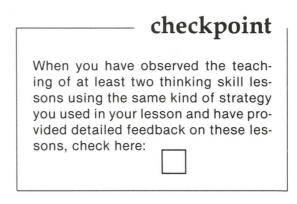

checkpoint

When you have observed the teaching of at least two thinking skill lessons using the same kind of strategy you used in your lesson and have provided detailed feedback on these lessons, check here: ☐

3. Reflect on, share with others, and summarize what you have learned about teaching thinking skills.

It is now time to pull together what you have learned about designing and teaching thinking skill lessons. You can then use what you have learned as guidelines in planning and teaching similar lessons in the future. One way to produce this summary is to reflect on each of the tasks you have engaged in so far. Take a few minutes and do this now, listing five or six things you would advise anyone who wanted to teach thinking skills well to do.

In order to elaborate or extend your summary or list of guidelines, you can compare your initial list to summaries produced by other teachers who have learned how to teach thinking skills by going through the same procedure as you have. For example, one group of teachers, after a week of intensive study, lesson planning, and demonstration teaching, produced the following list of guidelines to follow. Which of these are on your list? Which could have been? With which do you disagree? Why?

- Keep the focus on the skill—stay out of content, especially in introductory lessons.
- Keep the preview (introduction) short—3 to 4 minutes at best—in each lesson.

- Know your skill.
- Know your students and their previous experience with the skill.
- Model the skill or have a student good at it model it.
- Be sure to give the students time to think and talk about how they believe they did the skill.
- If you start out using an inductive strategy and it isn't working, switch to a more directive strategy.
- Use language the students understand.
- Get a variety of routines or procedures for doing the skill on the board—try not to converge on only one.
- Be sure in early lessons on the thinking skill that the students are familiar with the content used in the lesson.

You may also compare what you have learned about teaching thinking skills to what the teachers whose essays appear in Part III of this handbook report they learned. These teachers followed the same procedure you have to produce their lessons, some of which are presented in Part II. Then they tried them out with their colleagues acting as students or with their own students or those of another teacher. In reflecting on this experience, they provide useful insights into what it is like to try something new for the first time and what they learned about teaching thinking skills. You may find their reflections informative as well as encouraging. By comparing your experience with theirs, you can add to what you have learned about teaching thinking skills as you completed this chapter. Read Part III and then, with a colleague who was engaged in this same process, list a dozen things you believe any teacher should do—and/or avoid—who wants to teach thinking skills as effectively as possible.

checkpoint

When you have shared with your colleagues your experiences in teaching the type of thinking skill lesson using the teaching strategy on which you have been working so far, and have summarized in some detail useful guidelines to follow whenever teaching such a lesson, check here: ☐

You can use the procedures you have just completed to learn other teaching strategies for the kind of skill-teaching lesson that you are learning to design or for learning how to design other kinds of skill-teaching lessons as well. If you wish to concentrate on one of these other lessons or strategies, go back to the beginning of this procedure (p. 70) and repeat it again for that strategy or kind of lesson. Remember that the references under each step of the procedure key information in Appendices B, C, and D to the various strategies or lessons you may wish to learn how to use if you are interested in the direct teaching of thinking skills. You can use the appropriate information in these pages to guide you through the procedure to learn more about the lesson or strategy you have chosen to study.

SUMMARY

Having completed this section of the handbook, you should now be able to:

1. Examine any given lesson plan or observe the teaching of any thinking skill lesson and identify which principles of thinking skill instruction were included in or omitted from the lesson.

2. Examine a given lesson plan or observe the teaching of any thinking skill lesson and identify the steps that were included, omitted, or in need of improvement in a specific skill-teaching strategy.

3. Design and write detailed lesson plans for teaching different kinds of thinking skill lessons, each employing an instructional strategy appropriate to the skill-teaching function of the lesson.

4. Explain in detail to someone who is not familiar with the teaching of thinking how to design and write a lesson that will provide instruction in a thinking skill appropriate to a given stage in a research-based framework for thinking skills instruction and guide them in preparing such a lesson.

A well-structured lesson that applies research-based principles to teaching a thinking skill is a key to the effective teaching of thinking skills. Being able to distinguish effective thinking skill lesson plans from ones likely to be ineffective or inappropriate, and to design and write effective thinking skill lesson plans lie at the heart of such teaching. When you have mastered these skills, you will be well on your way to achieving excellence in teaching thinking skills.

Endnotes

1. Hilda Taba, "Teaching of Thinking," *Elementary English* 42:15 (May 1965), p. 534; Edward M. Glaser, *An Experiment in the Development of Critical Thinking* (New York: Bureau of Publications, Teachers College, Columbia University, 1941), p. 69; Howard Anderson, ed., *Teaching Critical Thinking in Social Studies* (Washington, DC: National Council for the Social Studies, 1942), pp. v–vii.

2. Walter Doyle, "Academic Work," *Review of Educational Research* 53:2 (Summer 1983), pp. 155–199; Barak V. Rosenshine, "Synthesis of Research on Explicit Teaching," *Educational Leadership* 43:7 (April 1986), pp. 60–69; Michael I. Posner and Steven W. Keele, *Skill Learning*, in Robert M. W. Travers, ed., *Second Handbook of Research on Teaching* (Chicago: Rand McNally College Publishing Company, 1973), pp. 805–831.

3. David N. Perkins and Gavriel Salomon, "Are Cognitive Skills Context-Bound?" *Educational Researcher* 18:1 (January–February 1989), pp. 16–25; Herbert J. Klausmeier and J. Kent Davis, "Transfer of Learning," *Encyclopedia of Educational Research* (New York: Macmillan, 1969), pp. 1483–1493; Bryce B. Hudgins, *Learning and Thinking* (Itasca, IL: F. E. Peacock, 1977), pp. 142–172.

4. Barak V. Rosenshine, "Teaching Functions in Instructional Programs," *Elementary School Journal* 83:4 (March 1983), pp. 335–352; Hudgins, *Learning and Thinking*, p. 146; Posner and Keele, "Skill Learning."

5. Hudgins, *Learning and Thinking*; Posner and Keele, "Skill Learning"; Robert J. Sternberg, "How Can We Teach Intelligence?" *Educational Leadership* 42:1 (September 1984), pp. 38–50; Edward de Bono, "The Direct Teaching of Thinking as a Skill," *Phi Delta Kappan* 64:10 (June 1983), pp. 703–708; Arthur Whimbey, "Teaching Sequential Thought: The Cognitive Skills Approach," *Phi Delta Kappan* 59:4 (December 1977), pp. 255–259.

6. Posner and Keele, "Skill Learning"; Hudgins, *Learning and Thinking*, pp. 92–99; Jane Stallings, "Effective Strategies for Teaching Basic Skills," in Daisy G. Wallace, ed., *Developing Basic Skills Programs in Secondary Schools* (Alexandria, VA: Association for Supervision and Curriculum Development, 1983), pp. 1–19; Rosenshine, "Teaching Functions"; Doyle, "Academic Work."

7. Klausmeier and Davis, "Transfer of Learning"; Hudgins, *Learning and Thinking*, pp. 142–169; D. N. Perkins, "Thinking Frames," *Educational Leadership* 43:8 (May 1986), pp. 14–15; Doyle, "Academic Work"; Ann Brown, Joseph C. Campione, and Jeanne D. Day, "Learning to Learn from Texts," *Educational Researcher* 10:2 (February 1981), p. 18.

8. Carl Bereiter, "How to Keep Thinking Skills from Going the Way of All Frills," *Educational Leadership* 42:1 (September 1984), pp. 75–78; Posner and Keele, "Skill Learning"; Hudgins, *Learning and Thinking*, pp. 92–99; Doyle, "Academic Work."

9. Carl Bereiter, "Elementary School: Necessity or Convenience?" *Elementary School Journal* 73:8 (May 1973), pp. 435–446.

10. Thomas H. Estes, "Reading in the Social Studies—A Review of Research Since 1950," in James Laffery, ed., *Reading In the Content Areas* (Newark, DE: International Reading Association, 1972), pp. 178–183.

11. Barry K. Beyer, *Practical Strategies for the Teaching of Thinking* (Boston: Allyn and Bacon, 1987).

12. Rosenshine, "Teaching Functions"; Stallings, "Effective Strategies"; Posner and Keele, "Skill Learning"; Whimbey, "Teaching Sequential Thought."

13. Barry K. Beyer, "Teaching Critical Thinking: A Direct Approach," *Social Education* 49:4 (April 1985), pp. 297–303; Rosenshine, "Teaching Functions"; Hudgins, *Learning and Thinking*, pp. 92–99.

14. Posner and Keele, "Skill Learning"; Bruce Joyce and Beverly Showers, *Power in Staff Development Through Research on Training* (Alexandria, VA: Association for Supervision and Curriculum Development, 1983); Rosenshine, "Teaching Functions."

15. Hubert Dreyfus, "Expert Systems Versus Intuitive Enterprise," paper delivered at George Mason University, Fairfax, VA, May 29, 1984; Doyle, "Academic Work"; Posner and Keele, "Skill Learning."

16. Posner and Keele, "Skill Learning"; Doyle, "Academic Work"; Hudgins, *Learning and Thinking*, pp. 92–99.

17. Hudgins, *Learning and Thinking*, pp. 142–169.

18. Hudgins, *Learning and Thinking*; Doyle, "Academic Work."

19. Bereiter, ''How to Keep.''

20. David Perkins and Gavriel Salomon, ''Teaching for Transfer,'' *Educational Leadership* 46:1 (September 1988), pp. 22–32.

21. Joyce and Showers, *Power in Staff Development*.

chapter 3

Preparing Thinking Skill Assessments

Anything worth teaching in depth is worth assessing. This is especially true of thinking skills. In the eyes of most students, continued assessment serves two important purposes. Classroom tests give value to what is being assessed. That is, whatever is to be tested serves as a signal to students as to what is worth learning. In a word, tests motivate learning. Second, test results can also reveal areas where improvement is needed—they help students become aware of gaps in their knowledge so they can, if they wish, direct their efforts at closing these gaps. Thus, tests help students prioritize and focus future learning efforts.

Assessment serves equally valuable purposes for teachers. Periodic end-of-unit and course assessments can identify the degree of student learning as well as the effectiveness of instruction. Used throughout a class or course, testing or other types of formal or informal data gathering about how well students carry out selected thinking skills guide and inform teaching. Assessment can serve diagnostic and formative purposes as well as summative functions.

Indeed, the diagnostic function of assessment is particularly important in the teaching of thinking skills. Identifying how well your students are learning a skill in the course of instruction enables you to adjust your teaching to meet their learning needs. Carefully structured end-of-unit or periodic thinking skill tests can provide information useful in reteaching a skill. Furthermore, assessing how well your students can carry out a specific thinking skill *before* you begin your teaching helps you in your planning. Such preteaching assessment can distinguish students who have some degree of proficiency in the skill to be taught from those who have little or none at all. This enables you to group or pair some of the former with some of the latter in any cooperative or group skill-learning activity. Diagnostic assessment also enables you to use scarce instructional time efficiently, because it enables you to focus your efforts on teaching only those thinking skills in which students appear to be deficient rather than on attempting to teach them what they already know and do fairly well.

Finally, preteaching assessment serves an important instructional or learning function. Pretests help students—indeed, they encourage students—to forecast what they are supposed to learn. By assessing student proficiency in selected thinking skills *at the beginning* of a course or unit, you alert students to important learning goals of the teaching that will follow. By combining with this diagnostic assessment a comment about the importance of learning thinking skills in the class, course, or unit, you can actually increase student awareness of what to attend to in the class.

Assessing student proficiency in a thinking skill is thus an integral part of teaching thinking skills. Such assessment should be frequent and continue throughout your course. It should use content from whatever subject has served as a vehicle for teaching the skill to be assessed. One useful way to do this is to attach the assessment of thinking, at least at the intermediate and secondary levels, to the unit or grading period tests that you probably give regularly. Repeated assessment of the thinking skills you are teaching can thus help you adjust your teaching—and students adjust their learning—of thinking skills as the semester progresses. Being able to design and prepare a variety of tests or instruments for assessing student thinking in your classroom are skills you can use throughout your teaching.

Currently, there are few instruments you and other classroom teachers can use regularly to assess thinking skills you might wish to teach. Of the dozen or so standardized thinking skill tests readily available, it is not likely you will find any that assess all or even half of the thinking skills you might wish to teach to your students—unless, of course, you selected these skills to teach precisely because they were assessed by a specific instrument. Although textbooks are often accompanied by testing booklets or programs, few if any of these assess thinking above the levels of recall, translation, or interpretation.

Consequently, if you are serious about teaching thinking skills in your course, class, school, or district, you will probably have to prepare your own instruments to assess student proficiency in these skills. This will be true especially for assessing student proficiency in the thinking skills you teach in your own class or course during the year.

So, if you are to become as effective a teacher of thinking skills as possible, you should be able to prepare your own assessment instruments for use in your own teaching. Or, at least you should be able to select, with a critical eye, from among commercially available thinking skills tests those most appropriate to your students, the skills being taught to them, and the subject area where these skills are used. This chapter will help you develop your abilities to do these things. Specifically, when you complete this chapter and have practiced with your colleagues what you have learned, you should be able to:

1. Identify the extent to which a given thinking skill assessment instrument assesses proficiency in a specific thinking skill.

2. Write a test or other type of instrument to assess student proficiency in a thinking skill or skills of your choice that meets the criteria of effective thinking skill assessment at different levels of instruction and learning.

3. Explain in detail to someone unfamiliar with thinking skill assessment

how to judge the quality of any thinking skill assessment instrument like the ones you have developed.

4. Explain in detail to someone unfamiliar with thinking skill assessment how to prepare a thinking skill assessment instrument for use with his or her students in a subject of his or her choice.

The following pages will assist you in achieving these objectives. Figure 3.1 outlines the procedures and the sequence in which they are presented. You should find these procedures and the accompanying information, as well as sample skill tests in Part II and the guidelines for creating such instruments in Appendix E, useful in helping you design, write, and evaluate instruments to assess student proficiency in the thinking skills you wish to teach. The major written product that will emerge from this chapter will be an instrument you can use to assess student proficiency in and your teaching of the thinking skill you have been focusing on throughout the preceding chapters.

As in Chapters 1 and 2, each of the learning segments in this chapter concludes with a *Checkpoint*. Each *Checkpoint* signals an end to a particular task and offers you an opportunity to pull together what you have learned to that point, to reflect on it, and, if you wish, to take a break before continuing. These *Checkpoints* may thus serve as learning goals and, when completed, mileposts to mark your progress through this chapter.

---

note

Each of the sets of thinking skill materials in Part II contains an instrument for assessing student proficiency in the thinking skill that is the subject of that set. This instrument is designed to be the first test students are to take after being introduced to and having received guided practice lessons a number of times in a given thinking skill, but before that skill has been transferred or elaborated. These tests are based on guidelines for assessing thinking skills presented in Appendix E. You may wish to refer to these sample tests as you proceed through Chapter 3. You may even find it useful to skim some of these tests now—*before* starting this chapter—so you can see what these instruments are like. When you complete Chapter 3, you should be able to prepare tests like these as well as other kinds of assessments for skills you wish to teach.

DESIGNING AND WRITING THINKING SKILL ASSESSMENT INSTRUMENTS

You can use a variety of techniques to assess your own proficiency in teaching thinking skills as well as student proficiency in carrying out these skills. Indeed, researchers and test developers are presently designing a number of new kinds of instruments and techniques precisely for this purpose. These include product and process assessment procedures, process portfolios, performance assessments, group and individual assessments, and new forms of paper-and-pencil assessments.[1] As these are tested in actual practice and refined, they may be of great value for classroom teachers. At the moment, however, perhaps the most reliable and practical assessment techniques for classroom teacher preparation

Figure 3.1 Chapter 3—Learning Modules and Procedures

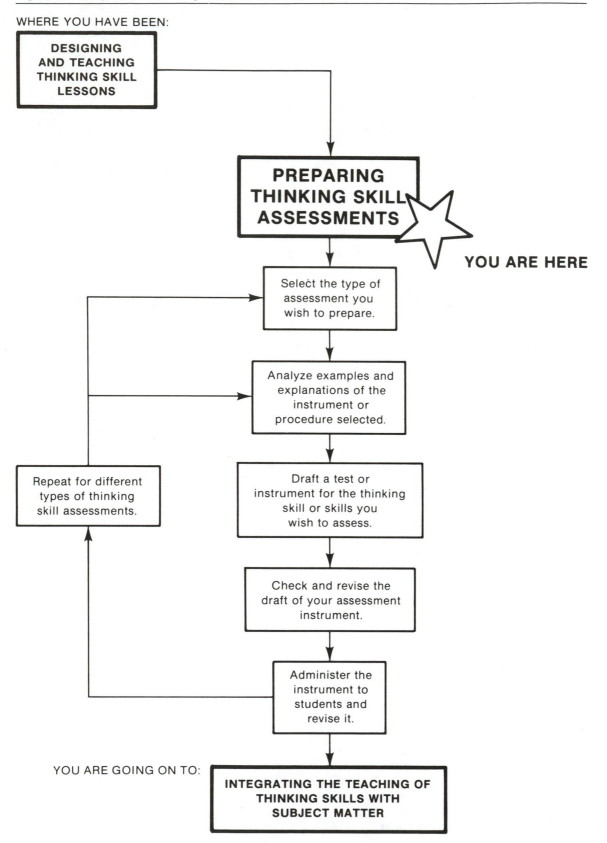

WHERE YOU HAVE BEEN:

DESIGNING AND TEACHING THINKING SKILL LESSONS

PREPARING THINKING SKILL ASSESSMENTS

YOU ARE HERE

Select the type of assessment you wish to prepare.

Analyze examples and explanations of the instrument or procedure selected.

Repeat for different types of thinking skill assessments.

Draft a test or instrument for the thinking skill or skills you wish to assess.

Check and revise the draft of your assessment instrument.

Administer the instrument to students and revise it.

YOU ARE GOING ON TO:

INTEGRATING THE TEACHING OF THINKING SKILLS WITH SUBJECT MATTER

and use remain objective paper-and-pencil instruments. This chapter will help you learn how to prepare such instruments.

To be most effective—that is, to best motivate students and to provide feedback appropriate for their learning and your teaching—assessment of student proficiency in thinking should meet at least two criteria. First, it should be continuous throughout the semester, year, or however long your course or class. Such testing should be done at least every marking period and at the midpoint and end of every semester. Ideally, it could be done on the examinations concluding and/or preceding each unit of study your students undertake or at the end of each marking period.

Second, the instruments used to assess student thinking should vary in structure and content according to where the students are in learning the skill to be assessed. That is, a test for a newly introduced thinking skill—one on which the students have been focusing for only the past three or four weeks or so—ought to differ considerably from a test assessing performance on a number of thinking skills introduced and practiced over the preceding several months. And a test on a number of thinking skills introduced the previous year and reinforced and elaborated in your class this year ought to differ considerably from the preceding types of tests. Learning how to construct each of these three kinds of instruments is not difficult, but it does take some time.

A test on a newly introduced thinking skill should focus exclusively on the skill and use data from that portion of the course just completed by the students. This test, consisting of five or six items, may be attached to, precede, or follow the regular unit test usually used to assess student learning of that content. Figure 3.2 shows in general what a six-item thinking skill test of this type might look like. This six-item instrument might include two items *about* the skill, one calling for a definition of it and the other calling for recognition that it is being used; three items that require students to *apply* the skill to data they know something about and to show how they did it; and finally, an item asking them to *explain* to a novice *how to do the skill.* This test format is explained in detail, with full-page examples, in Appendix E (pp. E-2–E-11). Each of the sets of thinking skill materials in Part II includes a sample test of this type.

A test on a number of thinking skills newly introduced and practiced for some time in your course may take a quite different form from the preceding test. It, too, can be part of, precede, or follow a regular unit content test and can use subject matter studied up to that point in the course. However, the questions can be fewer in number and structured as conventional multiple-choice items if you wish. Figure 3.3 presents what a test of this type might look like. Note that question 1 in each item requires use of the same skill, question 2 in each item requires use of the same second skill, and so on. Again, this kind of test is explained in detail with examples in Appendix E (pp. E-11–E-13).

Observational instruments may also be used to assess student proficiency in thinking skills. Appendix E provides an explanation of one type of these instruments. You may wish to read this Appendix now, or you can wait and study each section of it as you follow the procedure presented below to learn how to write such instruments of your own.

You can learn how to write any instrument or procedure to assess student proficiency in thinking skills by doing the following:

1. Select the type of procedure or instrument you wish to use to assess the skill you have been "teaching."

2. Analyze examples and explanations of the kind of test, assessment instrument, or procedure you wish to prepare.

3. Draft such an instrument for the skill you have selected to teach to your students.

Figure 3.2 A Format for Assessing Student Proficiency in a Newly Introduced Thinking Skill

UNIT I—TEST FOR THE SKILL OF CLASSIFYING

1 Which of the following best defines the skill of *classifying*?
a) to arrange things in the order in which they occurred
b) to put together things having a common characteristic or characteristics
c) to invent a theory

2 Which of the following show(s) information that has been classified?

    a) A   b) B   c) C

A

As the Indians approached, we put down our muskets and stood up. We recognized the one known as Red Feather clearly. As he came toward us he raised his right hand to salute. Captain Smythe returned the salute and held out the blue blanket. Red Feather smiled and clapped his hands together, shouting to his warriors. They lowered their bows and lances. We had made friendly contact!

B

The original colonies had different kinds of governments. Connecticut and Rhode Island, under charters, selected their own officials. Others, like Pennsylvania, Maryland, and New Jersey, had been granted to individuals known as proprietors. Some colonies, including New York and Georgia, were controlled by appointees of the King; these colonies were known as Royal colonies.

C

Spanish	*English*	*French*
Coronado	Cabot	de Champlain
Cabrillo	Hudson	Cartier
deSoto	Drake	Joliet
		LaSalle

---

3. The following words were commonly spoken by inhabitants of London, England, around the year 1750. Classify these words so you can identify what life was like for these Londoners at this time and show *all your work*. Then answer the question below.

customs house	journeyman	stock exchange
lottery ticket	workhouse	alehouse
malaria	milkmaid	mugger
apprentice	cesspool	pauper
almshouse	typhoid	gin
watchman	dockworker	poor house
coffee house	butcher	cow
weaver	smallpox	liquor
squire	debtors' prison	master
gambling house	wool-comber	night soil
chimney sweep	typhus	police court

Circle the letter preceding whichever of the following is/are probably true about life in London around 1750.

a) Most Londoners lived like rich people.
b) Life in London was unhealthy and unsafe for many people.
c) Farming was a way of life for most Londoners.

---

4. The items listed below were recovered from a dried-up well near a place where people lived in late eighteenth century America. The place of origin of each item is indicated, where known. Classify these items in some way that would help tell you about the people who used these items. *Be sure to show how you classify these items.* Then answer the question at the bottom of the page.

1 iron candle chandelier (France)	1 horn-handled knife (America)
3 pewter mugs (Germany)	8 perfume bottles (France)
18 copper buttons (America)	1 pocket knife, mother-of-pearl handle (England)
	9 medicine bottles (England)
7 pewter spoons (America)	1 iron hoe (America)
3 hand painted, porcelain plates (England)	
1 pewter plate (Germany)	11 wine decanters (France)
2 westerwald stoneware chamber pots (Germany)	1 silk glove
1 porcelain teapot (China)	3 bone-handled tooth brushes
5 whiteware hand-painted plates (France)	3 hand-painted pearlware plates (China)
3 bone-handled forks (England)	7 hand-painted porcelain tea cups (England)
2 stoneware milk vessels (America)	3 porcelain cups (China)
1 pewter fork	2 printed silk cloths (China)
8 liquor bottles (England)	1 leather shoe (England)
3 soda glasses	2 bone-handled hair brushes

Circle the letter preceding the phrase that best completes this sentence: The people who once used the items on the above list almost certainly

a) made a living as craftsmen.
b) lived on the western frontier.
c) were upper class, wealthy.

5. Classify the information in the following paragraph to answer this question: What was the economy of the thirteen colonies like before the American Revolution? *Show all your work.*

By 1763 the thirteen colonies were sending many products overseas. Lumber, tar, fish, rum — a drink made from molasses — and furs went from Massachusetts, New Hampshire, Connecticut, and nearby colonies. Pennsylvania, New York, Delaware, and neighboring colonies shipped iron, iron kettles and tools, flour, lead, woolen cloth, and hats as well as furs and livestock. The Carolinas, Virginia, and neighboring colonies shipped tobacco, indigo — a plant from which a dye was made — rice, and farm products like grain, beans, pork, and horses.

Now, complete the following:

Based on how you processed the above items, write one sentence describing the economy of the thirteen American colonies just before the American Revolution. In another sentence explain why your first sentence is accurate, based on the data above.

1. _____

2. _____

---

6. In the space under the data below, give *specific*, detailed directions that a fifth grader could follow to classify the *names* in order to answer this question: "What was colonial culture like by 1775?"

Name		Name	
Phyllis Wheatley	poet	Cotton Mather	minister/scientist
Benjamin Franklin	printer/inventor	John Copley	painter
Benjamin West	painter	Jonathan Edwards	minister/author
Sarah Kemble Knight	author	Roger Williams	minister
David Rittenhouse	astronomer	Anne Bradstreet	poet
John Peter Zenger	editor		

END OF TEST

Source: Barry K. Beyer, *Practical Strategies for the Teaching of Thinking* (Boston: Allyn and Bacon, 1987).

Figure 3.3 A Format for Assessing Student Proficiency in Several Thinking Skills

Name _____ Class _____ Date _____

Directions: For each of the three paragraphs below, there are four incomplete statements. Indicate the option that best completes each statement by circling the letter that precedes the option of your choice.

A

The Egbas and Yorubas were the main actors in these merciless conflicts. They also were the main sufferers from them. They were once the most peaceful and civilized tribes in the country, famous for their agriculture and trade. Fighting with their neighbors and with each other ruined them. When I arrived, many of the Egbas and Yorubas felt sick of war and the slave trade. They wanted peace and prosperity.

1. According to this excerpt, the Egbas and the Yorubas were recently involved in:

   a) changing their religion.
   b) civil war.
   c) starting to trade with Europe.
   d) outbreaks of contagious diseases.

2. The excerpt suggests that the Egbas and Yorubas were:

   a) the only civilized people in the country.
   b) the most warlike of all people in the country.
   c) famous as fishermen and traders.
   d) two of several groups living in the region.

3. According to this excerpt, its author:

   a) fears the Egbas and Yorubas.
   b) is unfamiliar with the Egbas and Yorubas.
   c) sympathizes with the Egbas and Yorubas.
   d) dislikes the Egbas and Yorubas.

4. The best title for this excerpt is:

   a) Trade among the Egbas and Yorubas.
   b) From War to Peace.
   c) Egbas versus Yorubas.
   d) The Fruits of War.

B

The Dutch claimed to have purchased the island for just $24 worth of beads and trinkets. But the Indians insisted they had not sold the island. Frequently, Indians would come across the river to hunt on their favorite hunting grounds on the island. When they did so, settlers would often shoot at them, killing or injuring some. Sometimes the barbarous Indians would return under cover of darkness to burn outlying farmhouses—and butcher their inhabitants. Once, Dutch farmers crossed the river to teach them a lesson, killing dozens of Indian women and children as well as the few warriors they could catch.

1. This account indicates that the early inhabitants of this area:

   a) traded with one another.
   b) considered the sale of land to be final.
   c) carried on fighting even after the island was sold.
   d) were victims of outside events.

2. This account indicates that the Indians and Dutch:

   a) differed in their interpretation of what the sale of land meant.
   b) refused to have anything to do with each other.
   c) deliberately misled each other.
   d) treated each other as equals.

3. The author of this account probably was:

   a) an Indian who lived there.
   b) a European observer living at the time.
   c) a historian writing more than 100 years later.
   d) a Dutch settler living on the island.

4. The best title for this account would be:

   a) Aborigines of the New World.
   b) European Exploitation of Native Americans.
   c) Cultures in Conflict.
   d) Civilization in the New World.

C

The Aztecs were the most powerful and feared people of Mexico. They continuously raided other cities and despoiled the countryside. Our arrival saved thousands from enslavement and torture at their hands. Once terrified of the fierce Aztecs, the natives now joined us in our march toward the city of Montezuma. They warned us about Aztec traps and ambushes. Our guns and artillery seemed to give them renewed courage to stand up to these butchers. Divine will had made us their salvation!

1. During the time described in this account, the peoples of Mexico:

   a) lived in peace and prosperity.
   b) distrusted foreigners.
   c) traded with people far away.
   d) fought among themselves.

2. According to this account, the Aztecs were:

   a) natural-born rulers.
   b) one of several different peoples living in Mexico.
   c) regarded by all Mexicans as superior.
   d) the most civilized of all Mexicans.

3. Whoever wrote this account:

   a) admired the Aztecs.
   b) was a religious person.
   c) was a leader of Mexicans who opposed the Aztecs.
   d) was a trained military leader.

4. The best title for this account is:

   a) Civil War in Mexico.
   b) Empire of the Aztecs.
   c) The Invasion of Mexico.
   d) New Life Comes to Mexico.

4. Check and revise your draft.

5. Administer the test or instrument or carry out your procedure at an appropriate place in your teaching of the skill, analyze the results, and revise it for later use.

This chapter presupposes an understanding of objective testing and the ability to write objective test items, especially multiple-choice and skill-testing items. If you understand such tests and possess these item-writing skills, you should proceed with this section. If you do not, however, you may wish to do some further study of both before proceeding. Being able to write thinking skill tests like those presented here requires some prior knowledge and experience in test writing. Having this knowledge and experience will certainly make your progress through this chapter easier and most productive.

1. Select the type of assessment you wish to prepare.

Three types of assessment instruments are worth exploring and considering for use in your classroom teaching of thinking skills. They are discussed, with examples, in Appendix E:

> Objective test for assessing a recently or newly introduced thinking skill, Appendix E, pp. E-3–E-11.
>
> Objective test for assessing several thinking skills that have been taught, practiced, and transferred over an extended time, Appendix E, pp. E-11–E-13.
>
> Instruments for recording observation of student thinking behaviors, Appendix E, pp. E-14–E-17.

To begin the process of preparing a thinking skill assessment, select the type of procedure or instrument you wish to prepare. Ideally, it should be designed to assess proficiency in the thinking skill on which you have been working in Chapters 1 and 2. When you have completed this chapter, you will then have an assessment procedure or instrument you can use in your own teaching. Unless you have some other plan, it would be most worthwhile if you focused here on preparing the first test listed above—an objective test for assessing a recently or newly introduced thinking skill. Such a test will be most immediately useful to you.

---

checkpoint

When you have selected the thinking skill or skills you wish to assess and the type of thinking skill assessment you wish to prepare, write this information on the lines below and check here:

☐

_____
thinking skill(s)

_____
type of assessment

2. Analyze examples and explanations of the instrument or procedure selected.

Before trying to prepare your own version of the type of assessment instrument or procedure selected, find out as much as you can about it. This can be done by analyzing one or more examples of it. For example, if you wish to become familiar with a test to assess a newly introduced thinking skill, you can:

1. Examine a model or sample of this type of test or instrument.
2. Read, listen to, and discuss an analysis and/or explanation of the sample or of the test in general.
3. Analyze additional examples of the same type of thinking skill test.

These same three steps can be used to examine any assessment instrument or procedure. As a result of doing these things, you will see what the specific instrument should look like. The analysis and explanation will clarify the nature and function of the different items on the instrument, the way in which the items are sequenced, and the rationale underlying the instrument. The sample instrument can then serve as a model for your own instrument to assess whatever thinking skill or skills you wish to assess, including perhaps the skill you introduced in the lessons designed in Chapter 2.

Step 1. *Examine a model or example of the instrument.* Carefully study a sample of the type of assessment instrument or procedure you wish to develop. Skim it first to note the kinds of items and general format. Then, put yourself in the position of test taker or instrument user. Read the items again carefully and identify what each item requires you to do to answer the question or complete the assigned task. When you have done this, review again the overall sequence of items and general structure of the instrument. You can find samples of three different kinds of thinking skill assessments in Appendix E:

For a newly introduced skill, pp. E-3–E-5, E-10

For several thinking skills, pp. E-11–E-12

For observed thinking behaviors, pp. E-15–E-16

Other kinds of thinking skill assessments may be found in other sources.[2]

Step 2. *Analyze the instrument.* After reflecting on what the test or instrument is like, listen to or read an analysis or explanation of the test or instrument. Why has it been constructed the way it has? Look especially for:

- The purpose or function of each item.
- The kind of mental operation called for by each item.
- What each item does or requires one to do to complete it.
- The relationship of each item to the other items and to the instrument as a whole.

Analyses of the following kinds of thinking skill assessment instruments may be found in Appendix E:

For a newly introduced skill, pp. E-3–E-11

For several thinking skills, pp. E-11–E-13

For observed thinking behaviors, pp. E-14–E-17

Reflect on or, if possible, discuss with others who have analyzed this same instrument the explanation and the results of your analysis. Conclude by identifying what you would have to do to write a test or instrument like this appropriate to the thinking skill or skills you plan to assess.

Step 3. *Analyze additional examples of this instrument.* After you have completed your initial analysis, you may wish to look at other examples of this kind of instrument. In Part II of this handbook, you will find examples of instruments for assessing student proficiency in a number of different thinking skills at a variety of grade levels in different subject areas. These tests were designed to be administered to students who have only recently been introduced to the skill and have been learning it for the preceding three to four weeks or so. They are modeled after the sample test presented on pages E-3–E-5 and E-10 in Appendix E.

By analyzing several of these, you can observe the general features of this type of assessment. Also note the variations made in the model in order to adapt it to students like those you wish to assess and perhaps using content similar to that you want to include on your test.

When examining other sample instruments, avoid looking at any that deal with the thinking skill(s) for which you have elected to write an instrument so that you don't get "boxed in" by what you see. At this point, you should be collecting information and ideas for creating your own version of this kind of assessment instrument. You will have an opportunity later to study a similar instrument for the thinking skill or skills that you plan to assess.

---

checkpoint

When you have examined several examples of the kind of thinking skill assessment instrument you propose to design and can explain to a peer the ingredients of such an instrument, check here: ☐

---

3. Draft a test or instrument for the thinking skill(s) you wish to assess.

Working with a partner, if possible, prepare a draft of the kind of test or other assessment instrument you have chosen to prepare. You can do this most effectively by doing the following:

1. Make a plan for the test or instrument, specifying what each item on the test or component of the instrument will be like.
2. Check the plan, or have it checked by others, to ensure that it will

result in a valid, reliable test of the thinking skill on which it is supposed to focus.

3. Write a complete draft of the actual test items or instrument.

As you draft your thinking skills assessment instrument, refer as often as you wish to samples or models of the instrument you are preparing and to guidelines for preparing it. If necessary, you may make your test items and structure virtually identical to those of the model you are using, with changes only to meet the attributes of the skill(s) you seek to assess and to the ability levels of your students. However, be sure to put the items and directions into language easily understood by your students. Don't introduce major variations on any model yet. Instead, replicate as faithfully as possible—given your knowledge of the abilities of your students—the kinds of items and stucture of the model. You can produce your own instruments later, once you have become accomplished at producing this type of test or instrument. To complete the task of drafting this instrument:

Step 1.

Make a plan. Begin designing your test (if it is to be an objective test) by preparing a plan of what each test item will assess and what it will be like. Figure 3.4 presents an example of one such plan for a test to assess student proficiency in a new thinking skill—classifying information—as introduced in an American history course. In fact, this plan is for the instrument presented in Figure 3.2 and is described in detail in Appendix E, pages E-3–E-5. Notice that to complete a plan like this one, you need to identify the types of questions to be asked (left-hand column) and then to note the specific features that each test item will include. You do *not* have to write the actual items at this time, however. The plan in Figure 3.4 shows this completed information for a six-item test on classifying.

Figure 3.5 presents a blank planning chart like that presented in Figure 3.4 that you can use to plan the initial two or three tests on any new thinking skill you may wish to introduce to your students. It indicates what you have to consider in preparing such an instrument. After writing the name of the skill on the line at the top of the chart, you can simply fill in ideas for items for each of the questions that will constitute this kind of test. For example, if you were preparing a test on the newly introduced skill of comparing, in the blank square opposite ''Skill Definition'' you could write what the question should be like, such as ''Which of the following best defines the term *compare*?'' with a note that you want it to be a three-option multiple-choice item. Similarly, in the blank opposite ''Application #1'' you might write ''paragraph describing two different environments'' and ''students to compare/contrast by listing similarities/differences'' or some other appropriate specifications. The rest of the plan could then be completed in similar fashion. From this completed chart of specifications, you can then write the actual test item.

Figure 3.6 presents an example of a plan for a test to assess student proficiency in a number of previously introduced and taught thinking skills. This plan is for the test presented in Figure 3.3. This particular kind of thinking skill test is also explained in detail in Appendix E. To complete this plan, its author decided on a format consisting of three separate items, each built around different data and each consisting of four multiple-choice questions, much like items that can be found on reading comprehension tests now currently in use. As the plan indicates, he then filled in his ideas about the kind of data, its form, and its potential source for each of the three test items. Finally, he indicated the skill

Skill: *Classifying*

Type of Question	Item Specifications

Skill Definition	multiple choice—
	  3 options defining: — sequencing
	                              — classifying
	                              — inventing

Recognition of Example	3 choices:
	  — paragraph on sequence of events
	     when colonists meet Indians
	  — types of colonial governments - examples
	  — lists of explorers by sponsoring country

Application # 1	words spoken in London about 1750 What was life in London like then?
Application # 2	items recovered in archeological dig dating c. 1750—Alexandria, VA. — and place of origin What were the owners like?
Application # 3	paragraph - giving products of the 13 colonies—can be grouped as farm, forest, sea What do these tell about colonial economy?
Metacognitive Application	list of colonial poets, authors, scientists — name and specialty What was colonial culture like?

Figure 3.5 Planning Chart for a Test to Assess Any Newly Introduced Thinking Skill

Skill: _____

Type of Question	Item Specifications
Skill Definition	
Recognition of Example	
Application # 1	
Application # 2	
Application # 3	
Metacognitive Application	

Figure 3.6 A Plan for a Test to Assess Multiple Thinking Skills as Taught in a History Class

Test Items	Item # 1	Item # 2	Item # 3
Data, Form, Source	Civil wars in Nigeria 19th century Paragraph—Crowder	Occupation of New York Colony—Dutch and Indians—Paragraph —Sources on colonial NY	Aztecs and Mexico When Spanish arrive— Indian conflicts Paragraph— Diaz
Skill 1.	M.C. translation	M.C. translation	M.C. translation
Skill 2.	M.C interpretation	M.C interpretation	M.C interpretation
Skill 3.	M.C. author point of view	M.C. author point of view	M.C. author point of view
Skill 4.	M. C. synthesis main idea "best title"	M. C. synthesis main idea "best title"	M. C. synthesis main idea "best title"

to be assessed by each question and, in the last question, the kind of question that would assess that skill. Again, note that this plan does *not* include any specific questions. To make the best use of your time—and to allow your mind to "incubate" ideas for these specific items—actual preparation of each test item should await preparation and review of your entire test plan.

Figure 3.7 presents a blank planning chart you can use to plan a test of any thinking skills of your choice in any subject of your choice. To complete such a plan for this type of test, you can start by writing in the space opposite "Data, Form, Source" and under each item number the kind of data you will provide

Figure 3.7 Planning Chart for a Test to Assess Multiple Thinking Skills as Taught in Any Subject Matter

Test Items	Item # 1	Item # 2	Item # 3
Data, Form, Source			
Skill 1.			
Skill 2.			
Skill 3.			
Skill 4.			

the students and where you can find them. It is not necessary to put those data here, however. Simply describe the data in a word and phrase. Then, in the numbered spaces under each item you can write the skill label of each skill you propose to require students to execute and the type of question (multiple choice, fill-in, true/false/correct, and so on) that will be written to exercise that skill.

Producing a plan for a thinking skill test *before* you write the actual item gives you an opportunity to lay out the entire test and check it over for flaws and workability, *before* your write any items, thus saving a great deal of time, effort, and possible frustration. Making such a plan for any thinking skill test results in much better instruments—and more valid and reliable results—than does making up a test as the items are written. You will find the charts in Figure 3.5 and 3.7 extremely useful in planning your own tests for the thinking skill(s) you have chosen to teach. Now you can complete a plan appropriate to your planned test by filling in a copy of the appropriate sample planning chart (if you are designing an objective-thinking skills test).

If you are planning an instrument to collect observational data about thinking behaviors, or some other type of thinking skill assessment, write your plan as a narrative or list, describing what each major component of the instrument might look like. Thus, for a behaviors checklist, you might indicate only that you plan to list the ten most common behaviors of skillful thinking on the left and a scale of frequency of observations of each behavior on the right. Providing an example of one item that would appear in each column would also be helpful. Such information should be sufficient for preparing the complete instrument once your plan has been checked against the model or against written guidelines for this type of instrument.

| Step 2. |

Check your plan. Once you have written your plan, check it against the test or instrument you are using as a model and/or the guidelines for such an instrument. If possible, have someone who is familiar with the kind of instrument you are designing check your plan to assure that each question or component will be easily understood by the students or instrument user and will provide a good opportunity for them to exercise the designated skill or complete the assigned task. Also check to ensure that each item will carry out the function called for by the instrument guidelines.

| Step 3. |

Write a complete draft of the actual instrument items or parts, including directions to the user. After you have revised your plan to fill in any gaps or correct any errors uncovered as a result of checking the plan, you can write the items and instructions that will constitute the test or instrument you are developing. It is especially important here to write the directions to the *test taker* or *instrument user* as well as the actual test items as they will appear on the completed instrument, so they can be checked by others to ensure their clarity.

At this point, it is not necessary to prepare your draft in the full-page format used in the model test to which you may be referring. You can write each test item on a 5″ × 8″ card, on a separate piece of paper, or on a word processor. This will allow you to shuffle or reorganize items and to make later changes without destroying any final structure. Once your draft has been checked and reviewed by others and you have received and examined their comments and suggestions, you can revise it and put it in its appropriate form.

---

checkpoint

When you have written a complete draft of your thinking skill assessment instrument and are ready to have others review it check here:

☐

---

4. Check and revise the draft of your assessment instrument.

If this is the first—or perhaps even the second—time you have ever written a test or assessment instrument like the one you have just completed, there could be some bugs in it. Therefore, you should check it and have others review it to be sure that it includes the kinds of items essential for the type of thinking skill test it is and that it meets the criteria of a good test. You can review and revise your draft by doing the following:

1. Compare your draft to a model or models of the kind of test or instrument you have made.
2. Have an instructor and/or several colleagues who are knowledgeable about this type of test or instrument review it for you.
3. Revise your test or instrument based on feedback received from these reviews.

To ensure that any flaws have been detected, you should use all of these procedures each time you design a new test, at least until you have mastered this type of test. After you have completed this review, you can revise your draft and put it into final form.

Step 1. *Compare your draft to a model (or models) of the test or instrument.* Compare your draft of the test or instrument to a sample or model of the kind of instrument it is supposed to replicate. If you are learning how to design a test for a newly introduced thinking skill, for example, you can use the sample test in Appendix E, pages E-3–E-5 or E-10, as a model against which to check your draft. If you are designing a test to assess a number of skills that students have been practicing for some time, you can use the sample items on pages E-11–E-12 of Appendix E as a model. The observation instruments on pages E-15–E-16 of Appendix E may serve as useful models of behavior assessments. Comparing each item on your draft with its counterpart on the model or sample and to the accompanying explanation will help you detect most errors or flaws.

In making this comparison, be sure that:

1. The directions to the students are direct and clear.
2. The data and form in which they are presented to the students will be familiar enough that they will not be confused by them.
3. Questions requiring students to execute the skill minimize the need to recall subject matter.

4. The sequence of items moves from the relatively simple to the more complex.

5. The responses to one item do not give away correct responses to other items.

6. The individual items measure the skill or procedural knowledge they are supposed to measure.

7. There are no gaps or irrelevancies in the provided data, questions, or directions.

8. The provided data do *not* overwhelm the students and will not require much time to read.

9. Any paper-and-pencil test gives students at least two and preferably three opportunities *to use* each thinking skill being assessed.

It may also be useful to compare your draft with other completed samples of this type of instrument, if any are available. For example, some of the tests in Part II of this handbook may be similar in type to yours, even though they assess different thinking skills. You can compare your draft to these tests. Examining these other tests will provide additional examples of the kinds of assessment items you should or could be including in your draft. By comparing these to yours, you can clarify what yours should be like, spot any flaws in yours, and correct them. These sample tests may also include some variations from the model that may also give you ideas for test items appropriate to the skill which is the subject of your test or instrument.

| Step 2. |

Have one or more colleagues knowledgeable about the type of test or instrument you are preparing review your draft. When you have written an assessment instrument, sometimes you can be so close to it that it is difficult to spot flaws in it. Thus, having someone else review it is very helpful in ensuring a top-quality final version. This reviewer should be someone knowledgeable about the kind of instrument you have drafted or someone who is, like you, learning how to prepare such an instrument. The reviewer can be helpful by (1) reading the instrument for structure and language errors and seeking especially to check out the nine points noted above, and (2) actually taking the test as a ''student'' or using a behavior observation instrument as an observer would. By attempting to answer the questions or fill in an observation instrument, the reviewer can provide you with insights as to clarity, reliability, and validity of the items and of the instrument as a whole.

| Step 3. |

Revise your test or instrument based on feedback received from these reviews. At this point, revise (rewriting if necessary) the entire instrument. This may consist of merely changing a few words or phrases or resequencing several items. However, it may consist of a major restructuring or rewriting of many of the items. The result should be a test or instrument that meets as precisely as possible the specifications and model of the test or instrument you are preparing. Recheck any of the items that you rewrite.

This is where you can put the items in your instrument into final form like that of the model. This means providing a place for the student's name and class period or date, and leaving enough space for student notes, written answers, computations, and so on. Once you have it written out, edit the assessment instrument for accuracy, grammar, spelling, sentence structure, and the like. Be especially sure it is legible and easily read.

---

checkpoint

When you have revised your draft thinking skill assessment instrument to incorporate feedback from your own review and that of your colleagues and/or an expert, check here:

☐

---

5. *Administer the test or instrument to students and revise it.*

The ultimate check on any test or assessment instrument you have prepared is how well it works and the extent to which it supplies the information it is supposed to provide. Only the intended audience—your students—can provide this information. So, you should administer or use the test or instrument at the appropriate point in your teaching of the skill you wish to assess with it. The results may be used for formative as well as (cautiously) summative purposes.

You can conduct this formative trial of an objective test in any of several ways. For instance, you could select an average student and have him or her take the test as you sit nearby to record what he or she does. You can even have the student report to you at regular intervals what he or she is doing mentally at any point. Or you can videotape a student taking the test, positioning the camera so as to catch facial expressions as well as what is being written; the two of you can then review the tape, discussing move by move what the student was doing as he or she completed the test. Either of these procedures can be repeated with several different students, if you wish. In fact, experts in formative evaluation suggest that such trials be given to at least one below-average student and one above-average student if you wish to spot any potential problems with the instrument. Revisions based on several one-on-one trial evaluations can help you produce a test that will minimize problems when it is finally used by larger groups of students.

Of course, you can also administer your test to an entire class of students in addition to the individual administration just described or in place of it. As the students are taking the test, be particularly alert to problems or questions that arise about any items, procedures, or tasks required. Note these for analysis later. Upon completion of the test, have the students comment on it, especially with regard to (1) any problems they had in completing it (asking for suggestions for remedying these), (2) anything on it they did not understand (asking them what should be done to clarify or otherwise eliminate the cause of the confusion), and (3) any ideas they have for questions that might be better suited to this test.

You can submit a behavioral observation instrument to a field test in roughly similar fashion. Have several other teachers use it to record their observations on the same student over a limited period of time. Then discuss with them any problems they had in using it. Comparing their entries or responses on the various items may also identify problems. Be particularly alert to items about specific examples of behaviors that unquestioningly indicate the kind of criteria/behavior listed on the instrument. You can use this information later in revising the instrument.

Once you have recorded student responses on your test or the responses on an observation instrument, you should analyze them. In doing so, you should look especially for items that confused those who did very well on the test as a whole, as well as for those items that discriminated against all, or failed to discriminate against any, who took the test. You can do this by scoring the student answers on the test. Then, sort student responses to your test into three groups: (1) those who did the best, (2) those who did the worst, and (3) those between these two groups. You should have a third of your students in each group. Next, compare the results on each test item of those in the top third of your class with those in the bottom third.

Any item on which the top third of your students did worse than those in the lowest third is likely to be flawed in some way because it failed to discriminate between those doing well and those not doing as well on the overall test. Often such items turn out to have something in them that confuses your better students. Any item in which students in each group do equally well (or poorly) also fails to discriminate and may need to be rewritten or even replaced. A careful analysis of the student responses to items on your test may well reveal items that need to be revised or replaced. By doing this, you can help to ensure the reliability and validity of your test.

The information you collect from a "field trial" of your test or observation instrument can now be used in revising it. The knowledge you gathered from your observation of the students taking the test or of others using the observation instrument (their reactions and your analysis of their responses) will provide clues to places or items that need eliminating, revising, or additions. Repeated administration of the instrument in other classes or over the next several years will enable you to build an even stronger instrument.

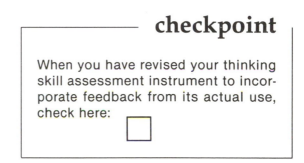

checkpoint

When you have revised your thinking skill assessment instrument to incorporate feedback from its actual use, check here: ☐

SUMMARY

Once you have completed this procedure for designing and preparing one type of thinking skill assessment instrument, you may wish to do one or all of three things: (1) You could repeat the procedure to prepare a modified version of that instrument, one designed to fit a particular type of exceptional student population or one that assesses several other skills at the same point of instruction. If you have prepared a test to be administered to students engaged in just learning the skill, you could then (2) prepare a second test of this same kind on the same thinking skill that could be administered in your course about six weeks from the time you would administer this initial test. Or (3) you could repeat the above procedure to learn how to design and prepare another type of thinking skill assessment altogether.

You can begin any of these tasks by consulting the following pages in Appendix E:

Objective test for assessing a newly introduced thinking skill, pp. E-3–E-7

A modification or elaboration of an objective test for assessing several newly introduced thinking skills, pp. E-7–E-11

Objective tests for assessing several thinking skills that have been taught and practiced for an extended time, pp. E-11–E-13

Instruments for recording observations of student thinking behaviors, pp. E-14–E-17

The procedure outlined above may be used to learn and practice designing any thinking skill assessment instrument or procedure.

Now that you have completed this chapter, you should be able to:

1. Identify the extent to which a given thinking skill assessment instrument assesses proficiency in a specific thinking skill.

2. Write a test or other type of instrument to assess student proficiency in a thinking skill or skills of your choice that meets the criteria of effective thinking skill assessment at different levels of instruction and learning.

3. Explain in detail to someone unfamiliar with thinking skill assessment how to judge the quality of any thinking skill assessment instrument like the ones you have developed.

4. Explain in detail to someone unfamiliar with thinking skill assessment how to prepare a thinking skill assessment for use with his or her students in a subject of his or her choice.

As noted earlier, assessment usually completes an instructional cycle. However, assessment just as often launches instruction. All assessment instruments may be used for diagnostic and instructional purposes, as well as to provide summative evaluation of learning and instruction. However they are employed, their use is integral to teaching and learning. Without what they can tell you, your decisions as to what to teach or reteach and when, where, and how to do so will not be as informed as they should be for effective instruction. By being able to design your own thinking skill assessment instruments or procedures, you become a more effective teacher of thinking.

Endnotes

1. See, for example, Joan Baron, "Evaluating Thinking Skills," in Joan Baron and Robert Sternberg, eds., *Teaching Thinking Skills: Theory and Practice* (New York: W. H. Freeman and Co., 1987), pp. 221–245; Robert H. Ennis, Jason Millman, and Thomas N. Tomko, *Cornell Critical Thinking Tests: Level X and Level Z* (Pacific Grove, CA: Midwest Publications, 1985), *Manual*; Richard J. Stiggins, Evelyn Rubel, and Edys Quellmalz, *Measuring Thinking Skills in the Classroom*, revised edition (Washington, DC: National Education Association, 1986/1988).

2. See, for example, Ennis, Millman, and Tomko, *Cornell Critical Thinking Tests.*

chapter 4

Integrating the Teaching of Thinking Skills with Subject Matter

Once you have learned how to teach the various kinds of lessons and use the strategies appropriate for teaching thinking skills, and feel comfortable in doing so, you will want to integrate instruction in thinking skills into your regular teaching. The sooner you can do this in a systematic, deliberate way, the better off your students will be. Without the modeling, explaining, guided practice, student reflection, and mediation you will now be able to provide or facilitate, your students are not likely to become as proficient as they could be in the cognitive skills needed to learn the subject matter you are trying to teach and which they are supposed to be learning!

Integrating instruction in thinking skills with subject-matter instruction involves mixing the two to the point where they complement and support each other. This means providing instruction in a thinking skill in which the students are less than proficient when the skill is needed by students to understand subject matter better. It also means helping students to use their growing repertoire of thinking skills to expand their learning in the subject matter being studied. And it means combining a variety of individual thinking skills into purposeful thinking strategies to accomplish complex subject-matter learning goals. Integrating instruction in thinking skills with instruction in subject matter, in sum, means using subject matter to learn thinking skills and also using thinking skills to learn subject matter. Better thinking and better subject-matter learning are the intended results. You can integrate the teaching of thinking skills with your regular classroom teaching of subject matter by attending continuously to: (1)

the relation of instruction in the thinking skill you have selected for teaching to the subject matter you are responsible for teaching, (2) the classroom climate in which your teaching of thinking is to be carried on, and (3) the role of dispositions—attitudes and values—in thinking.

This chapter focuses on these three important aspects of teaching thinking. Upon completion of this chapter, you should be able to:

1. Sequence instruction in thinking skills with instruction in any subject matter you teach.
2. Recognize, create, and maintain a classroom climate supportive of skillful thinking.
3. Recognize and model dispositions essential to skillful thinking.

The following pages will assist you in achieving these objectives. Figure 4.1 indicates the sequence in which they are dealt with here. Unlike the rather precise procedures presented in the preceding chapters, this chapter does not present a great deal of step-by-step learning for you to go through to achieve these objectives. Instead, the remainder of the chapter simply provides information you will find useful in formulating the conditions essential for creating and maintaining a thinking curriculum in your classroom and techniques that will be helpful in doing so. Periodic reference to these pages will help you keep these features in mind and remind you of what you can do to make them an integral part of your teaching.

Where appropriate, this chapter uses *Checkpoints* to mark off important topics with which you should be familiar or skills that you should refine. As in previous chapters, each *Checkpoint* signals an end to the focus on a particular topic or teaching skill and offers you an opportunity to reflect on what you have learned to that point, to pull it all together and, if you wish, to take a break before continuing. These *Checkpoints* will serve both as learning targets and, when completed, mileposts to mark your progress through these pages.

If you conscientiously and consistently employ the techniques of effective instruction in your teaching of thinking skills, they will contribute considerably to the success of your efforts to improve the thinking and subject-matter learning of your students. Only by integrating the teaching of thinking skills with the subject-matter instruction you provide can you ensure the success of your efforts to help your students become more skillful thinkers—in school and out.

WHAT YOU CAN DO TO INTEGRATE THINKING SKILL AND SUBJECT-MATTER TEACHING

Teaching thinking skills in skills classes (classes free of academic subject matter) is not nearly as effective in helping students learn to use these skills as is combining instruction in thinking skills with subject-matter teaching. One does not think without something to think about. By infusing instruction in thinking skills with the teaching of academic subjects, you can provide instruction in important thinking operations at a time when they are needed to accomplish subject-matter learning objectives—something that research indicates motivates skill learning as well as enhances subject-matter achievement. If your teaching of thinking skills is to be of any lasting value whatsoever to your students, it should be conducted in subject matter about which you wish students to learn and think.

Correctly done, the integration of subject matter and thinking skill instruc-

Figure 4.1 Chapter 4—Learning Modules and Procedures

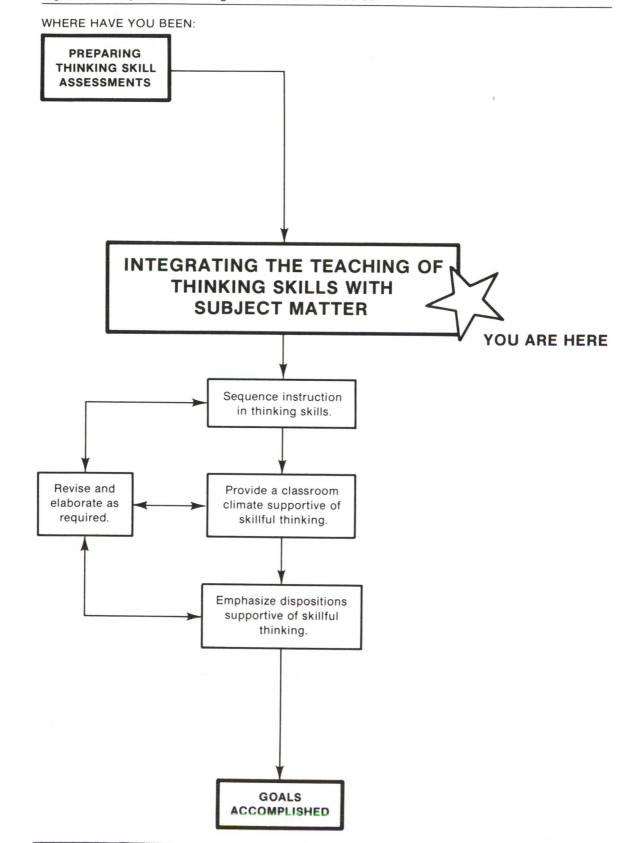

tion *uses* subject matter as a vehicle for learning and refining thinking skills. Such instruction also uses these thinking skills as tools for understanding subject matter. Thinking skills and subject matter use, build on, and reinforce each other. Proficiency in using the tools of thinking is as important as the mastery of subject matter. Both ought to be valued as major outcomes of learning in any classroom or curriculum.

Integrating the teaching of thinking skills in subject matter is not without difficulty, however. All too often attention to subject matter overwhelms skill teaching. Simply making students think as best they can to achieve a subject-matter goal, as you must by now realize, does not necessarily make them better at carrying out the operations that constitute skillful thinking. You must, on occasion, focus on the thinking skill being taught, using subject matter simply as the vehicle for employing the skill. This is especially true of lessons where you are introducing a new skill or initiating transfer of a skill, or lessons in which you are providing guided practice immediately following such introduction. Eventually, of course, you want students to be able to use a given skill, on their own and without your assistance, to process subject matter. At that point, focusing on subject matter becomes paramount. Getting your students to this point is a major reason for providing systematic attention to teaching thinking skills.

Thus, in integrating instruction in thinking skills with instruction in subject matter, you should, in your first few lessons on any new thinking skill, concentrate on the skill rather than on any subject matter-related learning that develops from its use. This is true even though your students use subject matter as a vehicle for carrying out the skill in that lesson and will learn something about it in the process. For example, in the lesson introducing the skill of classifying described in Appendix B, students used information about life in the thirteen American colonies to learn how to execute this skill. Although they learned about life in these colonies as a result of this lesson, the teacher had to keep the students' attention directed at the attributes of the skill of classifying. The *next* lesson, which focused on life in the thirteen colonies, was rich in subject-matter insight and learning precisely because students had concentrated on processing that subject matter in the preceding skill lesson. In subsequent lessons, students were able to classify data well enough on their own so attention could be given equally, first to how they carried out the skill and then to what they learned by so doing. Eventually, focus was given almost exclusively to subject-matter objectives while students applied this skill because they could do it well.

Integrating instruction in thinking skills and subject matter does not mean hiding instruction in thinking under cover of content or simply "making" students think. Rather, it means alternating focus sometimes on a skill and other times on the subject matter, but always using the skills and subject matter to carry subject-matter learning forward. To do this requires deliberate and systematic use of teaching strategies that provide direct instruction in these skills when such instruction is appropriate, as you learned in Chapters 1 through 3. As shown in Figure 4.2, it also requires careful attention to the sequencing of this instruction in thinking skills, to maintaining a classroom climate supportive of thinking in subject matter, and to "teaching" dispositions supportive of effective thinking. The following pages provide suggestions for ways to go about doing each of these in your classroom.

1. Sequence instruction in thinking skills.

In Chapter 1, you looked at or imagined a course of study, unit, or text to pick out places where a particular skill could be taught in a given subject. It was

Figure 4.2 Essential Requirements for Integrating Instruction in Thinking with Subject Matter

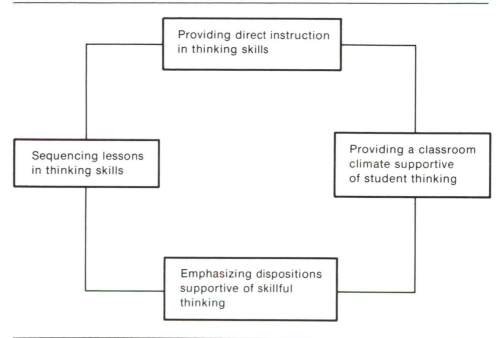

necessary to do this at that point in planning your skill-teaching lessons so you would know what content might be used in the lessons you had to design and what kinds of teaching strategies would be most appropriate for use with each lesson. This was a sort of mini-sequencing effort on your part, for it dealt with only a single thinking skill, and then only briefly. It is now appropriate to return to this task so you can explore ways to sequence instruction in a number of thinking skills in your course or class.

Sequencing thinking skills for purposes of teaching them in any subject— or across a number of subjects—can best be done as follows:

1. Survey your course (or courses) to find all the places where the skill can naturally be used by students to understand the subject matter.
2. Fill in any gaps in the sequence by creating opportunities for additional skill lessons, if any are needed.
3. Translate the skill-using opportunities identified into the kinds of lessons appropriate to skill teaching.
4. Repeat these steps for any additional thinking skill(s) to be taught in the class.

An explanation of how to carry out each of these steps follows, as do examples of each and illustrations or models you can use to assist you in your own sequencing of skill instruction.

Step 1.   *Identify opportunities for using the skill.* Assume you are going to provide instruction in one new thinking skill in a particular subject during one semester (or an entire year). The skill may have been included in your district program of studies, assigned by some curriculum directive, presented in your text, or simply chosen by you as an objective for the year.[1] This is a good place to start planning your skill teaching, whether you wish to teach just one thinking skill using the various skill-teaching strategies from introducing a new skill through guiding practice to transferring or elaborating a skill, or whether you are planning to teach multiple skills in a single course or subject-matter area. Such a sequence might require anywhere from 10 to 30 skill lessons, depending on the number of new contexts into which you wish to transfer these skills or the degree to which you wish to elaborate them.

Figure 4.3 illustrates how this initial step in sequencing a thinking skill for instruction can be carried out in any subject. You may recall this figure from Chapter 2. To prepare such a sequence, simply list in order the content lessons you will teach. A lesson can be thought of as any ''period-long'' instruction in a given subject, perhaps a class of 45 to 50 minutes or a module of 15 to 20 minutes, depending on how you organize instructional time. It may be thought of as textbook sections, or program of study modules, or sets of behavioral objectives grouped into ''teachable'' one-period units, or whatever way you wish to define it. But regardless of its origin, a lesson should consist of a learning segment defined in terms of content to be used or learned within one teaching period.

Next, skim the series of content ''lessons'' to find those lessons where students will or could use the skill you wish to teach to learn or use the content presented at that point in the sequence. By identifying these opportunities for

Figure 4.3 Identifying Lessons Where a Specific Thinking Skill Could Be Taught

LESSON:	1	2	3	4	5	6	7
focus on the thinking skill			✓		✓		✓

LESSON:	8	9	10	11	12	13	14
focus on the thinking skill		✓		✓			✓

LESSON:	15	16	17	18	19	20	21
focus on the thinking skill		✓					✓

LESSON:	22	23	24	25	26	27	28
focus on the thinking skill	✓		✓			✓	

skill use, you are really identifying places where actual instruction in the skill will be possible without interrupting the flow of subject-matter learning.

In looking for such opportunities, it is a useful rule of thumb to seek places at intervals just two or three lessons (days) apart—no more—following the introductory lesson, to maintain that interval for three of four lessons on that thinking skill, and then to gradually increase the interval between subsequent lessons on the skill to four or five lessons (days) and eventually even more. For instance, the first lessons following the introduction of a new skill may be spaced at two to three per week over three weeks or so, drop to one every four to six class days, and then to one a week or so, to a point where you think students have mastered the skill as introduced to them. If you plan to transfer or elaborate the skill, the sequence should then start over, although you would probably need fewer guided practice lessons following its reintroduction in order for your students to be able to do it on their own because they will already have been doing it.

Figure 4.3 outlines a sample sequence of 11 thinking skill lessons that could be offered over almost six weeks of teaching. Your own sequence may identify more or fewer lessons, depending on the complexity of the skill, the abilities of your students, and the extent you wish to transfer or elaborate it. In general form, however, it should look like that presented in Figure 4.3.

Step 2. *Fill in any gaps in the sequence.* As you review the sequence of places where skill-teaching lessons could be taught, you may notice gaps in the intervals between and frequency of lessons. The first five or six opportunities may not be spaced at the proper intervals—two to three lessons (days) apart. Therefore, you may have to insert a lesson or two in the skill, using material prepared by you especially to practice this skill. This material should be related to the subject of the lessons being studied. It is not desirable to step out of the subject matter being used at these points, for that takes precious time away from subject-matter study. Aside from interrupting the flow of such learning, it may also interfere with skill learning by introducing new content or contexts into the learning situation, thus confusing the students about the skill as well as the subject being studied.

When encountering gaps in the learning sequence, it is more useful to fill in these gaps with lessons using the same kind of subject matter students have been studying as a vehicle for executing the skill. These lessons may be presented as supplemental subject-matter activities—ones that move understanding of subject matter forward or provide more depth in it while simultaneously giving you an opportunity to provide the guided practice or independent use of the skill needed by students to master it. Thus, the gap between lessons 16 and 21 in Figure 4.3 needs to be filled in at some point with an opportunity for students to apply the skill being taught. You will note that the planned teaching sequence developed in Figure 4.4 includes this adjustment. Providing an appropriately spaced sequence of activities for teaching a new thinking skill is an important part of your planning and ought to be done carefully before you start preparing specific lessons.

Step 3. *Translate the skill-using opportunities into appropriate skill-teaching lessons.* Once you have decided where use of the skill by your students naturally fits the subject-matter lessons to be taught, you can decide what kind of skill-teaching

Figure 4.4 Sequence of Instruction in One Specific Thinking Skill

LESSON:	1	2	3	4	5	6	7
focus on the thinking skill			✓ Introduction		✓ Guided Practice		✓ Guided Practice

LESSON:	8	9	10	11	12	13	14
focus on the thinking skill		✓ Guided Practice		✓ Guided Practice			✓ Guided Practice

LESSON:	15	16	17	18	19	20	21
focus on the thinking skill		✓ Independent Use		✗ Independent Use			✓ Transfer or Elaboration

LESSON:	22	23	24	25	26	27	28
focus on the thinking skill	✓ Guided Practice		✓ Guided Practice			✓ Autonomous Use	

lesson would be appropriate for each opportunity. Figure 4.4 shows how the opportunities identified in Figure 4.3 have been translated into appropriate skill-teaching lessons. It identifies the type of skill lesson to be taught at each point in the sequence. The author of this sequence has assumed his students could demonstrate proficiency in the skill after just 7 lessons. Lesson 21 could then be devoted to transferring or elaborating the skill and that would be followed by another series of guided practice and independent use lessons. Presumably the skill will be further elaborated or transferred in subsequent lessons throughout the rest of the semester or year.

Of course, it should be noted that at this point this sequence is simply a guess, however well thought out, about how the teaching and learning will go. If necessary, lessons indicated in Figure 4.4 as independent use can quickly be transformed into additional guided practice lessons (or vice versa, if the students ''get it'' quicker than expected). Having a plan like this helps immensely in preparing lessons and gathering any special materials needed. But it does not require that it be followed to the letter. You should feel free to shorten or expand any skill-teaching sequence once you have launched your teaching.

Step 4.
Repeat these steps if you are planning instruction in more than one thinking skill. If you are going to teach more than one thinking skill, it will be necessary to sequence appropriate instruction in *each* skill exactly as you have done for a single thinking skill. For each additional thinking skill to be taught, you will

have to skim your text or course of study to identify where the additional skill(s) can naturally be used by students to understand the subject matter being studied, and then translate these teaching opportunities into appropriate skill-teaching lessons. You may have to create opportunities of your own for guided practice or independent use if intervals between skill-teaching opportunities are too far apart. Figure 4.5 illustrates a plan for providing instruction in four thinking skills over a series of 42 days (or lessons) in any subject.

Notice that the sequence of lessons in Figure 4.5 takes into account a new factor—the additional thinking skills you plan to teach. You must be careful in teaching thinking skills to minimize any interference that the learning of one new thinking skill can cause with learning other new thinking skills. Consequently, in sequencing a number of thinking skills for instruction, you must take care to avoid teaching several skills too close together, especially at the initial stages of instruction in these skills. Important lessons in one skill, such as introductory or transfer lessons, should not compete with similar lessons in another.

You must be concerned at this point with two kinds of thinking skills—those introduced in the preceding grade or subject, and those that you plan to introduce new in your class. If your subject area (or building or district) has a multigrade or subject scope and sequence of thinking skills to be taught, it is quite possible some of these will be introduced at a certain grade level (or subject) one year, and that instruction in them is to continue into other subjects or grades over the next year or so. Therefore, you may be expected to provide continued instruction in one or more thinking skills introduced earlier. In the past, such instruction has been called *reinforcement*, but this term is an unfortunate one because it implies simply coming back to the original skill. Yet our knowledge of any thinking skill changes as the skill is used repeatedly and in different contexts. Expertise in a thinking skill does not remain stagnant or unchanging but actually grows and develops over time. Continued instruction in a thinking skill facilitates the transfer of the skill to different contexts, and this elaborates or deepens knowledge of the skill attributes. Such continued instruction in a thinking skill introduced in earlier courses is thus as important as introducing new skills to your students.

The sequence of thinking skills in Figure 4.5 includes one skill (A) in which instruction is to be picked up from a preceding course (or year), and three other thinking skills (B, C, D) to be introduced and taught to varying degrees of completeness in your course. The "carryover" skill (A) can be introduced via a guided practice strategy or a transfer strategy. Both are useful for renewing familiarity with a skill after students have been away from it for some time. In this example, because skill A was taught in this same subject last year, it is to be practiced with teacher guidance twice before any other new skill (B, for example) is introduced. If thinking skill A had been introduced in another subject, however, a transfer strategy would have been most appropriate to initiate instruction here, followed by one or more guided practice lessons.

Once you have identified and sequenced any "carryover" skills for which you may be responsible, you can then turn to sequencing the thinking skills you plan to introduce as new skills for your students. As with the carryover skill, you must identify where in your course there will be natural opportunities to use each in learning the subject matter being studied. But as you translate these teaching opportunities into appropriate skill lessons, you now have to make sure you do not "bunch up" your teaching of these skills to the point where they interfere with student learning of them. Therefore, you need to stagger instruction in each, delaying the introduction of some until students have developed some familiarity with the first ones taught.

Thus, as Figure 4.5 indicates, Skill A, after being reviewed and used inde-

Figure 4.5 A Plan for Teaching Four Thinking Skills Over an 8-9-Week Period

LESSON:	1	2	3	4	5	6	7	8	9	10	11	12	13	14
Skill A		GP		GP	I		IU				IU	GP		IU
Skill B						GP			GP			GP		
Skill C			IU											I
Skill D														

LESSON:	15	16	17	18	19	20	21	22	23	24	25	26	27	28
Skill A	IU			T	IU	GP			GP	GP		GP	GP	
Skill B		GP	IU								T			
Skill C							GP							IU
Skill D														

LESSON:	29	30	31	32	33	34	35	36	37	38	39	40	41	42
Skill A					IU		IU	T		GP		GP	GP	
Skill B	GP			GP							IU			
Skill C		IU				IU			IU					IU
Skill D			I											GP

Key:
I   = Introduce
GP = Guided Practice
IU = Independent Use
T   = Transfer or Elaborate

118

pendently for five lessons is to be transferred to a new type of media or context. After being practiced in this new context and used independently, it is to be transferred and practiced some more. This pattern is likely to continue throughout the rest of the course. Skill B is to be introduced at the end of the first week of the class (assuming five lessons equals a week of teaching), and practiced, used, and transferred later, and so on. Instruction in skills C and D starts even later. Introduction of these latter skills could come even later in a course than suggested here, depending on where other skills are scheduled to be taught as well as where you can find opportunities in the subject matter for students to use the skills to learn subject matter. When sequencing multiple skills, it is useful to "think small" and "go slowly" in teaching thinking skills, especially if these skills are complex or involve abstractions of some degree of difficulty.

Regardless of which or how many thinking skills you choose to teach, careful planning and sequencing of your lessons will enable you to provide appropriate instruction in a skill at the most opportune time. This is not to say that instruction cannot or should not be spontaneous, however. Ideally, whenever students demonstrate an inability to execute a skill required to understand an important point about subject matter they are studying, you should drop the subject-matter focus of your lesson and give explicit attention to the thinking skill. Provide an introductory or transfer lesson on it and then plan some followup guided practice lessons in this skill if you expect your students to become proficient in it.

Being able to plan and carry out skill-teaching sequences successfully requires considerable experience in using strategies appropriate to each kind of lesson that can be used to teach new skills. Such experience comes only from training and education in these strategies and their carefully planned practice over and over again. Well-planned sequencing of thinking skill lessons can provide such experience and practice and help you develop your expertise at teaching thinking skills. Planning and sequencing are also indispensable to carrying out thinking skills teaching that your school or district mandates.

You can use the sequence planning form in Figure 4.6 to help you sequence your teaching of one or more thinking skills in your class. Simply duplicate as many copies as you will need for the number of skills you must teach and the number of lessons you will present. Fill in the skill names down the left-hand side and the lesson numbers on the blanks across the page. Then use these forms to complete steps 1 through 4 presented in this chapter, making whatever adjustments are required if you will be teaching several skills rather than one or picking up instruction in previously introduced skills as well as introducing instruction in new skills. Use of the procedure outlined here should help you integrate instruction in thinking with instruction in subject matter to the benefit of both.

checkpoint

When you have completed and explained to several colleagues a sequence for teaching four thinking skills over one semester in a subject you teach, and have revised it to incorporate their worthwhile suggestions, check here:

Figure 4.6 A Form for Sequencing Thinking Skill Lessons

LESSON: —   —   —   —   —   —   —   —   —   —

1. _____

2. _____

3. _____

4. _____

LESSON: —   —   —   —   —   —   —   —   —   —

1. _____

2. _____

3. _____

4. _____

LESSON: —   —   —   —   —   —   —   —   —   —

1. _____

2. _____

3. _____

4. _____

2. *Provide a classroom climate supportive of skillful thinking.*

If you expect your students to improve their thinking, you will have to provide instruction in an environment or climate that supports thinking. You cannot expect students to be willing, or even able, to think beyond the levels of simple recall and translation in a classroom that emphasizes primarily reception learning, lesson hearing, and testing for factual recall. Rather, a classroom climate conducive to thinking requires the processing of facts and information to produce new meanings, draw conclusions, infer relationships, develop new insights, make and test hypotheses, and reflect regularly on how and how well (how accurate, relevant, objective, and worthy) these procedures worked. It involves considerable student-to-content and student-to-student engagement and interaction. A thinking classroom encourages, stimulates, honors, and facilitates student learning by providing instruction in how to carry out the thinking operations required to engage in learning. Establishing and maintaining such a climate is essential if you wish to maximize the impact of instruction in the thinking skills you seek to teach.

You can develop and maintain such a climate in your classroom by attending to at least five things:

The physical layout of your classroom

Student behavior

Your behavior

Learning tasks and activities used

Instructional materials

Here, briefly, are some things you can do in each of these areas to provide a classroom climate supportive of student thinking.

Classroom Layout.   Since student thinking is greatly enhanced by student-to-student interaction and by the processing rather than the absorbing or reporting of information, your room should be arranged to facilitate these processes. Students should be seated so they face each other, not in theater-style seating with neat rows all facing front. A hollow square or circle of desks or movable tables that can be placed in a ''U'' shape will allow students to face each other and encourage such interaction. Movable desks or tables will permit frequent use of small-group activities, each with its own workplace. Removing the teacher's desk from its customary position at the front of the room to the rear or side of the room (as just another work station) will also allow for more interaction and cooperative learning. Where the physical arrangement of a classroom invites face-to-face discussion, group work, and cooperative inquiry, thinking is more likely to be fostered, stimulated, and thus engaged in by students and teacher.

Student Behavior.   Thinking involves great risk, especially for students whose prior achievement has been based on figuring out ''what the teacher wants'' and trying to give it to him or her. It is also risky for those who are often the objects of peer pressure not to get involved in classroom learning. Student behaviors that minimize risk in thinking should be encouraged, whereas those that inhibit it should be discouraged. Pairing and grouping students for cooperative learning activities requiring the use of new thinking skills or the solution of difficult problems can minimize any risk they may feel of being wrong in completing assigned tasks. Emphasis should always be on ideas or thoughts generated rather than on who comes up with them. Students must not criticize their peers personally for any ideas but must focus on the quality of the ideas offered and the processes by which they are generated. They should be helped to seek and offer clarification of the terms they use, to voluntarily define technical language, to seek and voluntarily give reasons and evidence in support of their claims, and to reflect critically on *their own* thinking as well as that of their classmates. They should focus not so much on what is right or what is wrong but on the proof or support provided for proffered conclusions or theories, on the assumptions that underlie them, and on the implications to which they lead.

Your Behavior.   You should use your role as teacher to model the behaviors that typify the skillful thinking that you want your students to exhibit. You should also demonstrate for your students how you execute significant thinking operations, explaining as you do the important *steps* you go through and *why* you do each one. Critically evaluate *your own thinking* and its products, and willingly change your mind when reason and evidence warrant it. By playing devil's advocate, you can also teach your students that looking at an issue from a variety of sides is an important component of skillful thinking.

You, too, should be willing to risk in your thinking—to voice as yet ill-formed thoughts and to submit your ideas to evaluation by the class. *You should reflect aloud on how you execute thinking operations.* Welcome and consider objectively new thoughts, including those contrary to your cherished beliefs of preferences. Instead of giving answers, facilitate your students' search for meaning by asking carefully structured questions, alerting students to the need for more information and providing instructive help when they need assistance in carrying out new or complex thinking skills. It is quite appropriate to give them information they may need if you have it and if searching for it interferes with other higher-level cognitive goals, but giving information should be a minor rather than central focus of your teaching efforts.

Learning Activities.   The classroom that best develops student thinking is one in which students have something worthwhile to think about! This means that students must engage in learning activities that go far beyond reporting what they read in the text or saw on television or found in the library. They must use that information to make new meaning out of it. This means that the substantive issues or topics studied must be structured so as to provide opportunities for—indeed, the necessity of—thinking at levels beyond simple recall. Students should actively work through problems; make decisions; critically evaluate hypotheses, information, and thoughts—their own as well as those of others; build concepts and generalizations; and raise and answer significant questions. Activities that enable students to *un*cover rather than cover are best suited to accomplishing these tasks.

You can do much to make activities such as these central to the teaching of any subject by organizing or structuring your units, subject, or course in a such a way as to make these activities a natural part of teaching and learning. For example, you may organize any topic or subject as a problem to be solved. In such an approach, student study is initiated by posing a problem, and then continued through the stages of hypothesizing solutions, testing, and retesting. Such an inquiry approach to teaching offers a rich, and probably the best, climate and context for teaching student thinking.

You can also do much to ensure student motivation and interest in such activities by making the topics and problems to be investigated of interest to your students. Ideally, your students should identify problems or topics about which they wish to know more. In many instances, knowledge of your students and your subject will allow you to preplan such topics. Questions habitually asked by your students or their predecessors will indicate possible choices here, as will persistent and timely human concerns (such as the relationship of individuals to authority or the role of rules in any community).

Questions can also be used to organize and structure a unit, topic, or course for skillful thinking. Questions best suited for this purpose are those that require students to process, evaluate, and make meaning of information rather than simply report or repeat this information. When these questions cue the use of specific thinking skills or require their use, they can stimulate and facilitate the kinds of integration of thinking skills with each other and with subject matter that typifies the most productive and supportive classroom climates for thinking. Whether these questions initiate such study or are used by you to guide this study, they can contribute significantly to integrating thinking and subject matter in your classroom.

These and other methods of structuring units and courses for thinking play an important role in *teaching* thinking. Not only do they create opportunities for students to employ selected thinking skills but they also create opportunities for you to provide explicit instruction in those skills that the students seem to have difficulty in carrying out. Every time you put students in a position of having to think or to use a particular thinking skill, you create an opportunity for you to explain, show, or otherwise teach them how to carry out the skill(s) needed to complete the assigned task. Taking advantage of these teaching opportunities is what the teaching of thinking skills is all about! The ways in which you structure your subject-matter study contributes much to a classroom climate conducive to student thinking.

Instructional Materials.   The materials you and your students use should assist them in developing their thinking as well as simply practicing it. And they should do this in the subjects you want your students to think about. Until recently, few instructional materials were available that did this. For example, most texts or workbooks simply made students think by putting them in situations where they had to think if they wanted to answer the assigned end-of-chapter or workbook questions. Few if any teaching guides provided any help at all for teachers who wished to help students learn how to carry out the thinking skills they needed to complete these tasks.

Now, however, increasing numbers of student texts, supporting instructional materials, and teaching guides that *teach* thinking skills in specific subject-matter areas are becoming available. For instance, some textbooks include specific instruction—explanations, modeling, guided practice, and cued questions—in how to carry out selected thinking skills to better understand the content they present. Instructor's guides also increasingly include teaching suggestions and information helpful in assisting students to improve their abilities to carry out these skills. The most useful of these materials integrate instruction in thinking skills with instruction in subject matter, and employ the basic skill-teaching principles that are explained in Chapter 2 of this handbook.[2]

Use of materials like these can enable you to take advantage of opportunities in your classroom study of the subject(s) you are teaching to actually teach your students how to do the thinking skills they need in order to learn what they are supposed to learn about these subjects. By using these, you not only can help maintain a classroom climate supportive of student thinking but you can also integrate instruction in thinking with subject matter.

checkpoint

When you have identified and listed below three specific things you can do to improve the climate for thinking in *your* classroom, check here: ☐

_____

_____

_____

3. Emphasize dispositions supportive of skillful thinking.

There is more to skillful thinking than technical expertise in carrying out a thinking task. To be an effective thinker, one must know *when* to employ appropriate thinking skills and *be willing to do so* on his or her own initiative. Helping students develop the dispositions typical of skillful thinkers, the attitudes and values that lead them *habitually* to employ the skills you teach at appropriate places and on their own, must be a continuing and conscious effort on your part and on the part of your colleagues. In your classroom and in all aspects of your contact with students, you should model the behaviors of skillful thinking, for they reflect these dispositions. And you should insist that your students do the same.

According to researchers, skillful thinkers are disposed, among other things, to:

- Seek a clear statement of a question or problem or claim.
- Use, and request that others use, precise language.
- Be less impulsive than they normally may be.
- Check their work.
- Persevere in carrying out a thinking task.
- Seek and give reasons and evidence in support of claims made.
- Be open-minded.
- Judge in terms of issues, purposes, and consequences rather than in terms of dogma or wistful thinking.
- Use prior knowledge.
- Suspend judgment until sufficient evidence is available.[3]

These and similar habitual ways of behaving reflect the high value that skillful thinkers put on objective truth and accuracy. For above all, thinking as making meaning honors meaning that stands the test of critical evaluation.

Thinking dispositions—as all aspects of affect—take time to develop. They are not acquired as the result of a single lesson or even as the result of a single unit or course of study. Nor can they simply be told to students and adopted as a result. Dispositions develop as the result of continued efforts to examine and reflect on the various behaviors generated by the dispositions that could be engaged in and on the consequences of these behaviors. You must consistently help students engage in such reflective examination and in the behaviors that enact these dispositions.

What can you do specifically to accomplish this objective? You can, on a regular basis:

1. *Model behaviors that demonstrate the desired dispositions.* You and your colleagues should exhibit the behaviors that reflect the dispositions of skillful thinking. For example, you should suspend judgments until you have as much relevant information as possible and you should make deliberate, explicit efforts to secure such information. Deliberately seek out a variety of points of view on an issue or topic. Articulate a number of alternatives in decision-making situations before considering any and making choices. Give your reasoning for assertions and decisions you make. In so doing, you should explain to your students why you are doing these things, and you need to be sure that your students recognize this demonstration of important aspects of thinking.

2. *Insist on student behavior that reflects the dispositions sought.* You and your colleagues should require your students to exhibit behaviors demonstrating the dispositions indicative and supportive of effective thinking, just as you do. Stu-

dents should be required to give reasons for their claims and decisions and to ask others to do the same, to generate alternatives before making choices, to seek out and explore a variety of points of view, to withhold judgment, and so on. Practice of such behaviors, even if at your insistence, can, in time, lead to internalization of the values implicit in these behaviors.

3. *Engage students in repeated activities that require use of these disposition-based behaviors.* Learning activities must consistently and continuously require students to exhibit behaviors related to skillfull thinking. One or two cases, instances, or opportunities to do so over the course of a semester or year are not sufficient even to begin to develop such dispositions. You must design and carry out activities in which students repeatedly seek out and discuss a variety of points of view, collect additional data, suspend judgment, and choose from a number of alternatives. These and related behaviors must be practiced in appropriate places over and over again across many grade levels and in many subjects.

4. *Reinforce behaviors that demonstrate the appropriate dispositions.* Behaviors illustrative of good thinking can be reinforced by explaining and demonstrating their value as well as by offering praise, grades, and other reinforcements for them. You need to be cautious in doing this, however, to ensure that such reinforcement clearly relates to the behavior, not to the student(s) exhibiting it. Few, if any, students can be or even may wish to be like another individual, but all can exhibit a valued behavior.

Urging someone to model, reinforce, and have students engage in behaviors that evidence these dispositions is one thing—identifying exactly which behaviors illustrate such dispositions is quite another. But some of these behaviors can be identified. For example, a group of experienced teachers in a thinking skills workshop, after observing students for some time, identified the following behaviors as possible indicators of these dispositions:

a. *Uses precise language*
   - asks for clarification of words used by classmates and teachers
   - uses correct names for objects and ideas (avoids slang)
   - uses technical terms for major thinking operations (for example, *alternative* or *option* for possible choices that could be made)
   - voluntarily gives examples and a definition in using new words or terms
b. *Is less impulsive*
   - reflects or pauses before answering
   - considers options thoughtfully before making a choice
   - reads directions thoroughly before acting and refers to them repeatedly
   - states a plan or makes an outline before acting
c. *Checks his or her work*
   - takes time to review a problem statement after working out an answer to a problem
   - reviews how an answer was derived
   - expresses a desire for feedback on how a particular answer was derived
   - compares his or her solution process to that of others
   - may erase or put a line through an initial response and put "correct" answer next to or in place of it
   - uses another operation to redo the problem
d. *Perseveres in carrying out a thinking task*
   - asks questions about process, if stumped

- asks ''what if'' questions about a task, when puzzled
- returns to an unresolved problem after being away from it for a time
- redefines or subdivides a problem

e. *Uses prior knowledge*
  - says, ''I remember that before we . . .'' in dealing with a new problem
  - applies content used in one class in another class
  - says, ''This reminds me of . . .''
  - uses sources used before to check answers

Of course, other behaviors evidence these dispositions, too, and can be identified with practice, careful observation, and analysis.

A word of caution about these behaviors needs to be offered here, however. No single behavior exhibited once or twice can be taken as evidence of any specific disposition. A disposition is an *habitual way of behaving*. Only a *pattern* of repetitive behaviors identified as indicators of a specific disposition should be accepted as evidence that a student is beginning to internalize that disposition. Knowing what specific behaviors may reflect certain sought-after dispositions is very helpful in directing students in class, but one must be cautious in interpreting from such behaviors exactly what they mean.

Yet—with this caution in mind—emphasis on the dispositions of skillful thinking, and the behaviors to which they give rise, is extremely important in teaching thinking skills. Techniques other than the four listed earlier can also be employed to help students develop these dispositions and behaviors. But there is more to developing such dispositions than the use of certain techniques. *When* these techniques are used is equally important. Attitudes, values, and dispositions are formed early in life. Indeed, in most cases, they are established rather firmly by the time youngsters enter their junior high school years. The implications of this are quite clear. Schools must start as early as possible to develop these dispositions if youngsters are to develop the affective support system requisite for effective use of the thinking skills you seek to teach.

This suggests that attention to thinking dispositions cannot be limited to any single grade or combination of several grade levels. If it is in the elementary grades that basic attitudes and dispositions are nurtured and developed, then a considerable effort should be made to teach thinking dispositions beginning in the primary grades.[4] Teachers throughout all grades can use many of the techniques outlined here to develop the dispositions listed earlier. These techniques should be used consistently across all elementary and secondary grades to develop and reinforce these and similar dispositions.

It should be noted that many of the dispositions that support and drive effective thinking run counter to the natural inclinations of novice thinkers and students of all ability levels. For students who find thinking difficult or who seem to abhor academic work of any kind, efforts to seek out additional data beyond those already in front of them or to seek alternatives beyond the first one that pops up are simply ''too much work.'' And these students are quick to point out they did not sign up for such work! Other students, often those categorized as academically talented, frequently find winning in argumentation preferable to finding the ''truth.'' They prefer to use their thinking skills to persuade others of the validity of a particular personal opinion rather than to establish what is true or accurate in as objective terms as possible. Respecting others, examining alternative viewpoints, analyzing data that challenge a preconception, and judging on the basis of evidence and reasoning rather than on the basis of dogma or personal bias often run counter to the preferred forms of behavior of many individuals.

There is no magic formula for helping students develop the dispositions supportive of effective thinking outlined here. Yet, this is an important part of the teaching of thinking. Initiating efforts to develop these dispositions at the earliest stages—in preschool programs or in the primary grades at the latest—certainly would help accomplish this goal. Providing instruction in appropriate thinking skills and offering opportunities to develop these operations in subject matter of immediate interest to these students may also underscore the value of such skills and dispositions. You can contribute to development of these dispositions by patiently explaining the long-range implications of sloppy "one-sided" thinking, of failing to use all the data available, or of not considering a variety of alternatives. This can also be accomplished by providing lessons where the results of such thinking can be examined by your students. Certainly, modeling and insisting on student behaviors that illustrate these dispositions will help, too. Developing dispositions supportive of effective thinking clearly is a challenge that requires a continuing and long-range effort by all teachers, parents, and students.

checkpoint

When you have identified three dispositions supportive of skillful thinking that you will seek to develop over the next year or in your first year of teaching, and have also identified two techniques by which you can help your students develop each, check here: ☐

SUMMARY

Having completed this chapter, you should now be able to:

1. Sequence instruction in thinking skills with instruction in any subject matter you teach.
2. Recognize, create, and maintain a classroom climate supportive of skillful thinking.
3. Recognize and model dispositions essential to skillful thinking.

No matter how skilled you may become at teaching thinking skills, your effectiveness will be enhanced (or limited) by the extent to which you integrate (or fail to integrate) instruction in thinking skills in subject matter, by sequencing your instruction appropriately, creating and sustaining a classroom climate supportive of thinking, and providing continued attention to the dispositions that underlie and sustain skillful thinking. Of course, other factors are also important in this effort, such as your understanding of the skills you seek to teach and your ability to provide the kinds of instruction and assessment required to develop proficiency in them. Your knowledge of subject matter is also of crucial import, for it is presumably in this context that you will or do provide instruction in thinking skills. Becoming a skillful teacher of thinking requires considerable knowledge and experience on your part as well as a high degree of commitment to the task.

CONCLUSION

You have now explored and practiced how to do four tasks essential to the effective teaching of thinking:

1. Identify and describe the critical attributes of any thinking skill you might wish to teach.

2. Design, write, and teach a lesson (or different kinds of lessons) that ''teaches'' a thinking skill, using a teaching strategy appropriate to your students, to the skill to be learned, and to the role of the lesson in a sequence of lessons on the skill.

3. Design and prepare one or more types of thinking skill assessments.

4. Integrate instruction in thinking skills in subject matter units, classes, or courses.

Obviously, much remains to be done in order for you to become proficient in applying these skills in your own teaching. You need to practice them repeatedly over a long period of time with the coaching and support of your colleagues who are engaged in this same endeavor. And you need continuously to reflect with them and on your own about what you are doing. Eventually you can become proficient in applying these skills and will feel quite comfortable in doing so.

All this, of course, will take time. But it will be time well spent. Not only will your present and future students benefit immensely from your successful efforts and investment but so will you. *Mastery of these teaching skills enhances your performance as a teacher as well as your skills as a thinker! What you have learned here will not only improve your skill as a classroom teacher but it will help you understand more completely the thinking skills and dispositions you may be teaching.*

Increasing your knowledge of and skill at thinking and adding to your repertoire of classroom strategies and techniques for teaching thinking frees you from the restrictions imposed on your teaching by having to rely on a limited knowledge or storehouse of techniques and strategies for teaching thinking. Learning how to identify the attributes of a thinking skill, to design and use strategies and lessons to teach these skills directly, to assess student thinking, and to integrate thinking skill and subject-matter teaching *empowers you* as well as your students. And that is a principal reason for attending to thinking skills in your school and classroom on a continuing, explicit, and systematic basis. Best wishes for success in your endeavors to help your students develop their thinking abilities to their fullest potentials and, by so doing, to reach higher levels of achievement in their school subjects and civic lives.

Endnotes

1. See Barry K. Beyer, *Developing a Thinking Skills Program* (Boston: Allyn and Bacon, 1988), pp. 103–122 and 194–211, for detailed descriptions of various approaches to selecting thinking skills for instruction and to developing thinking skill scope and sequences that extend beyond single subjects or grade levels.

2. The list of Selected Materials on the Teaching of Thinking that concludes this handbook includes a variety of commercially available materials for teaching thinking skills in different subjects that may be of interest or use to you.

3. Arthur L. Costa and Lawrence F. Lowery, *Techniques for Teaching Thinking* (Pacific Grove, CA.: Midwest Publications, 1989), pp. 89–102; Robert Ennis, "A Logical Basis for Measuring Critical Thinking Skills," *Educational Leadership* 43:2 (October 1985), p. 46; David R. Krathwohl et al., *Taxonomy of Educational Objectives—Handbook II: The Affective Domain* (New York: David McKay, 1964), pp. 181–185; Richard Paul, "Critical Thinking: Fundamental to Education for a Free Society," *Educational Leadership* 42:1 (September 1984), pp. 4–14; Barry K. Beyer, *Practical Strategies for the Teaching of Thinking* (Boston: Allyn and Bacon, 1987), pp. 19–20, 211–214.

4. For a K–12 scope and sequence of thinking dispositions and metacognitive skills, see Beyer, *Developing a Thinking Skills Program*, pp. 211–214.

part II

Sample Materials for Teaching and Assessing Thinking Skills

INTRODUCTION

The pages that follow contain teaching packets for selected thinking skills. Each packet contains:

- A description of the thinking skill to be taught
- A lesson plan for introducing the skill inductively to average or above-average students (or to any students, if the skill is an "easy" one)
- A lesson plan for introducing the skill directly or developmentally to below-average students (or to any students, if the skill is a "difficult" one)
- A lesson plan for providing guided practice in the skill
- A lesson plan for transferring the skill to a new setting, subject, or kind of data, or for elaborating the skill by adding new procedures or rules to it
- A test to assess student proficiency in the skill following its initial introduction and practice

These materials have been developed by outstanding beginning and experienced teachers for use in introducing and teaching specific thinking skills to students at selected grade levels, 6–12, in different subjects. They have been prepared by going through the procedures and following the guidelines in this handbook. All have been reviewed by other teachers and by specialists in teaching thinking skills, all have been taught, and all have been revised based on feedback generated by these reviews or applications. Thus, they reflect the realities of classroom practice as well as instructional theory and skill-teaching research.

You can use these materials in several ways. You can treat them as practical examples of what you need to know how to develop if you wish to teach thinking skills directly. They can also serve as models for you to follow in designing similar materials for use in your teaching of a thinking skill of your choice to students in your own classes. Additionally, analysis of these materials can also help you understand more about different strategies for teaching and assessing thinking skills.

These materials can also be used to teach selected skills in your own classes. They may be used as they are or adapted to your own students and own subject area. By using these lessons as *your* lesson plans—if they do match your own teaching interests or needs—you can gain some feel for what such teaching is like and you can even practice a bit how to carry it out in your classroom. The skill descriptions will be useful if you do not know much about these skills. The tests, if used with your students, can provide diagnostic information about the proficiency of your students in these skills as well as about their reaction to the type of assessment they represent. In other words, using these materials can be a shortcut to learning how to teach thinking skills in your own classroom.

Use of these teaching materials, however, should not be a substitute for learning how to produce your own descriptions, lessons, and tests for thinking skills you wish to teach to your students. These materials are simply an introduction to this task. Analysis and/or use of them must be followed by the construction and classroom application of your own similar materials. And it is with this intent that they are provided here. If you go through the procedures presented in Part I using appropriate materials from this part of the handbook, you, too, will be able to design, prepare, and use teaching materials like these in your own classroom. These materials are not meant as ends in themselves but as springboards for you to use to sharpen your skills at teaching thinking skills.

Before examining any of these materials, these words of explanation may be helpful:

1. The *skill descriptions* represent what their authors conceptualized as essential features or attributes of the skills described. These descriptions are the results of repeated efforts to apply the skills, and they reflect those applications as well as research into what others have written about these skills. They also reflect informed teacher knowledge of the skill. They are *not*, unless otherwise labeled, descriptive of how *students* at any particular grade level actually do the skill, but they can be translated into such descriptions. They are intended simply as guides to you and others who are teaching the skill and can be of considerable use in planning lessons, selecting learning materials, and designing assessments.

2. The *lesson plans* are models only. They are samples of how selected kinds of thinking skill teaching strategies might be used in specific grades or classes. Obviously, instruction in any thinking skill would not introduce that skill twice, nor would it consist of only three or four lessons. Two introductory plans are included in each set to illustrate how each would work with the same skill. If you choose to use these lessons, you would use only one of these introductory lesson plans unless you actually teach two different kinds of classes—one of mostly average to above-average students and the other of slower students. However, you should know how to write and teach both kinds of lessons because over the years you may have the need to use both or some combination of the two.

The guided practice lesson plan has been designed for a lesson to be offered about two or three days after the skill has been introduced by one of the preceding sample introductory lessons. More guided practice lessons, spaced out appropriately after this one, would be needed, of course, if teaching the skill to a high degree of proficiency is your goal—as it should be. The guided practice plan presented here can serve as a model for any of these additional lessons.

The transfer lesson represents one way to *initiate* transfer or elaboration of the skill after students have demonstrated on a test (like that included in each set) an appropriate degree of proficiency in the skill in the context in which it was originally introduced. Guided practice in the new context will then be required.

The lessons presented here are essential to effective instruction in these skills but they do *not* constitute all the lessons you will need to teach to develop the level of student proficiency you probably desire. Additional lessons providing guided practice (with decreasing amounts of guidance) and independent use of the skill will be needed following the guided practice lesson included in each set here. The lessons provided here will serve as models for preparing the former; your own experience and the guidelines in the Appendices will provide you with ideas for the latter.

Even though these lesson plans can hardly be considered as scripts, you may think they are more detailed than is necessary or than you are accustomed to preparing. They probably are. But such detail is necessary if you are to become familiar with the key steps in executing a teaching strategy or type of lesson that is new to you. Preparing such a detailed plan helps you simulate an actual lesson as it should be carried out. As pointed out in Chapter 2, such "anticipatory teaching" also helps rehearse and embed in memory the teaching routine you intend to follow if all goes as planned! This preparation makes it easier for you to actually carry out the strategy when you try to do so. The detail is especially useful to ensure that you do not skip any of the key steps in the strategy when you are teaching the lesson. You can cut back on the detail in your plans once you have internalized the elements of the strategy and can carry them out automatically.

3. The *thinking skill tests* provided here are intended to be used after the students, as a group, have moved from an introduction to the skill through a number of guided practice lessons on the skill and several lessons requiring them to apply the skill independently *before* the skill has been transferred or elaborated. Variations of this test format can be made for assessing proficiency after subsequent instruction for transfer or elaboration and for assessing several additional thinking skills rather than just a single thinking skill. As explained in Chapter 3, other kinds of assessments may also be used or designed.

In summary, the thinking skill teaching materials that follow can serve as models as well as tools for your own teaching of thinking. Careful study of and reflection on these skill descriptions, lesson plans, and tests can enable you to produce similar ones for your own teaching. They are presented by their authors as a practical way to provide serious, direct instruction in important thinking skills. And they work!

Skill-Teaching
Materials

Teaching the Skill of Problem Solving

*Sixth/Seventh Grades
Mathematics*

Cindy Abramoski

Middle School Teacher
Prince Georges County (Maryland)
Public Schools

Marijke deVries

Teacher Candidate
George Mason University

Peggy H. Recker

Teacher Candidate
George Mason University

SKILL DESCRIPTION

Label: Problem Solving

Definition: To find an answer, solution, explanation, or remedy for an unsettled matter

Synonyms: question-answering, solution finding, solving, re-solving

Steps:

1. Recognize a problem.
2. Represent the problem.
3. Plan/Choose a solution plan.
4. Execute a plan (solve).
5. Check answer/plan.

Rules:

1. When to problem solve?
   - when confronted with a problem or any matter requiring solution
2. How to start?
   - locate question mark to help identify the problem
   - circle key words or data that are given
3. What to do if . . .
   - you can't find a plan to solve the problem? Draw a picture (or table, graph, etc.).
   - your check does not match? Look back for computation errors.
   - your plan does not work? Try a new plan.

Knowledge:

1. Know the subject matter of the particular type of problem (e.g., knowing math facts and symbols, how to set up equations).
2. To check a problem, you use the reverse operation.
3. Know the *clues* to determine what type of problem it is (e.g., *altogether, and, how many in all,* etc., may signal an addition problem).

INTRODUCING THE SKILL OF PROBLEM SOLVING
An Inductive Lesson

Goal: To introduce the skill of problem solving

Objectives:

To state 5 major steps in problem solving

To state at least 1 important rule to follow in problem solving

To solve a problem using a systematic problem-solving strategy

Materials:

Word Problems #1 and #2

Teacher	Students
Preview	
1. State that the objective of today's lesson is to learn the skill of problem solving.	Listen
2. Write *problem solving* on the board.	
3. Ask for synonyms. May need to look at each word separately: *problem* and *solving.* Write synonyms on the board.	question, dilemma, conflict answering, remedying, resolving
4. Ask for examples of day-to-day experience that may present a problem and how it may be solved.	Solving word problems in math fight with friend—made up no lunch money—borrowed some
5. How might you define *problem solving?*	To find a solution to something or some problem; to look at a situation and come up with a solution
Execute	
6. Have Word Problem #1 written on blackboard. Instruct students to work individually to solve the problem.	Students work independently to solve the problem.
Have students then share their results with a partner and discuss their *methods* of solving the problem.	Students discuss, in pairs, *how* they obtained their answers.

Teacher	Students
7. Ask for responses from students: "What did you obtain for your answer?"	Answer: $27

Reflect

8. What did you *do* mentally to solve this problem?	Allow time for thinking.
What did you do first? Why?	Read the problem.
What did you do next? Why? Etc.	Asked what needs to be solved. Wrote down important given data (number of old stamps, number of president stamps, price of stamps, total spent).
What was your next step?	Drew a picture.
Why?	To get a clearer understanding of the givens.
What did you do next?	Chose operations of addition and multiplication to solve the problem.
Why did you choose these processes?	Looked for key words (*cost, each, altogether*).
What did you do after obtaining an answer?	Checked the answer by a reverse operation (subtraction/division).
Why?	To verify that answer was correct.
9. Ask for other ways students derived their answers. (It is important to have several examples of procedures.)	
Now, in your own words, review the general steps taken to solve the problem. Put responses on the board.	*Steps:* 1. Identify problem by locating question mark or key words (*how much, cost of each, altogether*). 2. Draw a picture or make a representation of the problem. 3. Decide how to solve the problem. 4. Solve problem. 5. Check answer.
10. How do you determine if the answer is correct?	*Rules:* 1. Look for key words or question marks. 2. Change representation of problem; change solution plan. 3. Always check for answer/plan. Use reverse operation.

Teacher	**Students**

Apply

11. Hand out Word Problem #2. Have students work alone using steps and rules on the board to solve the problem. Share *method* of solving the problem with a partner. Assist as necessary.

   Students work alone to solve.

   Share method/results with partner.

12. Have students report results.

Review

13. Ask: *How* did you solve this problem? What did you do first? Why? What next? Why? (etc.)

   1. Identified problem by locating key words (number of hours, rate of pay) to help identify needed operation.
   2. Made table; did operation (add).
   3. Another operation (multiply).
   4. Solved.
   5. Checked by reverse operation (subtract/divide).

In your own words, what are the key steps of problem solving?

   Steps:
   1. Identify problem.
   2. Draw a picture/table/representation.
   3. Decide how to solve.
   4. Solve.
   5. Check.

What rules are helpful to solving a problem?

   Rules:
   1. Look for key words.
   2. Check representation of problem.
   3. Change solution plan.
   4. Always check answer/plan.
   5. Use reverse operation.

14. Review synonyms and definition. Revise as necessary.

15. Have students write steps/rules in notebook after determining if synonyms and definition are satisfactory.

   Identify a problem.
   Represent it.
   Choose a plan.
   Carry out plan.
   Check plan/answer.

16. Ask for examples of places or times when this skill can be used in everyday life or school life.

   To find the cost of things.
   To see how much money is needed.
   To buy a wanted item.
   To fix things at home.

Materials for Introductory Problem-Solving Lessons

Word Problem #1

Kimberly collects stamps. She bought 5 old stamps with American flags on them and 4 stamps with pictures of presidents on them. She paid $3 for each stamp. How much did she spend altogether for these stamps?

Word Problem #2

Joe works at Wild World Amusement Park to earn spending money. He earns $10 per hour. How much did Joe get paid this week if he worked 8 hours Monday, 10 hours Wednesday, and 7 hours Friday?

INTRODUCING THE SKILL OF PROBLEM SOLVING
A Directive Lesson

Goal: To introduce the skill of problem solving

Objectives:

To state 5 major steps in problem solving
To state 2 important rules to follow in problem solving
To solve a problem using a systematic process of problem solving

Materials:

Word Problems #1 and #2

Teacher	Students
Preview	
1. State that the objective of today's lesson is to learn the skill of problem solving.	Listen
2. Write *problem solving* on the board.	
3. Ask for synonyms. May need to look at each word separately. Write synonyms on the board.	question, dilemma, conflict, answering, remedying, resolving
4. Ask for examples of day-to-day experience that may present a problem and how it may be solved.	Solving word problems in math fight with friend—made up no lunch money—borrowed some
5. How might you define *problem solving?*	To find a solution to something or some problem; to look at a situation and come up with a solution
Explain	

6. Explain the steps—list them on the board.
   a. Recognize a problem.
   b. Represent the problem.
   c. Plan/choose a solution plan.
   d. Execute a plan (solve).
   e. Check answer/solution plan.

Give the student some useful rules to follow:

Teacher	**Students**

a. If you can't find the problem, look for a question mark.

b. If you're not sure how to represent the problem, circle the key words or data that are given.

c. If you can't find a plan, draw a picture.

d. To check your answer, use the reverse operation.

Demonstrate

7. Show Word Problem #1 on overhead.

8. Walk the class through the steps to solve the problem, with student help as volunteered. Explain why each step is done as it is executed.

Review

9. Have students parapharase the steps and reasons for each step. Review the rules—have students discuss the importance of these rules.

    a. Recognize a problem (gives purpose).

    b. Represent problem (provides picture).

    c. Plan/choose a solution plan (provides a strategy).

    d. Execute a plan (solve) (gives an answer).

    e. Check answer/plan (checks for errors).

Apply

10. Project Word Problem #2 on overhead. Ask students to solve in pairs using the steps and rules just explained and demonstrated

11. Have students report and give answers.

    Possible answer: $250

Reflect

12. What did you *do* mentally to solve this problem?

Teacher	Students
What did you do first? Why?	Read the problem.
After reading, what did you do? Why?	Asked what needs to be solved.
Then what? Why?	Wrote down important given data (number of old stamps, number of president stamps, cost).
What was your next step? Why?	Drew a picture. To get a clearer understanding of facts.
What did you do next? Why?	Chose operations of addition or multiplication. Looked for key words (*cost, each, altogether*)
What did you do after obtaining an answer? Why?	Checked the answer by a reverse operation. To verify the answer.
13. Ask for other ways students derived their answers. (It is important to have several examples on the board.) Now, in your own words, state the steps taken to solve the problem. Write on board their responses.	*Steps:* a. Identify problem. b. Draw a picture or make a representation of the problem. c. Decide how to solve the problem. What operation? (add, subtract, etc.) d. Solve problem. e. Check answer.
14. List any rules that played a key role in solving the problem.	*Rules:* 1. Look for key words or question marks. 2. Change representation of problem; change solution plan, if not successful at first. 3. Always check answer/plan. Use reverse operation.
15. Have students write steps/rules in notebook.	
16. Have students review and revise skill definition.	To find a solution to a problem
17. Ask for examples of places or times when this skill can be used in everyday life or school life.	To find the cost of things To see how much money is needed To buy an item

> **note**
>
> *This type of introductory lesson may work best with below-average students (or with any students if the skill is very difficult).*

GUIDING PRACTICE IN PROBLEM SOLVING

Goal: To guide practice in the skill of problem solving

Objectives:

To state the major steps in problem solving
To state 2 important rules to follow in problem solving
To apply the skill of problem solving to find solutions to math problems

Materials: Word Problem #3

Teacher	Students
Preview	
1. State that the objective of today's lesson is to practice the skill of problem solving.	Listen
2. Write *problem solving* on the board.	
3. Ask for synonyms for:	
a. problem	a. dilemma, question
b. solving	b. answering, remedying, working out
c. problem solving	c. question answering
4. Ask for examples of when students had to solve a problem.	I was lost at the mall, so I went to the information booth. In math yesterday.
5. Have students define *problem solving*.	Finding an answer, remedy, or solution to an unsettled matter
Review	
6. What do we do mentally to solve problems? List steps on board. Give reasons for using each step.	*Steps:* 1. Recognize a problem (gives purpose). 2. Represent the problem (provides a picture). 3. Plan/choose a solution plan (provides a strategy). 4. Execute a plan (solve) (gives an answer). 5. Check answer/plan (checks for errors).

Teacher	**Students**
7. What rules are useful to follow? List rules on board.	*Rules:* 1. Locate the question mark to help find the problem. 2. Circle key words or data given. 3. If you cannot find a plan, draw a picture (or table, or graph).
8. What is helpful to know to solve problems? List knowledge on board.	1. Know the subject matter of the particular types of problem. 2. To check a math problem, you do the reverse operation. 3. Know the key rules to determine what type of problem it is (e.g., *and, all together, how many*) 4. Know some of the strategies for solving different types of problems (e.g., look for a pattern, construct a table, make a diagram)
9. What types of obstacles could you encounter in problem solving and how could you overcome them? List under rules on board.	1. If you can't find the problem look for the question mark. 2. If you're not sure how to represent the problem, circle data/key words. 3. If you can't find a plan, draw a picture (or graph, or table).

Execute

10. Have students, in pairs or groups, work to solve Word Problem #3.	
11. What did you get?	Possible answer: $49

Ponder

12. Have students state steps, rules, and knowledge they used to solve problem. Get several different procedures reported, if possible. Look for rules, procedures, or steps common to all procedures volunteered.	*Steps:* 1. Recognize the problem. 2. Represent the problem. 3. Plan/choose a solution plan. 4. Execute a plan (solve). 5. Check answer/plan. *Rules:* 1. Locate the question mark. 2. Circle given data/key words. 3. If you can't find a plan, draw a picture (or graph, etc.).

Teacher	**Students**
	Knowledge:
	1. Know subject matter of the particular problem.
	2. To check a math problem, you do the reverse operation.
	3. Know the clues to determine what type of problem it is.
	4. Know some of the strategies for solving different types of problems.
13. What changes or additions can we make to our definition? Make any changes in personal notes as well as on the board.	
14. Where else can we use problem solving in our day-to-day lives?	When fixing a disagreement with a friend In science experiments

note

In teaching this skill, additional guided practice lessons like this one will be needed. These additional lessons can use the same strategy that is used in this lesson. Students should also have several opportunities to use this skill on their own after *appropriate guided practice.*

Material for Guiding Practice in Problem Solving

Word Problem #3

Sue took her cousin to the mall on Saturday. She bought two blouses at $20 each, two pretzels at $1.50 each, and two tickets to the matinee at $3 each. How much money did she spend all together?

INITIATING TRANSFER OF THE SKILL
OF PROBLEM SOLVING
An Inductive Lesson

Goal: To initiate transfer of the skill of problem solving

Objectives:

To state major steps in problem solving
To state at least two important rules to follow in problem solving in science
To apply the skill of problem solving to science

Materials:

1 baggie powdered sugar
1 baggie baking soda
5 baggies table salt
5 baggies granulated sugar

Teacher	Students
(To set the stage for transfer of the skill of problem solving, bring to class two eggs that look alike, one raw, the other hard boiled.)	

Preview

Teacher	Students
1. Relate this lesson to the preceding lessons that dealt with word problems.	
2. We can use problem solving to solve problems outside of math, specifically, in science. Learning how to do this is today's goal.	
3. Write *problem solving* on the board.	

4. Ask for synonyms:
  a. problem
  b. solving
	question, dilemma, conflict
	answering, remedying, fixing
	answering questions

5. Ask students for times when they have used problem solving to solve problems:
  a. in out-of-school situations
 	
  b. in this course to date
Ask why this skill is useful.
	a. lost at mall—went to information booth
	b. solving word problems in math
	It applies to day-to-day activities.

Teacher	Students
6. Ask for definition of *problem solving.* Write it on board.	To find an answer, solution, or remedy for an unsettled matter

Review

7. Recall the word problems from math and how we used problem solving to obtain answers.	Kimberly's stamps Joe's job a Wild World Sue at the mall
8. What steps did we follow to obtain an answer to those problems? Post chart listing steps (when appropriate).	1. Recognize a problem. 2. Represent the problem. 3. Plan/Choose a solution plan. 4. Execute a plan (solve). 5. Check answer/plan.
9. What rules or clues did we feel were helpful in solving the problem?	1. If you can't find the problem, look for the question mark. 2. If you're not sure how to represent the problem, look for key words or data. 3. If you can't find a plan, draw a picture. 4. Check answer with reverse operation.
10. Tell the students that these steps and rules are very much applicable to nonmath problem solving, but they are subject to change as content area varies.	

Execute

11. Put students in groups. Give each group two baggies—one with sugar and one with baking soda. Ask them to find which is which. Several pairs of baggies could hold same substance.	

Reflect

12. What did you do to solve this problem? What did you do first? Why? Next? Why? etc. Have volunteers tell the process and steps they followed.	1. Recognized problem. 2. Chose plan. 3. Tried it—failed, so chose another plan. 4. Tried it.

Teacher	**Students**
	5. Repeated process.
	6. Got answer.
13. What did you do differently from the previous way?	Recalled what we thought we knew about what's in baggies.
	Used one plan after another until we got one that worked.
14. Get several different sequences on the board. Identify common steps.	

15. How is this the same as problem solving in math?	Same general steps:
	   Recognize problem.
	   Pick a solution plan.
	   Carry out plan.
	   Check answer.

16. How does it differ?	One general plan is to experiment:
	   Make hypothesis (its sugar).
	   Make plan to test hypothesis (if this is sugar, it will taste sweet).
	   Carry out plan (taste it).
	   If plan doesn't work, try another.

17. Review general problem-solving process for science.	1. Recognize problem. 2. Make hypothesis. 3. Set up experiment. 4. Collect data. 5. Conclude. 6. Check plan/solution.

Apply

18. Let's see if this process works. Have students divide into groups of five. Distribute baggies of salt and of sugar to each group. Apply steps to determine which bag contains salt and which contains sugar. Have one student record steps taken to solve the problem.	Divide into groups, follow problem-solving procedure. Jot down notes about discoveries. Obtain solution.

Review

19. Have student recorders report the procedure used to solve the salt/sugar problem.	*Method #1* 1. State problem. 2. Design/execute plan.

Teacher	**Students**
Write down on board at least two complete procedures used by students. Ask what did you do first? Why? Next? Why? (etc.)	3. Solved by tasting.
	4. Others tasted to check.
	Method #2
	1. Had a problem.
	2. Looked at bags for differences.
	3. Tried to tell by touch.
	4. Tasted contents of one bag (salt).
	5. Assumed other was sugar, but was also salt.
	Method #3:
	1. Identify problem.
	2. Hypothesize answer.
	3. Decide what can do to test hypothesis.
	4. Conduct the test.
	5. Check results and the experiment.
20. Which steps seemed least useful? If plan to smell didn't work, what did you do? Why?	Did not need to draw picture. Tried another plan.
21. If you did not know how salt or sugar was supposed to taste, feel, or smell, what could you have done? If you found first was salt how do you know other is sugar?	*Rules/Clues:* Might need more information. Might need to research. Never take anything for granted. DON'T ASSUME.
22. Which of the new rules could you use to solve the problem of telling which is which? We've used this skill of problem solving in math problems and now you have seen it related to science. What other times could we apply problem solving in our everyday life? Problem solving is an excellent skill to use in math and science, but we can also utilize the same steps to work through day-to-day situations that present a problem and require a solution.	Guess by appearance. Check by logical reasoning. NEVER ASSUME. Turning on switch—no light. Trying to start car.

note

This lesson should be followed by a number of guided practice lessons and several additional opportunities to apply the skill as presented in this transfer lesson.

FIRST TEST FOR THE SKILL OF PROBLEM SOLVING
Grade 6 or 7

Name _____ Date _____

1. Which of the following best defines the skill of *problem solving?*
   a. To guess what will happen next
   b. To find the answer to a question
   c. To rank a list of items

2. Circle the letter of whichever of the following is an example of problem solving.

A   **B**

Example A:
I came home from the grocery store. I put all of the groceries on the table. I put all of the fruits and vegetables into the refrigerator, all of the meats into the freezer, and all of the canned goods into the cabinet.

Example B:
One of the cans from my grocery bag had no label on it. What's in it? I compared it in size and shape to the other cans and still could not tell. I shook it and weighed it and still could not tell. I opened the can. I had soup for dinner.

3. Solve the following problem. Show *all* your work.

   Mrs. Wilson was returning library books for her children. The books were nine days late. Her son had checked out six books and her daughter had checked out four books. If each book costs five cents for each day it was late, how much did Mrs. Wilson have to pay?

4. Solve the following problem. Show *all* your work.

Mrs. Jones was buying some cookies. Chocolate chip cookies cost 50 cents each. Oatmeal cookies cost 75 cents each. Sugar cookies cost 80 cents each. If she bought one dozen of each kind, how much money did she spend?

5. Solve the following word problem. Show *all* your work.

Jeremy had some clothes to take to the cleaners. He had four shirts, three jackets, and five pairs of pants. How much was his dry cleaning bill if the cleaners charged $2 per shirt, $8 per jacket, and $4.50 for each pair of pants?

6. On a separate page, give *specific,* detailed directions that a fifth-grader could follow to solve the following problem.

The car wash in Jonesville is very busy. It washed 12 vans, 4 trucks, and 22 cars on Saturday. How much money did the car wash take in on Saturday if the charge for each van is $7, for each truck is $11, and for each car is $5?

Teaching the Skill of Decision Making

Seventh Grade
Language Arts—Social Studies

Jerome Robbins

Middle School Teacher
Seattle (Washington) Country Day School

SKILL DESCRIPTION

Label: Decision Making

Definition: To arrive at a decision after careful consideration of possible alternatives, probable consequences, and personal values

Synonyms: choosing, opting, judging, selecting

Steps:

1. Define the goal/purpose to be achieved.
2. Identify alternatives.
3. Analyze the alternatives in terms of consequences (short/long range); costs (real/personal); resources required; and so on.
4. Weight and rank the alternatives according to their consequences (for each consequence, assign an importance score: very important = 3, moderately important = 2, least important = 1) or rank each alternative by giving plus and minus values to each consequence for each alternative, etc.
5. Identify the top two or three alternatives.
6. Based on your reaction to the selected alternatives, review them for risks involved or any unanticipated consequences.
7. Make final choice.

Rules:

1. When to make decision?
   - in any "choice" situation, such as selecting a course of action to follow, something to believe, etc.
   - in attempting to resolve any problem involving values or divergent "potential solutions"
2. How to start?
   - brainstorm potential alternatives
   - establish criteria to be used and the relative weight of each
   - recall previous successful or comparable decision-making situations
3. What to do if . . .

- you are inclined early toward a specific solution? Look for additional options or for evidence against a favored option. Don't jump at the first seemingly "good" alternative that turns up!

Knowledge:

1. Understand sources of decision-making interference, including impulsiveness, conflict of interest/bias, and irrational persistence of key beliefs.

INTRODUCING THE SKILL OF DECISION MAKING
An Inductive Lesson

Goal: To learn the skill of decision making

Objectives:

To define decision making

To state some major steps in decision making

To make a decision by applying the steps and rules

Materials: Stories A and B

Teacher	Students
Preview	
1. Learning the skill of decision making is the objective of today's lesson. By the end of the lesson, you should be able to describe, at least tentatively, one or more ways to execute this skill.	
2. Write *decision making* on the board.	decision making
3. We are all making decisions many times each day, some more important than others. Give examples of decisions that have been made today.	What to wear to school What to do this weekend When to do my homework
4. Ask for synonyms. What are some other words that mean the same thing as making a decision?	selecting, choosing, deciding
5. State a tentative/working definition for *decision making.*	Arriving at a decision after careful consideration of possible alternatives, probable consequences, and personal values; the process of making choices; the process of selecting the (best) choice from among several alternatives
6. State or have students volunteer ways that decision making can be or has been used in personal experiences, important events, relationships, purchases, etc.	When to get up in the morning What to wear, what to eat Where to go on Saturday and with whom

Teacher	**Students**
7. Explain how decision making is useful and why it is worth learning:	
a. We are making decisions many times each day.	
b. When we are faced with difficult decisions, it is important for us to know that we have made the best decision for the circumstances and that we personally can live with that decision.	

Execute

8. Read Story A: What Should Graham Do?	Groups of 3-4 students read and decide
9. What do you think Graham should do? Why? Take several minutes to talk it over with those sitting around you.	

Reflect

10. What did you do mentally to arrive at a decision? How did you do it? List on the board various steps taken. What did you do first? Why? What did you do second? Why? What did you do next? Why? etc.	Students report what they did in their heads as they engaged in the process of decision making.
11. Have two or three students report the steps they followed in coming to their decisions. List these on the board. Help students rearrange steps in order completed, first to last.	Brainstormed alternatives available. Predicted otucomes of each alternative. Decided the "best" solution.
12. Ask students to tell any rules they followed.	1. Think of as many alternatives as possible before picking any. 2. Try to think of all the things that might happen if each alternative were chosen.

Apply

13. Read Story B: What Should Susan Do?	work in pairs, triads, or groups

Teacher	Students

Use what has been discussed about the skill of decision making to arrive at a decision for Susan.

Review

14. What did you come up with for Susan to do?

15. How did you decide?
Review the steps/procedures that seem to constitute the decision-making skill.
What did you do differently this time? Why?

    Students tell how they arrived at their decision.
1. Define the goal.
2. Identify alternatives.
3. Analyze the alternatives in terms of consequences.
4. Decide pluses or minuses of each.
5. Make choice.

16. Review any rules that seem to direct the use of the decision-making process.

1. Think of as many alternatives as possible first.
2. Think of all the consequences you can of each alternative.

17. Review or revise the definition of decision making.

Decision making is choosing the best thing to do after you have looked at all the things you could do.

18. Discuss where the skill can be used in personal or out-of-school situations.

Choosing my friends
Deciding how to spend my spare time
Picking classes for next year

— note

This type of introductory lesson may work best with average to above-average students (or with any students if the skill is very easy).

Material for Introductory Decision-Making Lessons

A
What Should Graham Do?

"Yes. . . . I do, sir, it was Tony Miller," said Ken. Graham felt a sinking feeling in his stomach. He walked slowly away from the Principal's office where his own brother—Ken, had just lied to the Principal. He could no longer hear voices—there was a pause as the Principal was probably wondering what he should do.

As Graham walked away, he recalled the comment his father had made at breakfast that very morning. "I'd love a nice silver pen. It seems that the plastic ones break or they run out," he had said. Graham and Ken had given each other a knowing look across the breakfast table, because they knew it was their father's birthday in three days. But when they had opened their piggy-banks and turned out their pockets, they had realized that they could not afford to buy a nice silver pen.

When Graham saw Ken steal the pen of the school clerk, it took him a little while to work out Ken's reason. Ken just wanted to please their father by giving him a gift he really wanted.

Graham didn't know what to do. He didn't think stealing was right, but the pen would make their father proud of them. Fortunately, only *he* had seen Ken take the pen, because his room was directly opposite that of the school clerk. Should I pretend I know nothing about it, thought Graham, or should I say something to Ken?

When the bell rang for recess, Graham couldn't find Ken. He then overheard that the Principal was speaking to every boy and girl in turn who had been seen in the area of the clerk's office that morning. Graham had turned pale. He wondered what Ken had done with the pen. If he had it in his pocket and he was searched—whatever would happen to him?

Graham had raced to the administration block to find Ken, but when he got there, he had heard Ken talking to the Principal. He had pressed himself flat against the wall so that he wouldn't be seen, and trembled a little. The Principal's voice was very stern.

Graham could still hear Ken's words: "Yes. . . . I do, sir, it was Tony Miller." Graham felt ashamed of his brother. He understood why Ken had stolen the pen—he only wanted to please his father. But now he had put the blame on another boy, a boy who was new to the school. Graham's first thought was to speak to Ken, but Ken wasn't likely to change his mind now—he was in too deep. He couldn't tell on his own brother—or could he?

What should Graham do?

From Laurie Brady, *Do We Dare: A Dilemma Approach to Moral Development* (Sydney: Dymock's Book Arcade, Ltd., n.d.). Reprinted by permission of the publisher.

B
What Should Susan Do?

"The winner," said the pleasant man in the blue suit, "is a girl from this very school . . . Susan Cavanagh." The school assembly burst into applause, and the Principal beamed with pride. Susan was almost pushed to the front of the assembly by her enthusiastic classmates. She felt confused, and she knew that her legs were trembling and that her face was a deathly white. She had to walk to the rough wooden platform and climb the six or so steps as the whole school watched her. The visiting man shook her hand, and so did the Principal.

Susan had won a composition competition organized by the local branch of the Apex Club. Boys and girls from all the primary schools in the district had entered compositions. They simply had to write on the subject, "How I'd Help the Needy." The prize was a free trip on the Hawkesbury River on a thirty-five-foot yacht for a whole day—and NOT just for the winner, but for his or her whole class.

It was little wonder, then, that Susan was so popular with her class. All her girlfriends were excited, and even the boys who usually had nothing to say to her couldn't do enough to help her. "I'll wear the captain's cap my dad gave me," said one boy, his eyes alight with excitement.

But Susan couldn't really share their happiness. She had only entered the competition to please her teacher, and she had left it to the last moment. She had set herself the task of writing her composition in her library period the day the competition entries closed. To her surprise, she had found an old dusty book, and had copied out a composition word-for-word.

Susan didn't know what to do. She felt that she had cheated. But if she said anything, she would get into trouble with the Principal and her parents; and if her classmates were stopped from going on their boat trip, they would probably never talk to her again.

That same day, Susan was told that the boy who came in second in the competition had cheated—his brother in high school had written his composition. Susan knew that if she owned-up, then this boy might be named the winner in her place. Anyway, why should she own-up when she was now so popular with her class?

What should Susan do?

From Laurie Brady, *Do We Dare: A Dilemma Approach to Moral Development* (Sydney: Dymock's Book Arcade, Ltd., n.d.). Reprinted by permission of the publisher.

INTRODUCING THE SKILL OF DECISION MAKING
A Directive Lesson

Goal: To introduce the skill of decision making

Objectives:

To define decision making
To state the major steps in decision making
To apply the skill of decision making to make a decision

Materials: Stories A and B

Teacher	Students

Preview

1. Learning the skill of decision making is the objective of today's lesson. By the end of the lesson, you should be able to describe, at least tentatively, one or more ways to do this skill.

2. Write *decision making* on the board.

   decision making

3. We are all making decisions many times each day, some more important than others. Give examples of decisions that have been made today.

   What to wear to school
   What to do this weekend
   When to do my homework

4. Ask for synonyms. What are some other words that mean the same thing as making a decision?

   selecting, choosing, opting

5. State or get a tentative/working definition for *decision making.*

   Arriving at a decision after careful consideration of possible alternatives, probable consequences, and personal values; the process of making choices; the process of selecting the (best) choice from among several alternatives

6. State ways that decision making can be or has been used in personal experiences, important events, relationships, purchases, etc.

   When to get up in the morning
   What to wear, what to eat
   Where to go on Saturday and with whom

Teacher	**Students**

7. Explain how decision making is useful and why it is worth learning:

   a. We are making decisions many times each day.

   b. When we are faced with difficult decisions, it is important for us to know that we have made the best decision for the circumstances and that we personally can live with that decision.

Explain

8. Explain the steps and list them on the board.

1. Determine your goal.
2. Identify all alternatives.
3. Identify consequences, costs, and resources needed for each alternative.
4. Choose the best alternative.

Demonstrate

9. Read Story A: What Should Graham Do? Put chart on board.

10. Walk students through the alternatives that Graham has for this situation. Write these on the chart under the heading "ALTERNATIVES."

11. Write the names of the characters in the story across a line and label "CONSEQUENCES." Draw lines down to complete a matrix.

12. Taking each alternative one by one, discuss the effects (consequences) that choosing it would have on each character and other factors.

ALTER-NATIVES	CONSEQUENCES				
	Graham	Ken	Tony	Cost	Resources Needed
confront Ken					
tell principal					
tell father					
?					

Review

13. Review the steps/procedures that constitute decision making. Review any rules that direct the

Teacher	Students

use of the decision-making process.

Cover the list of steps and have students tell what order we followed to arrive at our decision.

Example:
1. Define goal.
2. Identify alternatives.
3. Analyze the alternatives.
4. Make choice.

Apply

14. Read Story B: What Should Susan Do?
Use what has been discussed about the skill of decision making to arrive at a decision for Susan.

work in pairs, triads, or groups

Reflect

15. What did you come up with for Susan to do?

16. How did you decide it? What steps did you go through?
Review the steps/procedures that seem to constitute the decision-making skill.
Get several procedures on the board.

1. Gather data.
2. Define goal.
3. Identify alternatives.
4. Analyze the alternatives in terms of consequences, costs, resources needed.
5. Judge consequences.
6. Make choice.

17. Review any rules that direct the use of the decision-making process.

1. Brainstorm as many alternatives as possible.
2. Use a chart to check out consequences and alternatives.

18. Review or revise the beginning working definition of decision making.

Decision making is choosing the best alternatives from all the alternatives you have.

19. State where the skill can be used in personal or out-of-school situations.

Picking a topic for a report
Deciding when to call time out in a basketball game
Buying a new record

---

note

This type of introductory lesson may work best with below-average students (or with any students if the skill is very difficult).

GUIDING PRACTICE IN DECISION MAKING

Goal: To guide practice in the skill of decision making

Objectives:

To state the major steps in decision making
To apply the skill of decision making

Materials: Story C

Teacher	**Students**

Preview

1. Remind the students that becoming better decision makers is the objective of today's lesson.

2. Write *decision making* on the board and underline it for emphasis.

<u>decision making</u>

3. Ask for synonyms. What are some other words that mean the same thing as making a decision?

selecting, choosing, deciding

4. Define or have students define *decision making.*

Choosing after careful consideration of possible alternatives, probable consequences, and personal values; the process of making choices; the process of selecting the (best) choice from among several alternatives

5. Ask for ways the skill of decision making can be or has already been used in personal experiences, important events, relationships, previous classes, etc.

Making daily decisions
Resolving social, personal problems
Making choices of projects to do

Review

6. What do you do to make a decision?
What steps can you follow?

1. Determine your goal.
2. Identify alternatives.
3. Identify consequences and costs for each alternative.
4. Judge alternatives.
5. Make choice.

Teacher	**Students**
7. What rules are useful to follow?	1. Use a chart to list alternatives, consequences, cost, and resources needed for each.

	Conse-quences	Cost	Resources
Choice A			
Choice B			
Choice C			

2. Brainstorm as many alternatives as possible first.

Execute

8. Read Story C: What Should Keith Do?

9. Have students engage in the skill of decision making with reference to what they have discussed about it.

10. Have students briefly share the decision that they came up with.

Keith should . . .

Ponder

11. Go over the steps that they used to decide.
What did you do first? Why? Next? Why? etc.
Have several different procedures volunteered. Write them on the board.

Students tell how they arrive at their decisions

1. Define goal.
2. Identify alternatives.
3. Analyze the alternatives in terms of consequences, costs, and resources.
4. Judge alternatives.
5. Make choice.

12. Have the students:
   a. Predict where else this skill can be used.

   b. Identify cues to occasions when it is appropriate to use this skill.

a. Whenever I have to make a choice between two or more things.

b. buying a present for someone
   what topic to work on
   what TV show to watch

note

In teaching this skill, additional guided practice lessons like this one will be needed. These additional lessons can use the same strategy that is used in this lesson. Students should also have several opportunities to use this skill on their own after *appropriate guided practice.*

Material for Guiding Practice in Decision Making

C
What Should Keith Do?

Keith crept forward on hands and knees to see where the noise was coming from. It sounded like a scuffle of some sort, so Keith was careful to be as quiet as possible. Then he heard a voice, a little like that of Peter Johnson. Peering through some thick bush, he saw Peter and Warren Gibbs in a clearing.

Warren was twisting Peter's arm and calling him names. Peter was trying to get away, but the harder he tried, the rougher Warren became. Warren was the biggest boy in the school and a real bully. Most of the boys tried to keep away from him because he was always trying to start a fight.

Keith knelt behind some bushes wondering what to do. He had been itching to go down to the creek at the back of the school for a month, and finally he had plucked-up enough courage. The creek was out-of-bounds, and the Principal had warned the school several times not to be caught in the area of the creek. But Keith had heard that some boys from the high school had built a big dam there, which was full of tadpoles, frogs, and ferns. There were lots of flat pebbles there that could be sent skimming across the surface of the water.

That day, Keith was given his chance. He had been given free time for doing an errand for his teacher, and found himself in the playground by himself a minute before the lunchtime bell. Deciding that he would go to the creek, he had started to run toward the back fence, and wasn't about to look back over his shoulder. He had scrambled under the wire fence and had given a deep sigh when he was safely hidden by the bushes.

He had found the dam and had looked into the deep water, lying on his stomach on the grassy bank. The water was icy cold and the sun was hot. "This certainly beats playing catch in the playground," he thought to himself. It was then that he had heard the noises.

Now he was confused. Peter was nearly crying and Keith felt sorry for him. Peter was a boy who would do anything to help others—he always shared his snacks and lent his books. Keith knew that Warren would soon start punching Peter, and wondered if he should help. He was afraid that if he did, he too might be badly beaten and might find it hard to explain a bleeding nose or a black eye. But if he ran back to the school to get a teacher or the Principal, he himself would be in trouble for being out-of-bounds and breaking a school rule. He wondered whether he should sneak back and say nothing.

What should Keith do?

From Laurie Brady, *Do We Dare: A Dilemma Approach to Moral Development* (Sydney: Dymock's Book Arcade, Ltd., n.d.). Reprinted by permission of the publisher.

INITIATING TRANSFER OF THE SKILL OF DECISION MAKING
An Inductive Lesson

Goal: To initiate transfer of the skill of decision making

Objectives:

To state in the correct order the main steps involved in making a decision
To apply to an ill-defined situation the skill of decision making

Materials: Pencil, paper, and Word Problem #1

Teacher	Students

Preview

Teacher	Students
1. Learning the skill of decision making is the objective of today's lesson. By the end of the lesson, you should be able to describe, at least tentatively, one or more ways to execute this skill.	
2. Write *decision making* on the board and underline it for emphasis.	<u>decision making</u>
3. We are all making decisions many times each day, some more important than others. Give examples of decisions that have been made today.	Who to sit with at lunch Which book to select from the library for a report
4. Ask for synonyms. What are some other words that mean the same thing as making a decision?	selecting, choosing, picking, deciding
5. State or get a tentative/working definition for *decision making.*	Choosing after careful consideration of possible alternatives, probable consequences, and personal values; the process of selecting the (best) choice from among several alternatives
6. State some ways that decision making can be or has been used in your personal experiences, important events, relationships, etc.	When to get up in the morning What to wear, what to eat Where to go tomorrow and with whom

Teacher	**Students**

Review

7. Go over the steps and rules that constitute decision making.
   When is it useful to use the skill of decision making?
   What steps can we follow? Why do we do each?

   Whenever we have an opportunity to choose.
   1. Determine goal.
   2. Identify alternatives.
   3. Identify consequences and costs for each alternative.
   4. Judge alternatives.
   5. Choose best alternative.

   What can we do to help make this process work?

   Use a chart to list alternatives and consequences of each.

8. Have the students:

   a. predict where else this skill can be used.

      a. Wherever it is necessary to choose between two or more options.

   b. identify cues to occasions when it is appropriate to use this skill.

      b. buying a present for someone
         what topic to work on
         what TV show to watch

Execute

9. Have the students apply the decision-making process to a hypothetical situation. Group the students.
   Ask them to assume different family member roles (mother, father, sister, etc.) and to use the process from that role's perspective for the family decision of buying a new car.
   What did you decide?

   Using lists, charts, or diagrams, arrive at a decision.

Reflect

10. What did you do mentally to arrive at a decision.
    How did you do it?
    What did you do first? Why?
    What did you do next? Why? etc.

    Students report what went on in their heads as they engaged in the process of decision making.

11. Help students arrange steps in order completed, first to last.

Teacher	**Students**
12. Clarify the procedure and steps by asking students to tell any rules they followed.	1. Brainstormed alternatives. 2. Predicted outcomes for each alternative. 3. Set up criteria for judging "best" solution.

Apply

13. Use what has been discussed about the skill to complete a second task, if time permits. Work in pairs, triads, or groups. You are trying to save up enough money to buy a new cassette player. You have saved $100. The one that has all the features you want costs $125. Another model is on sale for $80 but does not have all the features you want. A friend has a used player with all the features you want, but no warranty, along with 10 extra tapes for $100. Which one would you buy? Why?	

Review

14. What did you do to come up with a decision? How did you do it? Why? Review the steps/procedures that seem to constitute decision making.	Students tell how they arrived at their decision. 1. Define goal. 2. Identify alternatives. 3. Analyze the alternatives in terms of consequences (criteria), cost, and other variables. 4. Weight and rank alternatives. 5. Make choice.
15. Review any rules that direct the use of the decision-making process.	1. Collect information as you need it throughout the process. 2. Think of as many alternatives as you can *before* analyzing any. 3. Consider long-range as well as short-range consequences.
16. Review or revise the beginning working definition of decision making.	Decision making is choosing from alternatives examined in the light of their consequences.

Teacher	Students
17. State where the skill can be used in personal or out-of-school situations.	In picking gifts In deciding whether to work after school or not

note

This lesson should be followed by a number of guided practice lessons and several opportunities to apply the skill as presented in this transfer lesson.

FIRST TEST FOR THE SKILL OF DECISION MAKING
Grade 7

Name _____   Date _____

1. Which of the following best defines the skill of decision making?
   a. To make a choice from among several possible choices
   b. To put together things having common characteristics
   c. To arrange things in the order in which they occurred

2. Circle the letter of whichever of the following shows that the skill of decision making was used.

A

Bill emptied all the contents of his dresser drawers onto his bed, looking for a pair of clean socks. As he put things back in the drawers, he put similar things together in each of the drawers.

B

Bill had $10 to spend on a new record album. He went to the record store with a list of his favorite albums. One of his favorite albums was on sale and he bought it.

C

Bill made a bet with Jim on Thursday night's football game. Bill was sure he would win because his chosen team had won the last three Thursday nights.

3. Assume you are going to buy a new bike. There are three different brands available, Brand X, Brand Y, and Brand Z. Brand X is sporty, great on trails, comes in red, green, or blue, and is expensive. Brand Y is lightweight, has twelve speeds, comes all colors, and is expensive. Brand Z has ten speeds, knobby tires for off-road riding, comes in black only, and is on sale for a moderate price. Which bike would you choose? Tell the reasons why you make that decision.

4. Assume your family is going on a vacation this next year. You have just won a contest that will pay the expenses. Taking into consideration what you know about each member of your family's wants, needs, interests, and resources, where would you choose for them to travel? Tell the reasons why you made this choice.

5. You are going shopping with a friend who is purchasing a new stereo. Explain or list, for your friend, in as much detail as possible, what steps to go through in order to make the best choice.

Teaching the Skill of Predicting

Eighth/Ninth Grades
Science

Jack Green

Science Program Specialist
Fairfax County (Virginia) Public Schools

SKILL DESCRIPTION

Label: Predicting

Definition: To state what you believe is most likely to happen next

Synonyms: anticipating, foretelling, projecting, forecasting

Steps:

1. State what you are going to make a prediction about.
2. Review what you know about what you are going to predict.
3. Review any personal experiences that relate to what you are going to predict.
4. If possible, collect and examine information about what you are going to predict.
5. State some things you think could happen.
6. State what you think will be the *most likely* to happen.

Rules:

1. When to predict?
   - in making hypotheses
   - in checking options while making decisions
   - in searching for evidence about a claim
2. How to start?
   - make a flowchart showing everything up to this point
   - ask: "What is most likely to happen next?"
3. What to do if . . .
   - several possibilities exist? Pick the one *most* likely to happen.
   - you naturally lean toward a specific outcome? Look for evidence against the fact that that outcome will happen.

Knowledge:

1. Ability to compare/contrast
2. Types of patterns (such as number progressions, space patterns, etc.)

INTRODUCING THE SKILL OF PREDICTING
An Inductive Lesson

Goal: To introduce the skill of predicting

Objectives:

To identify and state some procedures for making predictions
To state at least one rule to follow in making predictions
To make a prediction

Materials:

clear, 16-oz. plastic container (about 475 ml.) and lid
100 ml. graduated cylinder
ice
plastic bag
hot water
cold water
matches
Student Worksheet

Teacher	Students

Preview

Teacher	Students
1. Begin the lesson by stating the objective. Today we are going to think about how we make predictions.	
2. Write *predicting* on the board.	predicting
3. Give or ask students for examples: When getting dressed in the morning, you put on clothes that will keep you warm or cool depending on your prediction of what the outside temperature is going to be. When you set the alarm to wake up on a school day, you are predicting how long it will take to get ready and to travel to school.	
4. Ask students to give examples of how they use the skill of predicting.	Predicting how well I will do on a test. Predicting what team will win an intramural game.

Teacher	Students
	Predicting if you will like the hot lunch served at lunch today.
5. Ask for synonyms.	foretelling, projecting, making an educated guess
6. Define or have students define *predicting*.	Saying what you believe will happen next

Execute

Teacher	Students
7. Divided the class into pairs. Distribute worksheet to all students. Tell students to make a prediction about what will happen when you conduct the following experiment on forming a cloud.	
Experiment #1: Place ice in a plastic bag. Pour 200 ml. of cold water in the plastic container and close the lid. Place the bag of ice on top of the lid and observe what happens inside the container. Ask: What will happen?	
Assign one partner the role of "predictor" and the other partner the role of "recorder." Instruct the "predictor" to talk aloud about what mental steps he or she is using to make the prediction. The "recorder" is to write the steps used by the person making the prediction. Then exchange roles so that the "predictor" records and vice-versa, as the second student makes his/her prediction.	Several different sequences of steps could be generated by the students as they think about how they make a prediction. Possible steps stated by a "predictor":
	Ask: What am I going to predict? What will happen when I place a bag of ice on top of the container holding cold water?
	List what I know about this: Warm air meeting cold air forms a cloud.
The "recorder" should encourage the "predictor" to think aloud about how he or she thinks when predicting by asking such questions as "What are you thinking now? ... Now? ... Now? (etc.) How did you do or come to that idea?"	When warm moist air is cooled it can rain. Warm air rises and cold air sinks. I'm remembering what I know. When I put ice cubes in a glass of warm water, condensation forms on the side of the glass.
	Review all the facts and make a prediction: Cold water in the container cools the air in the container, and the ice on top

Teacher	Students

also cools the air. From what I know about cloud formation, I predict that there will not be much of a change in air temperature in the container, so no cloud will form.

Reflect

8. Ask volunteers to write the steps they used to make a prediction on the board. Have each explain and justify the sequence of steps listed. Emphasize that there is *no* "one right way" to make a prediction. Have the class compare the lists of steps written on the board. Ask others to volunteer how they did it.

If necessary, probe for steps by asking:
    What did you do first? Why?
    What did you do next? Why?
    etc.
Try to get several different lists of procedures on the board.

Possible Responses:
1. State what you are going to predict.
2. Review your knowledge about what you are going to predict.
3. Review any personal experiences related to what you are going to predict.
4. If possible, find information about what you are going to predict.
5. Based on reliable information and personal experience that relate to what you are going to predict, state what you think will most likely happen.

9. Have students list any general rules to follow when making a prediction.
Point out steps common to all procedures on the board.

Useful Rules to Follow:
1. Make two or three predictions and then choose the one that is most likely to occur.
2. Make sure you base your prediction on appropriate and reliable information.

Apply

10. Hand out the worksheet. Have students make predictions on what will most likely happen as a result of the following experiment:

Teacher	**Students**

Experiment #2: Pour 200 ml. of hot water into the plastic container, secure the lid, and place the bag of ice on top of the lid. (Condensation occurs in the container.) Ask: What will happen now?

Have students work in pairs and write their predictions on the worksheet after talking aloud to their partners. Pairs should switch roles after experiment #2 and do experiment #3 so each student can predict and record.

Experiment #3: Pour 200 ml. of hot water into the plastic container. Hold a lighted match inside the container for a few seconds. Blow out the match, quickly secure the lid and place the plastic bag of ice cubes on the top of the lid. What will happen next?

Review

11. Have students report how they made their predictions. What did they do first? Why? Next? Why? etc.
    List responses for each volunteer on the board or add to or alter what is already on the board.

Possible Responses:
1. Thought about what I was to predict about.
2. Recalled information about it.
3. Looked at the experiment.
4. Combined what I knew with what I saw to find any pattern.
5. Identified what happened in similar experiment and matched it to this one.
6. Said what would happen next.

12. Redefine predicting.

Predicting is telling what is most likely to happen or occur.

13. Get or give synonyms.

foretelling, forecasting, projecting

14. Explain to students that there are certain questions that indicate the thinking skill of predicting is required. These questions include: What will happen if? What could change in the future? Who will? When will? Where will?

Teacher	**Students**
Ask students to think of other questions or cues that indicate the need to employ the thinking skill of predicting.	
15. Ask sudents to give examples of how they use the thinking skill of predicting in everyday life.	Predicting if a new song will be a #1 hit. Predicting which line to the cash register in a department store will move the fastest. Predicting which new pair of pants you will look the best in before you try them on.

note

This type of introductory lesson may work best with average to above-average students (or with any students if the skill is very easy).

Material for Inductive and Directive Introduction Lessons

**Student Worksheet: Classroom Experiment—
Cloud Observation Sheet**

PREDICT	OBSERVE
Experiment 1	
Experiment 2	
Experiment 3	

INTRODUCING THE SKILL OF PREDICTING
A Directive Lesson

Goal: To introduce the skill of making predictions

Objectives:

To state some procedures for predicting
To state at least one rule to follow in making predictions
To make a prediction

Materials:

clear, 16-oz. plastic container (about 475 ml.) and lid
100 ml. graduated cylinder
ice
plastic bag
hot water
cold water
matches
Student Worksheet

Teacher	**Students**

Preview

Teacher	Students
1. Begin the lesson by stating the objective. Today we are going to think about how we make predictions and state the major steps we use when predicting.	
2. Write *predicting* on the board.	predicting
3. Explain to students that they use the thinking skill of predicting every day. Give examples: When getting dressed in the morning, you put on clothes that will keep you warm or cool depending on your prediction of what the outside temperature is going to be. When you set the alarm to wake up on a school day, you are predicting how long it will take to get ready and travel to school.	

Teacher	Students
4. Ask students to give examples of how they use the skill of predicting.	Predicting how well I will do on a test or quiz. Predicting what team will win an intramural game. Predicting if you will like the hot lunch served at lunch today.
5. Ask for or give synonyms.	foretelling, making an educated guess, projecting
6. Define or have students define *predicting.*	Saying what you believe will happen

Explain

7. Explain that predicting can be broken down into steps. One way of doing this is as follows:
   1. State what you are going to predict.
   2. Review your knowledge about what you are going to predict.
   3. Review any personal experiences that relate to what you are going to predict.
   4. If possible, research information about what you are going to predict.
   5. Based on reliable information and personal experiences that relate to what you are going to predict, state what you think will most likely happen.

Useful Rules:
1. Make two or three predictions and then choose the one that is most likely to occur.
2. Make sure you base your prediction on appropriate and reliable information.

Demonstrate (Experiment #1)

8. Give each student the Worksheet. Place the ice in the plastic bag. Pour 200 ml. of cold water in the plastic container and close the lid.

Teacher	**Students**

Explain to the students that you are going to demonstrate the steps you just gave them for making a prediction.

Step 1. *State what you are going to predict.*

I am going to predict what will happen inside the plastic container when I place the bag of ice on the container that contains 200 ml. of cold water.

Step 2. *Review your knowledge of what you are going to predict.* (If you choose, have students participate in this step.)

I know the following:

• Ice is formed from water at 32 degrees Fahrenheit (0 degrees Celsius).

• When water vapor turns into water this is called condensation.

• When water turns to water vapor this is called evaporation.

• Warm air holds more water vapor than cold air.

• Warm air rises and cold air sinks.

Step 3. *Review any personal experiences that relate to what you are going to predict.*

• When I put ice cubes in a glass, condensation often occurs on the outside of the glass.

• When I take a hot shower, water vapor condenses on the bathroom mirror.

• After a summer rainstorm, I sometimes see water evaporating from puddles.

Step 4. *If possible, research information about what you are going to predict.*

Look in an encyclopedia under the topic of clouds and read about

Teacher	**Students**
cloud formation, or ask students what they know about condensation and evaporation. (Check accuracy of student information and clarify any misconceptions.)	
Step 5. *Based on reliable information and personal experiences related to what you are predicting, state what you think will most likely happen.*	
I predict that a little bit of condensation will occur on the lid of the plastic container right under the bag of ice. I also predict that no condensation will occur on the side of the container.	
9. Place the bag of ice on the lid of the plastic container containing the cold water and wait one minute. Observe what happens to determine the accuracy of the predictions. Discuss reasons for the accuracy or inaccuracy of the predictions.	

Review

10. After demonstrating the steps for predicting, ask the students to review the steps and make suggestions for adding steps or changing the order. Emphasize that there is *no* "one right way" to follow when you use the thinking skill of predicting.	
Ask students to pick out really important steps:	1. Concisely state what you are going to predict.
	2. Know something about what you are going to predict.
	3. Check your information to make sure it is current and reliable before you make your prediction.
	4. Identify a number of things that *could* happen.

Teacher	**Students**

Apply

11. Have students make predictions on what will *most likely* happen as a result of the following experiments.
    Do each experiment slowly, telling them what you are doing.
    Have students write their predictions on the worksheet.

    Experiment #2 Pour 200 ml. of hot water into the plastic container, secure the lid, and place the bag of ice on top of the lid. (Condensation occurs in the container.)

    Experiment #3 Pour 200 ml. of hot water into the plastic container. Hold a lighted match inside the container for a few seconds. Blow out the match, quickly secure the lid, and place the plastic bag of ice cubes on the top of the lid.

Reflect

12. Have students reflect on how they made their predictions. Ask for volunteers to report the steps or rules they followed to make their predictions. Again, if necessary, ask: What did you do first? Why? Next? Why? etc.	1. Start by saying what you are going to predict. 2. Review knowledge and personal experiences about what you are predicting. 3. Check on reliability of information. 4. Make two or three predictions based on reliable information. 5. Choose the prediction you believe will happen and be able to justify your choice.
13. Explain to students that there are certain questions that indicate the thinking skill of predicting is required. What are some of these questions? Tell some, if none are volunteered.	What will happen if? What could change in the future? Who will? When will? Where will?
14. Review the definition, if necessary.	Telling what is most likely to happen next

Teacher	**Students**
15. Ask for synonyms.	foretelling, forecasting, projecting
16. Discuss how the skill of predicting is used in conjunction with other thinking skills such as generalizing, testing a hypothesis, and developing models. Where can we use this skill?	Predicting can be used in conjunction with other thinking skills to solve problems. In everyday life we use the skill of predicting in a variety of ways including the following: To estimate how long it will take to complete a task To determine if we have a chance at winning a game To select food from a menu that you believe will taste good To get into a line that will move the quickest

---

note

This type of introductory lesson may work best with below-average students (or with any students if the skill is very difficult).

GUIDING PRACTICE IN PREDICTING

Goal: To guide practice in the skill of predicting

Objectives:

To state the major steps when making predictions
To state two important rules to follow when making a prediction
To make a prediction

Materials:

1.5-volt battery
#48 lightbulb
15 cm. (6″) of insulated copper wire with 1 cm. of insulation stripped from each end

Teacher	Students
Preview	
1. Begin by stating the objective. Today we are going to practice making predictions.	
2. Write *predicting* on the board.	predicting
3. Give examples: Explain to students that when they make choices from a menu, they are predicting that the food they choose will taste good and satisfy their hunger.	
Ask students to give examples of how they use the skill of predicting.	Predicting if it will storm hard enough to call off school. Predicting if your friends will like your new clothes.
4. Ask for synonyms.	foretelling, projecting, anticipating
5. Define *predicting*.	Saying what you believe will most likely happen
Review	
6. What steps can we follow to make a prediction?	1. State what you are going to predict.
	2. Review your knowledge about what you are going to predict.

Teacher	Students
	3. Review any personal experiences about what you are going to predict.
	4. If possible, research information about what you are going to predict.
	5. Based on reliable information and personal experiences about what you are going to predict, state what you think will most likely happen.
7. What rules are useful to follow?	1. Make two or three predictions then choose the one that is most likely to occur.
	2. Base your predictions on appropriate and reliable information.
8. What is helpful to know in order to make a prediction?	Events that took place in the past that relate to what you are predicting.
9. What kinds of obstacles or problems could occur that could affect your prediction? How would you overcome them?	Incorrect information; a sudden and expected change of events. Overcome them by checking information.

Execute

Teacher	Students
10. Ask students to predict which pictured diagrams are complete circuits that will light the bulb.	

Ponder

Teacher	Students
11. Go over the steps, rules, and knowledge that constitute making this and any prediction. Ask students to identify the most important things to do to make a good prediction. List these on the board.	1. State what you are going to predict.
	2. Review your knowledge about what you are going to predict.
	3. Review any personal experiences about what you are going to predict.
	4. If possible, research information about what you are going to predict.
	5. Based on all this information, state what you think will probably happen.
	6. Tell what is *most likely* to happen.
12. What rules are useful to follow?	1. Make two or three predictions then choose the one that is most likely to occur.
	2. Base your predictions on appropriate and reliable information.

Teacher	Students
13. What problems or obstacles occur when you make a prediction? How can you handle these?	Lack of information Do more research before making a prediction. Keep prediction tentative!
14. Give or get synonyms.	foretelling, anticipating, educated guessing, projecting
15. Define or have students define predicting.	Say what you believe will happen
16. In what instances in everyday life do you use the skill of predicting?	Predict how long it will take to do your homework assignment. Predict what you will get on a test based on the amount of time you study and knowledge of the subject. Predict who will win the game based on your knowledge of the abilities of the players.
17. When do you use the skill of predicting in science?	Scientists continually predict what may happen. They then set up experiments to determine if their predictions are correct.

note

In teaching this skill, additional guided practice lessons like this one will be needed. These additional lessons can use the same strategy that is used in this lesson. Students should also have several opportunities to use this skill on their own after appropriate guided practice.

INITIATING TRANSFER OF THE SKILL OF PREDICTING
An Inductive Lesson

Goal: To initiate transfer of the skill of predicting to a nonexperimental activity

Objectives:

To state the major steps when making predictions
To state two important rules to follow when making a prediction
To make a prediction

Materials: Weather maps from the local newspaper for the five previous days

Teacher	Students
Preview	
1. Begin the lesson by stating the objective. Today we are going to use the skill of predicting to make predictions about what the weather will be like 24 and 48 hours from now.	
2. Write *predicting* on the board.	predicting
3. Give examples: Explain to students that when they choose a course to take they are predicting that the course they choose will be good and satisfy their goals.	
Ask students to give examples of how they use the skill of predicting.	Predicting in July what major league baseball team will win the World Series in October. Predicting what kind and how many fish you will catch during the fishing trip.
4. Ask for synonyms.	foretelling, projecting, anticipating, making educated guesses
5. Define *predicting*.	Saying what you believe what will most likely happen
Review	
6. What steps can we follow when predicting?	1. State what you are going to predict. 2. Review your knowledge about what you are going to predict.

Teacher	**Students**
	3. Review any personal experiences about what you are going to predict.
	4. If possible, research information about what you are going to predict.
	5. Based on this information state what you think could happen.
	6. Tell what is *most likely* to happen.
7. What rules are useful to follow?	1. Make two or three predictions then choose the one that is most likely to occur.
	2. Base your predictions on appropriate and reliable information.
8. What is helpful to know in order to make a prediction?	Events that took place in the past that relate to what you are predicting
9. What kinds of obstacles or problems could occur that would affect your prediction?	Incorrect information; a sudden and expected change of events
How would you overcome them?	Research

Execute

10. Review the weather maps from the five previous days. Have each student predict what the weather will be like 24 hours from now, and write his or her prediction on chart paper that can be displayed at the front of the room.	Student responses will depend upon local weather conditions.
	1. When it is hot and humid out and cold air approaches from the west, it usually rains and thunderstorms occur.
	2. The weather maps indicate that a cold front is approaching and the weather is hot and humid.
	3. The five-day weather forecast calls for showers and thunderstorms.
	4. I predict that it will be raining 24 hours from now and the temperature will be a few degrees cooler.

Reflect

11. Ask volunteers to tell what went on in their heads as they made a prediction.	A student response could be: "I reviewed my personal experiences before reviewing facts. Then I followed the other steps we reviewed. I only made one prediction. It may be better to make two or three and choose the one that makes the most sense."

Teacher	**Students**

12. Ask students to tell what they did first and why, next and why, and so on.

    List answers to *what* under steps, to *why* under rules.

13. Have several volunteers tell how they did it.

Apply

15. Have the students review the weather maps and predict what the weather will be like in 48 hours—two days from now.

16. Have them write the predictions about highs and lows, humidity, winds, and so on, and hand them in. They can be used in two days.

Review

17. Ask for volunteers or call on students to demonstrate/explain what they did in a step-by-step manner when they made their predictions.
    Get several descriptions.

    "I stated what I was going to predict. I reviewed information on the weather maps. I tried to remember what happened last time we had similar weather conditions. I looked up weather predictions in the *Farmers' Almanac.* I then made three predictions and chose hot and sunny as the most likely weather 48 hours from now."

18. As a summary, ask students to again define the skill.

    Saying what you believe will most likely happen

19. Have the students state synonyms.

    an educated guess, anticipating, projecting

20. Ask students to state when predicting can be used in everyday life.

    To help you determine how someone will act in a new situation.
    To help you study for tests by anticipating what questions will be on the exam.

note

This lesson should be followed by a number of guided practice lessons and several additional opportunities to apply the skill as presented in this transfer lesson.

FIRST TEST FOR THE SKILL OF PREDICTING
Grade 8 or 9

Name _____ Date _____

1. Which of the following best defines the skill of predicting? Circle the correct answer.
   a. To make a wild guess
   b. To state what you believe will most likely happen
   c. Explain something that just happened

2. In which of the following is the speaker making a prediction? Circle the letter of the correct answer.

Speaker A:
It seems to me that the proper way to arrange these animals is by size. This mouse is the smallest. Let's put it first. The bunny is the largest. Let's put it at the other end. Now—the turtle is bigger than the mouse, but smaller than the bunny. So—I wonder where I can put it?

Speaker B:
I have to buy cat food for next week. Last week my cat ate 5 cans of food, but he wasn't feeling very well. He's acting better now, though. The week before last he ate a can a day, I think. In fact, every week I can remember he ate at least 7 cans of food. I think I better buy 7 cans of food.

Speaker C:
How do I know what will work best? John says the red one will. Susan says the blue one will. I don't even know if they are the same size. But I do know the red one will last longer. And the blue one is cheaper. I can get two blue ones for the price of the red one!

3. Based on the information below, which of the following is an appropriate prediction? Circle the letter of the best prediction.
   • The temperature outside suddenly drops ten degrees.
   • Dark cumulus clouds are rapidly moving in your direction.
   • The weather report calls for scattered thunderstorms.
   • Thunder is heard in the distance.

   a. I predict that it will not rain today.
   b. I predict that it will start raining within the next half hour.
   c. I predict that it will not start raining until tomorrow.

   Tell why prediction you picked above is the best prediction.

4. Make a prediction about which team will win the baseball game based on the following information:
   • Team A has a very good pitcher who strikes out eight or more batters each game.
   • Team B are all good batters and rarely strike out.
   • Team A only has a few good hitters.
   • Team B does not have any good pitchers.
   • The players on Team B are better fielders than the players on Team B.
   • Team A's record is 10 and 2. Team B's record is 5 and 4.

   PREDICTION: _____

   Tell why the prediction you made is the best prediction.

5. Which of the following would *not* be a good prediction based on the following information. Circle the answer of the best response.

On Friday, for the past four months, the school cafeteria served a salad tray with one of the following main meals: spaghetti, fish, or tuna salad sandwiches. Two weeks ago the cafeteria served spaghetti as the main course. Last week they served tuna sandwiches as the main course.

a. This Friday the school cafeteria will serve a salad tray and fish.
b. This Friday the cafeteria will serve pizza.
c. This Friday the cafeteria will offer a salad tray.
d. This Friday the cafeteria will not serve tuna sandwiches as the main course.

Explain why the answer you selected is most likely the correct answer.

6. In the space below, give specific directions that a third-grader could follow to make a prediction about what food a puppy and a rabbit would eat based on the following information.

Dogs and cats eat meat. Cows, rabbits, and horses eat plants. If a puppy and a baby rabbit were given the following foods, predict which foods each would eat.

a. lettuce
b. hamburger
c. grass
d. slice of ham

Write or list your directions here:

Teaching the Skill of Detecting Bias

Ninth/Tenth Grades
World History

Barry K. Beyer

Professor of Education
George Mason University
Fairfax, Virginia

SKILL DESCRIPTION

Label: Detecting Bias

Definition: To identify an inclination for or against that inhibits an impartial judgment

Synonyms for bias: a preference, slanted view, partiality, one-sideness

Steps:

Procedure A:
1. State your purpose.
2. Identify clues to look for.
3. Take the material apart piece-by-piece or line-by-line to find the clues.
4. Identify patterns among or consistency of the clues found.
5. State evidence to support patterns found.
6. State the extent of any bias found.

Procedure B:
1. State your purpose.
2. Examine the data.
3. Predict any bias when identifying first clues.
4. Search for corroborating or contrary clues.
5. Identify patterns among or consistency of the clues found.
6. State the results of the search: biased or not?

Rules:

1. When to search for bias?
   - in judging the accuracy of a source or statement
   - in identifying an author's point of view
2. How to start?
   - pick one clue and look for it, then pick another and search for it, etc.
3. What to do if . . .
   - we find little bias? Compare it to another piece of material on the same topic.

Knowledge (clues):

1. "Loaded" or emotionally charged words
2. Overgeneralizations
3. "Loaded" or rhetorical questions
4. Imbalance in presentation
5. Opinions stated as facts
6. ...

INTRODUCING THE SKILL OF DETECTING BIAS
An Inductive Lesson

Goal: To introduce the skill of detecting bias

Objectives:

To state some major steps in analyzing written data to detect bias
To list at least three clues to the existence of bias in a written source
To detect bias in a given source

Materials: Excerpts A and B

Teacher	Students
1. Relate today's lesson to the previous lesson on the Industrial Revolution. So far we have discussed the cause of this revolution and how it developed. Today we can look at its results.	
2. The Industrial Revolution affected people in many ways. One way to understand these effects is to examine accounts written by people of that time. However, because people often feel strongly about something, their accounts of it could be *biased.* A biased account may not be completely accurate or truthful. So, before believing what we read, we should analyze any written source to see if it is biased. Learning how to do this will be our goal today.	

Preview

Teacher	Students
3. Write *bias* on the board.	bias
4. Ask for or give several synonyms for bias.	prejudice, slant
5. Ask for or tell where you cold find examples of biases.	Newspaper editorials or letters to the editors Political speeches Advertisements

Teacher	**Students**
6. Ask for or give some examples of bias you have heard or seen.	Might prefer chocolate ice cream over all other flavors even though tasted only a few May be partial toward certain type of auto although never tried all makes of autos
7. Define or get a definition of *bias.*	A preconceived preference, a slanted view, a one-sided view (usually un-tested)

Execute

8. Hand out Excerpt A. To determine the accuracy of a source, we have to see if it is biased. If it is, we have to decide what the biases are. Read this. It was written around 1820 in England. Is it biased?	students read individually
9. Ask what the bias is.	Very anti-factory owners, anti-factory system in general; is sympathetic to workers

Reflect

10. Pair the students. Have them tell each other how they found any bias in Excerpt A:	
a. Have them tell the steps they went through.	Skimmed it, spotted clues, etc.
b. Have them tell any clues they found to bias.	Loaded words—"creatures"
Allow only several minutes for this.	
11. Have volunteer students or pairs report to the entire class.	*One Possible Procedure:*
12. Probe by asking: What did you do first? Why? Next? Why? Next? Why? etc. List responses to "what" on the board under *steps*—to "why" under *clues.*	1. Stated my goals—to see if it's bi-ased. 2. Read it to see if there was bias. 3. Got the idea from words in first few sentences it was biased against owners.
13. Get several different processes de-scribed, if possible. Review steps common to most.	4. Read on to see if this idea was cor-rect. 5. Found more words sympathetic to workers—anti-owner

Teacher	Students
	6. Decided it was biased against owners.
14. Ask what the clues were to bias.	Loaded words like *creatures, doomed* Exaggeration like "not a moment"

Apply

15. Define or have students define *bias* again. Distribute Excerpt B. It was written about the same time as Excerpt A and in England. Pair students to search for bias. Refer to steps and information on the board, as they wish.	A preconceived or untested preference that slants one's view of things
16. Report any bias found in Excerpt B.	This excerpt is pro-factory owner.

Review

17. Ask how they did it. What did you do first? Why? Next? Why? Next? Why? etc.	May repeat procedure on the board and/or offer alternative procedure:
18. Ask for additional ways to detect bias. Write procedures on board.	1. Stated my goal—to see if there was bias.
	2. Remembered clues to look for—words like *creatures, exaggerations.*
	3. Read sentence-by-sentence, looking for clues.
	4. Found some clues—*never/always/exhilarating.*
	5. Noticed they formed a pattern in favor of children working in factory.
	6. Decided this was biased in favor of factory work for children.
19. What clues can we look for to find bias?	Loaded words absolutes—exaggeration images—positive or negative
20. Help students summarize what they have found out about *bias.* Have them:	
a. define *bias*	a. an untested preference or slanted view
b. give synonyms	b. slant, one-sided

Teacher	**Students**
c. tell when its useful to look for bias	c. We search for bias in using sources in order to see whether or not they are objective and thus accurate—like when reading a newspaper, watching a TV documentary or news show, listening to anyone.

21. Write clues/steps/rules in notes.

Assignment

22. Assign students to bring in one example of a biased account (perhaps from a newspaper editorial, letter to the editor, etc.).

---

note

This type of introductory lesson may work best with average to above-average students (or with any students if the skill is very easy).

Materials for Introducing Lessons in Detecting Bias

EXCERPT A

Some of the lords of the loom employ thousands of miserable creatures in the cotton-spinning work. The poor creatures are doomed to toil day after day fourteen hours in each day in an average heat of eighty-two degrees. Can any man with a heart in his body refrain from cursing a system that produces such slavery and such cruelty?

These poor creatures have no cool room to retreat to, not a moment to wipe off the sweat, and not a breath of air. The door of the place wherein they work, *is locked except* at tea time. If any spinner be found with his *window open,* he is to pay a fine.

For a large part of the time the abominable stink of gas assists in the murderous effects of the heat which the unfortunate creatures have to inhale. Children are rendered decrepit and deformed and thousands upon thousands of them die before the age of sixteen.

Adapted from William Cobbett, *Political Register, 52* (November 20, 1984).

EXCERPT B

I have visited many factories and I never saw children in ill-humor. They seemed to be always cheerful and alert, taking pleasure in the light play of their muscles—enjoying the mobility natural to their age. The scene of industry was exhilarating. It was delightful to observe the nimbleness with which they pieced the broken ends as the mule-carriage began to recede from the fixed roller beam and to see them at leisure after a few seconds' exercise of their tiny fingers, to amuse themselves in any attitude they chose. The work of those lively elves seemed to resemble a sport. They evinced no trace of exhaustion on emerging from the mill in the evening; for they skip about any neighboring playground.

Abridged from Andrew Ure, *The Philosophy of Manufacture* (London, 1861).

INTRODUCING THE SKILL OF DETECTING BIAS
A Directive Lesson

Goal: To introduce the skill of detecting bias

Objectives:

To state some of the major steps in analyzing a written source for bias
To list at least three clues to the existence of bias in a written source
To identify bias in a written account

Materials: Excerpts A and B

Teacher	Students
Preview	
1. Relate today's lesson to the previous lesson on the Industrial Revolution. So far we have discussed the causes of this revolution and how it developed. Today we can look at its results.	
2. The Industrial Revolution affected people in many ways. One way to understand these effects is to examine accounts written by people of that time. However, because many people often felt strongly about the impact of the Industrial Revolution, their accounts of it are often biased. A biased account may not be completely accurate or true. So, in using written accounts, before you can believe them you need to see if they are biased.	
3. Write *bias* on the board.	bias
4. Ask for or give synonyms.	slant, prejudice, partial view, one-sidedness
5. Ask for or tell where you cold go to find examples of bias.	Newspaper editorials, letters to the editor, ads, etc.
6. Ask for examples (or give some) of bias.	Preference for chocolate ice cream over all other flavors Preference for a certain kind of car

Teacher	**Students**
7. Define *bias*.	A slanted view, a preconceived preference that slants one's view of things
8. State that learning to detect bias is the goal of today's lesson.	

Explain

9. List on board or project on overhead and explain:	

Steps:
1. State your goal or purpose—to see if there is bias.
2. Recall some clues to look for.
3. Examine the information line-by-line or piece-by-piece to find these clues.
4. Decide how the clues connect to each other. Is there a pattern?
5. Judge the extent of the pattern.
6. State your judgment.

Clues:
1. loaded words (*labor* instead of *work*)
2. overgeneralization (All—every—never)
3. loaded questions (Even an idiot would know this, right?)
4. omissions or errors

Demonstrate

Teacher	**Students**
10. Hand out Excerpt A. It was written around 1820 in England. Demonstrate steps and clues with Excerpt A. Lead students through the steps above. Have them help find some clues. Tell why each step is taken as it is done.	*Clues:* loaded words (*doomed, curse, cruelty*) overgeneralization (have *no* cool room, etc.)

Review

Teacher	**Students**
11. Have students paraphrase steps and clues on the board.	*One Procedure:* 1. State goal.

Teacher	**Students**
	2. Think of possible clues.
	3. Read line-by-line to find clues.
	4. See if the clues form a pattern—on one side.
	5. If so, state the bias.

Apply

Teacher	**Students**
12. Distribute Excerpt B. It was written around the same time as Excerpt A, also in England. Have students, in pairs, examine it to see if it is biased.	
13. When students have completed their searches, have several report their findings with evidence. Accept only a few responses.	*Clues:* Words (*cheerful, pleasure, exhilarating, nimbleness*)

Reflect

Teacher	**Students**
14. How did you determine any bias? What did you do first? Why? Next? Why? Next? Why? etc. Get several procedures on the board.	In addition to procedure explained above, might suggest: 1. Read material. 2. Get impression it is biased from words used in first few lines. 3. Read on to check it out— to confirm this idea. 4. Find more clues to this bias and none against it. 5. Decide it is biased and what the bias is.
15. Revise or review clues to bias.	loaded words overgeneralizations omissions of evidence one-sidedness image created (positive/negative)
16. Conclude by writing common steps, rules, and clues in notebooks; give a device for remembering how to find *bias,* such as:	

Teacher	Students

B egin with data
I dentify needed clues
A nalyze data piece-by-piece to find clues
S earch for patterns
E stablish evidence for pattern(s) found
S tate the bias(es) found

17. Ask for:

a. definition

b. examples

c. synonyms

d. when to look for bias

a. a preconceived or untested preference that slants one's view of things

b. a "Redskins'" fanatic

c. slant, one-sided

d. in using sources in order to determine objectivity and accuracy in reading newspapers, watching TV news

Assignment

18. Assign students to bring in an example of a bias—a letter to the editor from a local newspaper, etc.

note

This type of introductory lesson may work best with below-average students (or with any students if the skill is very difficult).

GUIDING PRACTICE IN DETECTING BIAS

Goal: To guide practice in the skill of detecting bias

Objectives:

To state the major steps in at least one procedure for detecting bias
To state three important clues to look for in detecting bias in written documents
To determine the degree or nature of bias in a written document

Materials: Excerpts C and D

Teacher	Students
1. Relate this lesson to previous lesson. Now that we know what they said, we can use these documents to learn more about European views of the Americas. First, however, we need to examine these documents to see if they are biased.	

Preview

Teacher	Students
2. Write *bias* on board.	bias
3. Ask for synonyms.	one-sided, slanted
4. Ask for examples of places you can find biases: a. out of school b. from previous classes	a. letters to the editor, political speeches b. testimony about factory conditions
5. Define *bias*.	A slanted point of view
6. In this lesson we can practice our skill of detecting bias.	

Review

Teacher	Students
7. What can we do to detect bias? What steps can we follow? First? Why? Next? Why? etc.	*One Procedure:* 1. State your purpose. 2. Recall useful clues to bias. 3. Search data piece-by-piece to find clues.

Teacher	Students
	4. Identify a pattern or side supported by clues.
	5. State the bias, if any.
8. What *rules* are useful to follow?	1. Look for bias when someone is trying to persuade you.
	2. To start, hunt for loaded words.
9. What *clues* are helpful for detecting bias?	1. Loaded words
	2. Rhetorical questions
	3. Overgeneralizations
	4. One-sidedness
10. What kinds of obstacles could occur in trying to detect bias? How would you overcome them?	If no obvious bias, examine another source representing another view.

Execute

11. Have students examine Excerpts C and D to see which is the more biased.	
12. Have several volunteers tell which is more biased and why.	

Ponder

13. Have students report the steps, rules, and clues that constitute detecting bias. Add or revise as appropriate.	
a. When is it useful to search for bias?	a. When your source is unidentified or unknown.

b. What steps can we follow? Get several procedures, if possible. Ask: What can we do first? Why? Next? Why? Next? Why? etc.	b. Possible Procedures:
	  1. State purpose.
	    Recall useful clues.
	    Search data line-by-line to find clues.
	    See if there is a pattern.
	    State any bias found.
	  2. State your purpose.
	    Read.
	    Form impression.
	    Read further, looking for clues to check it out.
	    Look for evidence against your impression.
	    State your findings.

Teacher	**Students**

c. What are some useful clues to bias in written materials?

1. Loaded words
2. Exaggerations
3. Loaded questions
4. One-sided presentations
5. Images presented

14. Make any needed changes or additions to skill attributes in notes.

Content Discussion

15. Now that we have searched for bias, let's find out what we can say about European views of the Americas.

note

In teaching this skill, additional guided practice lessons like this one will be needed. These additional lessons can use the same strategy that is used in this lesson. Students should also have several opportunities to use this skill on their own after appropriate guided practice.

Materials for Guiding Practice in Detecting Bias

EXCERPT C

Pleasant scences of spring-like beauty, a luxuriance, where fruits and flowers lavish their fragrance together in the same bough! That is the tropics! There, nature animates all life and reigns in vegetable and animal perfection. There, nature flows in wild splendor and uncultivated maturity. I contemplate the years I passed in that terrestial Elysium. The simple food which my solitude afforded sweetened my rural life. My enjoyment was never broken by those cares and perplexing fears which pride and folly create in the lives of populous communities. The fertile soil produced all the food people need in abundance. Fish was in great plenty. The flocks and animals were numerous, the trees loaded with fruit. I never wanted for anything. Who but a fool would not be refreshed by such mildness of clime and land, such beauty and such luxury?

Adapted from *The Works of John Fothergill, M.D.* (London, 1784).

EXCERPT D

The tropical lands invite and repel. The fertile but often shallow soil produces fruits and spices, foods and flowers in abundance. One can wander the land finding food aplenty as it is needed. Little need be done to cultivate what grows so naturally. However, trying to grow indigo or rice or cotton in any quantity is difficult. If luxurious plants grow in abundance, weeds and grasses grow even more abundantly so one is obliged to clear the fields continuously in order to allow one's own crops sunlight and space to grow. This work can be hard at times, especially in the heat and humidity. And this work is constant. Neglect to weed even a week or two and a well cultivated field becomes overgrown with dense vegetation.

The winds often blow gentle as spring breezes bringing to all the fragrance of flowers. But they also bring the hurricanes with their devastating rainstorms and floods. One cannot let the beauty of the region blind one to its imperfections.

Adapted from Peter N. Stearns, Donald R. Schwartz, and Barry K. Beyer, *World History: Traditions and New Directions* (Menlo Park, CA: Addison-Wesley Publishing Company, 1989), p. 363.

INITIATING TRANSFER OF THE SKILL
OF DETECTING BIAS
A Directive Lesson

Goal: To initiate transfer of the skill of detecting bias

Objectives:

To state the main steps in one procedure for detecting bias
To list at least four clues to bias in a film
To identify bias in a film

Materials: Film Excerpts A and B

Teacher	Students
1. Relate this lesson to the preceding lesson. Today we have two short films made in and about Dimbaza, the place we read about yesterday. Let's use them to learn more about this place. As we do be especially alert to any evidence of bias.	

Preview

Teacher	Students
2. Write *bias* on the board.	bias
3. Ask for synonyms.	slanted, a stacked deck, loaded view
4. Ask for examples.	My dad's opinion about the best base-ball team Our newspaper's view about . . .
5. Define *bias.*	A slanted or one-sided view of something

Review

Teacher	Students
6. How do we analyze data to see if they are biased? What *proce-dure*(s) can we use? Probe for as specific steps as possible.	1. State our goal—to find evidence of bias. 2. Recall the clues to bias, such as loaded words, exaggeration, one-sidedness, and so on. 3. Go over the data piece-by-piece to find evidence of these clues. 4. Identify any pattern in this evidence.

Teacher	Students
	5. Match this pattern to our criteria for bias.
	6. State whether or not the source is biased—and what the bias is!
7. What *rules* are useful in searching for bias?	1. Look for a consistent use of loaded words, rhetorical questions, and other clues on the same side.
	2. Look for bias if the author is unknown to us.
	3. Think BIASES and the steps these letters stand for.

Explain

Teacher	Students
8. Explain how to use this skill with films—something students haven't done before. Focus on new *clues* to look for. (Steps remain about the same.)	Some new clues to look for: 1. Mood of background music 2. What narrator says compared to what pictures show 3. Type, tone of voice of narrator 4. Use of color; black/white

Demonstrate

Teacher	Students
9. Project portion of Film A. Point out or have students describe music mood or sound and how it differs from pictures shown. Stop film frequently to discuss mood and to compare narration to pictures shown. Play sound track without projecting picture—then show picture without sound.	Music is in contrast to picture. Narration says one thing, picture depicts something different.

Review

Teacher	Students
10. Have students review or paraphrase clues to look for and steps to use.	1. State purpose. 2. Look/listen to film. 3. Compare music to what is shown; narration to pictures. 4. Notice use of color, kinds of words used by narrator. 5. See if pattern emerges—if it is one-sided or not. 6. If it is, state the bias found.

Teacher	**Students**

Apply

11. Project portion of Film B. Have students (in pairs) look for evidence of bias.

Note use of black and white as contrasted to color to present "good" versus "bad" interpretation; use of loaded words; use of overgeneralizations.

12. Give pairs time to discuss what they see/hear. Show second time.

13. Have several volunteers report their findings and tell the reasons for these.

Reflect

14. Have students explain what they did mentally to identify any bias. Ask: What did you do first? Why? Next? Why? Next? Why? etc. What clues can you search for?

1. Stated purpose—to identify bias.
2. Recalled what to look and listen for, including mood/tone of music, type of narrator voice, use of color, use of words, possible omissions, and how these contradict or match each other.
3. Viewed/listened carefully to find any of these clues.
4. Looked for a pattern.
5. Relooked to confirm ideas.
6. Stated the bias found.

15. Review synonyms of *bias*.

slant, one-sided

16. Review definition of *detecting bias*.

Identifying slanted points of view

17. Ask for places where it is useful to search for bias.

In reading textbooks
Listening to people talk

18. Ask where this can be done in out-of-school life.

Reading, newspapers, watching TV news, movie documentaries

Assignment

19. Watch given TV film tonight. Is it biased? Be prepared to justify your answer tomorrow.

---

note

This lesson should be followed by a number of guided practice lessons and several additional opportunities to apply the skill as presented in this transfer lesson.

FIRST TEST FOR THE SKILL OF DETECTING BIAS
Grade 9 or 10

Name _____ Date _____

1. Circle the letter that precedes the best definition of detecting bias:
   a. Finding things that share similar characteristics
   b. Identifying a slanted or one-sided view of something
   c. Distinguishing relevant from irrelevant data
2. Circle the letter of which speaker has most likely just finished analyzing something for *bias.*

A   B   C

Speaker A:
Look! I think this section connects directly to the first sentence. It gives examples of the topic. Then, I think this last section gives an explanation of the second part of the topic. It all ties together if you can relate these parts to each other like this.

Speaker B:
The items you placed here are all the same. They are all examples of profits. But the items you put over there are all expenses. So they are similar to each other. These items here seem to be all mixed up. What do you call them?

Speaker C:
Well, you certainly made your point. You surely showed us the good side of dogs as pets. But don't dogs have any bad points? I mean, after all, some dogs have been known not to be very friendly to at least some people!

3. The following account was written in 1757. Examine it to see if it reveals any bias on the part of its author. Indicate by marking on the account and/or by writing in the space below any evidence that shows whether it is or is not biased.

Nature has placed in America only children who have not yet become men. When Europeans arrived in the West Indies they found not one single American who could read or write; even today there is not one who can think. These brutes are insensible to everything. Their laziness prevents them from attending to instruction. Deprived of both intelligence and perfectibility they can only obey the impulses of their crude instincts. Their unpardonable weakness forces them either into slavery where it keeps them or into a savage existence they are too cowardly to quit.

QUESTION: Circle the letter preceding the answer:

The above account (a) is not biased, (b) is biased against Americans, (c) is simple propaganda.

4. This excerpt is from a letter written in 1750. Analyze it to see if its author reveals any bias about the subject it is about. Then answer the questions that follow the excerpt.

Our city is a place of evil, the home of only thieves, murderers and brigands. These heartless souls prey on rich and poor alike, taking whatever they please whenever they wish. Violence is their trademark. Hardly a day goes by when I do not see a pocket picked or a gentleman attacked and beaten by ruffians. I have seen bloodied bodies in rutted streets and even floating in the Thames. Danger lurks in every alley. Death is often close at hand.

a. What is the author's bias, if any?

b. What evidence is there that this account shows or does not show a bias?

5. The account below was written in 1760. Analyze it to see if its author has any bias about his or her subject. Then answer or complete the items that follow.

There are several views about the local natives. Some settlers believe them naturally to be liars and thieves. Indeed, these savages never say the truth. They are quick to take unguarded food or wood or pelts. A few settlers excuse this behavior by saying the natives simply consider these items products of their land which they feel they never gave away in the first place. What utter nonsense. To sign a treaty giving land in return for other goods and then to claim the land was never given up is outrageous. The natives here clearly are deceivers of the first order. Never trust them.

a. What is this author's bias, if any?

b. Give evidence from this excerpt that proves this account shows a bias or does not show any bias:

6. In the space under the 1750 account below, list, write, or give a *specific, detailed procedure* and any other information that an eighth-grader could use to detect any bias in this account.

My dear sir, Where will this all end? You claim that sending the dregs of our society to our American colonies will relieve us of a great burden. Perhaps it will. Certainly it will reduce overcrowding in our prisons. It will also reduce the cost of feeding these laggards. We shall finally be rid of the lower elements who contribute nothing to our society.

But tearing them from their families—if they have any who would claim to be so? And putting them on those tiny, leaking wooden ships to be savaged by the galeswept sea? Are these not new burdens? Do you mean for us to carry these matters of conscience forever?

Think what may happen if they do survive in the hostile lands abroad! Will they not cause us expense there, too? Will we not have to protect them—and our lands—from the French or Spanish armies? Could any intelligent person believe that you solve a problem simply by putting it out of sight?

Teaching the Skill of Analyzing for Tone

Eleventh/Twelfth Grades
American Literature

Carolyn Kreiter-Kurylo

High School English Teacher
Fairfax County (Virginia) Public Schools

SKILL DESCRIPTION

Label: Analyzing for Tone

Definition: To break any form of communication down into its component parts to determine the speaker's attitude and feelings toward his or her subject

Synonyms for tone: mood, feeling, attitude

Steps:

1. State the purpose of analyzing for tone.
2. Break the form of communication (e.g., poem, short story, essay, newspaper editorial, painting) down into its component parts.
3. Select those elements that reveal the author's attitude or feelings toward his or her subject.
4. State in a single word (e.g., *approving, mocking, reverent, solemn*) what that attitude is. This is the tone.

Rules:

1. When to analyze for tone?
   - when conducting an analysis of any kind of communication
2. How to start?
   - examine the communication (e.g., read a poem)
   - break it down into its component parts
   - select those elements that reveal the author's attitude or feelings toward his or her subject and make separate lists of these elements
3. What to do if . . .
   - you want to know which elements reveal tone? They tell you something about the author's attitude toward his or her subject.
   - you want to know when to stop breaking the form of communication down? When you've listed all the components that suggest the author's attitude.
   - you want to determine tone from this list of elements? Find a single word that expresses the essence of what the elements suggest about the author's attitude/feelings.

Knowledge:

1. Definitions and understanding of various components typical of the different kinds of communication being examined. For example:

Poetry:
- Figurative language (metaphor, simile, personification, metonymy, symbol, allegory, paradox, overstatement)
- elements that comprise figurative language (diction, imagery)
- sound devices (rhythm, rhyme, meter, assonance, consonance, alliteration, onomatopeia)
- syntactical arrangement of words (style)

Visual Art:
- compositional unity (in figurative art consider theme, subject; in all art, including abstract and nonobjective, consider balance, harmony)
- elements (color, line, light/shade, volume, plane)

INTRODUCING THE SKILL OF ANALYZING FOR TONE
An Inductive Lesson

Goal: To introduce the skill of analyzing a poem for tone

Objectives:

To state some major steps in analyzing a poem for tone
To state at least two rules to follow in analyzing poetry for tone
To identify the tone of given poems

Materials:

Lawrence Ferlinghetti's poem "14"
Carolyn Kreiter-Kurylo's poem "Rosewood"
Theodore Roethke's poem "Night Journey"

Teacher	Students
1. Relate today's lesson to a previous lesson on analyzing Lawrence Ferlinghetti's "14" for diction and imagery. Ask students: What do the word choices and word pictures in "14" tell us about the speaker's feelings toward his topic? To determine this, first we need to know something about tone.	Listen.

Preview

Teacher	Students
2. Write *tone* on the board.	tone
3. Ask for examples of tone from students' daily lives.	A parent's disapproving tone of voice when my room has not been cleaned A friend's playful tone of voice when describing a party to be held soon
4. Ask for example of tone from literature read recently.	MacLeish's serious treatment of his subject in "Ars Poetica"
5. Ask for synonyms.	mood, feeling, attitude, intonation, voice
6. Define *tone* in context of poetry.	The poet's or speaker's attitude or feelings toward his or her subject
7. Now, what does it mean to analyze? Ask for or give synonyms.	take apart, break down

Teacher	**Students**
8. Ask for examples.	Determining what the opposing team does in certain situations Looking at designs to find the basic patterns
9. Ask for or give definition of analysis.	To take apart in order to identify the parts and how they connect to each other
10. Analyzing for tone is taking a piece of literature apart to determine the speaker or author's feeling or attitude about the subject. Today we will learn how to analyze a poem for tone.	

Execute

11. Ask students to take out their copies of Ferlinghetti's "14." Remind them that they have already studied this poem for diction, imagery, theme, lineation, and connotation. Pair the students and ask them to analyze it for *tone.*	
12. Have several volunteers report what they think the tone is.	A playful or whimsical tone

Reflect

13. Ask sudents what they did mentally to identify tone. Have several volunteers tell what they did first? Why? Next? Why? etc. Get several processes on the board.	*Responses:* 1. Read the poem. 2. Looked for images, word choice (diction), theme, line breaks. *Steps:* 1. State purpose of analyzing for tone (i.e., to determine the poet's or speaker's attitude/feelings toward his or her subject). 2. Break poem down into its component parts. 3. Select those elements that reveal the poet's or speaker's attitude/feelings toward the subject: imagery, theme, diction, lineation. 4. State in a single word what that attitude is. This is the tone.

Teacher	Students
14. Have students suggest when it is useful to analyze for tone and how to start the analysis.	Useful to do when trying to understand a poem. Start by reading the poem all the way through—sometimes you get a feeling for its tone.

15. Ask:
  a. How do you know which elements reveal tone?
 	
  b. How do you know when to stop breaking the poem down?
 	
  c. How do you determine tone from this list of elements?
	
	a. The elements, such as images and words used, tell you something about the speaker's attitude.
	
	b. When you've listed all the figurative language and sound devices that suggest the poet's or speaker's attitude.
	
	c. Find a single word that expresses the essence of what the poem's elements suggest about the attitude.

Apply

16. Distribute copies of Carolyn Kreiter-Kurylo's "Rosewood." Have students work alone using the rules and steps on the board to analyze this poem for tone. Circulate around the room to clarify points.	Possible elements students might select to determine tone:
	   diction
	   imagery (nature, music)
	   theme
	   rhythm
	Tone = reverent

17. Have students report and justify responses.	

Review

18. Review the steps used to analyze for tone:
  a. What are some steps you can take to identify the tone of a poem?
    Identify those common to several procedures volunteered.
 	
  b. When would you analyze for tone?
  c. Which elements of a poem determine tone?
	
	a. State what I am trying to do—my purpose.
	Identify things to look for.
	Search for them line-by-line.
	See if they create a general pattern/feeling.
	State in a word the essence of this feeling or attitude.
	
	b. In conducting a poetry analysis.
	
	c. Those that suggest the poet's or speaker's attitude/feelings toward the subject (images, words, theme).

Teacher	**Students**
d. How do you know when to stop breaking a poem down?	d. When you've listed all the components that suggest the attitude toward the subject.
19. Have students write steps/rules/elements (clues) in their notes.	
20. Review and revise definition of analyzing for tone, if necessary.	Analyzing for tone is searching for clues to an author's or speaker's feelings about or attitude towards his or her subject.
21. Have students bridge this skill to other appropriate situations. Where else can you use this skill?	Checking to see my teacher's mood before class starts Listening for the feeling created by a piece of music or song Analyzing a description of something
22. Assign Theodore Roethke's "Night Journey." Have students analyze this poem for tone and be prepared tomorrow to tell what they did to identify the tone.	

note

This type of introductory lesson may work best with average to above-average students (or with any students if the skill is very easy).

Material for Introductory Analyzing for Tone Lessons

ROSEWOOD
Carolyn Kreiter-Kurylo

I have never made a single cut
with the knife into this branch
of rosewood that I did not each
time more powerfully breathe in
the perfume of victory and
rejuvenation: noa noa!
— Noa Noa: The Tahitian Journal,
Paul Gauguin

I have learned to live with nature,
claim her sea, tear shellfish loose
from stones, sleep in a Maori hut
to gather the silence of a Tahitian night.
The moon pushes through bamboo reeds,
reaches me lowering breadfruit
from my mouth. I shape the light's
rays into a reedpipe, imagine music,
nothing between the harmony and sky
but the frail roof of pandanus leaves.
Outside women sing at the foot
of tufted bushes, their breasts:
melodies thrown back from the sway
of coconut trees. Behind them
a mountain speaks out; lush foliage
opens onto a plateau where rosewood
trees fragrance clouds with their vast
branches. As the cadence of my whittling
fills the air, the rosewood's perfume
escapes from peeled bark. I inhale
the purity, and with each breath,
wind rushes through my fingers.

INTRODUCING THE SKILL OF ANALYZING FOR TONE
A Directive Lesson

Goal: To introduce the skill of analyzing a poem for tone

Objectives:

    To state the major steps in analyzing poetry for tone
    To state at least 2 important rules to follow to analyze a poem for tone
    To identify the tone of given poems

Materials:

    Lawrence Ferlinghetti's poem "14"
    Carolyn Kreiter-Kurylo's poem "Rosewood"
    Theodore Roethke's poem "Night Journey"

Teacher	Students
1. Relate today's lesson to a previous lesson on analyzing Lawrence Ferlinghetti's "14" for diction and imagery. Ask students: What do the word choices and word pictures in "14" tell us about the speaker's feelings toward his topic? To determine this, first we need to know something about tone.	Listen

Preview

Teacher	Students
2. Write *tone* on the board.	tone
3. Ask for examples of tone from students' daily lives.	A parent's disapproving tone of voice when my room has not been cleaned A friend's playful tone of voice when describing a party to be held soon
4. Ask for example of tone from literature read recently.	MacLeish's serious treatment of his subject in "Ars Poetica"
5. Ask for synonyms.	mood, feeling, attitude, intonation, voice
6. Define *tone* in context of poetry.	The poet's or speaker's attitude or feelings toward his or her subject
7. Now, what does it mean to analyze? Ask for or give synonyms.	take apart, break down

Teacher	Students
8. Ask for examples.	Determining what the opposing team does in certain situations Looking at designs to find the basic patterns
9. Ask for definition of analysis.	To take apart in order to identify the parts and how they connect to each other
10. Analyzing for tone is taking a piece of literature apart to determine the author or speaker's feeling or attitude about the subject. Today we will learn how to analyze a poem for tone.	

Explain

11. Have the following listed on the chalkboard or on a transparency or handout.

    Steps for Analyzing a Poem for Tone:

    1. State the purpose of analyzing for tone.

    2. Break the poem down into its component parts—phrases and lines.

    3. Identify those elements or clues that reveal the poet's or speaker's attitude/feelings toward the subject.

    4. State in a single word what that attitude is. This is the *tone.*

    Useful Rules to Follow:

    1. Analyze for tone when trying to understand a poem.

    2. Always start by reading the poem as many times as needed to understand theme. Then break the poem down into its component parts.

    3. Select only those elements (imagery, diction, theme, metaphor, lineation, etc.) that tell you the poet's or speaker's attitude toward the subject.

Teacher	**Students**

Demonstrate

12. Ask students to take out their copies of Ferlinghetti's "14." Say: What is the tone?

13. Walk the class through the steps, analyzing for tone with student help as volunteered. Explain why each step is done as it is executed.

Review

14. Have students paraphrase the key steps in analyzing for tone and the reasons for doing each.

1. Tell what I am going to do—to analyze for tone.
2. Look at the poem line-by-line or phrase-by-phrase.
3. Search for clues to author's or writer's feeling, such as: words used, images created, theme stressed, metaphors.
4. State in a word what the tone is.

Apply

15. Distribute copies of Carolyn Kreiter-Kurylo's "Rosewood." Have students, in pairs, analyze for tone by using the rules and steps on the board.

Possible elements students might select to determine tone:
   diction
   imagery (nature music)
   theme
   rhythm
Tone = reverent

16. Have students report and justify their responses.

Reflect

17. Review steps in analyzing for tone.
   a. What are the steps? Ask: What can you do first? Why? Next? Why? Next? Why? etc.

   b. Why analyze poetry for tone?

a. State the purpose.
   Identify the elements to look for.
   Find the elements.
   State in a single word the speaker's attitude.

b. To determine the poet's or speaker's attitude/feelings toward the subject.

Teacher	Students
c. Which elements of a poem suggest tone?	c. Images, diction, theme, metaphor, lineation, etc.
d. How do you know when to stop breaking a poem down?	d. When you've listed all the components that suggest poet's or speaker's attitude toward the subject.
e. What is the definition of analyzing for tone?	e. Breaking a poem down into its component parts to determine the poet's or speaker's attitude toward the subject.
18. Write steps and guidelines for use of skill in notebooks.	
19. Have students tell where else besides analyzing poems they can analyze for tone.	In checking out a parent's mood before asking for something In checking how my teacher feels before requesting a change in the homework assignment or in a test In listening to a song

Assignment

20. Assign Theodore Roethke's "Night Journey" for tomorrow. Have students analyze it for tone and be able to tell how they figured it out.

---

note

This type of introductory lesson may work best with below-average students (or with any students if the skill is very difficult).

GUIDING PRACTICE IN ANALYZING FOR TONE

Goal: To guide practice in the skill of analyzing a poem for tone

Objectives:

To state the major steps in a procedure for analyzing a poem for tone

To state at least 3 important rules to follow in analyzing a poem for tone

To apply the skill of analyzing for tone to identify the poet's or speaker's attitude/feelings toward the subject

Materials:

"Pity This Busy Monster, Manunkind" by e.e. cummings

"Reflections on a Gift of Watermelon Pickle Received from a Friend Called Felicity" by John Tobias

Teacher	Students

Preview

Teacher	Students
1. Relate this lesson to the previous lesson on analyzing a poem for tone. Now that we know how to analyze a poem for tone, we can look at additional poems to determine the poet's or speaker's attitude/feelings toward the subject.	
2. Write *tone* on the board.	tone
3. Ask for synonyms.	mood, feeling, attitude
4. Define *tone* in the context of poetry.	The poet's or speaker's attitude or feelings toward the subject
5. Ask for examples of tone: a. from outside of school	a. A parent's disapproving tone of voice about a daughter's short skirt A young man's persuasive tone of voice that convinces his girlfriend to pay for his ticket to the movies
b. from previous classes	b. Ferlinghetti's whimsical tone in his poem "14" Carolyn Kreiter-Kurylo's reverent tone in "Rosewood"
6. Ask for synonyms and definition of analyzing:	

Teacher	Students
a. What are some words that mean the same as analyzing?	a. taking apart, breaking down
b. What does analyzing mean?	b. taking something apart to identify the parts and see how they connect to each other and to the whole
7. Ask for a definition of *analyzing for tone.*	Studying a poem or piece of literature to determine how the speaker or author feels about the subject

Review

Teacher	Students
8. Ask: What can we do mentally to analyze a poem for tone?	*One Procedure:* 1. State the purpose of analyzing for tone. 2. Break the poem down into its component parts. 3. Select those elements (imagery, diction, etc.) that reveal the poet's or speaker's attitude/feelings toward the subject. 4. State in a single word what that attitude is. This = tone.
9. What rules are useful to follow?	1. When conducting an analysis for tone, first read the poem. 2. Then. . . .
10. What is it helpful to know to analyze a poem for tone?	The various elements, such as diction and lineation, that reveal the poem's tone
11. What kinds of obstacles could occur in analyzing a poem for tone, and how would you overcome them?	Students may not understand the connotative meaning of a word. They should find a dictionary (denotative) definition of that word. Then determine the connotative meaning from the word's placement (context) in the poem.

Execute

Teacher	Students
12. Pair students and ask them to analyze e. e. cummings' "Pity This Busy Monster, Manunkind" for tone.	

Teacher	**Students**

Ponder

13. Review what the students did mentally to carry out the skill. Ask:

　　a. What did you do to identify the tone of the poem? What did you do first? Why? Next? Why? Next? Why? etc.

　　b. Have several volunteers tell the procedures they used and tell why they did what they did. List the steps on the board.

　　c. Accept a number of procedures and help the class look for common elements in them.

One Possible Procedure:

1. Stated my purpose—to identify the tone.
2. Recalled some clues to tone (diction, imagery, metaphor, etc.).
3. Looked at the poem line-by-line to see if I could find these clues.
4. Determined how they added up—the impression they gave.
5. Stated the tone in a word.

Another Possible Procedure:

1. Knew I was to look for tone.
2. Read the entire poem.
3. Noticed certain words repeated, certain metaphors.
4. Got an idea of the tone.
5. Reread the poem carefully looking for other cues to see if my idea of the tone held up.
6. It did, so I stated the tone.

14. Ask: When is it useful to analyze for tone?

In trying to understand the meaning of a poem

15. Ask: What words mean the same as:

　　a. tone?

　　b. analyzing?

　　a. mood, feeling, attitude

　　b. taking apart

16. Ask for a definition of analyzing a poem for tone.

Taking a poem apart line-by-line to determine an author's or speaker's attitude toward his/her subject

17. Have students add to or modify their notes on analyzing for tone, as needed.

18. Help students think of where else is is useful to be able to analyze for tone or mood.

Checking out a person before asking him or her for something
Analyzing any work of literature
Looking at a painting

Teacher	**Students**

Content Discussion

19. Say to students: Now that we have discovered the tone of e. e. cummings' "Pity This Busy Monster, Manunkind," let's look at a poem with an entirely different tone. Turn in your books to "Reflections on a Gift of Watermelon Pickle Received from a Friend Called Felicity" by John Tobias.

20. Continued discussion of content.

---

note

In teaching this skill, additional guided practice lessons like this one will be needed. These additional lessons can use the same strategy that is used in this lesson. Students should also have several opportunities to use this skill on their own after appropriate guided practice.

INITIATING TRANSFER OF THE SKILL
OF ANALYZING FOR TONE
A Directive Lesson

Goal: To initiate transfer of the skill of analyzing for tone

Objectives:

To state the major steps in a procedure for analyzing for tone

To state at least two rules to follow in analyzing visual art for tone

To apply the skill of analyzing for tone in order to state the tone/mood of selected paintings

Materials:

A reproduction of *Crows Over the Wheat Field* by Vincent Van Gogh

A reproduction of *A Field of Poppies* by Claude Monet

Teacher	Students

Preview

Teacher	Students
1. Relate this lesson to the previous lesson on Van Gogh and his art. Ask students: What do the elements of Van Gogh's *Crows Over the Wheat Field* tell us about his feelings toward his subject?	
2. Say to the class: We can answer this question by analyzing for tone or mood. In the context of art, the term *mood* is used more frequently than *tone* to define the artist's attitude toward his or her subject and to depict the atmosphere of the art piece.	
3. Write *tone* on the board.	tone
4. Ask for synonyms.	mood, feelings, attitude
5. Ask for a definition of tone/mood in the context of painting.	The painter's attitude or feeling toward his subject
6. Ask for or give examples of tone: a. in out-of-school life	a. A parent's harsh tone of voice in telling a child to shut the door The mocking tone of a satiric editorial in the newspaper

Teacher	Students
	The playful shouts of children on a playground
b. in this course to date	b. Tone in poems, such as "14" by Ferlinghetti Tone in other forms of communication, such as short stories, editorials, etc.
7. Ask for a definition of analyzing (and for synonyms and examples, if necessary).	Analyzing is taking something apart to identify the parts and how they relate to each other and to the entire thing. It is like breaking down or separating.
8. Ask for a definition of *analyzing for tone.*	Taking something apart to identify how the author or speaker feels towards his or her subject

Review

9. Help the students review different ways to analyze a poem for tone—the steps and any rules to follow.	*One Procedure:* 1. State your purpose—identify tone. 2. Recall clues to tone—use of words, diction, imagery, lineation, metaphor 3. Read the poem line-by-line to find any of these clues. 4. See how the clues add up—the impression they give. 5. State the impression in a word or phrase—this is the tone.

Explain

10. Tell the students that this same skill can be used to better understand painting. We can analyze paintings for mood or tone.	
11. Explain that the process is the same but the clues you look for differ from those used in dealing with poetry. The clues to look for in analyzing a painting for mood include color, line, texture, theme, shape, figure-ground relationship, etc.	

Teacher	**Students**

Demonstrate

12. Using Van Gogh's "Crows Over the Wheat Field," show how the steps of analyzing for tone can be used to infer the mood communicated by the artist—his feeling toward the subject of the painting.

   Proceed step-by-step, explaining why each step is done as it is done as steps are projected on overhead.

Review

13. Have the students paraphrase the steps that have been demonstrated and define the clues they can look for.

14. Have several volunteer.

Possible Response:
1. State the goal of identifying the mood.
2. Recall clues to look for in determining mood of a painting.
3. Look at all parts of the painting to see if you can find these clues.
4. See what impression the combination of the clues gives.
5. State the mood of the painting.

Apply

15. Have the students work in pairs to analyze Claude Monet's "A Field of Poppies" for mood.

16. Have students report what they think the mood is.

serene, one of peacefulness

Reflect

17. Have students reflect on and explain how they determined the tone/mood of this painting.

Some may look at the painting and intuitively determine the tone/mood, focusing on the composition as a whole, rather than on its parts. Then they may go back to check out their "guesses" or try to follow the steps reviewed earlier.

18. Review the steps in the various procedures students are using.

Teacher	Students
19. Focus on the steps common to most of the procedures described —list these.	1. Think about the task—identifying mood. 2. Think about or recall clues to mood in painting. 3. Study the painting completely, searching for the clues. 4. See how the clues found add up. 5. State the general impression made by the clues as the mood.
20. Have students identify and explain some of the clues or elements of mood to look for in studying a painting.	Color, shading, lines, figure-ground relations, texture, color combinations, etc.
21. Have students review and, if necessary, revise the definition of *analyzing for tone.*	
22. Have students suggest where else they could use the skill of analyzing for tone or mood—and what clues they might look for in each.	A film (similar clues as colors, texture, composition of scenes, focus plus background music, dialogue, diction, etc.) Musical pieces—songs, etc. (looking for tempo, pitch, repeating melodies, rhythm etc.) Political speeches (looking for kinds of words and word patterns, tempo, facial expression, etc.)

Assignment

23. Assign two paintings to study for mood. Have the students be prepared to tell the mood tomorrow and also explain how they decided on their responses.

note

This lesson should be followed by a number of guided practice lessons and several additional opportunities to apply the skill as presented in this transfer lesson.

FIRST TEST FOR THE SKILL OF ANALYZING FOR TONE
Grade 11 or 12

Name _____   Date _____

1. Define *analyzing for tone.*

2. Here are two excerpts from an essay analyzing Robert Wallace's "Swimmer in the Rain." Circle the letter of the paragraph that best indicates *analysis for tone.*

A

"Swimmer in the Rain" is a light, delicate poem that creates a fragile image of man at one with nature. The speaker is somewhat transcendental in his attitude toward the natural world, with man being at one with it. The man exists, the rain falls, the marine life persists, and "wet is wet." Like the creek that becomes a mirror to the swimmer, the poem is a mirror to a reverent scene.

B

The form of the stanzas themselves—short and narrow—suggest the falling of the rain. We can see them as rain dropping down the page. Wallace frames his poem with the swimmer and "no one but him." By opening and closing his poem with the solitary swimmer, Wallace reminds us of the delicacy of the scene. "No one but him" is surrounded by the cool raindrops falling upon the water and the undisturbed natural world. We see that the poem's form comments on its meaning; just as the swimmer frames the natural imagery in the poem, he also exists as part of that world.

3. Analyze the following poem to determine its tone.

[Archibald MacLeish's "The End of the World" to be inserted here.]

a. Tone:

b. Which poetic elements suggest the poet's or speaker's attitude/feelings toward his or her subject?

4. Read the poem below carefully. Then, on your own paper, write detailed
   directions that a ninth-grader could follow to identify the tone of this
   poem.

THE LIE*
Carolyn Kreiter-Kurylo

I no longer remember why I shouted *merde*
in Latin class, thinking no one will understand,

even though the teacher did, peering
over her bright red spectacles. I held

my stance, a ninth grader, shy, and then began
to quiver, sank to my desk when she asked

if my father knew I used such language. *Yes,
ma'am,* I wanted to say. *He uses that word, too,*

except in English. That evening I feared
the phone would ring, wondered how I could

get my father to sign the one-hundred lines
I had to write. *Daddy,* I said, sliding my arms

around his shoulders, *I'll bet you can't sign*
this sheet of paper with your eyes shut.

I turned in the lines the next day,
his signature bold in the upper corner.

Tonight, nearly thirty years later, I wonder
if all lies are deceitful, or if some are

too clever to worry over. I think about
my father who has gotten the most out of life

by shutting his eyes to what he never cares
to see. Over the phone, he tells me he has

seen the Latin teacher at the grocery store.
Always full of talk, he says, and in the same

breath, asks if all is well. *Oh, yes,* I reply,
knowing he never held onto his children's lies.

SOURCES FOR POEMS AND PAINTINGS

Inductive Skill Introduction:

1. "14" by Lawrence Ferlinghetti (*A Coney Island of the Mind.* New York: New Directions Publishing Corporation, © 1958.)

2. "Rosewood" by Carolyn Kreiter-Kurylo (© 1988; included in text)

3. "Night Journey" by Theodore Roethke (*Collected Poems of Theodore Reothke.* New York: Doubleday & Co. © 1940.)

Directive Skill Introduction:

Same as above

Guiding Practice in the Skill:

1. "Pity This Busy Monster, Manunkind" by e. e. cummings (*Poems: 1923–1954.* New York: Harcourt, Brace, Jovanovich, © 1954.)

2. "Reflections on a Gift of Watermelon Pickle Received from a Friend Called Felicity" by John Tobias (*New Mexico Quarterly,* The University of New Mexico Press, Spring 1961.)

Transferring the Skill:

1. *Crows Over the Wheat Field* by Vincent van Gogh (Meyer Schapiro. *Van Gogh.* New York: Doubleday & Company, 1980, p. 131.)

2. *A Field of Poppies* by Claude Monet (*Impressionism.* By the editors of Realities. Secaucus, NJ: Chartwell Books, © 1973, pp. 96–97).

Test for the Skill of Analyzing for Tone:

1. "The End of the World" by Archibald MacLeish (*Collected Poems of Archibald MacLeish 1917–1952.* Boston: Houghton Mifflin, © 1952.)

2. "Musee des Beaux Arts" by W. H. Auden (*Collected Poems of W. H. Auden.* Ed. Edward Mendelson. New York: Random House, © 1940, renewed 1968.)

part **III**

Teacher Reflections on Launching the Teaching of Thinking Skills

INTRODUCTION

Learning new or different ways to teach something can be difficult and even frustrating. Trying to manage a class, teach a new subject or a particular thinking skill, use unfamiliar teaching strategies, and ask new kinds of questions are more than most of us can handle all at one time. Moreover, things don't always go as planned. When this happens, remember that it's not you who is at fault. It's the fact you are trying something new and perhaps rather complex. Don't get discouraged because a lesson doesn't work as intended on the first—or even second or third—try.

Experts claim that it may take up to 15 to 20 practices to feel comfortable in using a new skill and to execute it skillfully. This is as true of your learning to use new strategies to *teach* a thinking skill as it is of your students trying to master the thinking skills you seek to teach them. Learning new ways to teach takes time, effort, and skill. There will be setbacks along the way. Perhaps if you realize this, it will be easier to handle any frustrations or problems that do occur in this learning process.

Most of the teachers who designed the materials in Part II of this handbook experienced problems with these materials when they first actually tried to teach or use them. This was true of the lessons they tried to teach and especially true of their introductory lessons. Some of them have reflected on their experiences in introducing a thinking skill to students using an earlier version of the lesson plans included here. Reading what they did in teaching these lessons, what happened, how they felt, and what they learned may alert you to what you might expect when you teach such a lesson for your first time.

In reading these brief reflections, notice especially that these teachers *learned* from their experiences. Although the lessons may not have gone as they originally intended, they got ideas on what they should have done to make them work. The plans included here incorporate these changes. These teachers went on, rewrote these plans, and wrote and taught additional lessons using these and other strategies. Just as their students learned from their first halting and incomplete efforts to apply a new thinking skill and articulate how they did it, so, too, did these teachers learn from their initial efforts to introduce these skills and gradually become more skilled at teaching these and similar lessons. They didn't give up. In fact, they are alive and well—and teaching thinking skills with renewed confidence, enthusiasm, and sense of accomplishment. Learning how to teach thinking skills does take time and effort but is well worth both.

REFLECTIONS ON MY VERY FIRST TRY AT INTRODUCING THE SKILL OF DECISION MAKING BY ELIZABETH CALVERT

''*Write an inductive lesson plan* to introduce a thinking skill to your students.''
    Write a what?
    ''An inductive lesson is a lesson where you, as a teacher, are trying to help students find out more about how they do a skill.'' Great. I needed all the help I could get at this point. ''But, there is one pitfall.'' Oh, no. ''You take the chance during this lesson of teaching the skill wrong.'' How can you teach it wrong if you don't really know what it is? ''If it is taught wrong, you may have to spend an exorbitant amount of time undoing the incorrect learning that has been done.'' Wonderful.

I figured that I was not going to be able to do this by myself. And, as it turned out, neither was the person seated next to me.

So we became partners. And later we met at the library.

We labored over this lesson. We had not even defined any steps in the skill of decision making. But that is where we began.

We seemed to make it through the initial stages of designing an inductive lesson plan. We made it through the Preview stage but we got stuck at the Execute stage. We both had different ideas about the kinds of decisions that we should ask students to make and think about. I wanted to ask them something like: ''Here is a list of 50 items. You are on an island. You are going to be there for an unstated amount of time. You can only keep 15 of those items. What are you going to keep?'' My partner wanted to do something different. She wanted to have students make a decision about something that was relevant to them; something that was not so trivial. *She* was really an experienced teacher. I wasn't.

Addition of another period to the school day? I did not like it. It was an issue like abortion—too controversial and heated in our locality. It was an issue about which people automatically jump to their gut feelings. I did not want to deal with an issue that would get too involved. ''But,'' my partner stated, ''these are the kinds of things that kids and teachers are being asked to make decisions about.'' ''Yes, they are,'' I thought. ''They are being asked to make even bigger decisions at earlier ages. Drugs. Sex.''

So we went with the issue.

''Does anyone want to teach their lesson to us?''

Of course. I did. I was very proud of all the work that we put into this lesson. I was very confident that I knew what it was I was supposed to do. Sure, I will teach our lesson to the class. I will even go first.

Oh my, another decision. Will I ever get away from them?

Do not let my initial confidence deceive you. After I volunteered to do the lesson, my first reaction was, ''AAAAHHHH! What have I done? I'm going to screw it up. Everyone is going to learn the skill wrong. Then I am going to be up a creek with no paddle, no boat, and no life preserver!'' Of course, my language was not quite that.

That is when my rehearsal started. Anytime I would think about making a decision (i.e., driving my car, what to eat for dinner, whether or not to go to class), I would mentally go through the process that I took to reach the decision that I did. What did I do first? Why? Next? Why? Next? And so on!

I started to memorize what I was going to do when I stood up in front of the class for the first time. ''Hi, I'm Liz. Today we are going to learn. . . . '' Lousy introduction. I need an attention getter. Think. Think. Think. Just be relaxed. Be yourself. Do what comes naturally. Do not even rehearse an introduction.

I did not.

But I did rehearse the plan for our lesson. With an inductive lesson, there is quite a bit of improvising, so I was going to have to think quickly on my feet. Pressure. What do I do if the students do not tell me steps that are even remotely close to the steps that I have identified? They have to be close, don't they? Well, we were soon going to find out how close they were!

A week before I was to teach the lesson, I started to go over in my mind the major things that I needed to cover—synonyms, examples, definition, bridging at the end of the lesson. I did not want to leave anything out. As I would go to bed, I would say the lesson over and over until I fell asleep. Before I knew it, it was time to teach the lesson.

Teach the lesson!

I made myself some notecards to use in case I forgot something. I used them to check myself to make sure that I stayed on course with the direction of the lesson that we had written. I did not want to stray from it if I did not have to.

As soon as I started to teach our lesson, I felt really good. I wanted to laugh because I felt so good. I was nervous, sure, but I knew if I made a mistake that it was not going to cost me my life or anything like that. I just went up there and did what seemed to come naturally.

Introduction.   I wanted to get the students, actually my colleagues, into decision making. I asked them why they chose to sit where they were sitting—friends, tablemates, whatever. I let them know that they had just made a decision. Yes, I could see that this got their attention. Or were they just paying attention because I had enough guts to get up and do this? Who cares? At least they were listening to me.

Preview.   This part of the lesson was easy. I received many responses. Synonyms, examples, and definitions were easy to get. I found myself wanting to write down all the definitions that they gave me because most of them were pretty good. I asked if someone could give me a composite of the three that I had heard. No one could. This was frustrating. Next time, I know that I will write down one, maybe two, definitions. As I look back, there was no real need for me to spend as much time on the definition as I did.

Execute.   Easy. I asked the class to read an article that dealt with the addition of a seventh period to the school day and asked them to make a decision about it. *Fatal Error!* I knew it as soon as I said it. I knew there was going to be confusion. As it turns out, there was great confusion as to what decision they were being asked to make. Also, reflecting on the article that I handed out and on what was discussed after I did my lesson, I would really spell out, letter by letter, what decision it is that I want the students to make when I teach this lesson to my own students. I would choose something that was perhaps more trivial—maybe even use the same issue except have the article rewritten from a more objective point of view.

Reflect.   I never thought pulling teeth would hurt so much. Because I had obscured the decision, no one was very clear on their thinking. I had to "bait" every question—or so I felt. Only two people volunteered answers. What was I doing wrong? Frustration. So I wrote what I could on the board regarding steps people used. After about ten minutes of struggling, I decided to move on.

Apply.   I had my classmates resume the discussion that they were having on the issue of the addition of a seventh period to the school day. I gave them about ten minutes to do this. Here, I gave a sigh of relief. I felt that I no longer had to pull teeth and I could sit down—which I did. I listened in on the discussions that were taking place around the room and soon realized that in introducing a skill, I would not ever again use an example that was so heated and directly related to the students that they would get so caught up in the issue. I felt the "heat" was happening, but I was too far into it to turn back.

Review.   I knew at this point that I would have to bait the questions again, hoping that someone would get off of the issue. It happened, slowly and painfully. Next time, *no hot issues* for introduction of a thinking skill. I had learned my lesson—that was for sure.

I soon realized that I would shortly be running out of time, and sure enough, I was. I decided at that point to stop the discussion and refocus everyone's attention on the board, asking for more synonyms and examples. I also asked if anyone wanted to add or revise the first definition we had put on the board. They did not, so I asked one more time for students to bridge this skill. DONE!

As I reflected on the lesson plan that we wrote and I taught, I realized some specific things about an inductive lesson plan. First, it is a very hard lesson to teach. There is so much room for error if you, as a teacher, are not sure of what you are doing. If I were going to teach an inductive skill introduction again, I would research about four different sources to find out what they say about the skill I wanted to focus on. I would not like to go into the class cold.

Second, the content of the lesson cannot overpower the skill. The students need to be able to establish that they are talking directly about the process. The content is not as important. That was hard to do in my lesson. Controversial issues are great—for advanced students. These issues would be great at a guided practice lesson stage or maybe even later.

Finally, the next time I do an inductive lesson, I am going to add a step in which the students, before we reflect as a class on the process, *write* how they mentally did the skill. This, I would hope, would help them use the metacognitive skills that I want them to develop. By having them write first, maybe they would be more willing to volunteer their thoughts on how they did it rather than listening to someone else.

After reflecting on the whole process of choosing a skill and writing my first introduction to that skill, an amazing thing happened to me. I know more about decision making and where to look to find information about decision making than I ever thought anyone would want to know. And at the same time, I still don't know anything about the skill—I know more than most, but not like the experts.

I am finding myself consciously going through the steps of decision making when I have to make an involved decision. What am I going to do? What's the problem here? Well, I could do A or B or even C. I think I will do C. But what are the consequences? Which is best? What is my plan of action? How did the plan work? I dream about the steps. But that's not so bad, is it?

Knowing these steps is vital to my being able to teach them to a group of high school students. The more comfortable I am with the subject—in this case, the skill—the better teacher I am. The more I read about decision making, the more expert I feel I am becoming. Maybe someday I will write a book or an article on the process of decision making. Then, and only then, will I be recognized as an expert. For now, I have to settle for being in the car that leads to that destination.

Teaching a thinking skill is so vital, not only to academics but to everyday life. There are so many kids out there who don't like to think. It's like a microwave dinner—pull a TV dinner out of the freezer, pop it in the microwave. Ding. In four minutes they have the results. No so with making important decisions or any other complex thinking skill. The only machine that will do the thinking for them is their own mind. Thinking can be hard work. Who wants to work? Well, students might want to work instead of allowing a microwave to do the cooking for them if they could see and feel the gratification that comes when they can see and say, ''I did this myself!'' They thought of it and they are proud.

Pride. I thrive on it. I want people to be proud of me. I want people to say, ''That Liz, she really can think. She comes up with so many good ideas. Where did she learn to think?''

My answer: ''I thought of it myself.''

INTRODUCING THE SKILL OF DECISION MAKING: REFLECTIONS ON MY FIRST ATTEMPT BY JEROME F. ROBBINS

Decision making is a skill that can be taught in a great variety of subjects or content areas. I found the use of a moral dilemma story as the content for processing an interesting and stimulating one for both the students and myself. The real difficulty or challenge of using a moral dilemma as a vehicle for introducing this skill was that I had to be especially vigilant in maintaining the focus on the students' thought processes and keeping them directed toward the main parts of decision making. It would have been very easy to get sidetracked into collectively solving the dilemma. It seemed that the desire to solve the dilemma and discuss the alternatives and their worthiness was an overpowering temptation for some individuals. This tendency of the learners—to solve the dilemma rather than concentrate on the process—is something I had to keep in mind all through the lesson.

I chose to present my lesson inductively, as this approach involves the students almost immediately in doing the new operation. The students were experiencing firsthand the procedures and rules that seem to be implicit in how decision making works. I presented this lesson to students that were fifth-through seventh-grade age, were above average in intelligence, and had already demonstrated some proficiency in thinking. The first two steps of introducing and executing the skill went very close to my plan. The students generated appropriate synonyms: *choosing, deciding, selecting,* and came up with the working definition of ''to account for all the possibilities and choose the most favorable one.'' I made it a point to remind them that they were already using the skill everyday and that we were going to be practicing to become better decision makers. I emphasized that when faced with difficult decisions it is important for us to know that we have made the best decision for the circumstances and that we personally can live with that decision.

I chose to read the dilemma story ''What Should Graham Do?'' and have the class listen carefully to the reading. I could have had copies of the story for each person to read individually or to follow along with as I read it, but I felt at the time that just listening to the story being read with appropriate flow and emphasis by one person would be better as a whole-group experience. Before the reading, I had the students sit in pairs, triads, and groups of four so that they could discuss their reactions afterwards with little disruption or confusion about with whom to discuss it. After I read the story, the groups were given several minutes to respond and discuss together a solution for Graham. I wandered around the room, listening to their conversations but not interfering. When I sensed that most of the groups had either determined a solution or had at least generated several alternatives, I called for their attention.

I then asked for each group to respond orally with what they had resolved for Graham to do. As their choices were given, we listened to them but I did not put these choices on the board. I did not want the students to focus on the choices or cause attention to be diverted to the selection of the best choice. Instead, we began to reflect on the mental processes that the students were involved in that generated their decisions. As one student from a group verbalized the steps that they went through, I wrote the steps on the board and did not put them into any particular order—even though I encouraged the students to state them in the order that they had done them. When another student responded with her group's steps, I just added them to the list without separating any. After recording contributions from several students, I had them all review the list and put the steps into an order, mentally, thinking about steps that others had mentioned and where the steps might fit into their own process. At this time, students pointed out some of the steps listed as being similar or the same as others, so we combined or eliminated some of the steps until the students were satisfied with the list.

We then had about ten steps listed. Time was at a premium, so as one child told me an order for the steps, I wrote the number of the step to the left of it on the board, rather than taking the time to rewrite the steps in order. I did this again for several more students. Looking at the different orders, it was apparent that the students' concentration was on criteria for judging the best solution and not on identifying or generating alternatives. The children had done a superb job of trying to predict outcomes for each alternative, but had failed to see the important process that they had engaged in—that of coming up with their alternatives. At this time, I switched to a more direct approach, and pointed out to the students that actually listing alternatives or generating the options was a step in itself, and I added it to the list of steps.

We now needed to clarify these steps so that the class could apply the procedure to a new situation. I told the students that they had, in effect, come up with the steps that are considered to be useful in the decision-making process. But I wanted to collect these steps into a list of more general steps, which I then recorded on the board for the class. The first step was to define the task: "What should Graham do?" Step two, we decided, was to identify the alternatives, which the class had done but hadn't put a label on. Step three was to analyze the alternatives in terms of consequences or outcomes, and of criteria, which they very thoughtfully selected. The fourth step was to rank the alternatives according to their values, which they had also done. The last step was making the choice. I needed to paraphrase the students' thinking processes for them in order to help them put the steps into a logical sequence. My original approach had to be modified to include some direct presentation of material to assist the class in clarifying their experience.

I noticed after the lesson that many of the group's steps were related to setting criteria for judging their choices. Because I was running out of time, I was unable to pursue this aspect of their processing. I wanted the children to be able to apply the skill one time on their own before we closed the lesson. If I had had time, I would have discussed more about their setting criteria on personal values. I did mention several times there was no absolute right answer to the dilemma and that we were focusing on the process itself.

After quickly reviewing the skill steps, I handed out a copy of "What Should Susan Do?" and instructed the students to read it to themselves, go through the decision-making steps we had discussed, and, when ready, talk it over within their groups. In listening to their conversations, I noted that some came up with their decisions and then went back through the steps on the board and compared with each other how the steps fit with their own process. Others individually referred to the list and adhered to it step by step as they went through the process and then discussed this with their classmates.

During the review, again I let them respond briefly with their alternatives for Susan but held them to the task of reflecting on and reporting the processes of how they came to a final decision. Everyone seemed to feel comfortable with the list of steps and their order. We reviewed our working definition, making a few minor changes, and closed with the thought that making decisions is an everyday task and we can get lots of practice. The more we use the skill of decision making, the more comfortable and confident we will feel about the decisions we make.

How did I feel doing this lesson for the first time? I felt nervous, uncertain, and awkward. I was concerned that I might leave something out or miss a step in the lesson. When I first wrote my lesson plan, I could see the reasonableness and logic of an inductive strategy for introducing a skill were laid out and developed. But within the whole lesson there seemed to be just too much to keep track of comfortably. So I made an outline of the lesson written in large letters on notecards that I could lay on the cart in front of me or pick up and casually refer to during the lesson. I included key phrases and questions I didn't want to forget to use and also noted possible responses I was seeking from the students. On a separate card I listed the main steps of decision making. I made a note to myself to concentrate on the skill and not on the alternatives generated. Making the note cards helped a great deal as a review of the lesson for myself and took away the anxiety I felt of missing a step because I could refer to the notes during the lesson. Anyone presenting a skill lesson for the first time should make some notes to refer to during the presentation.

Adding to my nervousness was the fact that I was presenting the lesson to a group of students that I had not worked with as a class before. I had also invited another teacher into the classroom to observe the lesson. If I had it to do over again, I would suggest that in presenting a new skill or lesson for the first time one work with a group of students that he or she is familiar with and that no other observers be in the room. I would have felt more comfortable making a mistake had I been working with my own students without another teacher present.

Another observation I would like to share is that when nearing the end of classtime, I had a choice of giving the students the remaining time to complete the application of the skill step and eliminating the review, or of cutting their application short and doing the review step. I chose to stop them in the processing and complete the review as planned. I feel that it was extremely important and worthwhile to have done this. It brought the students' attention back to their original definition of the skill and gave them valuable moments to reflect on their beginning ideas and how their processing had changed or confirmed their thinking.

I enjoyed using an inductive strategy to introduce a skill for the first time as the students are deeply involved in learning, processing, and generating the ideas themselves. However, I would suggest that one be prepared to switch to a more directive strategy at any time during the lesson if the need arises. At one point, during this particular lesson, I had to intervene and give the class a step that I felt they had missed.

Overall, this lesson went as planned, with some direct input by me. The total lesson time was 40 minutes and I could have extended it another 10 minutes. This lesson could be done successfully with bright students as young as third-grade age and is certainly appropriate for any sixth- to eighth-graders in the context of language arts or social studies.

INTRODUCING THE SKILL OF CONCEPTUALIZING TO EIGHTH-GRADERS
BY SUZANNE GARDNER

Conceptualizing is a complicated skill to teach. I've experimented with a variety of ways to introduce it. My favorite introductory lesson is about wolves. I wish I could say that I just sat down one day and whipped up the lesson, but it's more accurate to say the lesson composed itself as a result of a variety of experiences. In the Spring of 1987, the Smithsonian Museum had a magnificent display of Robert Bateman's wildlife paintings, which I went to see. While there, I purchased a poster-size copy of a wolf pack shown at twilight staring cautiously at the viewer(s). Bateman had managed to place the viewer, at least this viewer, in a hushed moment of awe. There was something about those wolves that made me feel they were as frightened by my presence as I was of theirs. I bought the poster for no other reason than to relive the experience of exchanging glances, through tree branches, with those wolves whenever I wished.

Months later, I was browsing through a book store and noticed a picture book about wolves by Jean Craighead George (author of the Newbery Award winner, *Julie of the Wolves*). In her story, a wolf had fallen prey to animals much smaller than himself because he had been wounded and separated from his pack. The situation seemed like an interesting turn of fate to me. Written in rhyme and based on a true event, it was a must for my book collection. I bought it without even thinking about the poster tucked away in my closet.

It wasn't until I started planning an ecology lesson that I saw a connection between Bateman's picture, George's book, and my skill-teaching goals. It occured to me that animals like the wolf have a ''bad rep'' and are somehow not deemed ''worthy'' of our concern. Everyone cares about a cute deer or rabbit, but what of the ''vicious wolf''? I concluded that concepts can play an important role in environmental issues. That's when I decided to introduce the skill of conceptualizing in my science class and realized that I already had everything I needed.

I was excited about the lesson. I wanted my students to learn how to conceptualize, how to invent their own concepts. I also secretly hoped to change their concepts about wolves—not just because I wanted to sensitize them to the plight of less popular animals but because I suspected that middle schoolers (particularly eighth-graders) could grasp the first steps in conceptualizing quickly and would benefit most from a focus on the way concepts are modified to fit new information. I wondered whether much of their maturational turmoil and confusion might actually be a result of a shift from accepting others' concepts to formulating their own.

I knew the focus was supposed to be on the skill instead of the topic, so I reserved use of the overhead and screen for the steps I would like to show the students. But I wanted a visual representation of the conceptual change I hoped would occur, so I decided to record their comments about the topic—wolves—on unruled easel paper. Besides, the resulting lists would serve as a word bank for practicing the skill.

I started, as usual, by writing the word *conceptualizing* on the board.

"Could anyone tell me what a concept is?" I asked, as I underlined the letters *concept* within the word.

"Mental image." *Perfect.* I wrote the words next to *concept.* "What does that mean?"

"The picture you have of something in your mind," another student offered, pointing to her head.

I nodded, "Can anyone think of another word for concept?"

"An idea or a belief about something?" a student suggested.

"What would conceptualizing mean then?"

"How we form a concept?" *The lesson has officially begun.*

I had a definition for the skill plus some synonyms. Now I wanted to provide some kind of motivation, to pique their interest in learning the skill of conceptualizing. I had a plan I hoped would set the stage: demonstrate to them that they've been conceptualizing all along and show them how useful it would be to have more control over the process. Obviously, I couldn't introduce "wolf" to eighth-graders as though it was a concept to which they had never been exposed. After all, students don't come to us with a blank slate. The mind is a meaning maker and I knew the students would have formed some sort of concept about wolves before this.

"I want you to consider what you already know about wolves. Take a few minutes to jot down words and phrases that are part of your mental image of wolves." The students started quickly; they were used to my asking them to do this sort of writing in their learning logs. On cue, when I announced it was time to share, they began responding. (I've always dreaded a supervisor's walking in at this time. No raising of hands, my back to the students, there's total relinquishment of control to students as I feverishly try to record answers being given.) I stepped back and looked at the end result, giving the students time to inspect it as well. *Dangerous, mean, vicious, cruel, long teeth, howl, meat eaters, lonely, mountains,* and more.

Just as I had suspected, the list was filled with words that had negative connotations.

"These words represent what you 'know' about wolves. How do you think you formed these ideas?"

They mentioned tales like "The Three Little Pigs" and "Little Red Riding Hood," things they'd heard about wolves, things they'd seen. *Good. They realize the features they attributed to wolves came from the way wolves were commonly depicted in these stories and pictures.*

"Now, I'd like you to look at this picture. What do you suppose is the artist's concept of wolves? What might he be trying to say about wolves through his picture? Jot down any new words and phrases that come to mind."

As I walked around the room with the poster of Robert Bateman's painting, I felt a sudden sense of doubt. *What if they don't see what I saw in the picture? What if the picture merely confirms their present ideas?* There was silence, except for the scratchings of pens and pencils on paper as the students wrote their responses. It seemed like a long time before I asked them to contribute to a second list, which I again recorded on easel paper. *Cautious, soft, packs, frightened, timid, dog-like*—words that showed wolves in a slightly different light had been elicited by the painting. Doubt was replaced by relief. I posted this second list next to the first.

"As you can see, concepts can change. Why would it be useful to learn how to conceptualize?"

"So we don't get the wrong idea about something." Others nodded.

"Conceptualizing is something we do all the time, yet we're usually not aware of it. Look at this list of steps involved in this process and tell me which of them you've already done this morning.'' *Usually, I prefer inductive introductions, but the experiential parts of this lesson would take so much time that I'd opted to use a directive lesson instead.*

''We thought of examples.'' *Step 1.*

Silence. *I wonder if they know what ''attributes'' are.*

''What did you do with those examples?''

''We thought about the things the examples had in common.'' *That's it. Step 2. Press for more.*

''What do you mean 'things'?''

''You know, characteristics.''

''What other words can be used for characteristics?''

''Features.'' ''Qualities.'' ''Traits.'' (*But not ''Attributes.''*)

''If you thought about common characteristics, features, qualities, or traits, then you did Step 2—you found attributes the wolves shared.''

I explained the remaining steps generally used to conceptualize—grouping the attributes in some way (Step 3) and identifying a pattern of relationships among these attributes presented as a tentative model (Step 4). I placed the students in groups of four and asked them to use the two lists of attributes to compose a team concept about wolves. First, they were to group the attributes. Then, they were to form their ''tentative model.'' Supplying each team with a sheet of easel paper, I explained their concept could be represented by any form they preferred—web, outline, or paragraph.

They had fifteen minutes to work, while I circulated to observe their progress. This was a slight departure from normal directive lessons. *Would the class be able to follow the steps without my actually demonstrating each one? Time would tell . . . and time was running out.*

The students would have to share their concepts tomorrow. I asked each group's reporter to explain what their group had done to accomplish their task of conceptualizing. Listening for the steps, I pointed to each on the board as it was mentioned. I listened for variations, too, acknowledging them as such. The bell rang and students filed past me as I wondered about what I'd planned to do next—emphasize the final two steps in conceptualizing: applying their model to more examples (Step 5) and refining it (Step 6). *Would it work or was it a waste of their time?*

We started the next day's period by reviewing the objective—to learn the skill of conceptualizing—as I flashed the steps involved in carrying out this skill on the screen. Then we recalled synonyms for this skill and thought of examples of how or when we had developed concepts before. The steps we settled on included:

1. Identify examples of a particular phenomenon.
2. Compare and contrast the examples to identify common attributes.
3. Classify, group these attributes.
4. Determine the pattern revealed by the groups of attributes to formulate a generalized mental image (model) of the phenomenon.
5. Apply the model to a variety of examples.
6. Refine, modify, or otherwise adjust the model.

Could anyone define *concept*? Could they describe how they'd used the steps yesterday? Next, each group shared its concept about wolves. Though the manner in which they depicted their mental image varied, the content was quite similar. Then, it was time to turn to an important rule about conceptualizing: View the phenomenon being conceptualized from as many different points of view as possible when identifying its attributes. I asked the students to listen while I read the story *The Wounded Wolf* to see whether it evoked any new thoughts about the wolves.

"First, I'd like to read the dedication. During his ten-year study of wolves in the Alaskan wilderness, scientist Gordon Haber, Ph.D., observed the leader of a wolf pack save the life of a wounded wolf. What does this inscription tell you about the story?"

"That it's something that actually happened?"

"And what kind of person reported the event?"

"An expert—someone who's studied wolves for a long time."

"So, do you expect this story to represent wolves accurately?"

Of course they do. The stage is set.

The room was unusually quiet as I read to them about a wolf whose life was saved from predators by his pack's leader bringing him food until he regained his strength. When I finished, I asked whether they'd developed any new impressions of wolves. What words might they add to a third list that were different from the first two?

"They communicate."

"Yeah, they're like a community."

"They're vulnerable."

"They're loyal to each other."

They voiced these new attributes with a tone of surprise. *I did it!* I'd successfully orchestrated an experience for the students where they actually modified their mental image of wolves by applying it to additional examples (Step 5). To confirm that, I asked each team to revise their concept models. Then we talked about Step 6 in conceptualizing. I was careful to avoid the words *last step* because conceptualizing is really a never-ending, recursive process. In fact, one student stated that for me, in simpler terms.

The two periods had been well spent. The class had articulated a list of steps for conceptualizing that could be applied not only to other animals but could be transferred to ecosystems and biomes. Later, they would be ready to conceptualize such complex ecological issues as the conflict between spotted owl conservationists and the logging industry in the American Northwest. For now, I was satisfied that they seemed to understand how one conceptualizes. They'd also learned that the process is a continuous one, since new examples frequently result in changes, and that getting plenty of information as well as different perspectives is important in forming accurate concepts. At least, I hoped they knew all that. I'd gotten so caught up in the students' excitement, I'd forgotten to revisit the skill description one last time. The period had ended with the focus on the content, their concept of wolves and how it had changed. I would have to post the steps and rules for future reference and remember always to bridge the skill next time. But we were well on our way to learning how to conceptualize!

REFLECTIONS ON INTRODUCING A THINKING SKILL TO MY NINTH-GRADERS BY CYNTHIA WOOD

Although each lesson I teach during the year is important, perhaps none demand as much time and attention as those taught during the first week of school. During those critical five days, students decide if they like me and often if they will do the work they are assigned for the remainder of the year. Consequently, in preparing for "new" ninth-graders, I spend considerable time selecting lessons that will interest them and that will provide them with some degree of academic success.

This year was no exception. Abandoning some super "fun and games" activities that had worked exceptionally well in previous years, I decided to use new lessons that would get us into significant content material immediately. The first activity was a worksheet—short, accurate, and, I mistakenly believed, clearly written—entitled "The Drifting Continents." I asked my students to read the short selection in class and to answer four questions that required relevant information in the reading.

The results were disastrous. Students wrote incorrect answers not only because of misleading headings in the selection but also because of careless reading and their inability to recognize relevant information. After grading that first assignment, I became determined to teach the skill that would enable my students to recognize relevant information.

Before I taught the first lesson in this skill, I made several decisions about the materials and activities I would use. Since I hoped that my students would become involved immediately in the skill procedure, I decided to use an inductive strategy to guide their first experience in learning the thinking skill of *determining relevance*. The materials I prepared were lists of terms and phrases that focused on three important groups in prehistoric times—hunters and gatherers, settled farmers, and city dwellers. This was material with which my students were familiar—a critical consideration since when first encountering a new skill students must focus on the new thinking skill and not become distracted by unfamiliar content.

From the introduction until the final discussion, the lesson went very well. My students were very attentive and seemed to recognize the importance of learning the procedures and rules basic to this skill. In the introductory step of the lesson, students were actively involved in trying to provide accurate synonyms, to form a clear, concise, accurate definition, and to recognize instances when the skill could be used.

To be sure that the lesson focused on the skill and not content, I gave only a short time for completing the first activity sheet. Students worked in small groups of four or five and selected from a list of terms and phrases those that were relevant to prehistoric hunters and gatherers. Responses were quickly shared, and then students turned their attention to reflecting on what they had done.

Discussion was lively, and I was very pleased with student responses. Several students volunteered to share the procedures they had used in performing this skill, and I wrote their responses on the board. I was pleasantly surprised at the clarity they used in expressing their thought processes. They easily recognized that a number of steps were used to perform this skill, ordered these steps, and explained the thinking they had done with surprising ease.

A problem did develop during this phase of the lesson that bothered me but apparently didn't worry my students at all. They were not able to state specific criteria they used to identify relevant information, nor was I able to elicit any. Their answers to my question, "How did you know the information was relevant?" was "Prior knowledge. We remembered what we learned and just knew what terms were relevant." I tried more questions that didn't work well either and finally decided that, at this stage, identification of specific criteria wasn't critical to continuing the lesson.

Students then completed a second activity sheet on settled farmers as we moved into the fourth step of the lesson strategy. Students worked in pairs and volunteered to share their answers when the entire class reconvened. I felt it was important to leave adequate time to review steps and rules, to revise the skill definition, and to provide additional synonyms. Again, I was very pleased with the discussion and felt that students made some excellent suggestions as we thought of other times the skill could be used. Homework, providing a third opportunity to use the skill, was assigned. I felt certain that students were confident that the homework would present no problems for them.

All in all, the lesson was a success. For fifty minutes my students were actively involved in learning a skill that they recognized as being valuable and that they could use in numerous other circumstances. I had anticipated a higher degree of inattentiveness, but my students stayed on task and concentrated on the activities and reflection with a high degree of involvement and interest. I was very comfortable teaching the skill since my plans reflected a procedure that worked very well.

I have thought very seriously about any changes I will make when I introduce this skill next time. I will definitely start it earlier in the year, since recognizing relevant information is one of the first and most important skills I ask my students to use. I have also toyed with the idea of using pictures or slides as the material for the introductory lesson, because that will provide my students with more concrete data with which to work.

Since teaching this lesson, I have also introduced the skill of decision making to my students. The introductory lesson, the guided practices, and the subsequent activities using this strategy have been very successful. My students love these types of lessons and, much to my delight, improve and handle more easily each new activity. If I had not been absolutely convinced before this that direct attention to critical thinking skills and strategies should be included in my course, I am now. Recognizing that students will benefit from teaching that emphasizes critical thinking, I believe, is the first requirement for the successful revision of any course. It can't be denied that considerable planning time is needed to prepare a first-time lesson in any thinking skill. But the results are well worth the time invested. A commitment is also needed to "rethink" and probably revise "tried and true" lessons and to include time for new thinking skill lessons and activities in plans that already include too-much-to-do-in-too-little-time. However, I'm firmly convinced that students benefit immensely from the teaching of thinking skills and strategies. We do our students a grave disservice if we fail to provide this crucial instruction for them.

REFLECTIONS ON MY FIRST ATTEMPT
TO INTRODUCE THE SKILL
OF ANALYZING FOR TONE
BY CAROLYN KREITER-KURYLO

On the day that I taught the skill of analyzing for tone, my English students had just emerged from a weekend of Scholastic Aptitude Tests, a weekend filled with the ordeal of thinking analytically and critically for three—as they put it—interminable hours.

As I glanced around the room and saw the pained expressions students often times give teachers when the lesson seems unpalatable, I knew I had my work cut out for me.

Since it is the practice in my school district to state a lesson's objectives at the outset of the period, I briefly summarized what I hoped to accomplish. Basically, I told the class that we would be building on their previous knowledge of how to analyze poetry to learn how to analyze a poem for tone. I also noted that, to date, no class member had been able to determine the tone of every single poem we had examined, so a lesson such as this would help them recognize how to identify the tone of poems we would be studying this year.

I then wrote on the board the word *tone*, asking the class to supply synonyms. Students immediately responded with *mood* and *feeling*, two responses I anticipated. I thought that my art students might be able to tell the class what the word *tone* implies in the field of painting; however, this question met with blank stares so I dropped it and, instead, asked for a definition of tone as it relates to poetry. To my surprise, only one student knew the answer: the poet's or speaker's attitude/feelings toward his or her subject.

At this point, I stumbled on a key to teaching the concept of tone. I asked for examples of tone from real-life events. When I was again met by blank stares, I walked over to the door, opened it, then approached one of my most reticent students and demanded in a condescending tone of voice that she shut the door. Since my students had never heard me raise my voice, they were taken aback momentarily, but quickly caught on to the message revealed through my role playing. A lively discussion ensued during which students supplied numerous examples of teachers' using condescending voice commands, parents issuing sarcastic reminders to clean up a room, friends speaking to one another in a surly manner, or a priest taking vows with reverence in his voice.

The lesson I had planned to teach was an inductive approach to analyzing tone. However, what I found happening at the beginning of the lesson was a tendency on my part to lapse into more directive skill instruction. I attribute this partly to the fact that the fifty-minute period might not be enough time for students to respond cogently to every question I wanted to ask. Thus, I found myself pitching in and disseminating information I had hoped to pull from the students. The next time I teach this lesson, I plan to follow a more inductive design.

I was now ready to pair the students and let them examine Lawrence Ferlinghetti's poem, ''14,'' for tone. I gave students approximately five minutes to do this, while I circulated around the room to listen to their analyses. When I brought the class back together, we reported all of the possible responses (whimsical, light, playful), after which I asked the students which poetic elements in ''14'' suggest its tone. As expected, they replied that the imagery (playful, surrealistic), the diction (simplistic word choice), and lineation (whimsical arrangement) suggest a playful or whimsical tone. The comments of some, however, made me aware of one of the pitfalls when analyzing a poem for tone—that is, students focus on only a part of a poem.

I was amazed by the number of students who were unable to verbalize what mental steps they had taken to execute this skill. Only a few were able to say that they took the poem apart or examined its parts or selected those elements that revealed the poet's attitude toward his subject. No one mentioned that he or she read the entire poem first even though that's what they did. Very few were able to articulate how they had determined the tone of Ferlinghetti's poem.

After rearranging the steps according to what transpired first, second, third, and so forth in their thinking, I asked several review questions: When do you analyze for tone? How do you begin? How do you know which elements reveal tone? How do you know when to stop breaking the poem down? After some help from me, it appeared everyone was ready to practice the skill using a new poem.

This time, I distributed copies of my own poem, "Rosewood," a monologue in the voice of the artist, Paul Gauguin. Students read the monologue to themselves and then proceeded to analyze it for tone. The entire class agreed that the tone was reverent, calm, or pensive. When asked how they determined this, nearly everyone was able to point to specific words, images, and the theme itself as evidence of the tone of "Rosewood." Many students appeared pleased that they had been able to discover the tone so easily on their second try.

Unfortunately, the bell rang before we were able to finish reviewing the skill by going over the steps again. Also, there was no time to assign Theodore Roethke's "Night Journey," a poem I assigned later to the students as a springboard for review.

If I were to teach this lesson again, in addition to the changes I have already mentioned, I would extend the lesson to include two fifty-minute periods. As any high school teacher realizes, a fifty-minute period consists of, at best, only forty-plus minutes of instruction and even that is interrupted by announcements from guidance or the office. The second class day would allow (1) the necessary time for students to reflect before responding to questions and (2) adequate time for additional practice of the skill. Ideally, because of the intricate nature of poetry, I believe students should initially have no less than three or four practice poems, preferably each with a different tone. The skill should then be practiced at regular intervals throughout the remainder of the year.

I would also use the extra time to model how to analyze for tone *after* students had tried their own hands at the skill. I would use one of my own poems since I best understand how I achieved the desired tone. While modeling how to analyze for tone, I would "think aloud" so students could see the mental steps I take in executing this skill.

Finally, and most important, I would have my students spend the last five minutes of class during the second day of instruction reflecting in a journal entry on what they learned during the lesson(s), what was clear, what was not clear, and what analyzing for tone is in their own words. This "think" writing would give me a clear sense of what I, as a teacher, need to clarify, while offering students a chance to make sense of their own thinking.

If I were to offer a word of advice to anyone trying to teach this skill, it would be this: To start, bring in a published poet to talk about how he or she establishes tone in a particular poem. Select a poem that is accessible to all students—one the poet feels comfortable discussing in terms of tone, and one that will leave the students in awe of this writer's accomplishments. In doing so, you will not only be introducing an extremely valuable skill to students but you will also be enhancing their appreciation of the content used to teach that skill. Conclude by letting students brainstorm all the possible instances when such a skill could prove useful in their everyday lives. This extends the skill beyond the classroom, which is exactly where we hope our students will benefit from its use. And, of course, whatever enthusiasm you and your visiting poet display will be contagious, even on those days when your students enter the classroom and look at you, as mine did that day, as if to dare you to teach them anything that's worth their while.

SUMMARY

What typically happens to teachers who use a new strategy for teaching a thinking skill for the first time to their students? The teachers' experiences you just read, although dealing primarily with strategies for introducing a thinking skill, provide some answers to this question. Their experiences are not unlike those you will probably have when you try using a new teaching strategy for introducing or guiding practice in or initiating transfer of a thinking skill in your class or course for the first time. Among the things these teachers learned, and that you might learn, too, the following three seem especially significant.

- *A Need to Know More about the Thinking Skill*

Those using new skill-teaching strategies for the first time often realize how little they know about the thinking skill they are attempting to introduce. No matter whether they used an inductive or a more directed skill-introducing strategy, they feel uninformed about the key attributes of the skill being introduced or taught; they realize they needed to know certainly more than a dictionary definition or simple paragraph description of the skill. Without such knowledge, teachers feel unsure about what student responses or contributions to reinforce or even, in some cases, to acknowledge. Of course, having tried to identify skill attributes prior to teaching a skill lesson proves helpful. But teaching the lessons still points up gaps in one's understanding of the skill and the fact that until teachers have articulated such an understanding and clarified it they will feel rather unsure of the key attributes of the skill they are trying to teach.

This reaction is quite understandable. You are likely to share this same feeling when you teach your lessons for the first several times. Knowledge of any skill deepens and becomes more sophisticated as you have repeated occasions to apply it, reflect on it, and attempt to articulate just exactly how you carried it out. Since, until now, you have probably not thought much about your own thinking, you may not be as conscious and knowledgeable about these skills as you would like to be or as you need to be to help novices understand how to execute them. But as you teach more lessons on any skill and as you listen to your students reflect on and share how they do it, you will become more knowledgeable about it. Several years from now, after you have taught many lessons on the skill, you—for one—will know a great deal about the skill!

- *Risks Involved in Inductive Teaching*

A second thing often learned by trying new thinking skill-teaching strategies like those presented in this handbook is the risk inherent in using a new teaching strategy for the first time, especially an inductive teaching strategy. When a student tries to explain how he or she believes a skill was executed and gives an utterly confusing or patently dysfunctional way of doing it, many other students are likely to adopt this procedure or what they understand it to be. Helping them *un*learn this procedure and generating more effective ways to carry out the skill can take an enormous amount of instructional time. According to some researchers, it could take as few as 5 tries to become somewhat proficient in a new skill if it is learned accurately initially. However, if it is "mislearned" initially, it could take as many as 53 tries to develop this same level of proficiency. Although it may seem easier to use an inductive strategy if you subscribe to a developmentalist philosophy of teaching, and while such a strategy may lead to the "best" learning, you must be aware of this risk and be able and willing to devote the time necessary to undo any damage done by any misunderstanding of the skill attributes resulting from this approach.

Most teachers who experience these unfortunate results of an inductive lesson indicate they would prefer to use a directive or developmental strategy (see Appendix B for a detailed explanation and examples of these strategies) for introducing a thinking skill. Such strategies allow a teacher to guide and direct student understanding of the skill, especially in terms of key attributes about which the students may be confused and about which the teacher may feel uncertain.

The use of an inductive strategy also reinforces a teacher's desire to know the skill he or she is trying to introduce *before* using this strategy to introduce it to students. It is very confusing to try to learn inductively a thinking skill you are also inductively introducing to students for the first time. Doing two new operations at the same time is exceedingly difficult and confusing for teachers as well as for students. To help you over this hurdle, it may be wise to use a directive or developmental strategy in introducing new skills until you are familiar enough with these thinking skills to give full attention to carrying out an inductive teaching strategy.

This is not to downplay the value of an inductive introduction of a thinking skill. Using such a strategy makes it easier to begin teaching thinking skills because it appears you do not have to know so much about the skill or try to explain it in as much detail as you have to do in using a directive strategy. Use of an inductive strategy also honors students. It says, in effect, ''You already know something about this skill, so let's try it and see what we know about it. Then we can refine it, fill in the gaps, and go on from there.'' Inductive strategies involve the students more actively with reportedly longer-lasting results in what they are learning. But inductive teaching is, for many, difficult to do. You will have to decide which strategy you wish to use. In the long run, you should be able to use any of several different strategies, depending on the prior experience of your students and the complexity of the skill you wish to introduce. Starting inductively but being able, whenever trouble looms, to switch into a more directive or developmental strategy may be the ideal way to introduce any new thinking skill.

- *Awareness of Prerequisite Skills*

Finally, as a result of their initial efforts to introduce a thinking skill, these teachers often became aware of certain other thinking skills that seemed to be prerequisite to the thinking skills they were introducing. This is usually an unanticipated but very useful (if unsettling) consequence of such lessons. In this way, some teachers have discovered that if students can't classify information or objects very well, it may be that the problem lies in the students' lack of skill in observing (attributing) or in comparing/contrasting. If students cannot hypothesize very well, it may be they have not yet become proficient at predicting and sequencing. Clearly, one's ability to classify or hypothesize is enhanced by being skilled at these other operations. Teaching them before or in conjunction with teaching the target skills may be most helpful to novice thinkers.

You are likely to share this experience, too. It is virtually impossible to predict exactly all the skills needed to execute the more complex thinking operations you may choose to teach. Introducing such complex skills can even serve to alert students to the need to learn these prerequisite or enabling skills. It motivates. Actually, more complex operations provide a framework for hooking together instruction in the component operations of which they consist.

This is not to say you should try to identify and teach any and all ''prerequisite'' skills before introducing any rather complex ones. It simply is an explanation of what often occurs in trying to teach a new thinking skill and the role such an effort may play in identifying other skills that need to be learned. When the occasion demands, it is very useful to be able to suspend a lesson in one skill and either show students how to execute an enabling skill or switch into a lesson directed at that skill instead.

Other Things Learned in Teaching Thinking Skills for the First Time

In using new approaches to teach thinking skill lessons, you can learn other things about teaching, students, thinking, and even yourself. A primary-grade teacher recently summarized some of these by noting:

> I learned to keep it simple for my first graders! When I teach another introductory lesson I will reduce the steps in the thinking skill to a maximum of three at most. I will keep the lesson itself short. My students can't stay with anything very long. I learned also that when some students can't *tell* me how they did a thinking skill, many of them can *show* me how they did it. As they do that many can even explain *why* they did it that way. They really are brighter than a lot of us give them credit for.
>
> I also learned that content and product easily get in the way of learning a thinking skill. I, as well as my students, frequently slipped into talking about the subject matter being used in the lesson instead of keeping our minds on the skill and how to do it. When I try another introductory thinking skill lesson, I will have to work hard to keep us focused on the skill.

Another teacher who had designed and taught a thinking skill lesson using strategies with which she was unfamiliar had this advice for anyone seeking to do the same for the first time:

> Be prepared for a loss of memory (yours) and a change of plans (theirs).

This advice pretty well summarizes what is likely, at best, to occur when anyone tries using new teaching strategies or teaching new skills for the first time.

Teaching thinking skills usually is a good learning experience for you, the teacher, as well as for your students. In fact, when teaching thinking skills, you are almost certain to learn *more* than your students! You can use what you learn to improve your teaching as well as your thinking—and theirs!

Appendices

Appendix A
Identifying Thinking Skill Attributes

By engaging in the process of reflective analysis, preferably with some colleagues, you can identify and describe some of the essential procedural features, or attributes, of any thinking skill. Learning how to employ this procedure, like learning any skill, requires repeated application of it followed by reflection on and analysis of how you carried it out. You can also learn better how to carry out this procedure by examining how other people have used it to identify the attributes of skills in which they were interested. By repeated attempts to use the procedure yourself, by examining how others execute it, and by analyzing the process, you can improve your own ability to use this method for determining what is in a skill.

Three examples of the reflective analysis procedure follow. You can examine each to identify how the procedure works in practice. As you do, remember to keep your focus on the procedure of reflective analysis rather than on the particular thinking skill it is being used to analyze. This procedure, you will recall, consists of three major steps:

1. Define the skill.
2. Do it—carry out the skill under study to complete a task.
3. Describe what you did mentally as you carried out the skill.

Here are examples of how this procedure of reflective analysis works:

Example #1   *Identifying Attributes of the Skill: Using an Index**

How can a group of teachers use the 3-D procedure to identify the attributes of the skill of *using an index?* Well, one group started by defining the skill. Looking at three different dictionary definitions of the word *index* suggest to them that an index is an alphabetical listing of the contents of something with page numbers where each piece of listed content can be found. Thus, they decided, *using an index* probably means to use an alphabetical listing of what is in a textbook or publication and where it can be found in order to locate something.

Next, each teacher in the group considered how one engages in the skill of using a textbook's index. Each tried finding, or imagining how to find, the page number in a science text where Boyle's Law is explained. And as they did this, they tried to remain aware of what they did mentally and why they did it.

What did they do to carry out this skill? Individuals actually executing this skill indicated that they went through the following procedure:

1. First, they decided to use the index (rather than to thumb through the book or to use the table of contents).
2. They then decided to look under *B* for Boyle's Law.

* Adapted from Barry K. Beyer, *Practical Strategies for the Teaching of Thinking* (Boston: Allyn and Bacon, 1987), pp. 48–50.

3. Next, they opened the text and flipped to the back to locate the index.
4. Upon finding the index, they went straight to the *B* section and then to *Bo* where they skimmed to find the entry *Boyle's Law.*
5. Finding the entry, *Boyle's Law,* they searched under this term to find the specific topic—in this example, its explanation—and then identified the page number(s) following this topic entry.

Having identified some of the procedural steps of which the skill *using an index* seems to consist, these teachers next turned to identifying, or attempting to identify, any procedural knowledge and/or rules that might have guided their execution of the skill they were analyzing. Their analysis of *why* they did what they did as they used the index suggested to them that individuals good at using an index possess certain knowledge that enables them to engage in this procedure effectively and efficiently. For example, they know what an index is and what it looks like. They know that an index is customarily found at the back of a book and that certain items such as people's names are listed surname first, whereas events or other items are listed first word first. They know that under each heading they can find related, subordinate headings—sometimes in chronological order, sometimes in alphabetical order, and sometimes in the order presented in the text. And they know the meaning of symbols, such as 114–117; 114, 117; and 114ff.

Those who are expert at using an index also seem to follow certain rules or heuristics in executing the skill procedure. For example, these individuals use this skill when they wish to find text information quickly. They initiate the task by deciding what particular search word they will hunt for. If they can't find that particular term or word, they identify synonyms or associated terms—in the case of this example, perhaps Combined Gas Laws, pressure, or so on—and search for them. They use the same "emergency" approach in searching for specific aspects of any subtopic if they can't find them under the main term they are using.

If these individuals cannot find the index, they flip to the Table of Contents to see if there is one and where it begins. And they know what

to do after they have identified the page numbers they seek. Individuals successful at using a textbook index, in effect, follow these guidelines as if they were rules to guide the way they go about using an index.

Additional tries at using an index in a variety of books to locate different kinds of information help to generalize this skill. The tentative description of the skill of using an index that often results from such reflective analysis might look like this:

Label: Using an Index

Definition: be able to find a given topic/name in an alphabetical listing of names, places, and subjects with the page number where each can be found in a book

Steps:

1. Decide to use the index.
2. Select key word to look for.
3. Flip to back of book.
4. Locate index.
5. Locate key word.
6. Identify appropriate subtopic (if sought).
7. Identify page number(s).

Rules:

1. When to use an index?
   • to find information in a hurry
   • to see what a book contains on a topic of interest
2. How to start?
   • pick a key word/label to find
   • flip to the back of the book

3. What to do if . . .
- can't find the index? Look in the table of contents to see if one is listed and the page where it starts.
- can't find the key word? Look up synonym or suitable alternate word.

Knowledge Needed:

1. Location of index
2. Nature of index (alphabetical list of topics with page numbers)
3. People are listed last names first
4. Subheadings may be alphabetical, chronological, in a sequence of events
5. Meaning of page symbols: 114–117, 114ff, etc.

Example #2   *Identifying Attributes of the Skill: Determining Relevance**

Suppose a teacher wishes to identify the major attributes of the skill of distinguishing relevant from irrelevant information. First, the teacher can look up several dictionary definitions of the terms *relevant/relevance* and *irrelevant/irrelevance* and then find some common synonyms for these terms. Upon so doing, the teacher may note that *relevance* commonly means ''related or pertaining to the topic at hand,'' while *irrelevance* usually means ''having no application to or effect on'' the topic at hand. Then a number of statements can be examined to see what in them is relevant to a stipulated topic. Upon completing this task those involved can reflect on how they executed the task, why they did what they did, and what they knew that enabled them to proceed as they did.

*From Barry K. Beyer, *Practical Strategies for the Teaching of Thinking* (Boston: Allyn and Bacon, 1987), pp. 55–58.

Suppose the following statement—written about the European discovery of a large city in the sixteenth century—were used to find how one goes about distinguishing relevant from irrelevant information. The task could be to determine the extent this statement is relevant to this claim:

The city described here would be easy to conquer.

Statement:

1   Then Montezuma. . .told (us) to look at his great city and all the other
2   cities standing in the water. . . .So we stood there looking, because that
3   huge accursed (temple) stood so high that it dominated everything. We
4   saw the three causeways that led into Mexico. . . .We saw the fresh water
5   which came. . .(by viaduct) to supply the city, and the bridges. . .at
6   intervals on the causeways so that the water could flow in and out from one
7   part of the lake to another. We saw a great number of canoes, some
8   coming with provisions and others returning with cargoes and merchandise;
9   and we saw too that one could not pass from one house to another. . .except
10 over wooden drawbridges or by canoe. We saw (temples) and shrines. . .
11 that looked like gleaming white towers and castles: a marvelous sight.
12 ...(We) turned back to the great market and the swarm of people buying
13 and selling. . .Some of our soldiers who had been in many parts of the
14 world, in Constaninople, in Rome. . , said they had never seen a market
15 so well laid out, so large, so orderly, and so full of people.[1]

In reading this statement one may have identified sentences beginning on lines 1, 3, 4, and 7 as relevant to the given claim. Sentences beginning on lines 2, 10, 12, and 13 may have been considered, initially at least, to be irrelevant to this claim. Analysis of why these choices were made can help articulate some of the key components of the skill of distinguishing the relevant from the irrelevant.

What is it one did to execute this skill—to determine what information is relevant or irrelevant to a given claim? In retrospect it seems on first thought as if one:

1. Restated the goal of the task—to distinguish what in the statement was relevant to the given claim from what is not relevant.
2. Read the statement sentence-by-sentence, even phrase-by-phrase, to identify what was relevant.

3. Judged the overall degree to which the statement as a whole was relevant to the given claim.

Why were certain sentences judged to be relevant? Sentences beginning on lines 1 and 3 seemed relevant because they explained or gave examples of how the island city related to the mainland and they implied that cutting the bridges would isolate the city. These sentences, in effect, seem to be evidence supporting the claim. Sentences beginning on lines 4 and 7 seem to be of the same type. They explain and give examples of how the city is linked to the outside world. Thus, those items judged to be relevant seem to be so judged because they give examples or explanations or details directly related to the given claim. It appears, then, that examples, explanations, and details may be three criteria of relevancy.

Discussion with others of how relevancy is determined can help further articulate and clarify some additional steps, principles, or rules to follow, and useful things to know in executing this skill. Repeating this task with several other claims and appropriately related information may add to one's insights into how this skill can be executed effectively. Such repeated efforts to use the skill and then to analyze retrospectively how it was executed might suggest eventually that someone accomplished in this skill might well carry out this operation by:

1. Stating the nature of the topic or matter at hand. By so doing, one sets up a criterion to keep on task.
2. Recalling or identifying various criteria to use in determining relevancy—criteria such as whether statements give details, examples, explanations, contradictions, or evidence directly related to (but *not* necessarily supportive of) the given claim.
3. Searching the statement piece-by-piece to find evidence of such criteria.
4. Matching each piece—each sentence—to the above criteria or other criteria that pop into mind.
5. Judging the degree to which the statement as a whole pertains or connects to the matter at hand.

Label: DETERMINING RELEVANCE

Definition: to decide whether something relates or pertains to the matter at hand

Synonyms: relevance: pertaining or related to, germane

Steps:

1. State the nature of the topic or matter at hand.
2. Recall or identify criteria to look for (that would make things relevant to the topic).
3. Take the material apart piece-by-piece to find evidence implied by these criteria.
4. Match each piece of the material to the identified criteria.
5. Judge the extent of the match—determine the degree of relevancy.

Rules:

1. When to determine relevance?
   - a specific topic is the matter at hand
   - there is a considerable amount of information
2. How to start?
   - restate the topic or matter at hand
   - recall criteria or clues of relevance
   - pick one piece of data and decide if it's relevant, telling why
3. What to do ....
   - if little appears relevant? Recall what we know about the topic or consult another source.
   - if material "contradicts" the topic? Negative evidence can be relevant, too!
4. What other skills to use this with?
   - identifying the elements of a problem
   - collecting information for writing on a topic

Criteria or Clues:

1. examples
2. explanations
3. details
4. reasons for or against
5. evidence for or against
6. something connected to

Figure A.1 A Tentative Description of a Thinking Skill

Like other procedures for identifying the major attributes of a thinking skill or strategy, this, too, has its limitations. There is obviously more to the skill of determining relevance than one or two tries at it may reveal. Initial analyses may not produce any recognizable rules or principles being followed, for example. Much depends on the media being used, the type of data involved, the informational and experiential background of the person executing the skill, and the purpose to which the skill is being put. However, reflective analysis such as this can produce at least tentative insights into some of the attributes and workings of any thinking skill or strategy. As one becomes experienced in using the skill and consciously reflecting on the process involved, understanding of it deepens. What this preliminary investigation can do in most cases is to enable a teacher to prepare at least a tentative description of a thinking operation as in Figure A.1. Using this description as a guide and perhaps as an initial target, the teacher can then introduce this operation to students in a direct, explicit fashion.

Example #3   *Identifying Attributes of the Skill: Detecting Bias* *

Suppose we wished to identify the major attributes of the skill of detecting bias in a written statement. First, we can recall or identify some common synonyms for *bias*, and look up several dictionary definitions of the term. Bias is commonly taken to be synonymous with preference, slanted view, or inclination. It is a slanted, often objectively untested, opinion about, or view of, something. A useful dictionary definition may be that a bias is an inclination for or against something that inhibits an impartial judgment. Then, after finding some written statements that may contain bias, we may start by analyzing a given statement to see if it shows evidence of bias. A history teacher might find the following statement useful for this purpose. It was written in England in the early nineteenth century. Is it biased?

1 Some of the lords of the loom employ
2 thousands of miserable creatures (i)n the
3 cotton-spinning work. *The poor creatures*
4 *are doomed to toil* day after day fourteen
5 hours in each day in an average heat of eighty-
6 two degrees. Can any man with a heart in his
7 body refrain from cursing a system that
8 produces such slavery and such cruelty?
9   These poor creatures have no cool room
10 to retreat to, not a moment to wipe off the
11 sweat, and not a breath of air. The door
12 of the place wherein they work, *is locked*
13 *except* at tea-time. If any spinner be
14 found with his *window open*, he is to pay a
15 fine.
16   For a large part of the time the abom-
17 inable stink of gas assist(s) in the
18 murderous effects of the heat which the
19 unfortunate creatures have to inhale. Children
20 are rendered decrepit and deformed and thou-
21 sands of them (die) before
22 the age of sixteen.[2]

In reading this statement, one does not go far before deciding that there is considerable bias in it. Seeing the word "Lords" may initially arouse this suspicion because the word may have perjorative connotations. Continued use of words such as "miserable creatures" or "poor creatures" (instead of laborers or workers) and of words like "doomed" and "toil" suggest an effort to arouse sympathy for laborers. The leading question starting on line 6 reinforces this sympathy, as does the over-generalization in lines 9–15—*no* cool room, *not* a moment, *not* a breath.

*Adapted from Barry K. Beyer, *Developing a Thinking Skills Program* (Boston: Allyn and Bacon, 1988), pp. 142–148.

Not one? The italicized words draw attention to the facts that the workers were confined and were punished if they altered the conditions of that confinement. The adjectives used in the concluding lines simply trigger additional sympathy for the workers. The general pattern of all these devices is to elicit sympathy for the workers; little if anything favorable about the mill owners can be found. This statement certainly appears to be one-sided!

Discussion with others of how one arrives at this conclusion or reflection on what one did to arrive at it helps articulate some aspects of the skill of detecting bias. Having reaffirmed the purpose of looking at the statement—to identify whether or not it is biased—one starts reading to look for evidence of bias. Such evidence seems to pop up almost immediately. Repeated use of emotionally charged words alerts us to the possibility of bias here. The leading question tells rather directly the author's preference, while at the same time putting the reader in a ''no win'' position of agreeing with him or, in fact, being inhumane—heartless! The author's use of italics further makes clear his position. As one reads, noting items like these, a pattern begins to emerge—repeated use of these devices seems to evidence a sympathy for the workers. The obvious lack of balance in the statement suggests rather strongly a negative attitude toward the mill owners who are presented as creating all the horrible conditions suffered by the workers.

What does one do, then, in executing the skill of detecting bias? In retrospect, it seems as if one may:

1. State the goal—to look for evidence of bias.
2. Read the data line-by-line or phrase-by-phrase to find indications of bias.
3. Look for any pattern or common relationship among these bias indicators.
4. Match the perceived pattern to some criteria of what constitutes bias.
5. Judge the extent to which bias seems to be found, and state the bias.

To understand this operation as completely as possible, it is worth doing it again. The following statement proves useful for this purpose. It, too, was written in England at about the same time as the preceding statement. Is this statement biased?

1 I have visited many factories and I never
2 saw children in ill-humor. They seemed to
3 be always cheerful and alert, taking pleasure
4 in the light play of their muscles—enjoying
5 the mobility natural to their age. The scene
6 of industry was exhilarating. It was de-
7 lightful to observe the nimbleness with which
8 they pieced the broken ends as the mule-carriage
9 began to recede from the fixed roller-beam and
10 to see them at leisure after a few seconds ex-
11 ercise of their tiny fingers, to amuse them-
12 selves in any attitude they chose. The work
13 of those lively elves seemed to resemble a
14 sport. They evinced no trace of (exhaus-
15 tion) on emerging from the mill in the evening;
16 for they skip about any neighboring play-
17 ground.[3]

From the previous experience, one recalls that bias is often revealed by excessive use of emotionally charged words (especially adjectives), by one-sided reports, by leading questions, and by exaggeration and overgeneralization. One can then search through this statement line-by-line looking for use of such devices. They seem to be there, but this time the bias seems to be a positive one, giving an impression that labor in these mills was akin to being at summer camp, a fun, invigorating, and stimulating experience! In doing this procedure a second time, it seems that recalling the different types of clues to bias is something that actually is often done between steps 1 and 2 in the original outline of the procedure. Thus, a more complete description of the procedure for detecting bias seems to be:

1. State the goal.
2. Recall clues to bias—use of "loaded" words, "loaded" questions, rhetorical questions, overgeneralization, one-sidedness, and so on.
3. Go through the data line-by-line or piece-by-piece to find evidence of these clues.
4. Identify any pattern among these clues.
5. Match the pattern of clues to the recalled standards of what constitutes bias.
6. Judge the extent of the match.

Interestingly, what emerges from such reflective analysis is that different individuals may execute this—or virtually any—thinking operation in slightly different ways. For example, although many may agree that the process described above represents how they seem to do it, others might indicate that in trying to decide whether some written document is biased, they:

1. State the goal.
2. Start examining the data.
3. Find one or two clues to bias, such as a "loaded" word or two.
4. Guess there is a bias and what it is.
5. Search for corroborating clues.
6. Identify a consistent pattern in the clues confirming the inferred bias.
7. State the bias.

Additional procedures may also be reported. Neither of these procedure descriptions represents "the correct" procedure. Both are workable. Both are useful procedures that can be used to detect bias.

There is a knowledge component to this skill, as well. Knowing some of the devices, such as loaded words and one-sided presentations, indicative of bias provides clues to look for to detect bias as well as criteria for judging what we find or don't find. The clues noted in these example statements, of course, are not the only clues to or evidence of bias. When searching for bias in a newspaper, for example, position of

an article on a page, size of headline, and use of accompanying graphics may also give evidence of bias. Bias in a film might be revealed by the use of color vis-à-vis black and white, the way background music is used, and the content of the frames that accompany the narration. The skill of detecting bias in data is used with all kinds of media, audio as well as visual and written. Knowledge of these things about bias constitutes an important component of the skill of detecting bias.

In its most sophisticated form, the skill of detecting bias is certainly much more complex than it appears in this introductory encounter. As individuals become experienced in using this skill with a variety of media, their understanding of it deepens. Of course, the procedure by which this description of a thinking skill has been generated may not lead to the identification of any principles associated with the skill or of how the procedure may operate when used in other contexts. But enough has been identified here for a teacher to prepare at least a tentative description of this important thinking operation, as shown in Figure A.2. Using this description as a target, a teacher can then plan a sequence of lessons on this skill. Introducing this skill to a number of classes will provide additional insights into the key attributes of the skill which, in turn, will provide a useful springboard for learning this skill.

In generating a description of the key attributes of any thinking skill, the first step in this process, as illustrated here (*defining the skill*), helps to develop a mental set appropriate to executing the skill. Brainstorming synonyms first or looking them up in a dictionary or thesaurus assists in this process by making it easier to articulate a reasonably accurate definition. Checking this definition against several dictionary definitions and revising it to include the key parts of these definitions is also appropriate at this point. In some instances, identifying examples of a skill (e.g., in the case illustrated here, examples of a "bias") make it easier to generate both synonyms and an accurate definition.

After doing or executing the skill with one or two colleagues, those involved can discuss what they did in their heads as they engaged in doing the skill. As they *discuss* this, they should list what they report under "steps," "rules," and "knowledge." By collecting what is recalled under these headings, it is easier to identify the key attributes of the skill being analyzed. These headings can also serve as search cues by which

DETECTING BIAS

DEFINITION: Finding a one-sided or slanted view for or against something

bias: preference, slanted view, partiality, untested inclination that inhibits an impartial judgment

STEPS

Procedure A

1. State your purpose.
2. Identify the clues to look for, including
   - "loaded" or emotionally charged words
   - overgeneralizations
   - "loaded" or rhetorical questions
   - imbalance in presentation
   - opinions stated as facts
3. Take the material apart piece-by-piece or line-by-line to find the clues.
4. Identify patterns among or consistency of the clues found.
5. State evidence to support patterns found.
6. Judge the extent of the bias.

Procedure B

1. State your purpose.
2. Skim data/object.
3. Predict the bias when identifying first clues.
4. Search for corroborating clues
   - "loaded" or emotionally charged words
   - overgeneralizations
   - "loaded" or rhetorical questions
   - imbalance in presentation
   - opinions stated as facts
5. Search for a pattern in the clues.
6. State the bias found.

RULES

1. When to search for bias?
   - when an account seeks to persuade
   - in judging the accuracy of a source or statement
   - in identifying an author's point of view
   - . . . .

2. How to start?
   - pick one clue and look for it, then pick another and search for it, etc.
   - . . .

3. What to do if . . . .
   - you find little bias? Compare it to another piece of material on the same topic.
   - the vocabulary is unfamiliar? Use a dictionary to clarify meanings.
   - . . . .

KNOWLEDGE

1. Of clues to or criteria of bias
2. Of the subject of the "account" being analyzed

Figure A.2 A Tentative Description of a Thinking Skill

individuals may probe their memories to assist in recalling what they did or thought as they executed the skill. By use of this three-step 3-D process of *define, do,* and *discuss,* teachers and others can identify, at least tentatively, some of the key attributes of virtually any thinking skills and strategies.

NOTES

1. Reprinted with permission from *Bernal Díaz, The Discovery and Conquest of New Spain,* translated by J. M. Cohen (London: Penguin Books, Ltd., 1975), pp. 234–235.

2. Adapted from William Cobbett, *Political Register LII* (November 20, 1824). Italics in the original.

3. Adapted from Andrew Ure, *The Philosophy of Manufacturers: Or An Exposition of the Scientific, Moral and Commercial Economy of the Factory System of Great Britain* (3d ed.) (London: H. G. Bohn, 1861), p. 301.

Appendix B
Strategies for Introducing Thinking Skills

Each of the stages in a framework for teaching a thinking skill or strategy serves an important function in helping students to develop proficiency in that operation. However, the introductory stage may well be the most important. For most students this is the first formal instructional encounter with a new thinking skill or strategy. What happens during this encounter goes a long way in helping students understand it. If this introduction is frustrating because a new skill seems impossibly abstract or complex or irrelevant, students may well avoid future opportunities to apply the skill which they take up only half-heartedly, or they may attempt to shortcut it in a way that negates its effective use. Consequently, teachers should give careful attention to how, where, and in what form they introduce new thinking skills and strategies in classrooms.

At times some teachers introduce a new skill simply by throwing the students into a task that requires its use as best they know how, providing a bit of exhortation or encouragement and concentrating thereafter upon the substantive insights—the answers—generated through use of the skill by those who can execute it. Unfortunately, little understanding of the skill itself results from such introductions, for at least two reasons. There is usually no effort to reflect on, or to provide actual instruction in, how to execute it. Moreover, the focus of such lessons remains almost completely, if not wholly, on subject matter.

A more effective way to introduce a new thinking skill or strategy in any course makes the thinking operation itself the subject and content of the lesson. Although the lesson may use subject matter regularly studied in the course as a vehicle in which to employ the skill, the teacher seeking to enhance student understanding of the skill should keep student attention continuously and consciously on the skill being introduced.

An introductory lesson in a thinking skill or strategy presents teachers with their first opportunity to employ what should be done (as indicated by research and thoughtful skill teaching experience) to help beginners understand a skill. The main purpose of such a lesson is to help students see the operation as a skill—by feeling what it is like to engage in a simplified version of it and by becoming aware of some of its key attributes. It is in such a lesson that modeling of the operation can most profitably occur, that the specific components or attributes of the operation can be articulated by the students, and that the operation can be performed in a risk-free, supportive environment. For many thinking operations such a lesson may well be sufficient to launch very effective and rapid learning of the newly introduced skill, via subsequent guided practice; for other operations, especially those that upon first encounter appear to be very complex, such a lesson may serve mainly to increase awareness of the value of the skill and to stimulate a felt need to become better at executing it.

Lessons introducing a new thinking skill usually require thirty to fifty minutes, depending on its complexity and the abilities and prior experience of the students. Any of a number of teaching strategies can be used to conduct such lessons. These strategies range from inductive, student-directed strategies on the one hand to rather didactic, teacher-

From Barry K. Beyer, *Practical Strategies for the Teaching of Thinking* (Boston: Allyn and Bacon, 1987), pp. 87–137.

directed strategies on the other. Some strategies combine elements of both. The inductive strategies allow students, in effect, to articulate for themselves the main attributes of the thinking operation being introduced and to elaborate and refine these attributes with subsequent guidance and practice. In the most directive strategies, teachers or other models present the key attributes of a new skill right at the start so that students can replicate them and elaborate them while practicing the skill in subsequent lessons. A strategy combining elements of both the inductive and directive strategies can be used to heighten motivation, to accommodate more complex skills or subject matter, or to respond directly to varying ability levels and learning styles of the students. Each of these types of strategies is useful in introducing new thinking skills and strategies.

AN INDUCTIVE STRATEGY

An inductive introduction to a thinking skill involves students almost immediately in executing the new operation in order to identify the main procedures, rules, or criteria that seem to be implicit in how it works. Such a strategy is most useful with average to above-average students, students with considerable background in the subject matter being used, and students who have already demonstrated some proficiency in thinking. It is also useful when the thinking operation itself is relatively uncomplicated. What emerges from this type of lesson is the students' initial view of the operation.[1] While there is some risk that a skill or strategy first developed in this way may confuse more than enlighten, a properly conducted such an introductory lesson can, in effect, set up a hypothetical model of the operation for students to flesh out in subsequent practice by applying it with the guidance of teacher and peers.

In general, introducing a new thinking operation inductively consists of having students engage in the operation on their own, working perhaps in pairs or small groups to identify whatever procedures or rules they find themselves using. Once they have identified and discussed such attributes, the lesson continues with a second application of the operation and concludes with an explicit review of what has been dis-

covered about it. Such a lesson need not be a special event, breaking the subject-matter sequence, nor need it be conducted in a "subject-matter free" context. It can—and indeed should—be presented when using the new operation is clearly necessary for understanding the subject matter or for accomplishing a subject-matter objective.

In conducting an inductive introductory lesson, a teacher can guide the class through five steps:

1. First, the teacher introduces—or previews—the new thinking operation in the context of the subject matter being studied.
2. Then the students execute the operation as best they can to complete a short assigned task.
3. Next, students reflect on and share what they did in their minds as they executed the operation.
4. Another opportunity to execute the new operation follows in which students consciously try to use what they have discovered about it to complete a second task.
5. Students conclude by again reporting on what they believe they did in their heads to execute the new skill or strategy and what rules they seemed to follow in carrying it out.

By conducting lessons through these five steps of *preview, execute, reflect, apply, review,* teachers can provide the kind of introduction to a thinking skill or strategy that lets students begin where they are in terms of what they know about it and that raises to a level of consciousness what they do in executing it. Follow-up lessons providing guided practice can build on what emerges to elaborate, flesh out, and even correct the attributes of the operation identified in this lesson.

Applying the Strategy

To demonstrate and clarify the details of this inductive strategy, an example of this strategy follows. Suppose an American history teacher is charged with the responsibility of teaching the skill of classifying informa-

B-2

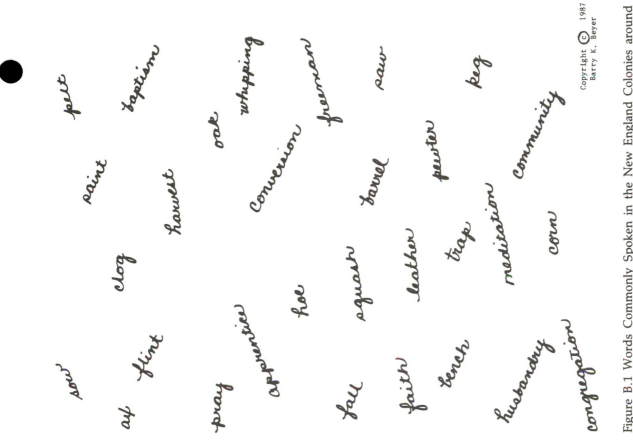

tion into self-invented categories.* This skill could be introduced early in the typical fifth or eighth grade American history course, perhaps at the point where students are supposed to learn the characteristics of life in England's American colonies just prior to the American Revolution. Students will be motivated to learn this skill when introduced in this context because being able to classify information will obviously help them achieve the given subject-matter objective. To introduce this skill at this point, then, a teacher could use the inductive strategy as follows.

After introducing the topic of the lesson—"life in the thirteen colonies around 1750"—and relating this topic to the students' previous study of the period, the teacher can set the substantive purpose for studying the skill by posing a question requiring student use of the skill. Such a question might be, "What was life like in the thirteen English North American colonies around 1750?"

To launch study of the skill itself, the teacher should then *preview the skill* and provide a rationale for studying it. This can be accomplished by presenting the class with some data to classify. In this case the words in Figure B.1 serve the purpose well. Pointing out that these words, presented as a handout or via an overhead transparency, were commonly spoken by the inhabitants of the New England colonies about 1750, the teacher can then ask the students to use these words to identify what life was like for these people at that time. The way these words are displayed, of course, is challenging to the students because, as some quickly point out, "These words are all mixed up. How can we make sense of them?"

Such a reaction accomplishes more than anything the teacher can say to introduce the value of the skill of classifying, a skill particularly useful in making sense out of disorganized data. At this point the teacher can tell

---

*Because it is important to use familiar, uncomplicated subject matter in introducing a new skill, we can use the skill of classifying as the subject for illustrating the introductory strategies presented here. This skill is quite straightforward for adults. The objective of the example lessons that follow is not to learn how to classify data but to understand how to execute the key steps in the particular skill-introducing strategy being illustrated. Rather than attending exclusively to the skill of classifying itself, the reader should focus on the teaching strategy being employed, for it is *teaching* skills that constitutes the focus.

Figure B.1 Words Commonly Spoken in the New England Colonies around 1750

the students this and state clearly that the lesson's objective is to learn how to execute the skill of classifying information. By the end of the lesson the students should be able to describe, at least tentatively, one or more ways to execute this skill.

At this point, the skill label *classify* can be written on the board and the teacher can underline it for emphasis. Synonyms (*group, sort, categorize*) can be then given—by the teacher or the students—followed by a simple working definition, such as, perhaps, "putting like things together." Since examples are useful in clarifying meanings, students could volunteer examples of anything from their school or personal experience that already have been classified. Examples might include telephone books—the yellow pages classify things by type of service or product offered; newspapers—they are divided into news sections, sports sections, comics, and even classified ads; students—they are grouped by grades or classes and, among themselves, into other categories; supermarkets—they have items grouped by type: dairy here, meat there, baked goods in another place, and canned vegetables somewhere else. Many things encountered daily have already been classified for ease in dealing with them.

At this point, without any instruction at all, the teacher can have the students *execute the skill*. In pairs or small groups they can put the words in Figure B.1 into categories or groups that will tell them what life was like in New England around 1750, at least for the people who commonly spoke those words. While executing this task, students will probably attend mainly to the substantive goal—in this case the features of life in 1750 New England—but they will also make physical moves and statements that reveal what they are thinking as they carry out the task. Some of these will be remembered when the task is completed. Throughout this activity the teacher may move around the classroom observing what is going on, perhaps encouraging some, but *not* explaining to anyone how to execute the task. This task is one students are to do on their own.

Having grouped most of the words on the handout, students then should *reflect* aloud on what they have been doing and how they have been doing it. The ensuing discussion should focus on the skill of classifying itself rather than on what the students found out about life in colonial New England. Yet to give substantive value to the activity, the teacher

might initiate the discussion by having students report for a minute or two on several categories they invented, on the words they placed in each, and on what they infer from each category about life at this time. However, detailed discussion and analysis of these responses should wait until the next class period. At this point, attention should focus as much as possible on what the students did, in as much step-by-step detail as possible, to put these words into groups.

Talking about what went on in their minds while executing a thinking operation is a difficult task for most students, especially initially, because it requires them to stand outside of their heads and be alert to what is going on in them, something to which most students are not accustomed. Most students above the fourth grade level, though, will be able to report some things they do or did, such as, "First, I read—skimmed—the words. Then I found two that were the same—*hoe* and *ax*—and then there were more tools, like *trap* . . . so . . . Then I started on another group—*baptism*, *faith*, and others. . . .But then later I broke the tools down into farming things, hunting things, and building things." Other students might indicate that first they skimmed the list of words and that, as they did so, categories of words seemed to jump out at them, such as religious words, farming words, and so on. So they then went back to find and list all the words related to each of these labels. Still other students may indicate that after hearing what their goal was and skimming the data, they looked at each word, recalled its meaning and a category to which it belonged, and marked it with some symbol or number to indicate its category. Then they went back to connect or list all those in the same category together and even, once or twice, to combine two categories (farm tools and farm crops, for example) to make a single category (such as farming).

As students report, elaborate on, and rework what they did or heard being done, the teacher can list their remarks on the chalkboard under *steps*, *rules*, and *knowledge used* columns as appropriate. In this way the teacher and students can gradually build a list of key attributes or components of this skill, as articulated by the students. What emerges is a tentative, first impression of some of the key procedures in which one engages in classifying data, some rules that may guide the execution of this skill, and some things students know about the skill or data to which

alien	apprentice	compact
faith	banish	wheelbarrow
exile	loft	clapboard
saw	musket	flint
ball	cold	community
net	shingles	freeman
heresy	conversion	writ
chimney	trap	pelt
cannon	discipline	shovel
thatch	covenant	bean
kettle	powder	maple
live	court	bedstead
sabbath	stranger	meeting
corn	bench	squash
will	pray	clay
barrel	ax	saint
keg	cloak	muskrat
wind	sandy	oak
harvest	fall	berry

Figure B.2 Words Commonly Spoken in the Middle Atlantic Colonies around 1750

it *was* applied that make it possible to execute the skill. A variety of procedures will be described, partially at best, as may be two or three rules—like putting data they didn't understand (such as the word *clog*) or data that they couldn't handle (perhaps *whipping*) into a category they called miscellaneous to work with later. At this point the goal is to get several different ways to execute this skill on the board for all to see, and to encourage students to articulate as many attributes of the skill as they can.

Students can now *apply the skill* again. Using the procedures, rules, and other items just discussed and on the board, they can, in pairs or alone this time, execute the skill a second time, using words like those in Figure B.2, that were commonly spoken by colonists living in the Middle Atlantic colonies around 1750. Unlike the items on the initial list, these words appear to be organized, but, as students are quick to point out, not in a useful fashion. Besides, they complain, there are too many words. Classifying data thus proves to be a useful operation when one has so many data that it seems impossible to learn or use them all; these data can be made meaningful, however, if they are grouped into fewer, more easily processed and remembered "chunks" or categories. Thus, students can proceed to classify these words into categories to determine what life was like in the Middle Atlantic colonies just before the American Revolution. Again, the teacher can move about the room offering assistance, encouraging, and this time suggesting how students can proceed to execute this skill.

To conclude this lesson, students should *review* what they have found out about the skill. They may initiate this final step in the strategy by reporting several categories they made out of these words and what each category implied about life in 1750 for the people using these words frequently. But again, as in the reflection step, focus should be constantly on the skill and its identified attributes. Students may report that they followed one or more of the sequences of procedures already listed on the board or that they did so but added or modified some steps or rules. For example, they may indicate that after finding just two words that seemed similar, they wrote the similarity as the label for the group and *then* wrote under it all the other words on the list fitting this label; they probably repeated this process until they had made several categories of words.

Others might indicate that after just glancing at these words they decided to use their previous categories because, since this task and data were similar to the initial task, they thought the earlier categories would work here, too. And they did, to a point.

After volunteering any additional procedures used, rules followed, or knowledge used, and after raising any questions about the skill, students can refine the working definition given at the beginning of the lesson. They can describe some places in the course to date where the data they used had already been classified (in the chapter on explorers, for instance) and report some instances in their out-of-school activities where this skill may be most useful (perhaps in categorizing the advantages and the disadvantages of choosing any particular activity when deciding on what to do on Saturday). Some key procedures and rules can be entered into their notebooks or put on butcher paper or on the bulletin board to display for later reference.

A follow-up assignment could then be to classify a list of words commonly spoken in Maryland, Virginia, Georgia and the Carolinas about 1750 in order to identify the key features of life there at that time. In the next class session, students and teacher can review how these words were classified. Then they can focus on the subject matter they have been studying by using the substantive products of all three classifying activities to probe in detail the nature of life in the thirteen colonies on the eve of the American Revolution. The class can continue subject-matter learning and go back to practicing the newly introduced skill of classifying in a day or two when the data to be used in class make it appropriate to do so.

Analyzing the Strategy

Figure B.3 outlines in some detail what should be done at each of the five major steps in this inductive introductory strategy to carry it out effectively. This outline can serve as a guide in writing a teaching plan for any lesson in any subject where a teacher wishes to introduce a thinking skill using this inductive strategy. The following explanation of the more important features of this strategy will clarify what ought to occur in each step and the importance of each.

In using this inductive strategy, a teacher first sets the substantive context of the lesson and then introduces the thinking skill or strategy which the lesson is to introduce. First, the teacher places the lesson in the context of the subject matter under study and gives, or has students invent, a subject-matter task—in this case, "What was life like for these people in 1750?"—that makes it useful for them to learn a particular skill. Then the teacher shifts the focus of the lesson to the skill itself. Such an introduction serves two purposes: it places the lesson in the subject-matter context of the course and gives purpose to learning about the skill to be introduced.

Giving a few minutes of concentrated attention at this point to the skill is important for both pedagogical as well as psychological reasons. Pedagogically, by writing the skill label—"classify"—on the board, adding synonyms and a tentative definition, and discussing some examples

STEP 1 PREVIEW THE SKILL

State that "learning" the skill is today's objective.
Give the skill label/name.
Give synonyms.
State a tentative/working definition.
State ways the skill can be or has been used:
• in students' personal experiences,
• in school activities,
• in this course.
Explain how the skill is useful and why it's worth learning.

STEP 2 EXECUTE THE SKILL

Use the skill (as best one can) to accomplish a task.
Work in pairs, triads, or groups.
Use subject matter familiar to students and appropriate to course (or if necessary, from students' experience).

STEP 3 REFLECT ON WHAT WAS DONE

Students report what went on in their heads as they engaged in the skill.
Identify the key steps/rules used and sequence of each.
Clarify the procedure and any criteria used.
Focus on the skill and its attributes.

STEP 4 APPLY SKILL TO NEW DATA

Use what has been discussed about the skill to complete a second task.
Work in pairs, triads, or groups.
Use subject matter appropriate to the course but in the same structure and media as in Step 2.

STEP 5 REVIEW THE SKILL

Report on what students did in their heads as they applied the skill.
Review the steps/procedure that seem to constitute the skill.
Review the rules that direct use of the skill as well as when its to be used.
State the relationship of this skill to other skills.
Review or revise the skill definition.
State where the skill can be used in personal or out-of-school situations.

Figure B.3 An Inductive Strategy for Introducing a Thinking Skill or Strategy

briefly, the teacher reinforces the stated goal of the lesson—to "learn" at an introductory level a specific thinking skill, in this case classifying.

Psychologically, the four or five minutes required to complete this introduction to the new skill or strategy helps students develop the mental set necessary for what they are about to do—execute the operation. Whenever individuals decide to do something, psychologists report, the mind searches long-term memory to bring into short-term memory for immediate use anything it knows related to the task to be undertaken.[2] It uses various cues in making this search. If all a teacher does to aid students to search their memories is to use a single skill label, the students' search may be limited to that one cue, the skill label. Adding synonyms, a definition, and examples in effect provides additional potential cues for those who may have something stored away in the past experience associated with *any* of these cues. The time devoted to this "cueing" allows time for the search and for students to develop the set or readiness to engage in the skill. Too many times teachers fail to help students develop the set needed to execute a skill. This attention to the skill in introducing it counters such an omission. In teaching a new thinking operation, especially in the early lessons, teachers should launch their instruction by introducing the skill as described here so that students can develop the set they need to have some success at executing the skill.

In conducting this part of an introductory lesson, the teacher may wish to involve students as much as possible. Students can volunteer synonyms for the skill label or simple definitions of the skill and even examples of its use. But the teacher should not strain to get these out of the class. In the case of complex or unfamiliar skills, this often proves impossible, so the teacher should be prepared to supply them directly. The point of the introduction is not to play guessing games with these skill descriptors but to get as many up on the chalkboard as possible in a brief time as cues for students trying to recall whatever they may know about the skill so that they can better understand or use it.

It is most useful for students to execute a newly introduced skill (Step 2) in pairs, triads, or small groups. This minimizes any risk involved. Those unable to do the skill can ride the coattails of those who can. This "teaming" also allows for some peer teaching, as those more familiar with

the skill usually step right in and do it, occasionally even explaining to their partners why they are doing what they do.

Once students have some experience in lessons of this type, one or two of them can be assigned as observers to record what other students do or seem to do as they execute the new skills, but this is not absolutely necessary. Such a procedure does serve to alert students to the kinds of thinking operations that may be going on as others in the groups or triads actually execute the skill. It also provides a number of resource people somewhat more prepared than other students to discuss, after this part of the lesson has been completed, how the skill was carried out. But when such an activity is first used (as in the above example with the skill of classifying), it is just as useful to have all students engage in doing the skill and later all take part in reconstructing what they did.

Students' reflecting on and verbalizing (Step 3) what they did in their minds as they executed this skill is a key step in this, as in any, introductory strategy. This activity requires students to engage in metacognition, to look inside their heads to report what went on there in the course of—in this example—forming categories of data.[3] At this point students must attempt to explore how they executed the skill and to articulate any rules they seem to have followed or special knowledge about the skill they used.

The teacher can initiate this step by discussing briefly—without writing anything on the board—ideas about life in 1750 New England generated by the groupings made by the students. But most of the class discussion at this point must focus on the skill. It is the skill that is to be "learned" in this lesson, not information about the subject; that information can be the focus of the next day's lesson. For the moment, it is crucial for students to hear how others did the skill and to share with them how they did it, for there is no "right" way to execute a skill, though some procedures are more efficient and productive than are others. Talking about the skill and hearing others talk about it are among the most effective devices in the initial stages of learning any thinking operation.

In the final two steps of this teaching strategy, students use what they have done, heard, and articulated to execute the skill again (Step 4), and then once again share with each other how they did it and what they have found out about the main attributes of the skill (Step 5). The skill definition offered at the beginning of the lesson can be revised here to reflect what has been learned, and perhaps additional synonyms will be volunteered. References can be made here, too, about where students can use this skill in other classes or out-of-school as well as where they have used it previously in the text or in their own course. The lesson concludes as it started, with emphasis on the skill, its attributes and uses. A follow-up assignment using the skill once more provides one more opportunity to begin to make it part of a student's intellectual repertoire.

Reviewing the Strategy

This inductive introductory strategy allows students and teacher to ''discover'' or at least become more conscious of the major steps, knowledge, and rules that constitute the skill being introduced, albeit perhaps only at a beginning and probably an incomplete level. Its use allows field-independent students to share their intuitive insights with their more field-dependent peers who rely more often on explicit directives to complete such tasks. It also requires field-independent students to become more conscious of how they think, thus giving them even more control over their own minds than they might otherwise develop. And, most important of all, this strategy allows teachers to introduce a thinking skill even when they themselves are not clear about its operations, rules, or special knowledge. In effect, this strategy allows students to ''teach'' the teacher as well as one another how to execute the skill. Conducting several inductive introductory lessons in the same skill in the same day will contribute immensely to a teacher's knowledge of how to do and how to explain a skill, thus making it much easier to use another, more direct introductory strategy when introducing this same skill another time.

This inductive strategy appeals to many teachers for a variety of reasons. Chief among these is belief that whatever students figure out on their own, as they do in using this strategy, they learn better. Indeed, research indicates that self-invention or student induction of thinking skills and strategies may lead to better retention of whatever operations are ''discovered.'' However, this same research indicates that such an approach to learning thinking skills and strategies can also easily result in the invention of dysfunctional skills and strategies and a commitment to

these that inhibits learning more useful, effective ways to execute these operations.[4] Thus, this inductive introductory teaching strategy must be used judiciously. It is not for all students nor for all times nor for all skills. Selection of the right teaching strategy for introducing a thinking operation must take into account the abilities of the students, their previous experience in using the operation to be introduced, the complexity of the operation, and the type of subject matter being used to introduce it. In many instances, especially for slower students or novices or in the case of complex thinking operations, more direct expository strategies will be more effective and appropriate in introducing a new thinking skill or strategy.

A DIRECTIVE STRATEGY

In introducing a new thinking operation, sometimes it is more efficient or effective, in terms of student learning, for teachers to be much more direct in their instruction than if they used the inductive introduction strategy. Such occasions include those when the thinking skill or strategy to be introduced is very complex, when the students may be less able than average students, or when the students have had no previous experience with the operation at all—when they are truly beginners or novices. In instances such as these, teachers can use a rather didactic introductory strategy.[5] For want of a better label, this introductory strategy can be called a directive strategy.

Analyzing the Strategy

With the directive strategy, the teacher plays a much more expository role than with the inductive strategy described above. This directive strategy presents the key attributes of the new thinking operation directly to the students right at the start of the lesson.[6] Thereupon, the students use whatever data have been provided them to execute the operation themselves in an effort to replicate it as it has been introduced. In so doing, they in effect test out the procedure and rules already presented and may even discover or invent additional ones. But the teacher retains almost complete control of what is to be learned about the new operation, first by presenting its key attributes; second by controlling its application; third, by accepting or rejecting student ideas about how it works; and, finally, by providing a standard description of the operation to conclude the lesson. A directive introduction actually minimizes student input at this initial stage of learning a new thinking skill or strategy. It does so in order to provide a common base on which students can elaborate with later guidance, practice, and reflection. In effect, this strategy has students execute a new thinking operation as others more proficient in it than they do it, before they—the students—try to execute it on their own.

In introducing a thinking operation using a directive strategy, a teacher guides students through six steps:

1. First, the teacher previews the operation in the context of the subject matter being studied, just as in the inductive strategy.
2. Next, the teacher explains in some detail the key steps, in sequence, that constitute the operation's procedure as well as important rules and other information relating to the operation.
3. Then, the teacher, with student assistance as volunteered, shows in step-by-step fashion just how the operation is executed—how the procedures are employed in sequence, how major rules work, and how specific criteria or cues are used.
4. At this point students discuss the demonstration, reviewing how the attributes of the operation are illustrated by the demonstration.
5. Then the students, with teacher guidance as necessary, apply the operation following as closely as possible the way it was demonstrated and explained.
6. Finally, the students reflect on how they executed the operation, focusing on the key procedures, rules, and knowledge that constitute the newly introduced operation.

By moving through these six steps—*preview, explain, demonstrate, review, apply, reflect*—teachers can initiate student understanding of a new, often complex, thinking skill or strategy. This directive strategy allows teachers to control the various features of an operation as they are introduced, presenting a simplified version of it before presenting its

more complex or sophisticated nuances. This approach can minimize confusion and provide all students a common baseline of knowledge about a new thinking operation on which to build in subsequent lessons. It also satisfies a commonly expressed desire of beginners and less able students faced with a seemingly impossible task to "show me what you want me to do" before they are willing to risk doing it. Figure B.4 identifies the key operations that constitute each of the major steps in this teaching strategy. Teachers can use this outline as a guide in planning or evaluating lessons to introduce any thinking operation employing this directive strategy.

Applying the Strategy

A teacher can use a directive strategy just as easily as an inductive strategy to introduce any thinking operation. For example, in introducing the skill of classifying information in the imaginary American history lesson described above, a teacher using the directive strategy could start exactly as with the lesson using the inductive strategy. The teacher should *preview* this skill at precisely the same point in the class and for the same purposes as in that example (Step 1). The four- to five-minute introduction of the skill should focus on the skill label—*classify*, provide synonyms, generate a tentative definition, and point out some examples from the everyday experiences of the students in the class. But after this initial introduction, the lesson should differ considerably from a lesson using the inductive approach.

Instead of having the students apply the skill immediately after its brief introduction, in this directive strategy the teacher should *explain* carefully the key attributes of the skill (Step 2). In this instance, for example, the teacher might project an overhead transparency showing some of the key rules and/or steps constituting the skill as executed by "experts." The teacher could thus point out that to classify data some experts:

1. State their goals—what they hope to find out by classifying the data.
2. Skim the data to see what's there.

3. Recall the meaning of the data.
4. Select one piece of the data—or let these data "jump up" and select them.
5. Find another piece of the data similar to the first.
6. Identify what it is that these items share and state that common feature as the label of a group (category/class).
7. Find all other items in this given information that fit in this group and put them under this label.
8. Repeat the process (Steps 4–7), forming new groups until all data have been placed in appropriate groups.
9. Subdivide some categories into more precise categories and/or combine others into larger, more encompassing categories.

Among the rules that might be pointed out are those about where such a skill can be used—as, for instance, when the data available appear to be disorganized (as in the word list in Figure B.1) or in an overwhelming amount (as in the list of words in Figure B.2). Students might also be advised that in encountering data they do not understand, they can put it aside in a category of "other" or "miscellaneous," to deal with after they have classified all other data, another useful rule followed by those experienced in executing this skill.

Next, the teacher should *demonstrate* just how this skill can be employed (Step 3). Using the list of words in Figure B.1 commonly spoken in New England colonies in 1750 and keeping the list of skill steps projected on the screen, the teacher can walk students through the skill to make several categories of items. Students can volunteer suggestions as they take each step: stating the goal (to find out what life was like in 1750 New England); skimming to report at random some of the words on the handout and stating the meanings of several of these words; selecting one word—any word—and finding another that is, to them, like the word just identified; and so on until a category of words is in place on the chalkboard. The steps can be repeated to make another category of words, if desired—and repeated several more times to make additional groupings. Then the teacher and students can *review* (Step 4) how they executed this skill thus far and how they followed the rules already introduced.

At this point (Step 5) the students can *apply* the skill as demonstrated

STEP 1 *PREVIEW THE SKILL*

State that "learning" the skill is today's objective.
Give the skill label/name.
Give synonyms.
State a tentative/working definition.
State ways the skill can be or has been used:
 • in students' personal experience,
 • in school activities,
 • in this course.
Explain how the skill is useful and why it's worth learning.

STEP 2 *EXPLAIN THE SKILL*

State the procedure constituting the skill in step-by-step sequence, explaining what one does and why for each step.
State key rules and "things to know" about the skill.

STEP 3 *DEMONSTRATE THE SKILL*

Lead the class step-by-step through the skill:
 • state the goal,
 • refer to each step in the procedure,
 • give reasons for doing each step.
Show how rules are carried out.
Use course subject matter familiar to the students (or, if necessary, from their experience)

STEP 4 *REVIEW WHAT WAS DONE*

Review the procedures and rules.
Review the reasons for each (as illustrated in the demonstration).

STEP 5 *APPLY THE SKILL*

Execute the skill with teacher guidance.
Work in pairs, triads, or groups.
Complete material used in demonstration or use new but same kind of data/media as used in Step 3.

STEP 6 *REFLECT ON THE SKILL*

Review the steps comprising the skill and the rules guiding its use.
Reflect on ways in which the skill is used and when it is appropriate to use.
State the relationship of this skill to other skills.
Review or revise skill definition..
State where the skill can be used in
 • personal or out-of-school situations,
 • coursework.

Figure B.4 A Directive Strategy for Introducing a Thinking Skill or Strategy

lesson on life in pre-Revolutionary America can thus continue just as in the preceding example.

Reviewing the Strategy

This teaching strategy may be used to introduce any thinking skill or strategy. However, unlike the case of the inductive strategy, in using a directive strategy to introduce a thinking skill or strategy the teacher must know the key attributes of the operation being introduced—and know them well enough to explain and demonstrate them for the students. In using this approach the teacher does not present these attributes as *the only* attributes of the skill. The attributes presented should be offered simply as one way some experts execute the skill—a way that can be used by students and modified by them as they become more proficient with practice in executing the skill. This strategy is most useful when teaching time is scarce and the thinking operation to be introduced is rather complex.

This directive skill-introducing strategy helps students begin to learn a thinking operation in two important ways. It accommodates the need or desire of some students to learn a workable way to do something and "get on with it." Many students have, rightly or wrongly, a low tolerance for ambiguity; trying to figure out inductively how to execute a new thinking operation may prove so frustrating that they simply "turn off" and withdraw or quit. Using this directive strategy thus eliminates or sharply reduces such potential frustration and keeps students engaged in the learning task.

Furthermore, while it may appear that the directive strategy does not allow students to articulate a variety of procedures for doing the new operation, as does the inductive strategy, use of this strategy does in fact quickly lead to such "personalization" of the operation.[7] The initial steps in this strategy do restrict students to one way of executing the new operation; however, at the point of application (Step 5), students frequently execute it *their* ways rather than exactly as demonstrated. Within one or two of the guided practice lessons that follow, students build on the base established by the demonstrated procedure to give their own twists to the skill or strategy being learned. In practice, presentation of a

to complete classifying the words used in the demonstration or to classify the words in Figure B.2. Working in pairs, perhaps, they can apply the skill as presented and demonstrated to put these words into categories of their own, with the transparency list of steps and rules still projected on the screen to guide them. To conclude the lesson (Step 6), the students can then *reflect* on the steps and rules they used and how they executed them; they can volunteer any other "rules" they seemed to have followed or any additional steps they executed. They need also to revise their definition of the skill to make it more precise or accurate, and they should suggest places in the text or course where they may have used data already classified by the textbook authors.

Finally, to end the class review of the skill, the teacher can present the students a saying or acronym or similar device related to the skill that will help them recall how to do it next time. In this case, the teacher could suggest that whenever it is time to classify data, students should think GROUPS, list these letters down the board (or on a sheet of butcher paper or on a transparency), and then after each letter write or project the step represented in classifying:

G oal stated

R ecall meaning of data

O rganize similar items together

U se the similarity as the group label

P lace all other items into groups and label each group

S ubdivide or combine and relabel groups

Students can copy this list of steps into their notebooks for future reference. If these steps are written on large sheets of paper or on a bulletin board for display, eventually the explanations can be removed, leaving simply the word GROUPS displayed for student reference in future lessons. The homework or seatwork assignment, if one is given, could have students classify a list of words commonly spoken in the Middle Atlantic or Southern colonies around 1750. The substantive flow of the

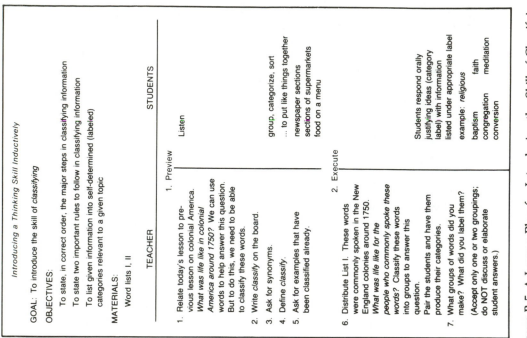

Introducing a Thinking Skill Inductively

GOAL: To introduce the skill of *classifying*

OBJECTIVES:

To state, in correct order, the major steps in classifying information

To state two important rules to follow in classifying information

To list given information into self-determined (labeled) categories relevant to a given topic

MATERIALS:

Word lists I, II

TEACHER	STUDENTS
1. Preview	
1. Relate today's lesson to previous lesson on colonial America. *What was life like in colonial America around 1750?* We can use words to help answer this question. But to do this, we need to be able to classify these words.	Listen
2. Write *classify* on the board.	
3. Ask for synonyms.	group, categorize, sort ... to put like things together
4. Define *classify*.	
5. Ask for examples that have been classified already.	newspaper sections sections of supermarkets food on a menu
2. Execute	
6. Distribute List I. These words were commonly spoken in the New England colonies around 1750. *What was life like for the people who commonly spoke these words?* Classify these words into groups to answer this question. Pair the students and have them produce their categories.	
7. What groups of words did you make? What did you label them? (Accept only one or two groupings; do NOT discuss or elaborate student answers.)	Students respond orally justifying ideas (category label) with information listed under appropriate label example: *religious* baptism faith congregation meditation conversion

Figure B.5 A Lesson Plan for Introducing the Skill of Classifying

model way to execute any thinking operation as included in this strategy turns out to be just the stimulus or springboard needed by students to engage in a difficult operation with enough insight and confidence to be able to do it—successfully—their ways.

INTRODUCING THINKING SKILLS AND STRATEGIES

Clear, explicit introduction of any thinking operation—whether it be a strategy of decision making or a micro-thinking skill such as classifying—is absolutely essential for helping students understand such an operation and how it might be executed. Either the inductive or directive strategies described in this chapter may be used for this purpose. Figure B.5 is a lesson plan using one of the two strategies employed in the sample lessons analyzed here. Which of these two skill-introducing strategies does this lesson plan employ?

Review the descriptions of each strategy in the preceding pages. Then study the plan in Figure B.5. As you read it, fill in each blank down the center of the plan with the name of the step in the strategy that describes the activities listed below that line. Then, on the blank after the title of the plan, write the type of strategy used in this lesson. Answers and a commentary may be found in a note to the reader on page B-14. If you have difficulty deciding which skill-introducing strategy is described in this lesson plan, discuss the sample plan with someone else who has also read the chapters. If you had no trouble identifying the steps in the lesson, and the strategy used in each step, then write a lesson plan using this strategy to introduce the skill of classifying in *your* favorite subject or class. Check it for accuracy by matching your plan with the appropriate guidelines presented here. This lesson plan and yours can then serve as models of lessons using this strategy to introduce any thinking operation in any subject or class.

There are, of course, other strategies equally well suited for introducing a new thinking operation. Most of these other strategies consist of some variation or combination of these inductive and directive strategies. One such alternative skill-introducing strategy is described next, and then goes on to analyze the essential features of those teaching

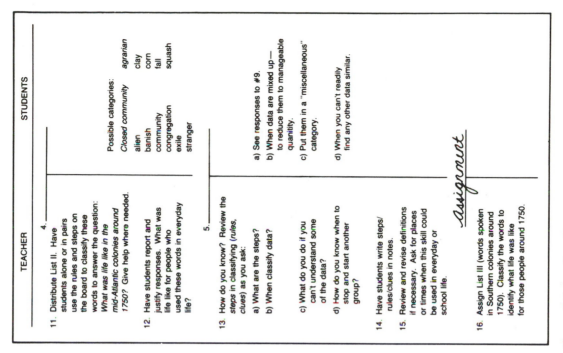

TEACHER	STUDENTS
11. Distribute List II. Have students alone or in pairs use the rules and steps on the board to classify these words to answer the question: *What was life like in the mid-Atlantic colonies around 1750?* Give help where needed.	Possible categories: *Closed community* *agrarian* alien clay banish corn community fall congregation squash exile stranger
12. Have students report and justify responses. What was life like for people who used these words in everyday life?	
13. How do you know? Review the steps in classifying (*rules, clues*) as you ask: a) What are the steps? b) When classify data? c) What do you do if you can't understand some of the data? d) How do you know when to stop and start another group?	a) See responses to #9. b) When data are mixed up—to reduce them to manageable quantity. c) Put them in a "miscellaneous" category. d) When you can't readily find any other data similar.
14. Have students write steps/rules/clues in notes.	
15. Review and revise definitions if necessary. Ask for places or times when this skill could be used in everyday or school life.	
Assignment	
16. Assign List III (words spoken in Southern colonies around 1750). Classify the words to identify what life was like for those people around 1750.	

Figure B.5 (*continued*)

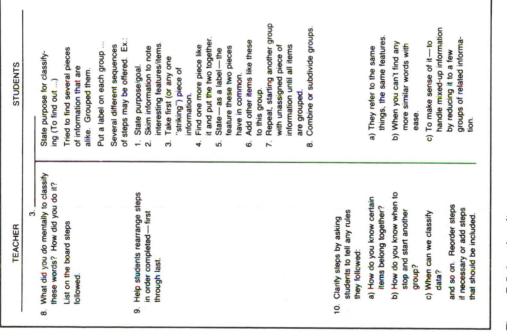

TEACHER	STUDENTS
8. What did you *do* mentally to classify these words? How did you do it? List on the board steps followed.	State purpose for classifying. (To find out ...) Tried to find several pieces of information that are alike. Grouped them. Put a label on each group ...
9. Help students rearrange steps in order completed—first through last.	Several different sequences of steps may be offered. Ex.: 1. State purpose/goal. 2. Skim information to note interesting features/items. 3. Take first (or any one "striking") piece of information. 4. Find one more piece like it and put the two together. 5. State—as a label—the feature these two pieces have in common. 6. Add other items like these to this group. 7. Repeat, starting another group with unassigned piece of information until all items are grouped. 8. Combine or subdivide groups.
10. Clarify steps by asking students to tell any rules they followed: a) How do you know certain items belong together? b) How do you know when to stop and start another group? c) When can we classify data? and so on. Reorder steps if necessary or add steps that should be included.	a) They refer to the same things, the same features. b) When you can't find any more similar words with ease. c) To make sense of it—to handle mixed-up information by reducing it to a few groups of related information.

Figure B.5 (*continued*)

strategies most effective for introducing any thinking skill or strategy in any subject to any students.

The inductive and directive strategies just described represent two prototypes from a range of strategies that can be used to introduce any thinking operation. Teachers can, of course, devise numerous variations on each of these prototypes. Moreover, the key elements of each can be blended into a third type of strategy that typifies those found midway in this range of strategies. This type of combined strategy can prove very useful with a wide range of students in introducing skills that students may have used earlier but in which they have only limited proficiency, or with skills of a modest level of difficulty, or with skills thought to be at a level of difficulty commensurate with the experience of the students. This skill-introducing strategy is best described as a developmental strategy.

A NOTE TO THE READER

The lesson plan in Figure B.5 involves students in executing a skill as best they can *before* discussing how it is done. This is the essence of the inductive strategy for introducing any thinking operation. After (1) previewing the operation, the teacher asks students simply (2) to attempt to carry it out. Only after trying it do they (3) reflect on and discuss how they executed it. Discussion focuses on the key attributes of the operation, especially the major steps through which students go in executing it and any principles or rules that they seem to be following in so doing. Then students (4) apply the operation a second time to new data—but data in the same form as that used in the initial effort. Finally, the students (5) review what they have learned about the operation. In this type of skill-introducing lesson, students do most of the work—they generate most of the substance of the lesson. What they have articulated about the new operation can be fleshed out, modified, and elaborated over the guided practice and other lessons that follow. This particular kind of introduction to a thinking operation is only one of several that could have been employed for this purpose.

What would a lesson plan look like that introduced the skill of classifying by using the other skill-introducing strategy described here? Figure B.6 presents such a lesson plan. Read it over to see if it includes the key steps in the directive skill-introducing strategy described in the preceding pages. Label these steps on the lines provided down the center of the plan.

Introducing a Skill

GOAL: To introduce the skill of *classifying*

OBJECTIVES:

To state, in correct order, the major steps in classifying information

To state two important rules to follow in classifying information

To list given information into self-determined (labeled) categories relevant to a given topic

MATERIALS:

Word lists I and II

TEACHER	STUDENTS
1.	
1. Relate today's lesson to previous lesson on colonial America. *What was life like in colonial America around 1750?* We can use words commonly spoken by early settlers to help answer this question. But to do this, we need to be able to classify these words.	
2. Write *classify* on board.	
3. Ask for synonyms. (What is it like?)	categorize/group/sort
4. Define *classify*.	...to put "like" things together
5. Give examples.	classify objects in room into people/furniture or students into boys/girls, short/tall, etc. sections in newspapers supermarket sections
Ask for other examples.	
2.	
6. Explain steps — *list on board* *Given specific information —* 1. State your purpose: What are you trying to find out? 2. Skim the information to note what's there. 3. Take one piece of information and search for one more piece like it. List these together. 4. State what makes these alike. Write this common feature above them as a label.	

Figure B.6 A Lesson Plan for Introducing the Skill of Classifying

Figure B.6 (*continued*)

TEACHER	STUDENTS
11. Have students report and give words from the list to justify one or two categories.	
12. Review steps in classifying. a) What are the steps? b) Why classify data?	a) See above Step 6. b) To make sense of it—to handle lots of information by reducing it to a few groups of related information.
c) How do you know when certain items belong together? d) How do you know when to stop and start another group?	c) They refer to the same thing, they have the same features, etc. d) When you can't find any more similar words with ease.
13. Write steps in "skills" book as list of rules.	
14. Show how to use GROUPS as a device to recall how to classify.	Get data. Relate two pieces together. Order a label. Use label to find other similar pieces. Pick another pair and repeat. Subdivide or combine.
15. Assign List III (words spoken in Southern colonies around 1750). Classify the words to identify what life was like for those people around 1750.	

Figure B.6 (*continued*)

---

5. Find as many other items as possible that fit this label and add to list.
6. Repeat this process with the next unassigned piece of information until all items are labeled in groups.
7. Combine and/or subdivide groups.

Useful rules to follow:

1. If you do not understand some item, put it in "miscellaneous" category and go on—but come back to it later to try to use it.
2. If a word means more than one thing, it can go in several categories.
3. ...

TEACHER	STUDENTS
7. Distribute List I. These words were commonly spoken in the New England colonies around 1750. *What was life like for the people who spoke these words frequently?*	3. *forests were important* ax *religious* barrel baptism clog congregation bench conversion fall faith oak meditation saw etc.
8. Walk the class through the steps, classifying items with student help as volunteered. Explain why each step is done as it is executed.	
9. Cover up list of steps on board and have students recall what was done and the reasons for doing each step.	4. As in item 6 above.
10. Distribute List II. These words were spoken frequently in the Middle Atlantic colonies around 1750. *What was life like for the people who spoke these words?* Classify these words to answer this question, using the steps and rules just explained and demonstrated.	5. Possible categories: *closed community* *agrarian* alien clay banish cold community corn exile fall heresy harvest stranger ... ...

Figure B.6 (*continued*)

A DEVELOPMENTAL STRATEGY

A developmental introductory strategy puts together the experimenting phase (Steps 1, 2 and 3) of the inductive strategy with the expository phase (Steps 2–6) of the directive strategy. It introduces a thinking operation by, first, involving students in applying it as best they can, knowing that they are likely to be less successful at it than they could be. After discussing with them how they did it and identifying any difficulties they had in engaging in the operation, the teacher then explains and demonstrates those rules or procedures that can be used to eliminate any difficulties encountered by the students. In effect, this strategy creates a discrepancy for the students between what they want or need to do and their current ability to do it and dramatically alerts them to this discrepancy. It then provides information and guided practice for helping them resolve the discrepancy on a need to know basis. Such a strategy incorporates basic principles of Piagetian-based developmental learning theory.[8]

In using this strategy, a teacher organizes the lesson as follows:

1. First, the teacher previews the new thinking operation, in the context of the subject matter being taught, just as in the inductive and directive strategies.
2. Then the students execute the operation as best they can without any instruction or teacher guidance.
3. The students then review what they have become aware of about the operation and identify places where they encountered difficulties.
4. Next, the teacher explains and demonstrates those procedures or rules that can be used to resolve the difficulties encountered.
5. The students, with teacher guidance as needed, then apply the operation again, incorporating what has been discussed and explained about it.
6. Finally, students and teacher reflect on and review how the operation can be executed and how the attributes given by the teacher make it easier to execute.

By moving through these six steps, the lesson creates a situation that provides its own motivation for learning. It also allows students to build their own representation of the thinking skill or strategy being introduced. Recognizing deficiencies in their knowledge of, or abilities to employ, the new skill, they incorporate into their version of it "expert knowledge" that increases their proficiency in its use. Insight into the operation "develops" as the lesson unfolds. Though an introductory strategy of this type often requires longer to execute than either of the strategies described earlier, it leads perhaps to better initial learning because it helps students resolve a cognitive dissonance that has been allowed to develop and involves inherently satisfying, active learning on their part.[9] Figure B.7 outlines the major steps constituting this developmental strategy.

Applying the Strategy

Rather than using either an inductive or directive strategy, a developmental strategy could have been used to introduce the skill of classifying data into self-identified categories in the imaginary American history class described in the preceding chapter. To do so, in the same topic or subject area as in that lesson, the teacher would begin (Step 1) by setting the subject-matter context exactly as in both the previously explained strategies. Then the teacher could *preview* in detail the skill to be learned. Writing the label on the board, finding and recording synonyms and a simple definition, and discussing briefly some examples of the skill in use help direct the focus of the lesson to the skill while assisting students to develop the mental set needed to deal purposefully with the skill.

As in the inductive strategy, students then execute the skill (Step 2). Working in groups or with a partner or two, they employ the skill with the same words listed in Figure B.1 to decide what life was like in the New England colonies around 1750. The teacher may move around the class to provide help with the data, if necessary, or to clarify the task, but should not provide instruction or assistance with the skill itself unless a student is absolutely stuck. In students' *reflecting* (Step 3) on how they actually executed the skill, discussion may well yield two or three different sequences of operations through which various students proceeded.

Analysis of these various sequences usually reveals that, as researcher Robbie Case points out, beginners or young students tend to be incomplete or inconsistent in the skill operations they employ rather than to employ incorrect operations.[10] Once the teacher has pointed out these omissions or inconsistencies, the lesson can then proceed—generally with rapt student attention—to how to remedy these difficulties.

By *explanation* and *demonstration* (Step 4) the teacher next can show what students can do to fill in any gaps in the skill or to remedy any inconsistencies. This may require explaining a rule used by experts to execute the skill, a rule that none of the students seemed to employ but one that, if used, makes the skill much more workable. Some youngsters, for example, have a hard time getting started in classifying data. Knowing that they have to match only two items to get underway is a useful "rule" for them. Others often fail to articulate the common feature of any pair of items they spot until after they have tried to collect all similar items; in so doing, they gradually alter or enlarge the initial category to the point where they lose focus and have to recategorize the data. When advised to state the common feature of an initial match of just two items—to make the category label at that point—students then have a specific label to use as a search tool in examining the remaining data. Thus, their search is more efficient and keeps the category with which they are working within reasonable bounds. By becoming aware of these missing rules or operations, students can then incorporate them into their conceptualization of the skill as they apply it once more.

In *applying* (Step 5) their revised descriptions of the skill with another similar data set, as with the words descriptive of life in the Middle Atlantic colonies around 1750 (see Figure B.2), students come to realize how useful the newly introduced attributes are. In the process, they gain additional insights into the skill. Students can then *revise* (Step 6) the key skill attributes thus discovered and tested, revise the skill definition, review synonyms, and discuss examples of how or where the skill has been or can be used in the course. The lesson can conclude with the same assignment as recommended in the sample applications of the inductive and directive strategies described earlier.

STEP 1 *PREVIEW THE SKILL*

State that "learning" the skill is today's objective.
Give the skill label/name.
Give synonyms.
State a tentative/working definition.
State ways the skill can be or has been used:
· in students' personal experience,
· in school activities,
· in this course.
Explain how the skill is useful and why it's worth learning.

STEP 2 *EXECUTE THE SKILL*

Use the skill (as best one can) to accomplish a task.
Work in pairs, triads, or groups.
Use subject matter familiar to the students and appropriate to course or from students' experience.

STEP 3 *REFLECT ON WHAT WAS DONE*

Report what went on in students' heads as they engaged in the skill.
Identify the steps and rules used and their sequence.
Clarify procedures or any criteria used.
Focus on the skill and its attributes.

STEP 4 *EXPLAIN/DEMONSTRATE*

State any key operations or key rules omitted or misapplied by students.
Give reasons for using these procedures or rules.
Demonstrate application of these operations or rules, explaining how and why each is used.

STEP 5 *APPLY THE SKILL TO NEW DATA*

Use the teacher-introduced procedures and rules with student descriptions of the skill to complete original or another task.
Students work in pairs or groups.
Use subject matter familiar to the students and appropriate to course, but in the same structure and media like that used in Step 2.

STEP 6 *REVIEW THE SKILL*

Report on what was done in students' heads as they applied the skill.
Review the procedures and rules that seem to constitute the skill.
State the relationship of this skill to other skills.
Review or revise the skill definition.
State where the skill can be used in:
· personal or out-of-school situations,
· coursework.

Figure B.7 A Developmental Strategy for Introducing a Thinking Skill or Strategy

Analyzing the Strategy

Figure B.8 presents a lesson plan employing this developmental strategy for introducing the skill of classifying within the sample American history lesson just described. This developmental strategy allows students to articulate what they know about this skill and then to become familiar with some of the rules or operations that flesh out their knowledge of it. The teacher's role in such a strategy is to help the students understand why their version of the skill is incomplete or doesn't work, to demonstrate and explain those operations or rules needed to make the skill operable, and to explain the reasons why these added elements are essential to the skill. The students, on the other hand, then have an opportunity to integrate this new information about the skill into their own understanding of the skill as they apply it in this lesson and in subsequent practice lessons. Both teacher and students need to know something about the skill for this strategy to be useful. The teacher needs to know enough about it to point out those bits of "expert knowledge" that students skip or abuse; students need to be able to engage in the skill to some degree so as to articulate at least a tentative version of it.

This strategy reflects developmental learning theories. The key to such learning consists of making students aware of a gap between what they need or want to do and their present abilities to do it. Learners learn, developmentalists assert, because of their internal motivation to close such gaps, to resolve perceived discrepancies.[11] Thus, thinking operations presented for learning using this strategy must be within the realm of student execution; if not, the resulting discrepancy between desired goal and current achievable goal may be so great as to "turn students off" and close down further learning. While this strategy relies on creating some degree of dissonance and perhaps frustration on the part of students, it can easily result in creating too much. Consequently, teachers planning to use the strategy need to be sure that the thinking operation introduced is within the ability level of the students. Often, such a determination can be made only with practice and as a result of a thorough knowledge of the students in a class. As yet, little guidance exists as to which thinking skills are best introduced to which students at what grade levels. Since all individuals engage in thinking to some degree, the key to working with novices or younger students may well be the *type* of

---

Introducing a Skill: A Developmental Strategy

GOAL: To introduce the skill of *classifying*

OBJECTIVES:

To state, in correct order, the major steps in classifying information

To state two important rules to follow in classifying information

To list given information into self-determined (labeled) categories relevant to a given topic

MATERIALS:

Word lists I, II

TEACHER	STUDENTS
Preview	
	Listen
1. Relate today's lesson to previous lesson on colonial America. *What was life like in colonial America around 1750?* We can use words to help answer this question. But to do this, we need to be able to classify these words.	
2. Write *classify* on the board.	
3. Ask for synonyms.	group, categorize, sort
4. Define *classify*.	... to put group like things together
5. Ask for examples that have been classified already.	newspaper sections / sections of supermarkets / food on a menu
Execute	
6. Distribute List I. These words were commonly spoken in the New England colonies around 1750. *What was life like for the people who commonly spoke these words?* Classify these words into groups to answer this question. Pair the students and have them write out their categories.	
7. What groups of words did you make? What did you label them? (Accept one or two groupings; do NOT discuss or elaborate student answers.)	Students respond orally, justifying ideas (category label) with information listed under appropriate label.

Figure B.8 A Developmental Lesson Plan for Introducing the Skill of Classifying

TEACHER	STUDENTS
Explain/Demonstrate	
11. If students skip an important step or rule or misapply it, point this out and explain how the step or rule should be applied — and why.	Perhaps point out: • usefulness of using a "miscellaneous" category for data not understood (such as "clog") • How to start the skill off by selecting one word at random, searching for another like it, and using the "likeness" as the category label • the importance of stating a group label as soon as two items have been "matched" and then using the label to help find other items that fit the group
Apply	
12. Demonstrate how these new or corrected rules and/or steps work, using List I.	
13. Distribute List II. Have the students in pairs use the rules and steps on the board as well as the new rules and steps to classify these words to answer the question: *What was life like in the Middle Atlantic colonies for the people who spoke these words around 1750?*	Possible categories: *closed community* *agrarian* alien clay banish corn community fall exile squash stranger ... ...
14. Accept one or two groupings suggested by students but do NOT discuss or elaborate on them.	
Review	
15. Review steps and rules in classifying: a) What are the steps? b) Why classify data? c) How do you know when certain data go together?	a) See above, Step 9. b) To make sense of it — to handle lots of information by reducing it to a few groups of related information. c) They refer to the same thing, they have the same features, etc

Figure B.8 (*continued*)

TEACHER	STUDENTS
Reflect	
	example: *religious* baptism faith congregation meditation conversion
8. What did you do to classify these words? How did you do it? List on the board steps followed.	State purpose for classifying (To find out ...) Tried to find several pieces of information that are alike. Grouped them. Put a label on each group ...
9. Help students rearrange steps in order completed — first through last.	Several different sequences of steps may be offered. Ex.: 1. State purpose/goal 2. Skim information to note interesting features/items 3. Take first (or any one "striking") piece of information 4. Find one more piece like it and put the two together 5. State — as a label — the feature these two pieces have in common 6. Add other items like these to this group 7. Repeat, starting another with unassigned piece of information until all items are grouped 8. Combine or subdivide groups
10. Clarify steps by asking students to tell any rules they followed: a) How do you know certain items belong together? b) How do you know when to stop and start another group? c) When can we classify data? and so on. Reorder steps, if necessary.	a) They refer to the same things, the same features b) When you can't find any more similar words with ease c) To make sense of it — to handle lots of information by reducing it to a few groups of related information

Figure B.8 (*continued*)

places in what is already written out. Other than this slight change, a teacher can employ the steps in this strategy to introduce any thinking operation just as similar steps in other introductory strategies are carried out. Figure B.7, as noted above, outlines these steps and can be a guide in preparing any lesson plan for using this strategy to introduce any thinking skill or strategy.

ESSENTIAL FEATURES OF SKILL-INTRODUCING STRATEGIES

The strategies for introducing any thinking operation described in this and the preceding chapter have many similarities. In general, these three strategies employ essentially the same teaching process. Figure B.9 makes clear these procedural similarities, showing that all of these strategies start with an extended, formal preview of the thinking skill or strategy being introduced. They then call for students either to execute the operation as best they can or to hear or see how it is executed by someone more expert in it than they are. Next, these three strategies ask students to reflect on or review how the skill was just executed so that they can verbalize its key attributes, especially the steps in a procedure by which it is carried out. After executing the operation a second time, students again review or reflect on its attributes and attempt to tie up the skill or strategy to their academic work and/or their out-of-school experiences. These activities constitute the core of any effective skill-introducing teaching strategy.

The procedures comprising these three introductory strategies incorporate those features of skill teaching that research suggests are most essential to launching effective learning of a new thinking skill or strategy. Understanding the nature of these key features allows a teacher to use these strategies to their maximum potential and to make useful adaptations in these strategies without sacrificing their crucial attributes.

TEACHER	STUDENTS
d) How do you know when to stop and start another group?	d) When you can't find any more similar words with ease.
e) ...	
16. Write steps and rules in "skills" notebook.	Get data
17. Show how to use GROUPS to recall how to classify data	Relate two pieces together Order a label Use label to find other similar pieces Pick another pair and repeat Subdivide or combine
18. Review and revise definitions if necessary. Ask for, or suggest, places or times when this skill could be used in everyday or school life.	

Figure B.8 (continued)

things about which we have them think—concrete rather than abstract—rather than the particular skills being taught.

In carrying out this developmental introductory strategy, the teacher conducts the class through the strategy, performing each step much as was done in the corresponding steps of the inductive and directive strategies—with one exception. In explaining and demonstrating the thinking operation being introduced (Step 4), the teacher needs to present only the new step(s) or rule(s). It is not necessary to treat the skill attributes in toto. What proves most useful here is to have the students first report their understanding of the skill attributes (Step 3) as the teacher records them for all to see—lists the procedures that comprise the skill in sequence and also lists any rules followed. Then, in adding new procedures or rules, simply insert these or add these to the appropriate

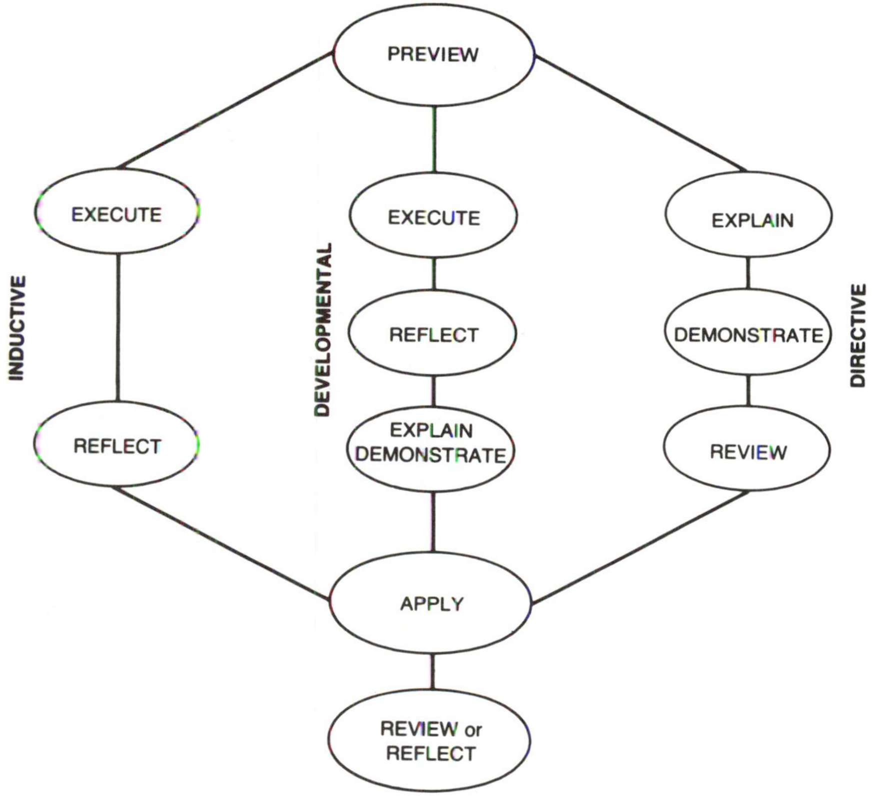

4. engage students in talking about how they think,
5. provide immediate, guided application of the operation,
6. build in cues useful in transferring the operation,
7. introduce instruction in the operation at a time when the operation is needed to accomplish a subject-matter task,
8. keep the data and media by which the data are presented the same throughout the introduction, and
9. keep the data or problem relatively simple and short.

Research and thoughtful practice indicate the importance of these factors in teaching and learning any thinking skill or strategy, especially in the initial introductory stages.

Focus on the Operation Being Introduced

In order to make it as easy as possible for students to deal with a newly introduced thinking skill or strategy and thus to enhance the learning of this operation, teachers need to minimize interference from competing input. While teachers may engage in the pursuit of several objectives simultaneously during a lesson, students apparently cannot attend si-multaneously to multiple stimuli or inputs and absorb or learn all of them equally well. Multiple inputs in addition to instruction in a new skill can interfere with skill learning. Such interference can be caused by other skills—especially recently introduced ones, by the subject matter being studied or used, and by the emotional content or implications of the subject matter.[12] Thus, a new thinking skill or strategy ought not to be introduced until students have achieved some proficiency in a previously introduced thinking operation. The emotional charge of the content being used or task being undertaken must not be so great as to distract from attention to the new skill. In introducing a thinking skill or strategy, teachers must be sure to eliminate or minimize the effect of other newly learned skills and strategies and the emotional or affective impact or difficulty of the subject matter.

For this same reason so, too, must teachers minimize attention to subject matter in introducing a new thinking operation. As difficult as this may be, the teacher must avoid virtually any discussion of subject matter

Figure B.9 Strategies for Introducing a New Thinking Skill or Strategy

In brief, the inductive, directive, and developmental introductory strategies all:

1. keep the focus on the operation to be learned,
2. model the operation,
3. articulate its key components or attributes,

whatsoever at this point in the teaching framework. Attention to subject matter normally seems to interfere with learning a skill, especially at the introductory stage of skill learning. Left to their own choices, most students elect to focus on subject matter, for after all that is what most teachers talk about, texts present, and classroom tests test! Minimizing or avoiding discussion of subject matter, of course, goes against the natural inclination of most teachers, who care deeply about and feel committed to teaching their subjects. However, for one lesson—this introductory one—it is absolutely crucial to keep any attention to content from interfering with the skill or strategy being introduced. Although students can use subject matter as a vehicle to begin learning about a skill, they should not discuss that subject matter *in this lesson*. For example, to give value to the task assigned the students and to initiate the mid-strategy reflection on or review of the skill (as initially demonstrated or tried in the sample lesson), the teacher can ask students to report briefly on what they found out about the topic (life in New England, in this case). But only two or three items need to be reported, and no discussion or elaboration should follow these reports. Discussion of what students learned about the subject by using the skill—in the case of the example used here, the nature of life in the thirteen colonies around 1750—can be the focus of the next day's lesson. In fact, it is often surprising to see how attention to the new skill in this introductory lesson seems to set up better recall of, and a more sophisticated understanding of, the subject matter in the next lesson.

All three introductory strategies place obvious and continuing emphasis on the thinking operation being introduced. In using any of these strategies, teachers must provide repeated cues to the effect that the new operation is what is to be focused on. In carrying out the preview step of each strategy (Step 1), for example, the teacher clearly indicates that beginning to learn the operation is the primary objective of the lesson in these ways: by giving explicit attention to defining the operation; by writing its label, synonyms, and definition on the chalkboard or overhead; and by stating or writing this as the objective of the day. *Nothing* to do with subject matter or other thinking skills should be written on the overhead or chalkboard. Rather, the teacher should write three headings on the board—*Steps, Rules, Useful Information*—and, under each, list what students offer as they reflect on or review how they

executed the operation. Of course, in explaining how to do the operation for the first time in using the directive strategy, the key steps and rules should be provided to the students via handouts or on the chalkboard or an overhead transparency. And in concluding an introductory lesson, focus should remain on the new operation. Students may need to redefine it or may have recalled synonyms not mentioned earlier. Discussion of examples of where this operation has been applied in the course earlier and where it can be later applied in the course or in daily life helps promote transfer as well as make the operation more relevant to the students. Just as an introductory skill lesson begins by focusing on the thinking operation to be introduced, so too should the lesson end with focus still on that operation.

Model the Thinking Operation

Research indicates that those who achieve a high degree of proficiency in any skill have seen it modeled or demonstrated, often repeatedly.[13] Modeling how an operation works is an extremely useful part of an introduction to any thinking operation because it allows students to actually see and hear how it is executed by someone more competent in it than are they. Such modeling need not be done only by the teacher, however; students good at a thinking operation can demonstrate how they do it. Written descriptions, such as sample problem solutions or narratives, are also useful for this purpose.

The introductory strategies presented all include modeling. In the inductive strategy, students' descriptions of how they engaged in the skill of classifying in effect present the required demonstration. Obviously, the results are by no means prescribed versions of the skill, but they serve as targets and pieces out of which students can construct or modify their own concepts of this skill. Both the directive and developmental strategies also call for demonstration of the operation being introduced—in these instances by the teacher or other "experts."

There is, though, more to modeling a thinking skill or strategy than simply doing something in an expert fashion. Students must be conscious that *someone is modeling* and that a *particular operation is being modeled*.[14] Simply to engage in a thinking task without alerting the students to the fact that execution of the task is being modeled is of little avail. Prior to demonstrating a thinking operation, the teacher needs to point out what is about to happen by explaining some of the key operations to be performed or rules that need to be followed and by alerting students as to what to look for. Before demonstrating the skill of classifying, for example, a teacher would find it useful to explain rules about how to start classifying and what to do in case one encounters troublesome data and to list in proper sequence some of the key elements of the procedure to be performed. As the skill is actually modeled, the demonstrator needs to explain what he or she is doing and why. And, upon concluding the demonstration, students and teacher should discuss what they have seen, especially the steps in the procedure, the sequence in which they were performed, and some reasons and rules for executing them. It is not enough simply to act out a behavior that students are to emulate. It is also important to call to the students' attention—to explain and to discuss with them—what is done, how it is done and why. Thus, demonstration of a thinking operation needs to be closely linked with explanation and discussion of the operation demonstrated.

Articulate Key Components

As a new thinking operation is demonstrated or used or after such demonstration or use, students need to have its major pieces, components, or attributes pointed out to them—or they need to do this themselves if they can. The strategies presented here each offer at least two opportunities to do just this. Novices learning a new operation naturally tend to fragment it and to concentrate on its major components. Allowing students to do this in the introductory lesson builds on a natural way of learning skills and meets very real learner demands regarding "What, exactly do I do?" and "How do I do it?" Discussing the key operations that constitute a skill, the key rules to be followed, and any useful information regarding it accomplishes this goal. While it is not necessary at the introductory stage to discuss every operation, rule, or bit of useful information, attention to the more important major attributes helps students identify these components of the operation and gives them more control over it.[15] Putting these components together and elaborating them follows gradually with guided practice.

Talk About Thinking

Research points out consistently that talking about what goes on in one's mind while engaging in a specific thinking operation or task, and hearing about what others do in their minds assist students in learning the operation.[16] Thinking about thinking—metacognition—is difficult, especially for individuals just being introduced to it. Verbalizing what one thinks, although even more difficult, helps students raise to a level of consciousness what they may intuitively know about the operation. By hearing others describe how they execute it, students discover new ways to engage in the operation. They find, too, that others in fact do similar things or that many people encounter obstacles similar to ones they encountered. Reflection on, and discussion of, what they believe they do or did in executing an operation not only help students isolate key operations but also leads to control of one's thinking. Thus, students find it easier to modify the ways they engage in thinking and to make their use of thinking operations more efficient and effective.

Each of the three strategies provides opportunities for students to talk about what they did as they executed the thinking skill being introduced. Not many students may choose to do so when these strategies are first employed. It is, after all, risky enough to tell what one thinks, let alone how one arrived at those thoughts, especially in situations where the products of thinking—answers—are traditionally judged right or wrong and these judgments are converted into grades with all the attendant consequences. Methods for facilitating student metacognition can be employed with students in the introductory lessons right after students try their hands at a skill for the first and second times in the course of these lessons.

In these introductory strategies student discussion of the new operation is as important, if not more important, than their actually executing it. The distribution of time for the various steps in each strategy is a measure of the importance of this step. The introduction of a new operation, Step 1 in each strategy, should require only four to five minutes. Student use of the operation should take up to six or eight minutes, enough to get into it and execute it. The focus here should be on doing the operation, not on completing any substantive task. So, whether or not the students actually process all the data they have been provided is not important at this point. Even less time may be desirable if the operation is particularly difficult or if the developmental introductory strategy is being used. While student levels of frustration at not being able to execute the operation well should not be allowed to reach intolerable or discouraging levels, some degree of frustration may be useful as a device for motivating further learning.

The largest single chunk of time in these strategies should be devoted to student reflection on how they executed the new thinking operation, perhaps fifteen minutes or more, for it is in doing this that they begin to raise to a level of consciousness their understanding of the operation. A second application of the operation can again be allocated six to eight or so minutes, enough time again to work through it at least once. Finally, five to ten minutes or so can be devoted to the review of what has been "discovered" so far about the operation and to making the assignment, if there is to be one. Of course, adjustments in this distribution of time may be required depending on the subject matter, nature of the operation to be introduced, and student abilities. It will require much more time to introduce such complex thinking strategies such as decision making or problem solving than it will to introduce a micro-thinking skill like classifying or synthesizing. But the point to remember is that a significant proportion of whatever time it takes should be devoted to student reflection and discussion of how they executed the operation being introduced.

Guide Application

It proves useful to have students apply a newly introduced thinking operation immediately after discussing a demonstration of it or an initial, unaided try at it. By so doing, students get an opportunity to apply or test out the insights they have gained about it or the procedures just demonstrated; thus, they begin to take ownership of these procedures. By minimizing delay between initial application or demonstration, discussion, and second application, teachers can reduce the impact of potential interference from all types of sources.[17]

In each introductory strategy, in its fourth or fifth steps, students apply (with teacher guidance as necessary) the new operation to, in effect, try or test out what they have heard or seen about it to that point.

With such an activity, followed by the ensuing review and discussion, students begin to enter this operation into memory, the first stage in learning a thinking skill or strategy. It is the first of a number of guided applications that they need to achieve proficiency in any thinking operation. When completed as part of an introductory lesson, this activity launches the sequence of skill learning lessons to follow. When the operation is applied to subject matter that is part of the regular course content and to a task that is relevant to the subject, it moves subject-matter learning along toward substantive course goals and satisfies oft-expressed student desires to "get on with it."

Build Cues for Transfer

Contrary to what most educators assume or would like to believe, transfer of thinking skills or strategies from one subject to another or from one context to another is neither automatic nor natural.[18] Most students do not as a matter of course or on their own transfer thinking operations learned in one area to another area. Failure to apply a thinking operation to a new but appropriate setting may, of course, be due to a low level of proficiency in how to engage in the operation. But, in many instances, transfer does not occur because students simply do not know that it is appropriate to use the operation in the new setting—they are not aware of the cues in the new setting that call the operation into play. And sometimes students fail to transfer an operation to a new setting because they do not know how to execute it in that setting.

Part of the task of teaching thinking operations is to teach the cues to setting, media, types of data, and tasks in which a particular thinking skill or strategy can be used. Classifying, for example, is appropriate to undertake whenever a task involves making sense of some data, as in inventing a topic sentence or synthesizing a generalization or conceptualizing or hypothesizing. Teaching students cues to these tasks helps set up transfer. Classifying can be done with numerical data, pictorial or graphic data, and data in forms other than the words used in the introductory lesson for illustrating the introductory strategies presented here. Students need to be alerted to this fact. In introducing a new thinking operation, teachers can move toward transfer by letting students know about or predict

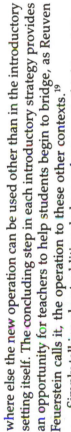

where else the new operation can be used other than in the introductory setting itself. The concluding step in each introductory strategy provides an opportunity for teachers to help students begin to bridge, as Reuven Feuerstein calls it, the operation to these other contexts.[19]

Simply talking about additional places where a new thinking skill or strategy is appropriate is, of course, not sufficient to ensure transfer. Skills are very much tied to the information and knowledge contexts in which they are applied. How one goes about classifying graphic data is not precisely the same as how one goes about classifying words. Students need repeated opportunities, with teacher guidance, actually to *apply* a previously introduced thinking operation with new data or new settings—as much to know that the operation is appropriate in these settings as to know how to execute it in these settings. Successful transfer of a thinking operation requires more than an initial introduction to it or discussion of where it can be well used. A start toward transfer can be made at the introductory stage and, by using these strategies presented here, teachers can and should undertake this task. But much more has to be done later for transfer actually to occur.

Introduce the Operation When It Is Needed to Learn Content

Thinking operations are not ends in themselves. They are tools with which individuals make meaning. Although not an inherent part of a skill introducing strategy itself, selecting *when* to introduce a thinking operation is as important as selecting the strategy to use. Introducing a new thinking skill or strategy can be most productive when the students need the operation itself to achieve a subject-matter goal and there is evidence that they are less proficient in the operation than they could be.[20] When introduced at these points in a course, instruction in the operation can move the subject-matter learning along just as the subject matter can serve as a vehicle for beginning to learn the new thinking operation.

In the imaginary lesson illustrating the use of these introductory strategies, the skill of classifying is needed to process the data (words) available for answering the question: What was life like in the thirteen English North American colonies around 1750? The teacher assigns the task, but the students quickly realize that they need some way to make

sense out of the assigned data. Learning how to classify these data is entirely appropriate and relevant at this point. In order to get the maximum learning in introducing a thinking operation, teachers need to pick very carefully those places in a sequence of lessons where the operation can best be introduced. Contriving subject-matter tasks that fairly cry out for the use of new thinking skills or strategies provides such places.

Keep the Data the Same

Too often, teachers try to teach a thinking operation by switching too soon the data, task, or context to which it is applied. Because thinking operations are tied closely to the contexts in which they are first introduced, students need to become proficient in them in one context before being confronted with new contexts.[21] It is inappropriate to show students how to do a skill or strategy or to have them try it initially with one data set and then on their next try to give them an entirely different data set in which to apply it. A lesson showing students how to identify a topic sentence cannot be productively followed by a lesson demanding that they write a topic sentence of their own without any instructional guidance at all, for these tasks are two quite different things, though they may both deal with topic sentences.

In the introduction of a new thinking skill or strategy, the data or context needs to remain constant throughout the introduction so that students can focus on the new thinking operation. For example, in the imaginary American history lesson on classifying, the type of data used in both the initial application or demonstration and the second application of the skill was the same in each strategy—words. In subsequent lessons on classifying, until the students demonstrate proficiency in the skill in this context, lists or collections of words should continue to serve as the data for practicing this skill. In order to develop initial proficiency with a thinking operation the kinds of data and media in which it is used must remain the same throughout the introductory lesson, and indeed for the practice lessons immediately following.

1. Be sure that students understand the lesson objective: learning a thinking skill or strategy.

2. Spend four to five minutes previewing the skill, including stating synonyms, examples, and a working definition, if possible.

3. Use media and content or subject matter with which students are already familiar, drawn from their own experiences or previously studied. Do not introduce a new skill with new data.

4. Keep the application or "doing it" parts of the lesson short — six to eight minutes each, at best

5. Eliminate or at least minimize the interference caused by:
   • other skills or strategies,
   • emotional or value-laden content, and
   • subject matter discussion.

6. Focus on the major components of the skill or strategy being introduced, especially on how the operation is executed and why.

7. Devote up to one-third of the lesson time to a reflective reporting, discussing and sharing what the students did in their heads to execute the skill.

8. In ending the lesson, involve the students in reviewing the key skill procedures, rules, and criteria identified so far and, if possible, provide a mnemonic device to assist them in remembering these.

9. Help students identify opportunities for using this skill or strategy in their out-of-school activities as well as in their academic work.

Figure B.10 Guidelines for Introducing a Thinking Skill or Strategy

All develop set on the part of the students, and all provide instructive input. These strategies not only involve the students in processing data but also provide opportunities to both teacher and students for checking learning. And in all these strategies teachers help students bridge what is being learned to things beyond that particular introductory lesson.

In addition, these three introductory strategies appeal to both teachers and students. They seem to accommodate different learning styles commonly found among students in most classrooms. The inductive strategy accommodates field-independent learners who often need little instruction to initiate a task and who plunge into a situation focusing

Keep the Data Simple and Short

The data to which students apply a new thinking operation initially should be neither voluminous nor too complex. To keep the focus on the operation, the data and task need to be rather straightforward and relatively short, not overwhelming. Excessive data to process get in the way of students' concentrating on how to execute the operation; and data that are too complex to understand turn attention to the data themselves and away from the operation altogether.[22] The data used in the American history lesson on classifying—lists of words—are neither complicated nor unduly long and involved. Students from fourth grade upward who have used these strategies and data are familiar with enough of the data to complete the assigned task without difficulty. The amount of data in each list can be processed in a reasonable time.

The point in an introductory lesson is not to produce fifteen or twenty different categories of words, nor to exercise the new operation repeatedly without interruption. Rather, it is useful to exercise the operation once or twice, or maybe three times—if it is a relatively simple one—and then discuss how it was done. The next application should also be limited to a few tries and then discussed. It is the discussion of how the new operation was executed as much as the actually doing of it that helps students begin to take command of a new thinking skill or strategy.

Figure B.10 summarizes basic guidelines for introducing a thinking skill or strategy. These guidelines apply to all three of the introductory strategies. A teacher following these guidelines will be able to help students become well-acquainted with a new thinking operation.

INTRODUCING THINKING SKILLS AND STRATEGIES

The three introductory strategies presented here prove valuable beyond the fact that they incorporate the findings of research on skill learning. They also meet the criteria of effective teaching identified by researchers and educators such as Walter Doyle, Madeline Hunter, Barak Rosenshine, and Jane Stallings.[23] Each strategy makes the learning objectives public right at the start of the lesson—no surprises with these strategies.

more on the whole than on its parts. These students often seem to know almost intuitively how to engage in a skill, even if imperfectly. Using this strategy allows these students to do the operation and then share with others how they did it.

The directive strategy, on the other hand, usually appeals more to field-dependent students who rely on teacher directions and environmental cues to complete a skilled task.[24] It also appeals to those learners characterized by a step-to-step, list-making orientation to remembering and learning. The developmental strategy accommodates those students ready to benefit from instruction in a specific operation by offering them an opportunity to articulate what they can do at the moment; it gives them a reason to want to do it better and then shows them how to do so, thus helping them grow intellectually in the process. Each of these strategies seems to speak to different learning styles.

Of even greater importance, these three strategies are well suited to introducing different types of thinking operations at different points in a students' schooling. The inductive strategy is useful with average to above-average students or with operations about which a number of students in a class may have some knowledge. The directive strategy, on the other hand, appears to be most useful in introducing rather complicated operations to even the most able students or any thinking operations to novices, beginners, or below-average students. The developmental strategy may well be most useful in helping students expand on, elaborate, or apply to new settings thinking operations that they were introduced to earlier or that they have not used for some time.

These introductory strategies also seem to appeal to different types of teachers because of differences in teaching styles. The directive strategy, for example, seems to match the preferred instructional style of an expository teacher. The inductive strategy, on the other hand, appears to suit inquiry-oriented instructors, and the developmental strategy is often the favorite of a constructivist, developmentally oriented teacher.[25] But using only strategies that fit one's teaching preferences is hardly justified considering the variety of thinking operations to be taught and the variety of students in most classrooms.

Even though these strategies may appeal to different teachers for a variety of reasons, any one seeking to teach thinking skills as effectively as possible should be competent in all of them and should employ them as needed according to the substantive task to be undertaken, the abilities and previous skill learning of the students, and the complexity or nature of the operation to be introduced. Any of these may be utilized in deliberately launching a skill lesson or, spontaneously, in the midst of a subject-matter lesson where students are apparently unfamiliar with an operation they are being asked to use. Variety in instruction is also an important consideration. Since all these strategies incorporate the features required of effective introduction to any thinking operation, any of the three can be useful in introducing a thinking skill or strategy. Any teacher should employ all three strategies as appropriate in introducing thinking skills.

As important as is the introductory stage in skill teaching and learning, it is but one of six stages through which students need instruction to achieve a high degree of proficiency in any thinking operation. The skill introducing strategies presented in this and the preceding chapter are very useful in this stage of the teaching of thinking, but they constitute less than 20 percent of what needs to be used to teach a thinking operation to any degree of proficiency at all. It is worth remembering that students do *not* command a thinking operation simply as a result of a single lesson built around one of the strategies. Repeated, follow-up, guided practice in the operation is also required. So, too, is its transfer to new settings and its elaboration in new, more sophisticated dimensions as well as repeated opportunities for its autonomous practice and use.

By using *all* of these strategies in the framework of skill teaching described earlier, teachers can help students become more effective and efficient in thinking skills and strategies.

NOTES

1. Ann L. Brown, Joseph C. Campione, and Jeanne D. Day, "Learning to Learn: On Training Students to Learn from Texts," *Educational Researcher* 10:2 (February 1981), p. 16.

2. John R. Hayes, *The Complete Problem Solver* (Philadelphia: Franklin Institute Press, 1981); Michael I. Posner and Steven W. Keele, "Skill Learning," in Robert M. W. Travers, ed., *Second Handbook of Research on Teaching* (Chicago: Rand McNally College Publishing Company, 1973), pp. 808–810, 821.

3. Brown, Campione, and Day, "Learning to Learn," pp. 14, 20.

4. Walter Doyle, "Academic Work," *Review of Educational Research* 53:2 (Summer 1983), pp. 168–170; David Perkins, "Thinking Frames," *Educational Leadership* 43:8 (May 1986), p. 8.

5. Arthur Whimbey, "Teaching Sequential Thought: The Cognitive Skills Approach," *Phi Delta Kappan* 59:4 (December 1977), pp. 255–259; Judith W. Segal and Susan F. Chipman, "Thinking and Learning Skills: The Contributions of NIE," *Educational Leadership* 42:1 (September 1984), p. 86.

6. Brown, Campione, and Day, "Learning to Learn," p. 18; Robert J. Sternberg, "Teaching Intellectual Skills: Looking for Smarts in All the Wrong Places" (Paper delivered at the Wingspread Conference on Teaching Thinking Skills, Racine, May 17–19, 1984, p. 16; Robert J. Sternberg, "How Can We Teach Intelligence?" *Educational Leadership* 42:1 (September 1984) p. 47.

7. Russell Gersten and Douglas Carnine, "Direct Instruction in Reading Comprehension," *Educational Leadership* 43:7 (April 1986), p. 77; Paul Chance, *Thinking in the Classroom: A Survey of Programs* (New York: Teachers College Press, 1986), p. 122.

8. Irving E. Sigel, "A Constructivist Perspective for Teaching Thinking," *Educational Leadership* 42:3 (November 1984), pp. 18–22.

9. Sigel, "A Constructivist"; Robbie Case, "A Developmentally Based Theory and Technology of Instruction," *Review of Educational Research* 48:3 (Summer 1978), pp. 439–463.

10. Case, "A Developmentally Based."

11. Sigel, "A Constructivist."

12. Arthur Whimbey, "The Key to Higher-Order Thinking Is Precise Processing," *Educational Leadership* 42:1 (September 1984), pp. 66–70; Michael I. Posner and Steven W. Keele, "Skill Learning," in Robert M. W. Travers. ed., *Second Handbook of Research on Teaching* (Chicago: Rand McNally College Publishing Company, 1973), pp. 808–810; Jane Stallings, "Effective Strategies for Teaching Basic Skills," in Daisy G. Wallace, ed., *Developing Basic Skills Programs in Secondary Schools* (Alexandria, Va.: Association for Supervision and Curriculum Development, 1983), pp. 1–19.

13. Posner and Keele, "Skill Learning," p. 824; David Pratt, *Curriculum Design and Development* (New York: Harcourt Brace Jovanovich, 1980), pp. 312–313.

14. Pratt, *Curriculum*, p. 313.

15. Robert J. Sternberg, "How Can We Teach Intelligence?" *Educational Leadership* 42:1 (September 1984), pp. 38–50.

16. Ann L. Brown, Joseph C. Campione, and Jeanne D. Day, "Learning to Learn: On Training Students to Learn from Texts," *Educational Researcher* 10 (February 1981), pp. 14–21; Sternberg, "How Can We. . ."; Arthur Costa, "Mediating the Metacognitive," *Educational Leadership* 42:3 (November 1984), pp. 58–62.

17. Posner and Keele, "Skill Learning."

18. Bryce B. Hudgins, *Learning and Thinking* (Itasca, Ill.: F.E. Peacock Publishers, 1977), pp. 142–172; David N. Perkins, "Thinking Frames" (Paper delivered at ASCD Conference on Approaches to Teaching Thinking, Alexandria, Va., August 6, 1985); Posner and Keele, "Skill Learning"; Sternberg, "How Can We. . ."

19. Reuven Feuerstein, *Instrumental Enrichment* (Baltimore: University Park Press, 1980).

20. Carl Bereiter, "Elementary School: Necessity or Convenience?" *Elementary School Journal* 73 (May 1973), pp. 435–446.

21. John McPeck, *Critical Thinking and Education* (New York: St. Martin's Press, 1981); Hudgins, *Learning and Thinking*, pp. 142–172; Posner and Keele, "Skill Learning."

22. Case, "A Developmentally Based"; Perkins, "Thinking Frames"; Alan H. Schoenfeld, "Can Heuristics Be Taught?" in Jack Lochhead and John Clement, eds., *Cognitive Process Instruction* (Philadelphia: The Franklin Institute Press, 1979), pp. 315–336.

23. Walter Doyle, "Academic Work," *Review of Educational Research* 53:2 (Summer 1983), pp. 159–199; Madeline Hunter, *Mastery Teaching: Increasing Instructional Effectiveness in Secondary Schools, Colleges and Universities* (El Segundo, Calif.: TIP Publications, 1982); Barak Rosenshine, "Teaching Functions in Instructional Programs," *Elementary School Journal* 83:4 (March 1983), pp. 335–353; Stallings, "Effective Strategies."

24. Doyle, "Academic Work," pp. 175–178; Peter Martorella, "Cognition Research: Some Implications for the Design of Social Studies Instructional Materials," *Theory and Research in Social Education* 10:3 (Fall 1982), pp. 1–16.

25. Sigel, "A Constructivist."

Appendix C
Strategies for Guiding Practice in Thinking Skills

Once introduced, a new thinking skill or strategy must be practiced until students can demonstrate proficiency in using it on their own. After the introductory lesson using one of the teaching strategies presented in Appendix B, teachers should provide a number of lessons in which students engage in this practice. To be most effective for skill learning, these practice lessons must be of two types. The initial practice lessons should provide instructive guidance along with the student practice of the new operation. Subsequent lessons can then provide opportunities for independent practice of the operation, ultimately in contexts where the students themselves must determine which thinking operations in their repetoire are the most appropriate to apply. These two types of practice lessons carry the teaching of thinking skills and strategies through the second and third stages of the six stage skill teaching framework.

GUIDED PRACTICE

In the practice lessons immediately following the introduction of a new thinking skill or strategy, teacher guidance should accompany student application of the operation being learned. In these lessons students should receive assistance in using the operation, should reflect on what they do as they engage in it, and should discuss its major attributes as well as what goes on in their heads as they execute it. Such activities can precede, accompany, and follow student use of the operation. At this stage of skill learning, students need to be conscious of how they execute the operation and to discuss how it can be executed *each time* they engage in it, if they are to take ownership of it.

A Strategy for Guiding Practice

Teachers can employ a number of strategies to guide student practice in executing a thinking skill or strategy. The key ingredient of any such teaching strategy is instructive guidance in how to carry out the operation being practiced. One basic strategy for providing such guidance consists of these four steps:

1. First, the teacher previews the operation to be practiced, just as in the lessons employing the introductory strategies described in Appendix B.
2. Then students and teacher review the operation to be used by reviewing what they know already about it—its key rules and procedures, and predicting how they will use these procedures and rules in this instance.
3. Next, the students apply the operation, monitoring how they execute it as discussed or planned in the preceding step.
4. Finally, the students reflect on what they did in their minds as they

Adapted from Barry K. Beyer, *Practical Strategies for the Teaching of Thinking* (Boston: Allyn and Bacon, 1987), pp. 139–150.

engaged in the operation and summarize what they have learned about it to this point.

This strategy requires about twenty minutes or so in an average subject-matter lesson for a thinking operation of average complexity. This leaves approximately half of a typical forty-five minute class period to then focus on the subject-matter learning that has occurred as a result of applying this operation. This strategy proves especially useful because it builds around what normally goes on in any subject-matter class where thinking operations are used to learn content. Its major step involves applying the operation to achieve a subject-matter objective (Step 3). To do this, the strategy adds three activities: a brief preview of the operation, a review of it before it is applied, and a follow-up, reflective discussion of it. Each of these three steps takes some time away from direct subject-matter learning; they, in fact, constitute direct *skill* teaching. However, rather than assume students will become proficient in a newly introduced thinking skill simply by using it to learn the subject and to discuss only the product of its use, this teaching strategy allocates some class activities and time to focus explicitly on the thinking operation before turning attention to what was learned about the subject through its use. This modest attention to the new thinking skill or strategy at this point seems to move students toward mastery more quickly than they would move simply if forced to use the skill on their own.

Figure C.1 outlines in detail what should be done to execute each of the major steps in a PREP strategy. This strategy could easily be used to guide practice in any thinking skill or strategy. We can illustrate its salient points by explaining how it could be used to provide guided practice in the skill of classifying information as this skill was introduced in the sample lessons in Appendix B.

Once the skill of classifying has been introduced as previously described, the teacher can identify a number of places in a course where it would be useful, for subject-matter learning purposes, to apply it. Almost immediately after studying life in the thirteen colonies, for instance, an American history course normally turns to the coming of the American Revolution. Students thus find themselves studying some laws passed by

---

STEP 1 *PREVIEW THE SKILL*

Remind the students that learning the skill is an objective of the course and lesson.

Help the students recall
- the skill label,
- synonyms,
- a simple definition,
- examples of where the skill has already been used.

Discuss the value of the skill.

Point out how use of the skill is helpful here.

STEP 2 *REVIEW THE SKILL*

Help the students identify key
- rules that direct the skill,
- steps in how the skill works,
- useful information about the skill.

Clarify any obstacles they may anticipate and how to overcome them.

Clarify how to start doing the skill.

STEP 3 *EXECUTE THE SKILL AND MONITOR*

Have students engage in the skill with reference to what they discussed about it.

Each may work with a partner who checks the executing of the skill.

Teacher provides help as needed.

STEP 4 *PONDER (REFLECT ON) THE SKILL*

Help the students identify the key attributes of the skill, including its
- rules,
- procedure,
- associated knowledge.

Have the students
- predict where else this skill can be used,
- predict other skills with which this skill can be used,
- identify cues to occasions when it is appropriate to use this skill.

Figure C.1 A PREP Strategy for Guiding Practice of a Thinking Skill or Strategy

England to control events and affairs in the colonies. This content offers a good opportunity to practice classifying data. As a preliminary activity, the teacher could have students list the key laws affecting the colonies enacted by the British Parliament after 1690 and identify what they said or did. Then the students would be prepared to classify these laws in order to infer just what England was up to or who in the colonies would be most directly affected by these laws.

Having thus provided a substantive context and purpose for classifying some data, the teacher can launch a guided practice lesson in this skill. To start, the class can *preview* the skill (Step 1) by writing its label—classify—on the board and by having students volunteer synonyms, a working definition, and examples of where the skill can be used and, indeed, was previously used in the course. The skill objective of the lesson needs to be stated explicitly, as does the rationale for using the skill as this point. Such an introduction customarily requires only four to five minutes at most; it serves the same purpose of goal setting and developing set as in the introductory strategies described earlier.

Next, teacher and students can (Step 2) *review* how the skill is executed and what they need to remember—in terms of operations, rules, and other knowledge—to execute it successfully. This requires a review—what they can recall from their introduction to the skill in the preceding lesson—as well as a prediction of how these attributes can be applied to complete the task assigned here. Students should be expected to be the major contributors at this point, but where there is doubt or confusion or error the teacher may also contribute. To aid in this review, the sequence of skill steps may be mapped or flowcharted or simply listed in sequence on the chalkboard or in student notes. About five to six minutes or so can be allotted to this step, less as students gain experience in applying the skill.

Next the students can *execute* the skill (Step 3) to complete the assigned subject-matter task. They may work alone or in small groups, concentrating on doing the skill, in this case actually grouping the various laws into any categories they choose to answer the assigned question. Or, they might work in pairs, with one student in each pair serving as a process monitor while the other member of the pair executes the skill.[1] The teacher can also provide assistance including demonstrating how to exe-

cute one or more of the steps constituting the skill, if necessary. Thus, at this point students execute the skill and monitor how they do it as they proceed.

Finally, students *ponder* and discuss what they did in their minds as they engaged in the skill (Step 4). With teacher assistance as needed, they can report and discuss the rules, knowledge, and procedures they used, suggesting modifications or additions as appropriate. They can also report obstacles they encountered, offering advice on how to overcome similar obstacles should they arise in future applications of the skill. Again, the teacher may interject suggestions or seek clarification of important steps in the skill procedure or any rules or principles relevant to the skill. This portion of the lesson can conclude with students predicting where else—in this course or elsewhere—use of this skill might be appropriate and the kinds of cues that would so indicate.

At this point, with about twenty minutes or so remaining in the typical class period, the class can turn to the various substantive products generated by the use of the skill. In terms of this illustrative lesson on English colonial laws after 1750, students could report the various ways they categorized the laws—in terms of the area of life each dealt with, as economic, political, and so on, or in terms of region affected, as the frontier, tidewater, and so on. They could also explain the insights inferred from the categories they made as they seek to answer the assigned subject-matter questions. And the class can then proceed to its study of the subject, to undertake another guided practice lesson in classifying data two or three days hence. Thus, in employing this particular teaching strategy, a teacher devotes about half of the lesson time to the thinking skill or strategy being practiced, with the remainder devoted to subject matter. Learning both the thinking operation and subject matter are legitimate goals of such guided practice lessons. Pursuing each goal explicitly and in sequence, however, is much more useful than in pursuing both simultaneously, with skill learning assumed to be implicit in a discussion of the subject at hand. Figure C.2 presents a lesson plan useful for carrying out the guided practice PREP strategy described here.

This strategy for guiding practice offers three opportunities for students to deal explicitly with any thinking operation—twice before they apply it (Steps 1 and 2) and once afterward (Step 4). Any of a number of

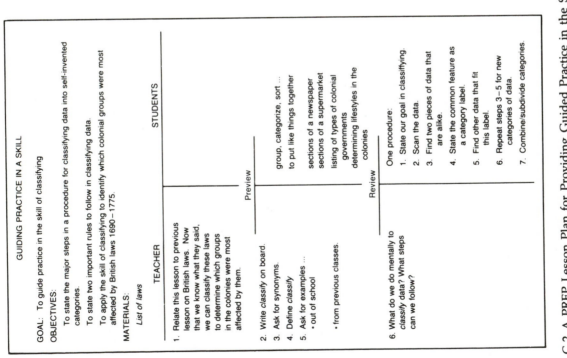

Figure C.2 *(continued)*

GUIDING PRACTICE IN A SKILL

GOAL: To guide practice in the skill of classifying

OBJECTIVES:

To state the major steps in a procedure for classifying data into self-invented categories.

To state two important rules to follow in classifying data.

To apply the skill of classifying to identify which colonial groups were most affected by British laws 1690–1775.

MATERIALS:

List of laws

TEACHER	STUDENTS
	Preview
1. Relate this lesson to previous lesson on British laws. Now that we know what they said, we can classify these laws to determine which groups in the colonies were most affected by them.	
2. Write *classify* on board.	
3. Ask for synonyms.	group, categorize, sort …
4. Define *classify*	to put like things together
5. Ask for examples … • out of school	sections of a newspaper sections of a supermarket listing of types of colonial governments
• from previous classes.	determining lifestyles in the colonies
	Review
6. What do we do mentally to *classify* data? What steps can we follow?	One procedure: 1. State our goal in classifying. 2. Scan the data. 3. Find two pieces of data that are alike. 4. State the common feature as a category label. 5. Find other data that fit this label. 6. Repeat steps 3–5 for new categories of data. 7. Combine/subdivide categories.

TEACHER	STUDENTS
7. What *rules* are useful to follow?	To start, take the first piece of these data and find another just like it …
8. What is it helpful to know to to classify data?	Some possible categories such as economic, political, religious, and so on … or occupations or types of government, and so on. If you don't understand some data put them in "miscellaneous" category
9. What kinds of obstacles could occur in classifying, and how would you overcome them?	If all data go in one category, —we need new category system.
	Execute
10. Have students, in pairs, put the laws into categories to answer the question: Which groups in the colonies were most affected by British laws?	
	Ponder (Reflect)
11. Go over the steps, rules, and knowledge that constitute *classifying.* • When is it useful to classify data? • What obstacles keep cropping up? How can we handle them? • What steps can we follow?	See items 6–9 above.
12. Make any needed changes or additions to skill attributes in notes.	
	Content Discussion
13. Now that we have classified these laws, let's find out who was most affected by them and why.	
14. Continued discussion of content …	

Figure C.2 A PREP Lesson Plan for Providing Guided Practice in the Skill of Classifying

techniques may be used to conduct these reviews. Before students apply the skill, they can review it in any of the following ways:

1. Recalling from memory the key attributes of the operation.
2. Referring to the steps and rules of the operation previously copied into their notebooks.
3. Reviewing the topic in which the operation was most recently used and recalling how they applied it in that case, listing what they did, in what sequence, and why.
4. Giving examples of where the operation could be used and explaining how they could execute it.
5. Responding to a scrambled list of key steps to be put into correct order.
6. Matching a list of rules to the appropriate steps.

To conclude any guided practice strategy, a teacher could also use one of the above activities or any of the following, in which students could:

1. Make a mobile depicting the key attributes of the operation.
2. Write a set of directions (in a paragraph, flowchart, or list) to younger students, telling them how to execute the operation.
3. Make a map or other type of diagram showing the key attributes of the operation and how they relate to one another.
4. Identify where else in their study of the subject or in their daily out-of-school life use of this operation might be appropriate.

These latter techniques could even become the basis of an additional lesson. Some students could produce products to be displayed around the room for others to use in subsequent applications of the operation. All these techniques or activities involve students in recalling and otherwise processing what they have learned to that point about a particular skill or strategy. Teachers can vary their use of these in order to fit activities to the ability levels of their students and to the complexity of the thinking skill or

strategy being studied as well as simply to bring variety to these steps of skill instruction.

This guided practice strategy could also extend over several class lessons with an intervening homework assignment. A teacher could introduce and have students review a thinking skill to be practiced and then let them apply it as homework, monitoring it as they work. To start the next class, students can review how they executed the skill and what they learned about it in so doing. Then they can turn to discussion and processing of the subject matter being studied, as outlined above.

The strategy described here can be modified in any number of ways as long as the essential introduction to the thinking skill and discussion of how it works are included. As a substitute for either the preview or review step, for example, a teacher might have students work in pairs, having one partner serve as the monitor, while the other actually executes the skill; in this arrangement it is the monitor's task to provide corrective guidance in how to carry out the operation as the partner actually executes it.

As students become experienced in employing the new thinking skill or strategy through repeated guided practice in applying it, the teacher can shorten and eliminate any of these ''guidance providing'' steps until the students simply engage in the operation without any explicit attention to it or any guidance at all. For instance, after several lessons employing all four steps of this strategy, the teacher might elect to shorten and then eliminate the introduction to the operation. After noting which operation is to be used and getting a definition of it from the class, the teacher moves the students immediately to executing it. After several additional guided practice lessons organized in this fashion, the teacher might even eliminate the follow-up discussion of how students executed the operation—save for discussion of any obstacles encountered in its use—and proceed immediately to discussion of the subject matter. In a later practice lesson the teacher might shorten and then eliminate the pre-discussion of the operation to be used altogether. By this time the students will have achieved the ability to use it autonomously. Gradually, over a number of guided practice lessons, the teacher can reduce the amount of explicit guidance or attention given the thinking operation. Thereafter, students use it without any guidance at all.

Key Features of Guided Practice

The guided practice strategy described here incorporates the major features of effective skill teaching also included in the introductory strategies described earlier. This strategy keeps the students focused on the thinking skill or strategy being practiced during the initial part of the lesson; involves them in talking about and reflecting on what goes on in their minds as they apply it; and bridges the operation to other settings. In addition, the skill is used when appropriate to substantive learning objectives and when the kinds of data—in the case of the example here, lists of items—are identical to those used in its introduction. To minimize interference, all guided practice lessons in the weeks following introduction of a new thinking skill or strategy should use only the kind of data used in the introductory lesson. Modeling, it should be noted, is not an essential part of practice at this stage, although a teacher can choose to demonstrate or have a student demonstrate any attribute of the new operation wherever necessary. Modeling might be especially appropriate, however, if the lesson were one of the first guided practice lessons in the operation following its introduction.

Research indicates that for practice to be most beneficial in learning thinking skills and strategies it should be frequent, intermittent, in small chunks, and accompanied by immediate feedback.[2] Translated into the framework for teaching thinking operations presented here, this means that at this second stage of the framework—that of guided practice—students must engage in a number of guided practice lessons spaced out over a period of several weeks following the introduction of a new thinking operation. How frequent such lessons should be is not known for certain. Certainly such frequency depends on the degree of student proficiency sought, the complexity of the skill, the abilities of the students, and the kinds of data and tasks with which the operation is used. It varies for each operation and for each student or group of students. But it is clear from skill teaching research and experience that the initial guided practice lessons should follow the introductory lesson closely, perhaps spaced over every three lessons or days for a week or two.[3] Relatively close spacing enhances recall of what was introduced. Subsequent prac-

tices might be spaced out over greater intervals with more intervening days or lessons devoted to other subjects or tasks. Guided practice lessons need to be scheduled until students demonstrate the level of continued proficiency that the teacher seeks. More intermittent spacing of skill practice serves to maintain skill proficiency better than does practice massed into a rapid-fire series of lessons right after a new skill or strategy is introduced.

For example, an American history teacher who has introduced the skill of classifying data into self-invented categories (as in the sample lesson in the preceding appendix) could plan a number of guided practice lessons in this skill over the weeks immediately following the introductory lesson, as data and tasks suitable for classifying occur. Such places might include study of the laws regulating colonial life between 1750 and 1776 and subsequent study of colonial reactions to these laws and to British reactions to colonial reactions, points of view regarding the relationship of the colonies to Britain, and battles fought during the American Revolution. Other opportunities also exist for students to classify information for better understanding the subject being studied in such a course. The point is that any thinking skill or strategy once introduced needs to be practiced or applied relatively frequently thereafter, with appropriate guidance and with the intervals between practices gradually lengthened as students begin to "get the hang of it."

No specific guidelines exist for the most appropriate length of any practice application of a thinking skill. Again, the length of such lessons will depend on student abilities, the subject-matter task, and complexity of the operation to be learned. Experience suggests, however, that practice applications should be relatively short, requiring twenty to thirty minutes or so for students in the intermediate grades upward. Students, of course, need time to reflect on and discuss how they execute a skill, but that portion of the lesson requiring use of the operation itself should not require prolonged exercise of it. What is needed as much as executing the operation are opportunities to discuss how it can be or was done. Those strategies that are most useful for guiding practice in a thinking operation are those that, in the space of a forty–fifty minute lesson, allow time to *carry out* the operation, to reflect on and *discuss* it, and also to *discuss what was learned about the subject* as a result of employing it.

Feedback is absolutely essential during this stage of skill learning. At this point students are still learning the new operation, so instruction in how to do it rather than testing how well students do it must remain the primary goal of any such lesson. This feedback can be provided in a variety of ways. It can, for example, be "feedforward." Research on effective problem solving indicates that individuals considered to be excellent problem solvers spend considerable time planning how to go about solving a problem before they actually engage in trying to solve it.[4] Planning how to execute any thinking skill or strategy actually makes its execution much more efficient and the effort much more productive. Consequently, instructive guidance in any thinking operation can be provided *before* students actually engage in it. This guidance feeds information about the operation forward and informs its application, while discussion of it after execution only informs its application next time—if the information can be remembered that long.

Instructional feedback may also occur while the thinking operation is being used as the teacher or a student's partner observes a student using it and provides immediate comments regarding omissions, inconsistencies, or errors the student makes. Or feedback may also follow the application of the operation as students report and discuss how they executed it, any rules that proved useful, particular operations they found useful, or anything that gave them difficulty and how that was handled.

By having students recall what they know about a thinking skill or strategy *before* they try to apply this skill or strategy and by helping them plan what they will do to execute it *before* they do it, teachers can provide the guidance necessary to make practice of a newly introduced thinking operation a learning rather than testing experience. By providing confirming or corrective feedback *during* and *after* application of a skill or strategy, students can sharpen their execution of it and deliberately attend to how it is carried out. The whole purpose of such feedback or feedforward is to help students become more conscious of how they engage in thinking so that they can take deliberate command of their mental abilities when they so desire. *Guided* practice helps accomplish this goal.

NOTES

1. Arthur Whimbey, "Teaching Sequential Thought: The Cognitive Skills Approach," *Phi Delta Kappan* 59:4 (December 1977), pp. 255–259.

2. Barak V. Rosenshine, "Teaching Functions in Instructional Programs," *Elementary School Journal* 83:4 (March 1983), pp. 340–343, 345–348; Michael I. Posner and Steven W. Keele, "Skill Learning," in Robert M. W. Travers, ed., *Second Handbook of Research on Teaching* (Chicago: Rand McNally College Publishing Company, 1973), pp. 816, 809–823; Jane Stallings, "Effective Strategies for Teaching Basic Skills," in Daisy G. Wallace, ed., *Developing Basic Skills Programs in Secondary Schools*, (Alexandria, Va.: Association for Supervision and Curriculum Development, 1983), pp. 1–19; Bryce B. Hudgins, *Learning and Thinking*, (Itasca, Ill.: F. E. Peacock Publishers, 1977), pp. 92–98.

3. Posner and Keele, "Skill Learning"; Hudgins, *Learning and Thinking*, pp. 96–98.

4. Benjamin S. Bloom and Lois J. Broder, *Problem-solving Processes of College Students* (Chicago: University of Chicago Press, 1950).

Appendix D

Strategies for Transferring and/or Elaborating Thinking Skills

To be proficient in a thinking skill or strategy means to be able to use that operation effectively and efficiently on one's own in a variety of appropriate contexts. To develop such proficiency requires more than simply introducing the thinking skill or strategy and practicing it in a single context.[1] It also requires instruction and guided practice in how and when to transfer the thinking skill or strategy from the context in which it was initially learned to the widest variety of contexts possible. The final three stages of the thinking skill teaching framework presented here focus on this crucial task.

Adapted from Barry K. Beyer, *Practical Strategies for the Teaching of Thinking* (Boston: Allyn and Bacon, 1989), pp. 163–178.

TEACHING FOR TRANSFER

To transfer a skill means essentially to be able to apply it effectively in a setting or with data other than the setting or data in which it was originally learned or experienced. Specialists in cognition, such as David Perkins, point out that transfer is of two kinds.[2] One, called "high road" transfer, consists of applying a skill learned in one setting to another quite different setting. The other—called "low road" transfer—consists of applying a skill learned in one setting to other rather similar settings. While "low road" transfer is the more likely to occur with minimum effort, neither kind of transfer occurs automatically.[3]

Thinking skills and strategies fail to transfer readily for several major reasons. The first has to do with the user's lack of knowledge about and expertise in the skill or strategy being employed. Thinking operations are very much tied to the contexts, subjects, and types of data with which they are initially used or experienced. Unless they are repeatedly applied—with reflection—in additional contexts or with other kinds of data, they are not likely to be generalized to the point of even appearing to be useful or applicable in a variety of contexts.

Thinking skills and strategies, for example, are often shaped by the media to which they are applied.[4] While their general procedures may remain substantially the same regardless of the media with which they are used, their knowledge components often differ. Ignorance of these varying knowledge components often inhibits effective application of the skill. For instance, detecting the bias of a newspaper or magazine differs considerably from detecting bias in a document such as a letter or speech or single article. While the procedure for detecting bias is generally the same in both instances, the clues one looks for differ because of differences in the media. In a newspaper, for instance, position on a page, size of the headline, and type of graphics associated with the articles are critical clues to bias, often moreso than the kinds of language used within any article. Unless one knows that these clues are important to look for in this instance, using this analytical skill may not be as productive as it otherwise could be.

Thinking skills and strategies are also very much shaped by the subject matter, disciplines, or content with which they are used.[5] Classifying biology data differs significantly from classifying historical data or parts of speech, not so much in the procedure employed as in the kinds of category systems most likely to yield useful insights about these different bodies of content. Knowledge of appropriate category systems in these instances is influenced more by knowledge of subject matter than by knowledge of the skill itself.

Thinking operations often fail to transfer for yet another reason. Many students fail to learn the cues that make use of a particular skill appropriate to different situations. Part of teaching and learning thinking operations involves identifying those cues or signals in a wide variety of situations that call for using particular skills or strategies. Again, this is essentially a matter of knowledge or information. In learning a thinking skill or strategy, students should explicitly deal with those elements in a number of settings that call for the use of the thinking skill or strategy they seek to master.

No thinking operation remains static, in the form in which it was initially used or learned. Like virtually all skills, thinking skills and strategies—or knowledge of and proficiencies in applying them—change and develop over time as individuals become more experienced in using them for a variety of purposes in a variety of contexts. In order to understand the utility of any particular thinking skill or strategy in a number of contexts, students must have generalized and elaborated its attributes. Generalizing a skill consists essentially of taking it beyond the specific parameters of the setting in which it was initially experienced.

As students apply a newly learned thinking skill or strategy, with reflection, to a number of new settings, they elaborate its key attributes. That is, they add to their knowledge of the cues that call it into use, of the criteria it might employ, of rules or principles specific to certain kinds of data, or even of certain procedural features to which one must attend under certain special circumstances. Elaborating thinking operations beyond their initial attributes helps students to understand some of the more complicated nuances of these operations, those not dealt with in the initial stages of learning these operations. As individuals elaborate a new skill or strategy, they begin to generalize its key attributes beyond specific cases or contexts to classes and categories of contexts. Those thinking

operations most thoroughly generalized and elaborated are most likely the ones students can and will transfer on their own.

Teaching thinking skills and strategies to transfer thus involves showing students (1) how to apply these operations in a variety of contexts—personal life experience contexts as well as academic subjects, (2) why it is appropriate to do so, and (3) the cues signaling that use of these operations is appropriate. To accomplish this, the thinking skill or strategy needs to be applied in new contexts where students can be introduced to attributes of it with which they are as yet unfamiliar.[6] Furthermore, this "reintroduction" needs to be followed by guided practice in applying the elaborated version of the operation in each of these new contexts and forms, and then by opportunities for its independent application in a number of different contexts. In effect, this instructional sequence repeats the first three stages of the skill teaching framework. Every time a previously introduced and practiced thinking skill or strategy is to be transferred, or elaborated, either in terms of its application or its attributes, it must be reintroduced, receive guided practice, and have independent practice in its new context or form.

Initiating Transfer and/or Elaboration

Teachers can launch their efforts to help students develop facility in transferring a thinking skill or strategy by conducting a single thirty to forty minute lesson similar to that used to introduce it. The strategies useful in introducing a new thinking skill—as illustrated in Appendix B—can easily be adapted for organizing such a lesson. All that is required is to add a new step early in each strategy, a step in which teacher and students review what they already know about the skill *before* they apply it in a new context or explore new attributes. For example, the inductive introductory strategy consisted of these five steps:

Preview

Execute

Reflect

Apply

Review

In following these steps, students can begin to articulate a beginning version of any thinking skill. However, by adding a *review* step between previewing and executing of the skill, this same strategy allows students to go over what they know about the skill in one context before they try to apply it in a new setting or add new attributes to it. Thus, an inductive strategy for initiating elaboration or transfer of a previously introduced thinking skill becomes:

1. Preview
2. *Review*
3. Execute
4. Reflect
5. Apply
6. Review

By carrying out each of these *six* steps, students can begin to learn new aspects or applications of a thinking skill or strategy to which they have been introduced earlier.

The *review* step added to this transfer/elaboration teaching strategy consists essentially of three tasks:

1. Students recall attributes of the skill or strategy as learned thus far, including:
   • its procedure
   • rules used
   • useful information about it.
2. Students describe how to execute the operation.
3. Students identify potential obstacles to smooth operation of the skill and possible ways to overcome the obstacles.

By having students complete this review before attempting to transfer or elaborate a previously introduced thinking operation, a teacher can help students develop the referents and set needed to facilitate such additional learning.[7]

Figure D.1 outlines in some detail how the inductive skill introducing strategy described in Appendix B works when modified to initiate transfer or elaboration of any thinking operation. This outline may be used as a guide for preparing lessons to launch any such effort with any previously introduced thinking skill or strategy. The essential difference between this version of the inductive strategy and the original version, it should be noted again, is simply the addition of a new second step wherein students review what they already know about the operation being used *before* they apply it or receive new information about it.

The directive and developmental strategies for introducing a thinking operation may also be altered, just as the inductive introductory strategy has been altered, for use in initiating the transfer or elaboration of any thinking skill or strategy. Figures D.2 and D.3 outline both strategies modified by the inclusion of the new step of *review*. Like the outlines of similar skill teaching strategies in this book, these outlines, too, may be used to prepare or conduct lessons to initiate transfer or elaboration of any thinking operation.

It seems unnecessary to illustrate the use of all these skill transfer/elaboration strategies here. However, the following brief explanation of how one of them might work in practice will clarify how all three can be successfully employed. A lesson using the directive strategy for transferring/elaborating a skill may best serve this purpose.

Suppose, as a continuation of the lessons on the skill of classifying used in the preceding chapters, an American history teacher wished to help students transfer this skill from use with written data to use with another medium. By this time in this history course, students may be studying the period midway between the War of 1812 and the Civil War, a period known to historians as the Middle Period! Numerous paintings by many famous artists of the period are available and can be used to develop insights into this period of America's past. Working with these paintings also offers an excellent opportunity to apply the skill of classifying, which the students, as a result of their preceding skill lessons, have generally

STEP 1 *PREVIEW THE SKILL*

State that "learning" the skill is today's objective.
Give the skill label/name.
Give synonyms.
State a tentative/working definition.
State ways the skill can be or has been used:
  • in students' personal experience,
  • in school activities,
  • in this course.
Explain how the skill is useful and why it's worth learning.

STEP 2 *REVIEW THE SKILL*

Students recall attributes of the skill as learned thus far:
  • operations,
  • rules used,
  • useful information about the skill.
Students describe how to execute the skill.
Students identify potential obstacles to smooth operation of the skill and ways to resolve the obstacles.

STEP 3 *EXPLAIN THE SKILL*

State any new procedures constituting the skill in step-by-step sequence, explaining what one does and why for each step.
State new rules and "things to know" about the skill.

STEP 4 *DEMONSTRATE THE SKILL*

Lead the class step-by-step through the skill:
  • state the goal,
  • refer to each step in the procedure,
  • give reasons for doing each step.
Show how the rules are carried out.
Use subject matter familiar to the students.

STEP 5 *REVIEW WHAT WAS DONE*

Review the procedures and rules.
Review the reasons for each (as illustrated in the demonstration).

STEP 6 *APPLY THE SKILL*

Execute the skill with teacher guidance.
Work in pairs, triads, or groups.
Complete material used in demonstration or use new but same kind of data/media.
Use course subject matter familiar to students but in same structure and media as in Step 4.

STEP 7 *REFLECT ON THE SKILL*

Review the steps comprising the skill and the rules guiding its use.
Reflect on ways in which the skill is used and when it is appropriate to use.
State the relationship of this skill to other skills.
Review or revise skill definition.
State where the skill can be used in:
  • personal or out-of-school situations,
  • coursework.

Figure D.2 A Directive Strategy for Initiating Transfer/Elaboration of a Thinking Skill or Strategy

STEP 1 *PREVIEW THE SKILL*

State that "learning" the skill is today's objective.
Give the skill label/name.
Give synonyms.
State a tentative/working definition.
State ways the skill can be or has been used:
  • in students' personal experiences,
  • in school activities,
  • in this course.
Explain how the skill is useful and why it's worth learning.

STEP 2 *REVIEW THE SKILL*

Students recall attributes of the skill as learned thus far:
  • operations,
  • rules used,
  • useful information about the skill.
Students describe how to execute the skill.
Students identify potential obstacles to smooth operation of the skill and ways to resolve the obstacles.

STEP 3 *EXECUTE THE SKILL—DO IT*

Use the skill (as best one can) to accomplish a task.
Work in pairs, in triads, or groups.
Use subject matter familiar to the students and appropriate to the course (or, if necessary, from students' experience).

STEP 4 *REFLECT ON WHAT WAS DONE*

Report what went on in students' heads as they engaged in the skill.
Identify the steps/rules used and sequence of each.
Clarify the procedure or any criteria used.
Focus on the skill and its attributes.

STEP 5 *APPLY SKILL TO NEW DATA*

Use what has been discussed about the skill to complete a second task.
Work in pairs, triads, or groups.
Use subject matter appropriate to the course and familiar to the students and in same structure and media as in Step 3.

STEP 6 *REVIEW THE SKILL*

Report on what students did in their heads as they applied the skill.
Review the steps/procedures that seem to constitute the skill.
Review the rules that direct use of the skill as well as when it is to be used.
State the relationship of this skill to other skills.
Review or revise the skill definition.
State where the skill can be used in personal or out-of-school situations.

Figure D.1 An Inductive Strategy for Initiating Transfer/Elaboration of a Thinking Skill or Strategy

mastered when applied to written data. A lesson initiating the transfer of this skill to a new medium is thus most appropriate at this point.

After establishing the subject-matter context of this lesson, the teacher can pose a significant question about America in the Middle Period and then point out that some paintings displayed at the front of the room or in a text can be used to help answer this question. The skill of classifying can be used to help make sense of these paintings as they might apply to the question at hand. So, to launch this transfer lesson, the teacher can (Step 1) *preview* this skill. Because students have been practicing this operation for some time, they will be relatively quick to provide synonyms, a working definition, and examples of how or where this skill has been used previously, outside of class as well as in. This same type of preview launched the original introduction to the skill and many of the follow-up guided practice lessons in this skill. Like these introductions, this reintroduction clearly establishes this skill as the major learning goal of this particular lesson while helping the students retrieve whatever they know about it so they can proceed to execute it with confidence.

However, before students try to apply this skill as they understand it to this new medium—paintings—they should *review* what they know about the skill already (Step 2), how to execute it, and any useful rules to follow. At this point, they can also predict any obstacles that might arise to its effective application and suggest ways to overcome these obstacles. This review of the skill is especially appropriate here because it focuses student attention on the basic procedure and rules constituting the skill; thus, it provides some guidance for executing it even in a new context. And by discussing obstacles that may arise in carrying out the skill and recalling or suggesting how to overcome them, students can be prepared for difficulties they may encounter in this new application.

Now the teacher can proceed to show students how to carry out this skill in a context in which they have not yet applied it. The teacher can point out and *explain* (Step 3) how this skill may have to be executed somewhat differently in applying it with a new medium. In this particular instance, the skill procedure remains essentially the same as when used with written data, but the features of the new medium to be classified—paintings—differ. Certainly the students can classify paintings in terms of their "content"—the kinds of people depicted, the landscapes, buildings,

---

STEP 1 *PREVIEW THE SKILL*

State that "learning" the skill is today's objective.
Give the skill label/name.
Give synonyms.
State a tentative/working definition.
State ways the skill can be or has been used:
• in students' personal experience,
• in school activities,
• in this course.
Explain how the skill is useful and why it's worth learning.

STEP 2 *REVIEW THE SKILL*

Students recall attributes of the skill as learned thus far:
• operations,
• rules used,
• useful information about the skill.
Students describe how to execute the skill.
Students identify potential obstacles to smooth operation of the skill and ways to resolve the obstacles.

STEP 3 *EXECUTE THE SKILL—DO IT*

Use the skill (as best one can) to accomplish a task.
Work in pairs or in groups.
Use subject matter appropriate to course and familiar to the students.

STEP 4 *REFLECT ON WHAT WAS DONE*

Report what went on in students' heads as they engaged in the skill.
Identify the steps and rules used and their sequence.
Clarify operations or any criteria used.
Focus on the skill and its attributes.

STEP 5 *EXPLAIN/DEMONSTRATE*

State any key operations or key rules omitted or misapplied by students.
Give reasons for using these operations or rules.
Demonstrate application of these operations or rules, explaining how and why each is used.

STEP 6 *APPLY THE SKILL TO NEW DATA*

Use the teacher-introduced operations and rules with student descriptions of the skill to complete another task.
Students work in pairs or groups.
Use subject matter familiar to the students and appropriate to course but in same structure and media as in Step 3.

STEP 7 *REVIEW THE SKILL*

Report on what was done in students' heads as they applied the skill.
Review the operations and rules that seem to constitute the skill.
State the relationship of this skill to other skills.
Review or revise the skill definition
State where the skill can be used in
• personal or out-of-school situations,
• coursework.

Figure D.3 A Developmental Strategy for Initiating Transfer/Elaboration of a Thinking Skill or Strategy

and so on—essentially the same type of attributes useful in dealing with words used in earlier classifying lessons. But paintings have their own attributes that also can be used to form categories, attributes related to composition, the use of color and perspective, figure-ground relationships, texture, and so on. Becoming aware of these aspects of the new medium will help students execute this skill better than if they remained ignorant of them. And so the teacher needs to explain some of these things about painting that will enable students to classify paintings more effectively. *Demonstrating* with some paintings (Step 4) exactly how one could classify these paintings, using such domain-specific knowledge, can alert students to the ways this information can shape the skill's execution.

After briefly *reviewing* (Step 5) key steps in classifying and any rules to follow in carrying out these steps, students can then classify additional paintings to answer the question at hand (Step 6). When finished, they can *reflect* (Step 7) on and report what they did in their heads as they adapted their understanding of the skill of classifying to this new situation. A revised description of important steps in executing the skill can be listed for all to copy, or several different descriptions may be listed. Any new rules "discovered" in the process may also be discussed and recorded, as may information about paintings that affect the use of this skill with them. Problems or obstacles seemingly peculiar to applying this skill with paintings can be explored, too. To conclude the lesson, students and teacher can then generalize about the skill and about those context cues, both written and visual, that may shape its execution. By so doing, students can begin to broaden their awareness of where this skill can be applied and how it might work in another setting. Follow-up guided practice in applying this skill with additional paintings and other visuals will further generalize the skill and facilitate its transfer to still other settings later.

Figure D.4 presents a lesson plan employing the directive transfer/elaboration strategy illustrated by the preceding lesson description. This lesson plan incorporates the essential features of the strategy outlined in Figure D.2. Interestingly, this directive strategy for initiating transfer or elaboration of a previously introduced thinking operation proves extremely effective, especially for average to below-average students.[8]

TRANSFERRING/ELABORATING A SKILL

GOAL: To initiate transfer of the skill of classifying.

OBJECTIVES:
To state in correct order the main steps in a procedure for classifying data.
To list at least three rules to follow in classifying paintings.
To apply the skill of classifying to state two features of a given set of paintings.

MATERIALS:
Three sets of paintings (six each).

TEACHER	STUDENTS
Preview	
1. Relate this lesson to the preceding lesson. What do these paintings suggest about American culture in the Middle Period?	
2. We can classify these paintings into different categories to answer this question.	
3. Write classify on the board.	
4. Ask for synonyms.	categorize, sort, group / to put like things together
5. Ask for definition of *classify*.	
6. Ask for or give examples of things already classified:	
• in out-of-school life,	newspaper sections / types of cars / seasonal clothing
• in this course to date.	lists of explorers / life in the 1750s / laws favored by different sections
Review	
7. Go over one or two procedures for classifying data—focus on steps and rules to follow	One procedure:
Procedures:	1. State the purpose of classifying.
	2. Scan the data.
	3. Find two items that have the same feature.
	4. State the common feature as a label for these two.
	5. Find all other data that fit under this label.
	6. Repeat Steps 3–5 until all data are in groups.
	7. Combine or subdivide groups.

Figure D.4 A Directive Lesson Plan for Initiating Transfer/Elaboration of the Skill of Classifying

TEACHER	STUDENTS
13. Review steps in different procedures, any rules followed, types of categories that prove useful	
14. Suggest other kinds of media with which this skill can be used and unique criteria that need to be applied.	

Figure D.4 (*continued*)

Many of these students find it frustrating and extremely difficult to "discover" inductively time after time how a particular skill can be successfully applied in a new context or with new data sets. Other, more able or experienced students also seem to prefer lessons employing this strategy at this point in learning a thinking operation; many of them, too, resent being asked continually to "discover" or invent everything they are expected to learn. In elaborating a skill, students seem to be more attentive and motivated when new attributes of the skill are explained and demonstrated or when the teacher demonstrates at the beginning the nuances of executing it in a new context. Even in applying the skill as demonstrated, the students often begin to adapt it so that such a presentation does not necessarily lead simply to mimicking or copying someone else's way of doing it.

As do the other skill introducing strategies presented here, these strategies initiating transfer incorporate attributes of effective skill teaching and learning explained in Appendix B. Each of these three transfer/ elaboration strategies keeps the focus of the lesson strictly on the skill being used; subject-matter products of this skill use can be the subject of the lesson immediately following. Each strategy includes modeling the new attributes of the skill: in the inductive strategy by "expert" students—in the other two by the teacher or other "experts." In each strategy students are given opportunities to see and hear the new attributes of

TEACHER		STUDENTS
Rules:		When you can't understand data, put them in "miscellaneous" category temporarily.
Discuss potential obstacles to successful classifying of paintings and how they might be overcome.		...
	Explain	
8. Explain how these procedures and rules for classifying can be used to classify the paintings in set #1 in order to answer the question about American culture. Point out attributes to use as categories that differ from those used in previous activities using verbal data.		Group the paintings with student help, focusing on composition, figure-ground relationships, color, texture, perspective as well as on objects shown.
	Demonstrate	
9. Demonstrate with set #1 the procedure and new attribute categories, inferring answers to the question once paintings are grouped.		Students volunteer attributes and categories as paintings are examined, following the procedure outlined in Step 7 above.
	Review	
10. Have the students briefly review the key steps used in classifying the paintings and the criteria appropriate to this medium. Review any obstacles encountered.		See above, Step 7.
	Apply	
11. Have the students, in pairs, classify the paintings in set #2 into categories related to texture, composition, and so on.		
	Reflect	
12. Have students reflect on and explain how they classified these paintings and why they did what they did to put them into groups. Focus on *steps* and *rules* or principles followed.		Some may use another procedure by starting with categories related to composition, for instance: 1 State categories in advance. 2 Find paintings to fit each category. 3 Combine or subdivide categories.

Figure D.4 (*continued*)

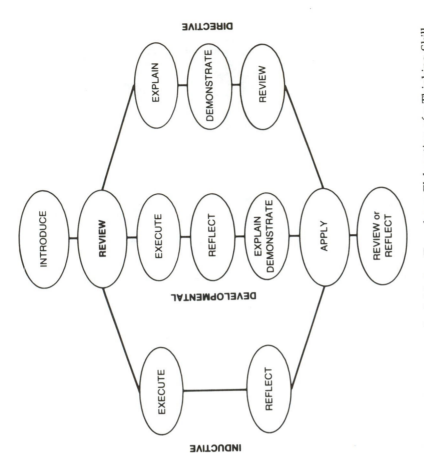

Figure D.5 Strategies for Initiating Transfer or Elaboration of a Thinking Skill

the skill articulated and to discuss what they did in their minds as they executed the skill. And each strategy provides for a second application of the skill immediately following discussion of how to make the skill work in the new setting or form. If properly used, each strategy also concludes with attention to transfer—to where else the skill has been or might be employed.[9] Figure D.5 summarizes the three different strategies presented here for reintroducing a thinking skill to initiate transfer or elaboration of that skill. Using one of these strategies enables teachers in a single thirty to forty minute lesson to launch transfer of a thinking skill or strategy learned in one context to another context and thus begin to help students elaborate or generalize it.

As noted above, the key ingredient in the strategies presented here for launching transfer or elaboration of a skill is the review (Step 2) of what the students know about the skill *before* they attempt to adapt it to a new setting or task or receive a demonstration and explanation of how to make the adaptation. This attention to the key attributes of the skill on the part of the students *before* they consider any modifications in its attributes or use not only makes them more confident of their ability to execute the skill but also helps them recall and make conscious the key operations they can use in employing the skill. This step, in effect, provides a starting place for modifying the skill. These strategies are a natural extension of the strategies previously used by the teacher to introduce any thinking skill or strategy.

Guided Practice

To complete the transfer of a skill to a newly introduced context or to assimilate the newly introduced or refined attributes of a thinking operation requires frequent, repeated, guided practice.[10] Initial practice of the operation in its elaborated form or new context must be accompanied by instruction and guidance. Teachers can use the general strategy for guided practice described in Appendix C to conduct these lessons and can carry out the strategy exactly as described there. This strategy, it will be recalled, involves (1) introducing the operation just as in each teaching strategy described here, (2) previewing how to execute it, (3) applying the operation, having students monitor their work as they proceed, and

(4) having students ponder how they executed the operation. A good portion of any lesson using this strategy, it should also be remembered, can then be devoted to the subject to which the thinking skill or strategy has been applied. As with any new thinking skill, students may need three or four or even more of these guided practice lessons in order to

achieve some degree of competence in this new form or application of the skill.

Autonomous Practice and Application

As students demonstrate increasing proficiency in executing a thinking skill or strategy in its elaborated form or new context, the amount of instruction and guidance can be reduced. After two or three guided practice lessons in the operation using all steps in this teaching strategy, the teacher might shorten, then drop, the preview step. Then, after several more practice lessons in it, the review step could be shortened, then dropped, with only the introduction and active monitoring of the skill as it is used serving as guidance. As students approach the desired level of proficiency, the teacher might even intersperse practice lessons in using the skill being learned in its original form or setting with continued but autonomous practice in the skill as elaborated. Eventually, students should get to the point of being able to execute the skill in its new form without any guidance or instruction at all.

Independent application of any thinking operation in many contexts is an important part of teaching a skill to transfer. In mastering a thinking skill or strategy, students must make decisions about which operations to use and under what conditions. At this final stage in the teaching of thinking, students need frequent opportunities to consider applying the operations being learned to a variety of contexts, some of which may not require using the operations and some of which may require using a number of other skills and strategies as well. Repeated practice in "exercises" obviously requiring use of the same skill is not enough to help students generalize and transfer a skill. For any thinking operation to become an integral part of a student's repertoire, students must have practice, with and without guidance, in deciding whether or not it is appropriate to use the operation in different contexts, as well as practice in actually applying the skill in these contexts.[11]

Teaching thinking operations to transfer is, thus, not something that can be completed in one lesson or probably even in one course. Rather, it requires attention over a sequence of lessons and courses. To help students transfer or elaborate a skill or strategy even into settings similar to that in which it was introduced requires repeated guidance in these settings. Thus, a skill like detecting bias in data, if introduced in a language arts context, needs to be elaborated by guided practice in social studies, journalism, science, and other settings. When initially teaching a thinking skill, a teacher must help students become aware of the cues they can look for in related settings that will call out the skill. In courses where students encounter these settings, teachers must also alert students to the presence of these cues as they provide reinforcement, transfer, and elaboration of the thinking skill introduced earlier.

To teach for "high road" transfer, teachers should help students generalize consciously and deliberately from the context in which the skill or strategy was originally developed, the cues and attributes of settings where the operation may be appropriately used. This can be accomplished by explicitly reintroducing the operation in such settings and providing instruction and guidance in how to apply it in some of these settings, by teaching generalized cues to such settings, and by showing students—and by giving them practice—in how to predict and monitor the application of the operation in novel settings. Teachers in a variety of subject areas thus need to combine efforts in introducing a thinking skill, teaching it to some degree of proficiency and then elaborating it in and transferring it to differing settings and to more sophisticated levels of operation.

NOTES

1. John McPeck, *Critical Thinking and Education* (New York: St. Martin's Press, 1981), p. 78.

2. David N. Perkins, "Thinking Frames" (Paper delivered at ASCD Conference on Approaches to Teaching Thinking, Alexandria, Va., August 6, 1985), pp. 14–15.

3. Bryce B. Hudgins, *Learning and Thinking* (Itasca, Ill.: F.E. Peacock Publishers, 1977), pp. 142–172; Herbert J. Klausmeier and J. Kent Davis, "Transfer of Learning," *Encyclopedia of Educational Research* (New York: Macmillan, 1969), pp. 1483–1495; Robert J. Sternberg, "How Can We Teach Intelligence?" *Educational Leadership* 42:1 (September 1984), p. 52.

4. Neil Postman, "Critical Thinking in the Electronic Era," *National Forum* 65:1 (Winter 1985), pp. 4–8, 17.

5. McPeck, *Critical Thinking*; Edward Feigenbaum and Pamela McCorduck, *The Fifth Generation: Artificial Intelligence and Japan's Computer Challenge to the World* (Reading, Mass.: Addison-Wesley Publishing Company, 1983), pp. 38, 56, 76–77; Walter Doyle, "Academic Work," *Review of Educational Research* 53:2 (Summer 1983), p. 168.

6. Doyle, "Academic Work," pp. 175–178; Hudgins, *Learning and Thinking*; Michael I. Posner and Steven W. Keele, "Skill Learning" in Robert M. W. Travers, ed., *Second Handook of Research on Teaching* (Chicago: Rand McNally College Publishing Company, 1973), pp. 816–823.

7. Posner and Keele, "Skill Learning," pp. 809–811, 821–822.

8. Doyle, "Academic Work," pp. 175–178; Peter Martorella, "Cognition Research: Some Implications for the Design of Social Studies Instructional Materials," *Theory and Research in Social Education* 10:3 (Fall 1982), pp. 1–16.

9. Posner and Keele, "Skill Learning," pp. 805–831; Doyle, *op. cit.*, pp. 159–199; Sternberg, "How Can We ...," pp. 38–50; Jane Stallings, "Effective Strategies for Teaching Basic Skills," in Daisy G. Wallace, *Developing Basic Skills Programs in Secondary Schools* (Alexandria, Va.: Association for Supervision and Curriculum Development, 1983), pp. 1–19.

10. Doyle, "Academic Work"; Posner and Keele, "Skill Learning"; Stallings, "Effective Strategies."

11. Carl Bereiter, "How to Keep Thinking Skills from Going the Way of All Frills," *Educational Leadership* 42:1 (September 1984), pp. 75–78.

Appendix E
Designing Thinking Skill Assessments

Two types of assessment are useful for this end. Teachers can include on their major paper-and-pencil tests items specifically directed at thinking skills and strategies and evaluated as such. And they can also use observational techniques to assess student thinking. Both methods provide data useful to making judgments about the quality—and changes in quality—of student thinking. By incorporating such practices into their testing procedures, teachers can gain valuable evidence not only about the learning of their students but also about the quality of their own instruction. What is even more important, such deliberate and publicly affirmed attention to thinking skills can provide significant additional motivation for students to attend to learning the thinking operations teachers seek to teach.[1]

PAPER-AND-PENCIL TESTS

Unfortunately, formal paper-and-pencil assessing of student proficiency in thinking is not a normal part of most classroom practice. Research suggests that less than 10 percent of most teacher-made classroom tests measure student performance above the level of simple recall.[2] Two reasons may account for this. First, most teachers view their primary function as teaching subject matter and simple subject-matter related skills. Second, since many teachers believe that students learn thinking skills automatically while processing subject matter, they assume that correct answers to subject-matter test questions indicate that students have mastered the thinking skills that teachers believe they have been teaching. This assumption is highly suspect.

Most teacher-directed classroom testing explicitly assesses subject-matter learning. Objective tests measure recall and recognition of facts and related information. Even essay tests—which some teachers claim to use as measures of thinking—commonly measure only subject-matter learning. Most teachers evaluate student essays on the basis of the kinds, amounts, accuracy, and relevance of information given as evidence in support of a claim, the number and kinds of sources cited, and the number and accuracy of the specific facts given, rather than on the basis of any discernible reasoning, critical thinking, or other thinking operations

"Will it be on the test?" Of all the student-asked questions heard in classrooms, this one may be the most common. For many students what is worth attending to and trying to learn is determined primarily by whether or not a teacher tests it. If topics or skills "covered" in class do not show up on end-of-chapter, unit, semester and/or final exams, students assume that they simply are neither important nor worth trying to learn. One way to give value to the instruction in thinking provided by the teaching strategies described in the preceding pages, while also diagnosing teaching and learning, is to devote a significant portion of school and classroom teaching to assessing student proficiency in the thinking operations being taught.

Adapted from Barry K. Beyer, *Practical Strategies for the Teaching of Thinking* (Boston: Allyn and Bacon, 1987), pp. 217–235 and 238–245.

used. The message to students is thus quite clear: facts, generalizations, and information are what count. Although one may use certain thinking skills and strategies to learn information, learning these skills themselves is hardly important, they presume.

If students are to develop more proficiency in thinking than they normally do, teachers must test directly—and appropriately—the thinking skills they teach.[3] Teachers can incorporate test items to measure student proficiency in thinking skills into every unit, mid-semester, and final exam they construct. In most cases, but not always, these tests consist largely of objective test items. To assess the thinking operations being taught in a course, a teacher can simply include with the subject-matter items on their regular tests a number of other objective items specifically dealing with thinking skills and strategies. These items can use the subject matter of the course. They can be mixed throughout a test or collected together in one section of the test so that students can clearly see the importance attached to learning the operations being taught. Such items can be objective types (multiple choice or completion or matching) as well as essay questions. They can include items about the skill or strategy—when it is to be used, rules that guide its use, and so on—as well as items that require students to execute it.

Any instrument developed to assess student proficiency in one or more thinking operations should be a challenge to students, but, as psychologist Robert Sternberg writes, it should be "a surmountable challenge."[4] That is, the task should stretch the student's thinking but not be impossible to complete successfully. And, as Sternberg cautions, the challenge itself should be in the thinking required to complete the item rather than in the knowledge needed to do so.

Tests for Newly Introduced Skills

For greatest impact on student learning, it may be best initially to cluster in a special section of a unit or semester test all questions assessing performance on a skill or strategy that has been the subject of considerable classroom attention. Not only will this format underscore for the students the importance of the specific thinking skills or strategies that have been taught, but it also reaffirms skill learning as an important

continuing goal of learning in the class. Once a teacher has "caught the attention" of the students in this manner and after students have been introduced to a skill over a period of several units in a course, test items on a particular skill or strategy may be scattered throughout the entire test or tested in conjunction with other skills, while the separate skill sections of the test focus on additional newly introduced or elaborated thinking skills.

The number of test items on a special thinking skills section of a unit or major subject-matter test should vary according to the extent to which a skill has been a subject of instruction in the course. Six objective items may provide an adequate measure of proficiency in any single skill or strategy that has been newly introduced (or transferred or elaborated) and practiced a number of times during the preceding several weeks. These six items should require students to (1) define the skill, (2) identify an example of the skill in use, (3) execute the skill several times, and finally (4) explain to others how to execute the skill. Assessing more than a single newly introduced or elaborated skill will require a combination of items that require these operations for each skill to be assessed. Thus, a mid-semester or final exam testing three such skills, for example, may consist of fifteen to eighteen objective items relating specifically to these three skills.

Suppose an American history teacher who had introduced and provided guided practice in the skill of classifying data wished to assess student proficiency in the skill on the first unit exam in the course. Six objective test items on this skill could be added in a special section to the objective part of this unit exam. Figure E.1 presents these items arranged as they would be on this test.

The first two questions on this sample test require students to define and identify an example of the skill. Question 1, requiring its definition, may be a multiple choice item if the teacher seeks only to measure recognition (as is done on this sample test) or a completion item if the teacher wishes to assess student recall of the skill definition. The latter type of question could simply ask students to "Define the skill of classifying. . . ." Question 2 calls for students to pick an example of the skill being used or a product of the skill's having been used. A variety of different questions could serve this function well, but the type of question

UNIT I—TEST FOR THE SKILL OF CLASSIFYING

1. Which of the following best defines the skill of *classifying*?

   a) to arrange things in the order in which they occurred.
   b) to put together things having a common characteristic or characteristics.
   c) to invent a theory.

2. Which of the following show(s) information that has been classified?

        a) A   b) B   c) C

A

As the Indians approached, we put down our muskets and stood up. We recognized the one known as Red Feather clearly. As he came toward us he raised his right hand to salute. Captain Smythe returned the salute and held out the blue blanket. Red Feather smiled and clapped his hands together, shouting to his warriors. They lowered their bows and lances. We had made friendly contact!

B

The original colonies had different kinds of governments. Connecticut and Rhode Island, under charters, selected their own officials. Others, like Pennsylvania, Maryland, and New Jersey, had been granted to individuals known as proprietors. Some colonies, including New York and Georgia, were controlled by appointees of the King; these colonies were known as Royal colonies.

C

Spanish	English	French
Coronado	Cabot	de Champlain
Cabrillo	Hudson	Cartier
deSoto	Drake	Joliet
		LaSalle

---

3. The following words were commonly spoken by inhabitants of London, England, around the year 1750. Classify these words so you can identify what life was like for these Londoners at this time and *show all your work*. Then answer the question below.

customs house	journeyman	stock exchange
lottery ticket	workhouse	alehouse
malaria	milkmaid	mugger
apprentice	cesspool	pauper
almshouse	typhoid	gin
watchman	dockworker	poor house
coffee house	butcher	cow
weaver	smallpox	liquor
squire	debtors' prison	master
gambling house	wool-comber	night soil
chimney sweep	typhus	police court

Circle the letter preceding whichever of the following is/are probably true about life in London around 1750.

a) Most Londoners lived like rich people.
b) Life in London was unhealthy and unsafe for many people.
c) Farming was a way of life for most Londoners.

Figure E.1 (*continued*)

Figure E.1 A Model for Testing a Newly Introduced Thinking Skill or Strategy

5. Classify the information in the following paragraph to answer this question: What was the economy of the thirteen colonies like before the American Revolution? *Show all your work.*

By 1763 the thirteen colonies were sending many products overseas. Lumber, tar, fish, rum — a drink made from molasses — and furs went from Massachusetts, New Hampshire, Connecticut, and nearby colonies. Pennsylvania, New York, Delaware, and neighboring colonies shipped iron, iron kettles and tools, flour, lead, woolen cloth, and hats as well as furs and livestock. The Carolinas, Virginia, and neighboring colonies shipped tobacco, indigo — a plant from which a dye was made — rice, and farm products like grain, beans, pork, and horses.

Now, complete the following:

Based on how you processed the above items, write one sentence describing the economy of the thirteen American colonies just before the American Revolution. In another sentence explain why your first sentence is accurate, based on the data above.

1. _____
2. _____

Figure E.1 (*(continued)*)

---

4. The items listed below were recovered from a dried-up well near a place where people lived in late eighteenth century America. The place of origin of each item is indicated, where known. Classify these items in some way that would help tell you about the people who used these items. *Be sure to show how you classify these items.* Then answer the question at the bottom of the page.

1 iron candle chandelier (France)
3 pewter mugs (Germany)
18 copper buttons (America)

7 pewter spoons (America)
3 hand-painted, porcelain plates (England)
1 pewter plate (Germany)
2 westerwald stoneware chamber pots (Germany)
1 porcelain teapot (China)
5 whiteware hand-painted plates (France)
3 bone-handled forks (England)

2 stoneware milk vessels (America)
1 pewter fork
8 liquor bottles (England)
3 soda glasses

1 horn-handled knife (America)
8 perfume bottles (France)
1 pocket knife, mother-of-pearl handle (England)
9 medicine bottles (England)
1 iron hoe (America)

11 wine decanters (France)
1 silk glove

3 bone-handled tooth brushes
3 hand-painted pearlware plates (China)

7 hand-painted porcelain tea cups (England)

3 porcelain cups (China)
2 printed silk cloths (China)
1 leather shoe (England)
2 bone-handled hair brushes

Circle the letter preceding the phrase that best completes this sentence:

The people who once used the items on the above list almost certainly

a) made a living as craftsmen.
b) lived on the western frontier.
c) were upper class, wealthy.

Figure E.1 (*continued*)

on the sample test appears to be most useful. In this sample, students are asked to choose from three different options the one or ones that most likely show(s) data that have already been classified.

Question 3, 4, and 5 require the students to execute the skill and to show how they did it. Plenty of space is provided around each question so that students can mark the data directly with circles and lines to connect items in the same category or with different symbols to identify items related to one another. Students can also use the space under the data in each selection to list items in groups, labeling each group. The key to this type of item, of course, is the requirement to "show your work," to indicate or even explain how and why the skill was executed as it was. Questions 3, 4, and 5 also contain a "check-up" request for students to infer a generalization or two about the data that they have classified.

Three opportunities are provided to demonstrate competence in the skill because at times the information to which a skill is applied can affect adversely how a skill is executed. One must allow for the possibility of students' not being able to execute a skill because of misreading or not understanding the given data. Several opportunities should thus be provided for using the skill; a teacher could consider passable a student's getting two out of three questions correct. It should be noted here that no specific instructions are given with these items that could either "give away" how to do the skill or limit any specific techniques that the students could use in executing the skill. Because asking students to group or list these items would hint at what they could do to carry it out, such hints need to be avoided. At best, the skill label used in class should be the action word in questions or tasks of this type only in the initial tests assessing the skill.

Probably the most difficult question in this sequence, question 6, requires students to know the skill well enough to explain to others how to execute it. Students may write their directions in paragraph form, make a list of steps and rules to follow, or draw and label a flowchart or other type of diagram to present these directions. When students direct their explanation to those younger and thus presumably less competent in the skill than are they, these directions tend to be in a clearer, more direct, simpler form than if addressed to the teacher or anyone else students suspect of knowing more about the skill than they do.

6. In the space under the data below, give *specific*, detailed directions that a fifth grader could follow to classify the *names* in order to answer this question: "What was colonial culture like by 1775?"

Name		Name	
Phyllis Wheatley	poet	Cotton Mather	minister/scientist
Benjamin Franklin	printer/inventor	John Copley	painter
Benjamin West	painter	Jonathan Edwards	minister/author
Sarah Kemble Knight	author	Roger Williams	minister
David Rittenhouse	astronomer	Anne Bradstreet	poet
John Peter Zenger	editor		

END OF TEST

Figure E.1 ((continued))

A cluster of test items like these suggested here offers many advantages in assessing student performance in thinking skills. In effect, this collection of items assesses three levels of proficiency. If a student answers questions 1 and 2 satisfactorily but cannot answer the remaining questions on this part of the exam, a teacher can reasonably assume that the student knows only a little about this skill and cannot do it well. For even if not familiar with the meaning of the data, a student could classify these words by first letters, by syllables, by number of letters, or by some other non-subject-matter criteria. A student who answers questions 1 through 5 but does not do well on item 6 shows a high degree of knowledge and proficiency in the skill in this type of context, but still not enough to be able to explain it satisfactorily to others. Any student who can complete the entire range of questions correctly may well have a very high proficiency in this particular skill, at least in this subject area and format.

In preparing such tests, teachers must give special attention to the kinds of data used with the questions and to the way these data are used. In devising items that require application of the skill to be assessed, teachers must especially guard against creating or selecting those that confuse or mix recall of subject matter or information with the thinking operations being tested. Figure E.2 illustrates this problem. It presents two test items, both designed to assess student proficiency in the skill of comparing/contrasting.[5] Yet item 1 requires students to recall information before they can process it to answer the question. Item 2 provides virtually all the information needed to answer the question. Students who fail to answer question 1 correctly may fail because they cannot recall appropriate information as much as because they cannot compare it correctly. Inferring that the skill of comparing is at fault in such instances could hardly be justified. As a rule of thumb, items that call for a student to apply any given thinking skills should be those like item 2 in this figure, providing data needed to answer the stated skill-applying questions. Such data can be presented in lists, graphs, maps, paragraphs, scripts, narratives, illustrations, and other appropriate formats. The key to minimizing interference in skill assessing, caused by a need to recall information or use other skills, is to provide all the information needed to answer a thinking skill question as part of the question or item.

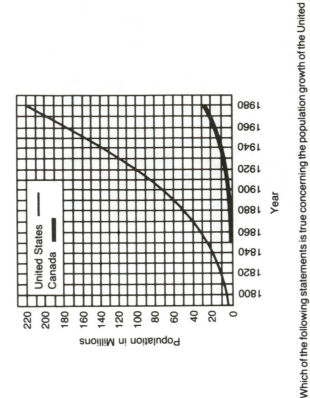

1. In the late nineteenth century, western vigilantes and southern Ku Klux Klan (KKK) members were similiar in what way?

   A. Both took the law into their own hands.
   B. Both were concerned with jury trials.
   C. Both were against violence.
   D. Both found jobs for immigrants.

2. Population Growth in the United States and Canada

   Which of the following statements is true concerning the population growth of the United States and Canada?

   • Both the United States and Canada are growing in population at the same rate.
   • The United States is growing in population more rapidly than Canada.
   • People do not like living in Canada.
   • There are more people living in Canada than in the United States.

Figure E.2 Questions Calling for Comparing/Contrasting

Furthermore, data used in skill application questions should be the same kinds of data and in the same format as those used in teaching the skill in class. But these data must *not* have been seen or used before in this form by the students. Students should be familiar with their meaning but should not have processed them in class exactly as they are to be processed on the test. To include as data in a particular thinking skills question data that the students already have worked with in learning that skill in class can invalidate the test. Student answers to such items are less likely to evidence proficiency in the skill that the items seek to assess than they are skills of simple recall or recognition. For the most valid and reliable test results, data included in thinking skills test items must not be the same data that students have used in practicing the skill in their classes but must be similar in form and method of presentation of classroom data.

To provide on a test data of a kind or in a form with which students are completely unfamiliar—especially on a test given early in the course of learning a thinking operation—is likely to result more in a measure of a student's ability to transfer a skill on his or her own than it is to be a measure of skill competency at this point. Keeping the data the same as that used in instruction provides a fairer and more valid measure of skill competency. As teachers help students elaborate a thinking skill and learn how to apply it in various settings, then test questions can use data representative of the variety of settings in which it has been taught.

The amount of data provided with thinking skill test items should also be relatively small. A cluster of items such as those in the model test (Figure E.1) will require much more then ten or fifteen minutes to complete; what time is allocated for the test must be devoted to processing data rather than simply reading it. Paragraphs, lists, and other types of data should, therefore, not be too long. What students do with the data is more important than how much data they process.

Teachers may wish to add more test items to these basic six. For example, a question asking for synonyms of a skill label or asking students to indicate a word that does *not* belong in a group of such synonyms might be suitable following question 1 on the model test. Two items requiring picking examples might be included instead of one, as on the model test here (question 2). In this case, the first of these two items could

illustrate use of the skill in a data set identical to the data set used in introducing a skill; the second of the two could provide a data set in a form identical to that used in introducing the skill but the data could be from other parts of the subject-matter unit being tested.

Application items (like numbers 3, 4, and 5 on the model test) can also be modified in a number of ways. It may be advisable to add one or two multiple choice questions at the bottom of each page after each major question as checks on how students processed the data. For example, the following items could have been included under question 3 of the model test in Figure E.1.

a) Which of the following might have been classified together?

  a) 1 and 2   c) 2, 3, and 4
  b) 1, 4, and 6   d) 2, 5, and 6

  1. police court   4. mugger
  2. chimney sweep 5. apprentice
  3. coffee house   6. watchman

b) What is it those items in your answer to the above question have in common?

In asking questions like these, teachers take some risk of limiting student options or of "giving away" certain categories. However, by giving only a few options, a teacher can steer students to provide a desired response and thus test knowledge. But such a question fails to allow students to truly generate their own categories. A more useful format for "check-up" items under questions like 3, 4, and 5 might thus be:

For one of the categories of information you have identified, explain why you have developed it as you did.

Notice the sequence of the data and tasks in questions 3, 4, and 5. The task and data in question 3 are virtually identical to those used in introducing the skill in class. The task in question 4 requires classifying but with data that students may not be familiar with, at least as a result of study in class. However, the general context of the data in the question resembles closely the topics being studied in the course and the subject matter of the test itself. Question 5 presents familiar data but in a paragraph format rather than in a list; the "listing" of data is, in fact, embedded in the paragraph. Such a change in data format presumes that students had used data presented in this second format prior to the test (as is the assumed case here). A progression of application items moving from an item as much as possible like those done in the class introduction of the skill being tested to the most recent elaboration of the skill may be a useful question sequence. But whatever sequence is used, it should be remembered that formats and data sets ought to be like those used with the skill in class up to the point of the test.

The items on this sample test presume student understanding of the data used. There is, thus, a risk that inability to execute the skill may reflect ignorance of the data rather than of the skill. Research clearly indicates that competence in a skill is enhanced by knowledge of the context or field in which it is applied.[6] Since this set of sample items is to be on a unit test for which students are to have studied, it seem reasonable to presume that students will recall enough about the data in these items to demonstrate proficiency in the skill. This is quite appropriate, especially since using a category of "miscellaneous" is a useful emergency rule students should have learned regarding how to handle unfamiliar or fuzzy data.

Where student knowledge of the data may not be presumed, some definition or description of the data needs to be supplied, as in question 6. To minimize interference with the skill caused by failure to know all the data used here, question 6 includes for each individual a significant attribute that can be used as categories for arranging them. Of course, the names themselves reflect the sex of each individual, and students may also recommend use of this distinction as a basis of classifying.

In the initial stages of teaching a skill or strategy, testing should concentrate on assessing proficiency in the operation as it has been introduced. This means essentially that the data used in the test items must be of the same type as that in which the skill was introduced and initially practiced. While it is tempting to produce a test to assess transfer, it is patently unfair and unproductive to do so until students have received instruction and guided practice in elaborating the skill in a number of related contexts or with a number of different types of data. Students

need experience and instruction in generalizing a skill to a variety of contexts before they can be reasonably expected to know enough to, or even voluntarily make, the transfer necessary to apply the skill successfully in a new context. Forcing students to make such a transfer before they have received appropriate instruction in how to do so and then giving students grades on the quality of the resulting performance may not only discourage students from further effort to learn the skill but merely confirm what we already know: transfer is not usually automatic. Results on such a test item would reveal more about the quality of instruction than about student proficiency in the skill being assessed.

As students receive more instruction and guided practice in applying a thinking skill or strategy in a variety of contexts and thus generalize it beyond the setting in which it was introduced, tests can more legitimately seek to assess proficiency at transfer. Tests for this purpose should not only provide "surmountable challenges" but also, according to educator Edys Quellmalz:

1. present tasks of significance,
2. require sustained thinking,
3. require integration of information used in a series of items, and
4. represent a range of generalized transfer tasks.[7]

Quellmalz recommends, for example, that test items for a particular skill include settings that are (1) life experience, (2) in subject-matter contexts and in (3) novel contexts. Thus, a test on classifying might present as items 3, 4, and 5 (1) a task involving classifying the items found in a garage or auto in an effort to identify something about the user of the garage or auto, (2) a task involving classifying a series of historical events (if the subject is history), and (3) a task involving classifying the ingredients of a structure found in the ruins of a "lost" civilization such as Atlantis or on Venus.

If each time this skill of classifying had been applied in class the teacher had been asking students to consider where this skill could be used in the context of their own school experiences, another application item could be added to the sample test presented here, an item that asks students to apply the skill with school-based data and "to show your

	A	B	C	D
1st period	Geography	Creative Writing	English Literature	International Relations
2nd period	General Math	Trigonometry	Introd. Spanish	French Literature
3rd period	Study Center	U.S. History	Algebra	Creative Writing
4th period	English Grammar	Gym/Study	Geography	Calculus
Lunch A	x		x	
Lunch B		x		x
5th period	Gym/Study	Physics	Study Center	Physics
6th period	General Science	Physics Lab	Gym/Study	Physics Lab
7th period	Typing	Spanish III	Biology	Typing
8th period	Introd. French	Typing	Biology Lab	Gym/Study

Figure E.3 High School Student Schedules

work''. For example, the following item might follow question 5 on the model test (Figure E.1):

(6). Four high school students were comparing their class schedules for the new school year. Process the information they reported so you can tell something about the kind of school which students A, B, C, and D attend and/or something about these students themselves. *Be sure to show how you processed this data.* (See Figure E.3.) Based on how you processed the data, write two sentences (1) describing the school attended by students A, B, C, and D or (2) describing the students themselves. Be sure to give a reason for what you say in each sentence.

This kind of item requires "transfer" of the thinking operation being assessed. Providing items using data typical of out-of-class contexts to which a skill can be legitimately applied should be done only if cues to these data have been previously introduced and used in class, at least in the early stages of teaching and testing a particular skill. On later tests additional items could require "transfer" to other data formats with clues similar to those discussed or used in class.

In sum, one specific format for a set of questions to assess proficiency in a newly introduced thinking skill or strategy (as with the skill of classifying used as an example here) consists of six items requiring, in sequence:

1. Definition of the skill
2. Identifying an example of the skill in use
3. Application of the skill
4. Application of the skill
5. Application of the skill
6. Explanation of how to execute the skill

The test presented in Figure E.1 illustrates how this six-item assessment format for a newly introduced thinking skill could be applied at the intermediate and secondary grade levels. However, this same assessment format can also be used to assess newly introduced thinking skills in the primary grades as well. Figure E.4 presents such a test for the skill of sorting, as classifying is usually called in these grades.

The six items on this test serve the same functions as do the six items on the instrument presented for older students. The first two require a definition (number 1) and recognition of an example of the skill in use (number 2). Items 3, 4, and 5 require the students to actually perform the skill, the essence of any effective skill assessment. In these items the students use objects that are similar, but not identical, to those they have presumably been using in class up to this point and with which they are familiar. Notice that the objects to be used in each item have multiple attributes so they can be sorted in any of several ways.

Item 6 requires students to, in effect, "tell" how the skill works, but here the student is asked to show how to do it because at this age verbalizing one's own thinking seems to be virtually impossible for these youngsters. As the student does show the teacher how to do it by actually manipulating the teacher's hand, the teacher can ask why he or she is being made to make each move the student wants him or her to make. This is about the closest a teacher-made thinking skill assessment can come to getting primary grade students to articulate their own thinking, which is the intent of this sixth question on this kind of thinking skill test.

Note that this test is designed as an individual test and is to be administered orally to each student in turn. If time does not permit this, however, the first five items can be administered to three students at a time. In this approach students could respond to items 1 and 2 by a show of hands. The three could then simultaneously sort the different objects in items 3, 4, and 5, trading objects in turn so each gets to sort objects in items 3, 4, and 5, three times. Item 6, however, would still have to be administered individually to each student.

With a few changes, this same test could easily be adapted for those students who can read and write. Instead of being administered orally, their test could be a paper-and-pencil test on which they circle the correct answers to items 1 and 2. Instead of working with actual objects on items 3, 4, and 5, students can be asked to circle or connect by lines,

---

TEST FOR SORTING

TO THE TEACHER: Administer this test orally to individual students. Read each item, 1–5, and record student answers and groupings on this page.

Student name _____ Date _____

TO THE STUDENT:
1. Tell me which of the following things I say tells what *sorting* is:
   a. finding an answer to a problem.
   b. putting things together that are alike.
   c. deciding what will probably happen next.

2. Tell me if each of these people are *sorting:*
   a. my brother putting silverware away in the drawer   yes/no
   b. my sister raking the leaves into piles in the yard   yes/no
   c. my uncle looking for a new car   yes/no

3. Here are some objects (a banana, a red apple, a red and a yellow ribbon, a red and a yellow flower). Sort these into groups.

4. Here are some objects (one red and one blue small toy car, one red and one blue large toy truck, one small red and one large blue toy airplane). Sort these.

5. Here are some other objects (6 keys of two different sizes, 3 silver-colored and 3 bronze-colored). Group these for me.

TO THE TEACHER: With each student individually, say:
6. *Here are some other objects* (one small green and one large orange plastic star, one large green and one small orange plastic square, one large green and one small orange plastic triangle). *Take my hand and show me how to sort these into groups.* (Ask the student to explain *why* he or she has you make the moves shown.) Record what the student says and does, for your records and later analysis.

Figure E.4 A Model Test for Assessing a Newly Introduced Skill in the Primary Grades

SAMPLE THINKING SKILL TEST ITEMS

A

The Egbas and Yorubas were the main actors in these merciless conflicts. They also were the main sufferers from them. They were once the most peaceful and civilized tribes in the country, famous for their agriculture and trade. Fighting with their neighbors and with each other ruined them. When I arrived, many of the Egbas and Yorubas felt sick of war and the slave trade. They wanted peace and prosperity.

1. According to this excerpt, the Egbas and the Yorubas were recently involved in:

   a) changing their religion.
   b) civil war.
   c) starting to trade with Europe.
   d) outbreaks of contagious diseases.

2. The excerpt suggests that the Egbas and Yorubas were:

   a) the only civilized people in the country.
   b) the most warlike of all people in the country.
   c) famous as fishermen and traders.
   d) two of several groups living in the region.

3. According to this excerpt, its author:

   a) fears the Egbas and Yorubas.
   b) is unfamiliar with the Egbas and Yorubas.
   c) sympathizes with the Egbas and Yorubas.
   d) dislikes the Egbas and Yorubas.

4. The best title for this excerpt is:

   a) Trade among the Egbas and Yorubas.
   b) From War to Peace.
   c) Egbas versus Yorubas.
   d) The Fruits of War.

Figure E.5 Sample Items to Assess Thinking Skill Proficiency in Multiple Thinking Skills

drawings or pictures of items that belong in the same group. Item 6 may still have to be administered orally, however, although it need not be given to every student but only to a representative sample depending on whether the teacher wishes to use the test results for diagnostic or summative purposes. Other variations of this primary grade version of this test format can be made, too. This six-item format for assessing proficiency in any newly introduced thinking skill can be used to assess proficiency in any thinking skill, in any subject area, at any grade level, from kindergarten onward.

One final point remains about test items of the type discussed here. Answering them requires considerably more time than is often allotted for conventional objective items designed to assess knowledge of subject matter alone. A six-item skill cluster like that described here may well require thirty minutes or so for many students. Thus, teachers may wish to administer this section of a unit test on a second day after students have completed the regular subject-matter segment of the test. But regardless of when it is administered, teachers should allow a reasonable time for students to complete it. At least on early administrations of items like these, time limits should not be restricting.

Tests for Multiple Thinking Skills

Thinking skills, of course, are rarely used singly or in isolation from one another. Thinking is a complex process involving a variety of skills and strategies. In order to resolve a problem, an individual may have to translate data, classify it and compare it to other data, and then infer a generalization about the unique feature(s) of a particular subject or phenomena. To assess student proficiencies in employing a variety of thinking skills or some combination of these skills, a teacher can construct multiple choice test items similar to those skill items used on major reading tests or on the Scholastic Aptitude Test. Each of these items can consist of a data set—a paragraph, map, chart, or table, for example—followed by a series of questions. Each question is designed to elicit the use of a particular thinking skill. Figure E.5 presents three such test items.

Like the data used in questions 3, 4, and 5 on the test presented in

B

The Dutch claimed to have purchased the island for just $24 worth of beads and trinkets. But the Indians insisted they had not sold the island. Frequently, Indians would come across the river to hunt on their favorite hunting grounds on the island. When they did so, settlers would often shoot at them, killing or injuring some. Sometimes the barbarous Indians would return under cover of darkness to burn outlying farmhouses—and butcher their inhabitants. Once, Dutch farmers crossed the river to teach them a lesson, killing dozens of Indian women and children as well as the few warriors they could catch.

1. This account indicates that the early inhabitants of this area:

   a) traded with one another.
   b) considered the sale of land to be final.
   c) carried on fighting even after the island was sold.
   d) were victims of outside events.

2. This account indicates that the Indians and Dutch:

   a) differed in their interpretation of what the sale of land meant.
   b) refused to have anything to do with each other.
   c) deliberately misled each other.
   d) treated each other as equals.

3. The author of this account probably was:

   a) an Indian who lived there.
   b) a European observer living at the time.
   c) a historian writing more than 100 years later.
   d) a Dutch settler living on the island.

4. The best title for this account would be:

   a) Aborigines of the New World.
   b) European Exploitation of Native Americans.
   c) Cultures in Conflict.
   d) Civilization in the New World.

Figure E.5 (*continued*)

C

The Aztecs were the most powerful and feared people of Mexico. They continuously raided other cities and despoiled the countryside. Our arrival saved thousands from enslavement and torture at their hands. Once terrified of the fierce Aztecs, the natives now joined us in our march on the city of Montezuma. They warned us about Aztec traps and ambushes. Our guns and artillery seemed to give them renewed courage to stand up to these butchers. Divine will had made us their salvation!

1. During the time described in this account, the peoples of Mexico:

   a) lived in peace and prosperity.
   b) distrusted foreigners.
   c) traded with people far away.
   d) fought among themselves.

2. According to this account, the Aztecs were:

   a) natural-born rulers.
   b) one of several different peoples living in Mexico.
   c) regarded by all Mexicans as superior.
   d) the most civilized of all Mexicans.

3. Whoever wrote this account:

   a) admired the Aztecs.
   b) was a religious person.
   c) was a leader of Mexicans who opposed the Aztecs.
   d) was a trained military leader.

4. The best title for this account is:

   a) Civil War in Mexico.
   b) Empire of the Aztecs.
   c) The Invasion of Mexico.
   d) New Life Comes to Mexico.

Figure E.5 (*continued*)

Figure E.1, the items in Figure E.5 are used to answer the questions that follow each. But unlike questions 3, 4, and 5 in Figure E.1, a series of different questions follows each set of data. Each of these questions accompanying the data requires students to employ a different thinking skill. Question 1 in each of the three items in Figure E.5, for example, requires students to translate the data provided in the given paragraph. Question 2 requires students to interpret the data, while question 3 assesses the reader's ability to analyze data to infer the author's frame of reference. And in question 4, respondents must synthesize what they have read to produce a generalization in the form of a title. Each of these four skills is assessed three times—once in each test item.

Questions such as these can be constructed for use in any subject area and be clustered at the end of a regular unit or other major subject-matter test to assess student proficiency in applying a variety of thinking operations that have been taught over the months preceding the test. A chemistry teacher, for instance, who has already taught skills of comparing, classifying, and generalizing may prepare five or six such items, each using different data sets followed by three or four questions. Of these questions, the first in each item could require translation, the second comparing, the next classifying, and the fourth generalizing. Thus, on such a test containing five, four-question items, five questions will assess proficiency on each of the four skills. From answers to these questions, teachers can infer students' proficiencies in each skill being assessed. Such inferences based on this type of test item are much less shaky than those based solely on conventional subject-matter tests.

An even more sophisticated format for a thinking skills test might resemble the Cornell Test of Critical Thinking developed by Robert Ennis and Jason Millman.[8] Such a test would include, as the data to be processed, a continuing narrative, a debate, a journal account, or an argument interspersed with questions, each requiring use of a particular thinking skill that has been taught. Questions can be keyed to a limited number of skills so that student proficiency in each can be assessed over several instances. Students answer the questions in a context of continuous thinking; they must apply many specific operations in order to resolve a problem, make a decision, clarify a argument, comprehend something, or develop a concept. Although extremely difficult to pro-

duce, such tests prove to be most intriguing to students and offer considerable internal motivation for completing them. The advent of the microcomputer and the possibilities of multiple branching based on student responses offer considerable potential for using tests like these for both teaching and assessing student proficiency in thinking.

Essay questions, too, produce some measure of student proficiencies in thinking skills and strategies. However, these essays must differ from traditional subject-matter essays and must be evaluated for the thinking they represent or report rather than solely for content accuracy or grammar. Several types of essay questions might be used for this purpose. Students can be asked to construct arguments to explain their evaluation of given statements or hypotheses, as for example:

To what extent do you agree or disagree with the claim—''Wars do not solve old problems—they merely create new ones''?

In answering questions like this one, students are expected to build an argument containing all the evidence of a good argument including an assertion, evidence, and reasoning. Analysis of a student's argument in terms of reasoning skills could serve as a useful assessment of proficiency in these skills.

Another type of essay might be based on the critical thinking essay developed by Robert Ennis and Eric Weir.[9] Here, given a series of paragraphs on a topic, students are asked to respond in a series of paragraphs of their own. The given paragraphs illustrate basic reasoning or critical thinking principles or faults, and student responses either judge these given statements or respond to them. Again, however, evaluation of such student writing must focus on the thinking skills evidenced by the writing rather than on the nature of the writing itself.

Two additional types of essays may also be useful measures of student thinking. Students can be assigned regular subject-matter essay questions to answer and, after having written their answers, can write a paragraph or two explaining what they did in their heads to invent their answers. These latter essays require students to articulate what thinking decisions they made and the reasoning behind such decisions. ''I think'' writing exemplifies such writing. The second type of essay consists of

is a prerequisite to effective use of observation for assessing student thinking.

Over the past several decades, researchers have identified a number of behaviors that characterize ineffective thinking.[11] Knowing these, teachers can then perhaps look for their behavioral opposites as indicators of more effective thinking. These thinking behaviors are primarily those indicative of the dispositions supportive of effective thinking outlined in the preceding chapter. Students good at thinking voluntarily cite evidence and reasons for claims they make and they ask others, including texts and other authorities, to do the same. They initiate questions, ones that ask why? how come? and so what? rather than simply calling for descriptive information. They deliberately seek out information in making decisions and constantly seem to want more of it before deciding. They deliberately generate many alternatives before judging or choosing any. They deliberately seek other points of view on a topic, issue, or question as a way of securing such information. They consult and cite reliable sources and insist that others do so, too. Consistent and persistent behaviors such as these can be interpreted as indicative of skillful thinking just as can be high scores on thinking skills tests.

Educator Arthur L. Costa has suggested a list of behaviors that he believes are indicative of an effective thinker. Such an individual, he writes:

1. Persists in a thinking task, applying alternative methods until a goal is achieved.
2. Deliberately plans how to execute a thinking task by clarifying goals, identifying givens, and carefully selecting methods and data.
3. Exhibits flexibility in thinking, approaching a task from a number of perspectives or angles.
4. Tells the steps engaged in when executing a thinking skill or strategy.
5. Identifies missing data in a problem-solving situation and how to locate it.

having students write a narrative explaining to another student, younger and less well informed and skilled than they, how to employ a selected thinking operation to complete a specific task. Of course, none of these types of essays should be included on any tests until students have written such essays as class assignments and have had opportunities to discuss and revise what they have written; otherwise, unfamiliarity with the answer format may interfere with execution of the skill or strategy.

Of all the methods teachers can use to assess student proficiency in thinking, explicit testing—in depth—of the thinking operations being taught in the classroom can be the most useful and powerful. Not only does such an assessment provide a more reliable measure of student skill learning than do most methods commonly used by teachers, but it also provides a measure of instructional effectiveness. Even more so, explicit testing of the skills being taught can also motivate student learning of such skills. Consistent and in-depth classroom paper-and-pencil testing of thinking skills and strategies can improve both teaching and learning of these skills.

OBSERVATION OF STUDENT BEHAVIOR

Besides using various types of paper-and-pencil tests to assess student proficiency in specific thinking skills and strategies, teachers can also look for patterns of student behaviors indicative of skillful thinking. By recording specific incidences of such behaviors over a year or so, teachers can develop another measure of student thinking. Consulting both observational data and test data, teachers are likely to get a thorough and realistic appraisal of the thinking proficiencies of their students—and of their own proficiency at the teaching of thinking.

Paper-and-pencil tests customarily reveal whether students get right—correct—answers. Observation can be a useful tool for providing information about how they go about developing those answers. Indeed, some educators assert that the ultimate assessment of student thinking is to identify what students do when they *don't* know an answer.[10] In both instances, knowing the behavior indicative of skillful thinking

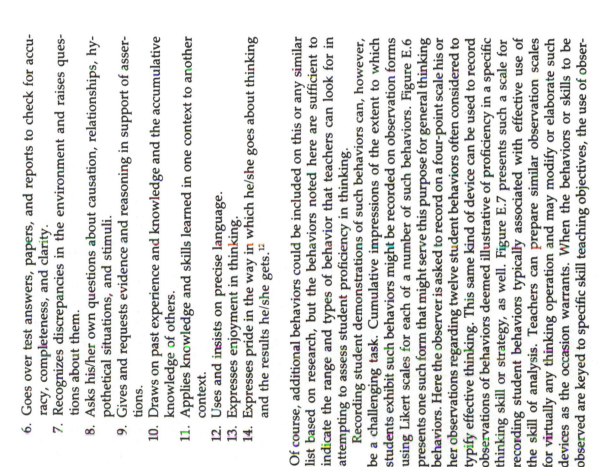

Figure E.6 Thinking Behavior Observation Report

6. Goes over test answers, papers, and reports to check for accuracy, completeness, and clarity.
7. Recognizes discrepancies in the environment and raises questions about them.
8. Asks his/her own questions about causation, relationships, hypothetical situations, and stimuli.
9. Gives and requests evidence and reasoning in support of assertions.
10. Draws on past experience and knowledge and the accumulative knowledge of others.
11. Applies knowledge and skills learned in one context to another context.
12. Uses and insists on precise language.
13. Expresses enjoyment in thinking.
14. Expresses pride in the way in which he/she goes about thinking and the results he/she gets.[12]

Of course, additional behaviors could be included on this or any similar list based on research, but the behaviors noted here are sufficient to indicate the range and types of behavior that teachers can look for in attempting to assess student proficiency in thinking.

Recording student demonstrations of such behaviors can, however, be a challenging task. Cumulative impressions of the extent to which students exhibit such behaviors might be recorded on observation forms using Likert scales for each of a number of such behaviors. Figure E.6 presents one such form that might serve this purpose for general thinking behaviors. Here the observer is asked to record on a four-point scale his or her observations regarding twelve student behaviors often considered to typify effective thinking. This same kind of device can be used to record observations of behaviors deemed illustrative of proficiency in a specific thinking skill or strategy, as well. Figure E.7 presents such a scale for recording student behaviors typically associated with effective use of the skill of analysis. Teachers can prepare similar observation scales for virtually any thinking operation and may modify or elaborate such devices as the occasion warrants. When the behaviors or skills to be observed are keyed to specific skill teaching objectives, the use of obser-

E-15

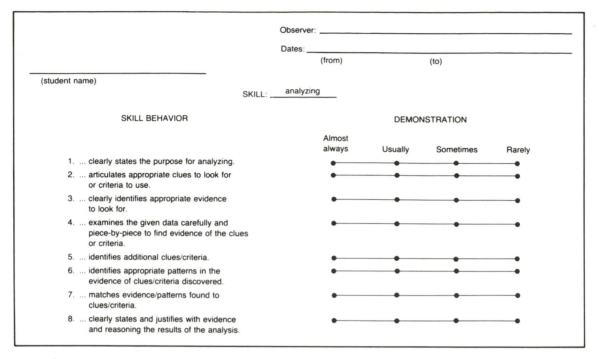

Observer: _____

Dates: _____
      (from)   (to)

_____
(student name)

SKILL: _____ analyzing _____

SKILL BEHAVIOR

1. ... clearly states the purpose for analyzing.
2. ... articulates appropriate clues to look for or criteria to use.
3. ... clearly identifies appropriate evidence to look for.
4. ... examines the given data carefully and piece-by-piece to find evidence of the clues or criteria.
5. ... identifies additional clues/criteria.
6. ... identifies appropriate patterns in the evidence of clues/criteria discovered.
7. ... matches evidence/patterns found to clues/criteria.
8. ... clearly states and justifies with evidence and reasoning the results of the analysis.

DEMONSTRATION

Almost always | Usually | Sometimes | Rarely

Figure E.7 Thinking Skill Observation Report

vational instruments such as these may be one useful way of assessing, for both formative and summative purposes, student learning as well as classroom instruction.

As attractive as such an approach to assessing thinking may be, however, problems exist in devising and using these observation instruments. First, the validity of such instruments and procedures needs to be determined. Beyond establishing a significant correlation between these instruments and other validated measures of thinking, this involves developing a consensus among potential observers about the kinds of behaviors to be noted. Indeed, it involves agreement on the extent to which the behaviors listed actually are evidence of effective thinking or are essential ingredients in any specific thinking operation to be assessed. It also requires attention to the degree of competence of the respondents in recognizing or recalling the use of such behaviors in the first place.

Furthermore, attending to student thinking behaviors requires more than merely noting the forms or content of such behaviors. It involves also noting the context of those behaviors—whether they are exhibited in familiar and previously experienced settings only or in novel and unfamiliar contexts as well. It is important to note also whether such behaviors are exhibited in response to teacher or other outside stimuli or are exhibited at the initiative of students themselves. Just as in paper-and-pencil testing, teachers employing observation to assess student thinking must look for patterns of voluntary thoughtful behavior in a variety of unfamiliar as well as familiar settings in order to judge the proficiency of student thinking.

Moreover, the logistics of using observation instruments, of virtually any kind, may well be overwhelming, especially if a single teacher is expected to complete one for each student he or she teaches or if an evaluation is sought from all teachers and other school officials for a large number of students in a school. Such an effort is likely to be rather forbidding, to say the least.

Finally, special efforts must be made to prevent abuses inherent in using observational devices such as these. Teachers must take care, for instance, *not* to reduce the points on the scales to numbers that can then be totaled and averaged across responses. They should make every effort to assure that student thinking behaviors are not put into the forms of numbers by which students can subsequently be classified and labeled. They must also be careful how they interpret data derived from such observations. At best, noting only patterns of behavior accumulated over time will be a valid interpretation. Data secured from a single observation will almost assuredly be inappropriate as a basis for describing or making judgments about a student's thinking or growth in thinking abilities.

In spite of serious problems in the use for summative purposes of observational instruments for assessment of thinking, these instruments may prove useful in other ways. They could be given directly to the students themselves, periodically, for self-assessment of their proficiency at thinking. Using the instruments in this way may serve instructional goals far better than assessment goals. Use of these instruments as a basis for student self-diagnosis early in a school year and periodically thereafter can alert students to the kinds of behaviors they *ought* to be exhibiting. Even if what they check on the accompanying scales remain suspect, the very fact that they know what the desired or expected behaviors are may motivate or otherwise lead them to adopt some of these behaviors. These instruments may also be provided periodically to parents so that they can note the behaviors of their children. And, even if parents choose not to use them, this may alert them to the school's goals in this aspect of the curriculum and thus serve a very useful public relations function. Indeed, allowing parents to contribute to the rating of student progress in thinking can educate parents about the kinds of thinking behavior they might reinforce at home and thus provide continuing support for such learning beyond the classroom.

SUMMARY

Without appropriate assessment we cannot know how skillful a student is at thinking or how effective a teacher is at teaching it. Nor can we know what needs to be attended to in order to improve either. By observing and testing directly the thinking behaviors and skills of students, teachers can sharply enhance both the teaching and learning of thinking. Making continuing and in-depth paper-and-pencil testing of these skills an integral part of each major subject-matter classroom test where thinking is being taught calls student attention to the importance of thinking as a legitimate learning and teaching objective. Such testing also provides diagnostic feedback about both the quality of student learning and teacher teaching. Without it, improvements in either are most difficult to come by.

Assessing student thinking is as essential a part of teaching of thinking as are the strategies and materials used in this teaching. Without it, the teaching and learning of thinking remain only half done. Unless teachers assess explicitly, continuously, and consistently the thinking skills they teach, the direct teaching of thinking is not likely to lead to the kinds of student proficiencies in thinking deemed most desirable today.

NOTES

1. Walter Doyle, "Academic Work," *Review of Educational Research* 53:2 (Summer 1983), pp. 185–186.

2. Richard W. Burns, "Objectives and Content Validity of Tests," *Educational Technology* (December 15, 1968), pp. 17–18; R.E. Stake and J.A. Easley, Jr., *Case Studies in Science Education: Report to the N.S.F.* (Urbana, Ill.: Committee on Culture and Cognition, University of Illinois, 1978), p. 11.

3. Edys S. Quellmalz, "Needed: Better Methods for Testing Higher-Order Thinking Skills," *Educational Leadership* 43:2 (October 1985), pp. 29–35.

4. Robert J. Sternberg and Joan B. Baron, "A Statewide Approach to Measuring Critical Thinking Skills," *Educational Leadership* 43:2 (October 1985), p. 43.

5. Peter Kneedler, "California's Assessment of the Critical Thinking Skills in History–Social Science." (Sample thinking skill questions distributed at The State of Thinking Conference, Detroit, Mich., October 28, 1985).

6. Alan Newell and Herbert Simon, *Human Problem Solving* (Englewood Cliffs, N.J.: Prentice-Hall, 1972); Doyle, "Academic Work," p. 168; Raymond S. Nickerson, "Kinds of Thinking Taught in Current Programs," *Educational Leadership* 42:1 (September 1984), p. 27; Ibrahim Q. Saadeh, "The Teacher and the Development of Critical Thinking," *Journal of Research and Development in Education* 3:1 (Fall 1969), p. 87; Robert J. Sternberg, "Teaching Intellectual Skills: Looking for Smarts in All the Wrong Places" (Paper delivered at ASCD Wingspread Conference on the Teaching Thinking Skills, Racine (May 17–19, 1984), p. 16.

7. Quellmalz, "Needed."

8. Robert H. Ennis and Jason Millman, *Cornell Critical Thinking Test, Levels X and Z* (Pacific Grove, Calif.: Midwest Publications, 1985).

9. Robert Ennis and Eric Weir, *The Ennis-Weir Critical Thinking Test* (Pacific Grove, Calif.: Midwest Publications, 1985).

10. Arthur L. Costa, "Teaching for Intelligent Behavior," *Educational Leadership* 39:2 (October 1981), p. 31.

11. Benjamin Bloom and Lois Broder, *Problem-solving Processes of College Students* (Chicago: University of Chicago Press, 1950); Reuven Feuerstein, *Instrumental Enrichment* (Baltimore: University Park Press, 1980).

12. Arthur L. Costa, "Thinking: How Do We Know Students Are Getting Better at It?" *Roeper Review* 6:4 (April 1984), pp. 197–198.

Selected Materials on the Teaching of Thinking

Instructional Strategies and Techniques

Barry K. Beyer. *Developing a Thinking Skills Program.* Boston: Allyn and Bacon, 1988.

Barry K. Beyer. *Practical Strategies for the Teaching of Thinking.* Boston: Allyn and Bacon, 1987.

Arthur L. Costa and Lawrence F. Lowery. *Techniques for Teaching Thinking.* Pacific Grove, CA: Midwest Publications, 1989.

Robert J. Marzano and Daisy E. Arredondo. *Tactics for Thinking: Teacher's Manual.* Alexandria, VA: Association for Supervision and Curriculum Development, 1986.

Richard A. Paul et al. *Critical Thinking Handbook: A Guide for Remodeling Lesson Plans in Language Arts, Social Studies & Science.* Rohnert Park, CA: Sonoma State University Center for Critical Thinking and Moral Critique, 1987.

Louis Raths et al. *Teaching for Thinking: Theory, Strategies and Activities for the Classroom.* New York: Teachers College Press, 1986.

Richard J. Stiggins, Evelyn Rabel, and Edys Quellmalz. *Measuring Thinking Skills in the Classroom,* rev. ed. Washington: National Education Association, 1988.

Instructional Approaches: Theory and Practice

Joan Baron and Robert Sternberg, eds. *Teaching Thinking Skills: Theory and Practice.* New York: W. H. Freeman and Company, 1987.

Barry K. Beyer. "Common Sense about Teaching Thinking Skills." *Educational Leadership* 41:3 (November 1983), pp. 44–49.

Ronald S. Brandt, ed. *Teaching Thinking.* Alexandria, VA: Association for Supervision and Curriculum Development, 1989.

Arthur L. Costa, ed. *Developing Minds: A Resource Book for Teaching Thinking,* rev. ed. Alexandria, VA: Association for Supervision and Curriculum Development, 1990.

Marcia Heiman and Joshua Slomianko. *Thinking Skills Instruction: Concepts and Techniques.* Washington: National Education Association, 1987.

Beau Fly Jones et al., eds. *Strategic Teaching and Learning: Cognitive Instruction in the Content Areas.* Alexandria, VA: Association for Supervision and Development, 1987.

Raymond S. Nickerson. "On Improving Thinking Through Instruction." In E. Z. Rothkopf, ed., *Review of Research in Education.* Washington: American Educational Research Association, 1988, Vol. 15, pp. 3–57.

Stephen P. Norris and Robert A. Ennis. *Evaluating Critical Thinking.* Pacific Grove, CA: Midwest Publications, 1989.

D. N. Perkins and Gavriel Salomon. "Teaching for Transfer." *Educational Leadership* 46:1 (September 1988), pp. 22–32.

Barbara Z. Presseisen, ed. *At Risk Students and Thinking: Perspectives from Research.* Washington: National Education Association and Research for Better Schools, 1988.

Robert J. Swartz and D. N. Perkins. *Teaching Thinking: Issues and Approaches.* Pacific Grove, CA: Midwest Publications, 1989.

Selected Instructional Materials Integrating Instruction in Thinking with Academic Content

Charles Barman et al. *Addison-Wesley Science.* Menlo Park, CA: Addison-Wesley Publishing Company, 1989. A K–6 science program including student texts, teaching guides, and thinking skill workbooks.

Barry K. Beyer, Jean Craven, Mary A. McFarland, and Walter C. Parker. *The World Around Us.* New York: Macmillan Publishing Company, 1990. Student texts, teaching guides, thinking skills blackline masters, workbooks, and tests in social studies for grades K–7. The series provides continuing, developmental, direct instruction in thinking skills integrated into content at each level.

James E. Davis and Phyllis Maxey Fernlund. *Civics: Participating in Our Democracy.* Menlo Park, CA: Addison-Wesley Publishing Company, 1991. A secondary-level civics text with continuing direct instruction in decision making and selected critical thinking skills, integrated with subject matter.

Beau Fly Jones et al. *Breakthroughs: Strategies for Thinking.* Columbus, OH: Zaner-Bloser, Inc., 1990. A series of 32 student activity booklets in science, social studies, and health topics for grades 1–8 using research-based teaching strategies to guide practice in thinking.

Kevin O'Reilly. *Evaluating Viewpoints: Critical Thinking in United States History Series.* Pacific Grove, CA: Midwest Publications, 1983/1990. A supplementary 4 student-book series, designed to teach selected critical thinking skills, with student worksheets, documents, and brief teaching notes.

Peter N. Stearns, Donald R. Schwartz, and Barry K. Beyer. *World History: Traditions and New Directions.* Menlo Park, CA: Addison-Wesley Publishing Company, 1991. A high school textbook integrating continuing, direct instruction in selected thinking skills with subject matter.

WANTED!

Have you designed and taught a series of lessons on a particular thinking skill that you would like to share with other teachers? If so, send your lesson plans, your skill test(s), and your skill description(s) to me at the address below. I will consider them for inclusion in the revision of or a supplement to this handbook. Essays like those in Part III that reflect on your experience in teaching one of your lessons for the first time are also welcomed!

REWARD OFFERED
if selected for publication!

Barry K. Beyer
College of Education and Human Services
George Mason University
4400 University Drive
Fairfax, Virginia 22030

Index